BIRDS
of
ATLANTIC
CANADA

LONE
PINE

Roger Burrows

The Publisher: Lone Pine Publishing
10145 – 81 Avenue
Edmonton, AB   T6E 1W9
Canada

Website: http://www.lonepinepublishing.com

National Library of Canada Cataloguing in Publication Data

Burrows, Roger, 1942-
    Birds of Atlantic Canada

    Includes bibliographical references and index.
    ISBN-13: 978-1-55105-353-0
    ISBN-10: 1-55105-353-5

    1.Birds—Atlantic Provinces—Identification. 2. Birds—Québec (Province)—Bas-Saint-Laurent-Gaspésie Region—Identification. I. Title.
QL685.5.A9B868 2002   598'.09715   C2002-910095-X

Editorial Director: Nancy Foulds
Project Editor: Genevieve Boyer
Editorial: Genevieve Boyer, Volker Bodegom, Amanda Joynt
Production Co-ordinator: Jennifer Fafard
Layout & Production: Alana Anderson-Hale and Tina Tomljenovic
Cover Design: Rod Michalchuk
Cover Illustration: Great Blue Heron, by Gary Ross
Illustrations: Gary Ross, Ted Nordhagen
Maps: Volker Bodegom
Separations & Film: Elite Lithographers Co., Edmonton, Alberta

We acknowledge the financial support of the Government of Canada through the Book Publishing Industry Development Program (BPIDP) for our publishing activities.

PC: P13

CONTENTS

ACKNOWLEDGEMENTS

Thanks are extended to the growing family of ornithologists and dedicated birders who have offered their inspiration and expertise to help build Lone Pine's expanding library of field guides. Thank you to the New Brunswick Federation of Naturalists, the Nova Scotia Bird Society, the Natural History Society of PEI, the Natural History Society of Newfoundland and Labrador and the Club des Ornithologues de la Gaspésie. In addition, Henrik Deichmann and Pierre Poulin were a great help in the preparation of this book. Thanks also go to John Acorn, Chris Fisher, Andy Bezener and Ross James for their contributions to previous books in this series. Last, but definitely not least, thank you to Gary Ross and Ted Nordhagen, whose skilled illustrations have brought each page to life.

DIVING BIRDS

Red-throated Loon
size 65 cm • p. 32

Common Loon
size 80 cm • p. 33

Pied-billed Grebe
size 34 cm • p. 34

Horned Grebe
size 34 cm • p. 35

Red-necked Grebe
size 50 cm • p. 36

Northern Fulmar
size 48 cm • p. 37

Greater Shearwater
size 48 cm • p. 38

Sooty Shearwater
size 44 cm • p. 39

Manx Shearwater
size 34 cm • p. 40

Wilson's Storm-Petrel
size 18 cm • p. 41

Leach's Storm-Petrel
size 21 cm • p. 42

Northern Gannet
size 94 cm • p. 43

Double-crested Cormorant
size 74 cm • p. 44

Great Cormorant
size 91 cm • p. 45

HERONLIKE BIRDS

American Bittern
size 64 cm • p. 46

Least Bittern
size 33 cm • p. 47

Great Blue Heron
size 135 cm • p. 48

Great Egret
size 99 cm • p. 49

Snowy Egret
size 61 cm • p. 50

Cattle Egret
size 51 cm • p. 51

Green Heron
size 47 cm • p. 52

WATERFOWL

Black-crowned Night-Heron
size 62 cm • p. 53

Glossy Ibis
size 60 cm • p. 54

Turkey Vulture
size 74 cm • p. 55

Snow Goose
size 78 cm • p. 56

WATERFOWL

Canada Goose
size 89 cm • p. 57

Brant
size 65 cm • p. 58

Wood Duck
size 46 cm • p. 59

Gadwall
size 51 cm • p. 60

Eurasian Wigeon
size 47 cm • p. 61

American Wigeon
size 52 cm • p. 62

American Black Duck
size 57 cm • p. 63

Mallard
size 61 cm • p. 64

Blue-winged Teal
size 39 cm • p. 65

Northern Shoveler
size 49 cm • p. 66

Northern Pintail
size 70 cm • p. 67

Green-winged Teal
size 36 cm • p. 68

Redhead
size 51 cm • p. 69

Ring-necked Duck
size 41 cm • p. 70

Tufted Duck
size 43 cm • p. 71

Greater Scaup
size 45 cm • p. 72

Lesser Scaup
size 42 cm • p. 73

King Eider
size 56 cm • p. 74

Common Eider
size 63 cm • p. 75

Harlequin Duck
size 42 cm • p. 76

Surf Scoter
size 48 cm • p. 77

White-winged Scoter
size 55 cm • p. 78

REFERENCE GUIDE

WATERFOWL

Black Scoter	Long-tailed Duck	Bufflehead
size 48 cm • p. 79	size 47 cm • p. 80	size 36 cm • p. 81

Common Goldeneye	Barrow's Goldeneye	Hooded Merganser
size 46 cm • p. 82	size 46 cm • p. 83	size 45 cm • p. 84

Common Merganser	Red-breasted Merganser	Ruddy Duck
size 63 cm • p. 85	size 57 cm • p. 86	size 39 cm • p. 87

BIRDS OF PREY

Osprey	Bald Eagle	Northern Harrier	Sharp-shinned Hawk	Cooper's Hawk
size 60 cm • p. 88	size 93 cm • p. 89	size 51 cm • p. 90	size 31 cm • p. 91	size 43 cm • p. 92

Northern Goshawk	Red-shouldered Hawk	Broad-winged Hawk	Red-tailed Hawk
size 59 cm • p. 93	size 48 cm • p. 94	size 42 cm • p. 95	size 55 cm • p. 96

Rough-legged Hawk	Golden Eagle	American Kestrel	Merlin
size 55 cm • p. 97	size 89 cm • p. 98	size 20 cm • p. 99	size 28 cm • p. 100

GROUSE-LIKE BIRDS

Gyrfalcon	Peregrine Falcon	Gray Partridge	Ring-necked Pheasant
size 58 cm • p. 101	size 43 cm • p. 102	size 32 cm • p. 103	size 71 cm • p. 104

REFERENCE GUIDE

GROUSELIKE BIRDS

Ruffed Grouse
size 42 cm • p. 105

Spruce Grouse
size 37 cm • p. 106

Willow Ptarmigan
size 39 cm • p. 107

Rock Ptarmigan
size 36 cm • p. 108

RAILS, COOTS & CRANES

Yellow Rail
size 18 cm • p. 109

Virginia Rail
size 26 cm • p. 110

Sora
size 23 cm • p. 111

Common Moorhen
size 34 cm • p. 112

American Coot
size 37 cm • p. 113

Black-bellied Plover
size 30 cm • p. 114

European Golden-Plover
size 28 cm • p. 115

American Golden-Plover
size 32 cm • p. 116

SHOREBIRDS

Semipalmated Plover
size 18 cm • p. 117

Piping Plover
size 18 cm • p. 118

Killdeer
size 26 cm • p. 119

Greater Yellowlegs
size 36 cm • p. 120

Lesser Yellowlegs
size 27 cm • p. 121

Solitary Sandpiper
size 21 cm • p. 122

Willet
size 39 cm • p. 123

Spotted Sandpiper
size 19 cm • p. 124

Upland Sandpiper
size 30 cm • p. 125

Whimbrel
size 45 cm • p. 126

Hudsonian Godwit
size 38 cm • p. 127

Ruddy Turnstone
size 24 cm • p. 128

Red Knot
size 27 cm • p. 129

Sanderling
size 20 cm • p. 130

Semipalmated Sandpiper
size 16 cm • p. 131

SHOREBIRDS

Least Sandpiper
size 15 cm • p. 132

White-rumped Sandpiper
size 19 cm • p. 133

Baird's Sandpiper
size 19 cm • p. 134

Pectoral Sandpiper
size 23 cm • p. 135

Purple Sandpiper
size 23 cm • p. 136

Dunlin
size 21 cm • p. 137

Stilt Sandpiper
size 22 cm • p. 138

Buff-breasted Sandpiper
size 20 cm • p. 139

Short-billed Dowitcher
size 29 cm • p. 140

Common Snipe
size 28 cm • p. 141

American Woodcock
size 28 cm • p. 142

GULLS, TERNS & ALCIDS

Wilson's Phalarope
size 23 cm • p. 143

Red-necked Phalarope
size 18 cm • p. 144

Red Phalarope
size 22 cm • p. 145

Great Skua
size 56 cm • p. 146

South Polar Skua
size 53 cm • p. 147

Pomarine Jaeger
size 55 cm • p. 148

Parasitic Jaeger
size 46 cm • p. 149

Long-tailed Jaeger
size 55 cm • p. 150

Laughing Gull
size 41 cm • p. 151

Black-headed Gull
size 39 cm • p. 152

Bonaparte's Gull
size 33 cm • p. 153

Mew Gull
size 42 cm • p. 154

Ring-billed Gull
size 49 cm • p. 155

Herring Gull
size 62 cm • p. 156

Iceland Gull
size 56 cm • p. 157

Lesser Black-backed Gull
size 53 cm • p. 158

Glaucous Gull
size 69 cm • p. 159

Great Black-backed Gull
size 76 cm • p. 160

Black-legged Kittiwake
size 44 cm • p. 161

Ivory Gull
size 42 cm • p. 162

Caspian Tern
size 53 cm • p. 163

Roseate Tern
size 33 cm • p. 164

Common Tern
size 37 cm • p. 165

Arctic Tern
size 40 cm • p. 166

Black Tern
size 24 cm • p. 167

Dovekie
size 21 cm • p. 168

Common Murre
size 43 cm • p. 169

Thick-billed Murre
size 46 cm • p. 170

Razorbill
size 43 cm • p. 171

Black Guillemot
size 33 cm • p. 172

Atlantic Puffin
size 32 cm • p. 173

Rock Dove
size 32 cm • p. 174

Mourning Dove
size 31 cm • p. 175

Black-billed Cuckoo
size 31 cm • p. 176

Yellow-billed Cuckoo
size 31 cm • p. 177

Great Horned Owl
size 55 cm • p. 178

Snowy Owl
size 60 cm • p. 179

Northern Hawk Owl
size 41 cm • p. 180

Barred Owl
size 52 cm • p. 181

Long-eared Owl
size 37 cm • p. 182

Short-eared Owl
size 38 cm • p. 183

Boreal Owl
size 27 cm • p. 184

Northern Saw-whet Owl
size 21 cm • p. 185

Common Nighthawk
size 24 cm • p. 186

Whip-poor-will
size 24 cm • p. 187

Chimney Swift
size 13 cm • p. 188

Ruby-throated Hummingbird
size 9 cm • p. 189

Belted Kingfisher
size 32 cm • p. 190

Yellow-bellied Sapsucker
size 19 cm • p. 191

Downy Woodpecker
size 17 cm • p. 192

Hairy Woodpecker
size 22 cm • p. 193

Three-toed Woodpecker
size 23 cm • p. 194

Black-backed Woodpecker
size 24 cm • p. 195

Northern Flicker
size 33 cm • p. 196

Pileated Woodpecker
size 45 cm • p. 197

Olive-sided Flycatcher
size 19 cm • p. 198

Eastern Wood-Pewee
size 16 cm • p. 199

Yellow-bellied Flycatcher
size 14 cm • p. 200

Alder Flycatcher
size 15 cm • p. 201

Willow Flycatcher
size 15 cm • p. 202

Least Flycatcher
size 13 cm • p. 203

Great Crested Flycatcher
size 22 cm • p. 204

Eastern Kingbird
size 22 cm • p. 205

Northern Shrike
size 25 cm • p. 206

Blue-headed Vireo
size 14 cm • p. 207

Warbling Vireo
size 14 cm • p. 208

Philadelphia Vireo
size 13 cm • p. 209

Red-eyed Vireo
size 15 cm • p. 210

Gray Jay
size 31 cm • p. 211

Blue Jay
size 30 cm • p. 212

American Crow
size 48 cm • p. 213

JAYS & CROWS

Common Raven
size 61 cm • p. 214

Horned Lark
size 18 cm • p. 215

Purple Martin
size 19 cm • p. 216

Tree Swallow
size 14 cm • p. 217

LARKS & SWALLOWS

Northern Rough-winged Swallow
size 14 cm • p. 218

Bank Swallow
size 13 cm • p. 219

Cliff Swallow
size 14 cm • p. 220

Barn Swallow
size 18 cm • p. 221

CHICKADEES, NUTHATCHES & WRENS

Black-capped Chickadee
size 14 cm • p. 222

Boreal Chickadee
size 14 cm • p. 223

Red-breasted Nuthatch
size 11 cm • p. 224

White-breasted Nuthatch
size 15 cm • p. 225

Brown Creeper
size 13 cm • p. 226

House Wren
size 12 cm • p. 227

Winter Wren
size 10 cm • p. 228

Sedge Wren
size 11 cm • p. 229

Marsh Wren
size 13 cm • p. 230

Golden-crowned Kinglet
size 10 cm • p. 231

Ruby-crowned Kinglet
size 10 cm • p. 232

KINGLETS, BLUEBIRDS & THRUSHES

Blue-gray Gnatcatcher
size 11 cm • p. 233

Northern Wheatear
size 15 cm • p. 234

Eastern Bluebird
size 18 cm • p. 235

Veery
size 18 cm • p. 236

Gray-cheeked Thrush
size 19 cm • p. 237

Bicknell's Thrush
size 16 cm • p. 238

Swainson's Thrush
size 18 cm • p. 239

Hermit Thrush
size 18 cm • p. 240

Wood Thrush
size 20 cm • p. 241

American Robin
size 25 cm • p. 242

Gray Catbird
size 23 cm • p. 243

Northern Mockingbird
size 25 cm • p. 244

Brown Thrasher
size 29 cm • p. 245

European Starling
size 22 cm • p. 246

American Pipit
size 17 cm • p. 247

Bohemian Waxwing
size 20 cm • p. 248

Cedar Waxwing
size 18 cm • p. 249

Tennessee Warbler
size 12 cm • p. 250

Orange-crowned Warbler
size 13 cm • p. 251

Nashville Warbler
size 12 cm • p. 252

Northern Parula
size 11 cm • p. 253

Yellow Warbler
size 13 cm • p. 254

Chestnut-sided Warbler
size 13 cm • p. 255

Magnolia Warbler
size 13 cm • p. 256

Cape May Warbler
size 13 cm • p. 257

Black-throated Blue Warbler
size 14 cm • p. 258

Yellow-rumped Warbler
size 14 cm • p. 259

Black-throated Green Warbler
size 12 cm • p. 260

Blackburnian Warbler
size 13 cm • p. 261

Pine Warbler
size 14 cm • p. 262

Prairie Warbler
size 13 cm • p. 263

Palm Warbler
size 13 cm • p. 264

Bay-breasted Warbler
size 14 cm • p. 265

Blackpoll Warbler
size 14 cm • p. 266

Black-and-white Warbler
size 13 cm • p. 267

REFERENCE GUIDE

WOOD-WARBLERS & TANAGERS

American Redstart
size 13 cm • p. 268

Ovenbird
size 15 cm • p. 269

Northern Waterthrush
size 14 cm • p. 270

Mourning Warbler
size 14 cm • p. 271

Common Yellowthroat
size 13 cm • p. 272

Wilson's Warbler
size 12 cm • p. 273

Canada Warbler
size 14 cm • p. 274

Scarlet Tanager
size 18 cm • p. 275

SPARROWS, GROSBEAKS & BUNTINGS

Eastern Towhee
size 20 cm • p. 276

American Tree Sparrow
size 16 cm • p. 277

Chipping Sparrow
size 14 cm • p. 278

Clay-colored Sparrow
size 14 cm • p. 279

Field Sparrow
size 14 cm • p. 280

Vesper Sparrow
size 16 cm • p. 281

Savannah Sparrow
size 14 cm • p. 282

Nelson's Sharp-tailed Sparrow
size 14 cm • p. 283

Fox Sparrow
size 18 cm • p. 284

Song Sparrow
size 16 cm • p. 285

Lincoln's Sparrow
size 14 cm • p. 286

Swamp Sparrow
size 14 cm • p. 287

White-throated Sparrow
size 18 cm • p. 288

White-crowned Sparrow
size 16 cm • p. 289

Dark-eyed Junco
size 16 cm • p. 290

Lapland Longspur
size 16 cm • p. 291

Snow Bunting
size 17 cm • p. 292

Northern Cardinal
size 21 cm • p. 293

Rose-breasted Grosbeak
size 20 cm • p. 294

Blue Grosbeak
size 17 cm • p. 295

14

BLACKBIRDS & ORIOLES

Indigo Bunting
size 14 cm • p. 296

Dickcissel
size 17 cm • p. 297

Bobolink
size 18 cm • p. 298

Red-winged Blackbird
size 21 cm • p. 299

Eastern Meadowlark
size 24 cm • p. 300

Rusty Blackbird
size 23 cm • p. 301

Common Grackle
size 31 cm • p. 302

Brown-headed Cowbird
size 18 cm • p. 303

FINCHLIKE BIRDS

Baltimore Oriole
size 19 cm • p. 304

Pine Grosbeak
size 23 cm • p. 305

Purple Finch
size 14 cm • p. 306

House Finch
size 14 cm • p. 307

Red Crossbill
size 15 cm • p. 308

White-winged Crossbill
size 16 cm • p. 309

Common Redpoll
size 13 cm • p. 310

Hoary Redpoll
size 14 cm • p. 311

Pine Siskin
size 13 cm • p. 312

American Goldfinch
size 13 cm • p. 313

Evening Grosbeak
size 20 cm • p. 314

House Sparrow
size 16 cm • p. 315

INTRODUCTION

Because of similar climate and habitat, many of the same bird species are found in New Brunswick, Nova Scotia, Prince Edward Island, the island of Newfoundland and the Gaspé Peninsula. Therefore, we have decided to include this entire region in one book. We occasionally make reference to Labrador as well, because of its proximity. When we mention "Atlantic Canada" or the "Atlantic provinces," we are referring to the whole region. The "Maritime provinces," however, denote only New Brunswick, Nova Scotia and Prince Edward Island.

BIRDING IN ATLANTIC CANADA

In recent decades, birding has evolved from an eccentric pursuit practised by a few dedicated individuals to a continent-wide activity that boasts millions of professional and amateur participants. There are many good reasons why birding has become so popular. Many people find it simple and relaxing, and others enjoy the outdoor exercise it affords. Some see it as a rewarding learning experience, an opportunity to socialize with like-minded people and a way to monitor the health of the local environment. Still others watch birds to reconnect with nature. These days, a visit to any of Atlantic Canada's premier birding locations, such as Forillon National Park, Grand Manan Island or the Codroy Valley, would doubtless uncover still more reasons why people watch birds.

American Bittern

We are truly blessed by the geographical and biological diversity of Atlantic Canada. Because the Atlantic Ocean moderates the climate, and Newfoundland bears the brunt of many of the worst storms, many birds remain in the Maritime provinces in winter. In addition to supporting a wide range of breeding birds and year-round residents, Atlantic Canada hosts a large number of spring and autumn migrants that pass through our region on their way to breeding and wintering grounds. In all, 477 bird species have been seen and recorded in Atlantic Canada, and more than 325 species make annual appearances.

Our region has a long tradition of friendly birding. In general, birders are willing to help beginners and involve novices in their projects. Christmas bird counts, breeding bird surveys, migration monitoring, birding lectures and workshops all provide a chance for novice, intermediate and expert birders to interact and share the splendour of birds. So, whatever your level, there is ample opportunity for you to get involved!

BIRDING BY HABITAT

Atlantic Canada can be separated into three biophysical regions or "bioregions": Great Lakes–St. Lawrence Forest (mixed forest), Boreal Forest (mainly coniferous forest) and Acadian Forest (maritime mixed forest). The large surface area of the Gulf of St. Lawrence and its shorelines arguably forms a fourth bioregion. Each bioregion is composed of a number of different habitats. Each habitat is a community of plants and animals supported by the infrastructure of water and soil and regulated by the constraints of topography, climate and elevation.

Simply put, a bird's habitat is the place in which it normally lives. Some birds prefer the open water, some birds are found in cattail marshes, others like mature coniferous forest, and still others prefer abandoned agricultural fields overgrown with tall grass and shrubs. Knowledge of a bird's habitat increases the chances of finding the bird or identifying it correctly. If you want to see shorebirds, head to the coast and avoid extreme low tide, when the birds are widely dispersed; if it's a variety of nesting songbirds you desire, then head inland, preferably early in the morning when most songbirds are in full song. Habitats are just like neighbourhoods: if you associate friends with the suburb in which they live, you can easily learn to associate specific birds with their preferred habitats. Only in migration, especially during inclement weather, do some birds leave their usual habitat.

BIRDING ACTIVITIES
Birding Groups

It is recommended that you join in on such activities as Christmas bird counts, birding festivals and the meetings of your local birding or natural history club. Meeting other people with the same interests can make birding even more pleasurable, and there is always something to be learned when birders of all levels gather. If you are interested in bird conservation and environmental issues, provincial and local natural history groups can keep you informed about the situation in your area and what you can do to help. Bird hotlines provide up-to-date information on the sightings of rarities, which are often easier to relocate than you might think. The following is a brief list of contacts that will help you get involved:

Organizations
New Brunswick Federation of Naturalists
277 Douglas Avenue
Saint John, NB
E2K 1E5
http://www3.nbnet.nb.ca/maryspt/NBFN.html

Nova Scotia Bird Society
Mary McLaren
c/o Nova Scotia Museum
1747 Summer Street
Halifax, NS
B3H 3A6
http://www.chebucto.ns.ca/Recreation/NS-BirdSoc/

Natural History Society of PEI
Michelle Johnson
PO Box 2346
Charlottetown, PE
C1A 8C1
http://www.gov.pe.ca/infopei/onelisting.php3?number=2388/

Natural History Society of Newfoundland and Labrador
PO Box 1013
St. John's, NF
A1C 5M3
http://www.nhs.nf.ca/

Club des Ornithologues de la Gaspésie
21 Bernatchez
Rivière-au-Renard, PQ
G4X 5A3
http://www.cogaspesie.org/

Hotlines
New Brunswick: (506) 384-6397
Nova Scotia: (902) 852-2428

Bird Conservation
Atlantic Canada is an excellent place to watch birds. After all, there are still large areas of wilderness here, including parks, wildlife reserves and public lands. Nevertheless, forestry and development for housing and recreation are threatening viable bird habitat throughout our region. It is hoped that more people will learn to appreciate nature in the form of birding, and that those people will do their best to protect the nature that remains. Many bird enthusiasts support groups such as The Nature Conservancy of Canada and Ducks Unlimited Canada, which help birds by buying and managing tracts of good habitat.

Landscaping your own property to provide native plant cover and natural foods for birds is an immediate way to ensure the conservation of bird habitat. The cumulative effects of such urban "nature-scaping" can be significant. If your

Red-winged Blackbird

yard is to become a bird sanctuary, you may want to keep the neighbourhood cats out; every year, millions of birds are killed by cats. Check with the local Humane Society for methods of protecting both your feline friends and wild birds.

Bird Feeding

Many people set up a backyard birdfeeder to attract birds to their yard, especially in winter. It is possible to attract specific birds by choosing the appropriate kind of food. If you have a feeder, you should keep it stocked through late spring. The weather may be balmy at this time of year, but birds have a hard time finding food before flowers bloom, seeds develop and insects hatch. In summer, the Ruby-throated Hummingbird can be attracted to your yard with a special feeder filled with artificial nectar (a simple sugar solution of one part white sugar and three to four parts water). Be sure to follow the feeder's cleaning instructions.

Bird baths will also bring birds to your yard, and heated bird baths are particularly effective in winter. Avoid bird baths that have exposed metal parts, because wet birds can accidentally freeze to them. In general, feeding birds is good, especially if you provide food in the form of native berry- or seed-producing plants grown in your backyard. Contrary to popular opinion, birds do not become dependent on feeders, nor do they subsequently forget to forage naturally. There are many good books written about feeding birds and landscaping your yard to provide natural foods and nest sites.

Nest Boxes

Another popular way to attract birds is to set out nest boxes, especially for chickadees and swallows. Not all birds will use nest boxes: only species that normally use cavities in trees are comfortable in such confined spaces. Larger nest boxes can attract kestrels, owls and cavity-nesting ducks.

Great Horned Owl

19

ATLANTIC CANADA'S TOP BIRDING SITES

There are hundreds, if not thousands, of good birding areas throughout our region. The following areas have been selected to represent a broad range of bird communities and habitats, with an emphasis on accessibility. Common birds are included in these accounts, as well as exciting rarities.

Kouchibouguac National Park

Kouchibouguac National Park is recognized for its variety of habitats and birdlife. Its 370 square kilometres contain extensive bogs, sand beaches, dunes, saltwater lagoons, salt marshes, rivers, boreal forests and hardwoods. A canoe offers the best chance to explore the inner reaches of the park, but there are a number of excellent hiking trails, too. In the northern section of the park, the Portage River and its estuary offer migrant and breeding birds, including Black-crowned Night-Herons as well as American Woodcocks. Another good site in the northern portion of the park is the Black River, where Hooded Mergansers stage with other waterfowl in autumn. The prime site in the southern section of the park is Kellys Beach, which provides access

Cattle Egret

to the huge tern colony at Tern Island near South Kouchibouguac Dune. It's best to visit Kellys Beach early in the morning to avoid the crowds and to view the shorebirds that stage in impressive numbers. Another must-visit location is Cap Saint-Louis, which is a good place to view migrant songbirds. The Wilson's Phalarope and the Whip-poor-will are regular summer residents of Cap Saint-Louis.

Cape Jourimain

Cape Jourimain's marshes, waters and bordering woods are part of a wildlife management area that is worth visiting year-round. Loons, grebes, cormorants and sea ducks migrate past the point and nearby Cape Tormentine in April and May. The extensive mud flats attract marsh birds, with Great Egrets and Snowy Egrets as regulars. Shorebirds appear in spring and may stay to nest. Shorebird sightings include regular Willets and Wilson's Phalaropes and enough Ruff sightings to suggest a future foothold for this species in North America. The greatest number of shorebirds appear in autumn, with the Hudsonian Godwit and the Short-billed Dowitcher as the featured species. Waterfowl are the most common birds in early winter. Cape Jourimain is the only place in Atlantic Canada where you can expect to tally three-figure counts of Golden-crowned Kinglets and Yellow-rumped Warblers on a Christmas bird count.

Fundy National Park

Much of Fundy National Park is covered by coniferous forests and bogs, making it a good place to look for boreal species. Extensive areas of mixed and hardwood forests attract more than a hundred nesting species. A short walk from Chignecto Campground to MacLaren Pond often uncovers flycatchers, swallows, warblers, mimic thrushes and sparrows. The campground area also attracts early winter flocks of Brown-headed Cowbirds, Common Redpolls and Pine Siskins, and sometimes Bohemian Waxwings and Red Crossbills. A number of short trails that are suitable for family walks offer an excellent selection of boreal species, including the 26 species of warblers that have been recorded in the park. Weather conditions may dictate the arrival and departure of migrant raptors, including Red-shouldered Hawks. Shoreline cliffs offer a good vantage point.

Fredericton

Fredericton is a very productive birding area year-round. The Fredericton Wildlife Management Area stretches from the mouth of the Nashwaak River to Princess Margaret Bridge. It includes a variety of habitats such as sandbars, muddy shores, riparian woodlands, fields and gardens. The Saint John River attracts many waterfowl in spring and autumn, as well as the odd Golden Eagle and Gyrfalcon; songbirds are common in summer. The 120-hectare Odell Park in the centre of the city is by far the best place to look for songbirds, which include Great Crested Flycatcher, Wood Thrush, Mourning Warbler, Scarlet Tanager and Baltimore Oriole, as well some boreal species. Barred Owls are present when Great Horned Owls are absent, and there is at least one resident pair of Pileated Woodpeckers. Fredericton is also known to have a large roost of Chimney Swifts and late August gatherings of Purple Martins.

Grand Manan Island

Grand Manan Island, and its neighbouring islets, is a maritime world in miniature. All birders should visit the northeast headlands at migration time. Not only can you see an unmatched variety of songbirds, but you can be assured of also seeing pelagic species in good numbers. Both the Northern Mockingbird and the Northern Cardinal both nest here. Red-headed Woodpeckers are regular with the parties of Northern Flickers in midautumn. Castalia Marsh has high counts of every common shorebird species from mid-July to mid-October. It also has more sightings of Long-billed Dowitchers and Stilt Sandpipers than any other site in New Brunswick. Long Pond, with good numbers of waterfowl and grebes offshore, also occasionally has Roseate Terns and Black Terns. The scrubby forests have nesting Boreal Chickadees and Blackpoll Warblers.

Great Crested Flycatcher

Brackley–Covehead Marshes

The central section of Prince Edward Island National Park is a rich mixture of beaches, dunes, tuckamore, mud flats and shallow lagoons, starting at Rustico Island and stretching to Covehead Harbour. Rustico Bay is a great place to observe waterfowl, shorebirds and marsh birds in spring. Northern Shovelers, Willets and terns nest by Covehead Harbour. As well, Nelson's Sharp-tailed Sparrows are easy to find in the short marsh grass. Shorebirds start to reappear in mid-July and spread out over the Brackley–Covehead salt marshes and flats until early November. Gull and tern flocks at Covehead Harbour in autumn are worth checking for rarities.

Kejimkujik National Park

Fresh water plays a major role in the life of Kejimkujik National Park, which is composed primarily of island-dotted lakes, ponds, marshes and bogs and a variety of rivers and streams. The park's main avifaunal features are its nesting birds of prey and the mix of boreal and southern hardwood species that are at the limits of their ranges. This park is a good place to look for owls, including the Northern Saw-whet Owl, and for accipiters, such as the Northern Goshawk. Local specialties include the American Woodcock, Whip-poor-will, Wood Duck, Hooded Merganser, Great Crested Flycatcher and Scarlet Tanager.

Gyrfalcon

Halifax–Dartmouth

Feeders are widespread throughout Halifax, especially close to Dalhousie University, so winter sightings are quite varied. Most of the bays remain open and retain loons, grebes, diving ducks and alcids through winter. As you walk along Halifax Harbour's famous "Sewer Stroll" in winter, it is worthwhile to look for Lesser Black-backed, Mew and Black-headed Gulls. Point Pleasant Park is one of the better places to look for migrating songbirds in May, but Spryfield and Herring Cove yield more sightings in autumn.

The most productive winter site in Dartmouth is Sullivan's Pond, a small freshwater pond that has attracted almost every duck known to occur in Atlantic Canada. Black-headed Gulls can be quite common along the waterfront, and they are sometimes joined by Lesser Black-backed, Laughing and Mew gulls. There are not as many feeders in Dartmouth, but spring and autumn migration can deposit flocks of songbirds in gardens and woodlots.

Wallace Bay

Canada Geese and most dabbling ducks are common here in autumn, and the later-arriving flocks of Ring-billed Gulls often attract a Black-headed Gull. The woodland and marsh trails provide access to breeding habitats for woodpeckers and songbirds; you may even notice some Hoary Redpolls among wintering flocks of Common Redpolls. Pugwash and River Philip are a short drive to the north and are well worth visiting in winter to see diving ducks, especially Barrow's Goldeneyes.

Cape Breton Highlands National Park

Most visitors are aware that the popular Cabot Trail runs through Cape Breton Highlands National Park, but very few make use of the excellent hiking trails, which access almost every habitat in the park. Chéticamp on the Gulf Shore has a variety of nesting marsh birds, Chéticamp Island has Great Cormorant, Black-legged Kittiwake and Black Guillemot colonies, and the Chéticamp River flood-plain is an excellent place to observe flycatchers and warblers. The Salmon Falls Trail offers raptors and a great variety of vireos and warblers.

By following the Cabot Trail northward you can check out the French Mountain trails for breeding boreal species and birds of prey. On the Atlantic coast, the Branch Pond Trail offers families of Ruffed Grouse and Spruce Grouse, as well as summering Greater Yellowlegs and Solitary Sandpipers. Middle Head has Red Crossbills and White-winged Crossbills. It also provides a view of a small Arctic Tern colony, which sometimes shelters a Black-legged Kittiwake or a Black-headed Gull.

Codroy Valley

The Codroy Valley offers the widest range of breeding species in Newfoundland. The best time to visit is in summer when nesting ducks and marsh birds can be spotted on the marshes and ponds and when songbirds can be found in the bordering fields and marshes. The best selection of birds is on the south bank of the Grand Codroy River, but side trips to O'Regans and Cape Anguille are recommended. On the way to Grand Codroy, stops at Cheeseman Provincial Park, Cape Ray and Mummichog Provincial Park are likely to turn up species that are rare elsewhere in Newfoundland.

Gros Morne National Park

Located 40 kilometres northwest of Deer Lake along Highway 430, Gros Morne National Park contains some of Atlantic Canada's most impressive scenery, including the Serpentine Tablelands and the forbidding Gros Morne itself. In fact, the first priority in summer should be to climb Gros Morne. The lower part of the trail offers a number of hardwood vireos, thrushes and warblers, while the upper section features boreal species. Willow Ptarmigans, Common Redpolls and White-crowned Sparrows nest on the lower slopes, but most people want to see Rock Ptarmigans, which requires a full climb. A descent by the loop trail offers the possibility of seeing nesting American Tree Sparrows. Rocky Harbour is the starting point for exploring the northern section of the park. Lobster Cove Head, Berry Head Pond, Green Point and Baker's Brook are all worth visiting, especially during migration periods.

Pileated Woodpecker

Snowy Owl

St. John's Metropolitan Area

The harbour and Quidi Vidi Lake are the two premier locations for observing gulls in winter. Quidi Vidi Lake also offers the possibility of sighting a Tufted Duck or a Eurasian Wigeon. Another must-visit winter site is White Hills, where scores of Snowy Owls share the dump area around White Hills with Northern Goshawks and occasionally a Golden Eagle or Gyrfalcon. In summer, a walk up the Rennie's River Trail from Quidi Vidi Lake leads to Long Pond, where the Sora is one of the many attractions. Feeders in the Pine Bud Avenue–Winter Avenue area of St. John's compete with the alder thickets near Cape Spear for the best early winter warblers and other lingering songbirds.

Cape St. Mary's

Cape St. Mary's has the second-largest Northern Gannet colony in North America after Île Bonaventure. It is certainly the most exciting site, because you must climb out onto a ledge just above the nesting birds on Bird Rock to see them. All the nesting alcids except Atlantic Puffins are found here, although it's best to make a short walk north of the Northern Gannet colony if you want to see Thick-billed Murres. Sea birds aren't the only summer attraction, because Rough-legged Hawks and Willow Ptarmigans are found on the barrens, and Least Sandpipers nest on the way to Golden Bay. Peregrine Falcons, shorebirds and vagrant songbirds can be found in autumn. Winter visits guarantee Harlequin Ducks and Long-tailed Ducks and often King Eiders and Purple Sandpipers. Saint Bride's is the nearest community. It is a good place to look for Hoary Redpolls among the winter redpoll flocks.

Rimouski

Rimouski's residents have many excellent places to visit to see birds. One of the sites closest to town and arguably the best is the saltwater marsh known as Marais de Sacré-Coeur with its series of well-maintained trails. All the marsh birds seen in Atlantic Canada can be expected here in spring and early summer, along with Snow Geese, whereas shorebirds and waterfowl are a late summer and autumn feature. Raptors are also common in migration, and gulls and diving ducks are common over winter. Three kilometres to the east of town, L'Anse-au-Lard is known for its autumn shorebirds and for pelagic species. Songbirds are a feature of Neigette,

Blue Jay

Sainte-Blandine and Saint-Anaclet south of town, with most regularly nesting species represented and concentrations of migrants in both May and August. This abundance of songbirds attracts raptors, including the Snowy Owl and the Boreal Owl.

Forillon National Park

Québec's easternmost national park occupies a rugged peninsula jutting into the Gulf of St. Lawrence. This makes Forillon an excellent place to look for pelagic species, waterfowl, raptors, alcids and shorebirds in the appropriate seasons. The combination of mountains, mixed and boreal forest, alpine tundra and shorelines makes Forillon the ideal place to spend a birding holiday. Hiking trails offer access to most of the different habitats.

Petit Gaspé is known for its nesting marsh birds and for a good selection of breeding songbirds. Penouille's sand dunes, salt marshes and cliffs are worth visiting any time of year for waterfowl, raptors and wintering birds. The Presqu'île Peninsula ends at Cap Gaspé, which is used by raptors as a migration landmark. Most of the park's breeding songbirds can be found in the peninsula woods, and its northern shore also has nesting sea bird colonies. To the north, Cap-des-Rosiers offers a good selection of migrating waterfowl and shorebirds, as well as some of the rarer songbirds.

Îles de la Madeleine

Located in the Gulf of St. Lawrence, 110 kilometres from Prince Edward Island and 95 kilometres from Cape Breton, the 12-island archipelago of Îles de la Madeleine can be reached by air from Québec or by taking the car-ferry from Souris, Prince Edward Island. This ferry offers an excellent chance to see many birds that are rarely seen from land. The relatively small size of the main island provides an opportunity to see many species of shorebirds in one location.

The most famous site in the archipelago, Bird Rock, actually lies 24 kilometres to the northeast, where 40,000 birds of a dozen species, mainly the Northern Gannet, make their summer home. Île Brion has nesting Common Eiders and some resident Black-backed Woodpeckers, as well as the occasional summering Snowy Owl. The settled islands are best known for their impressive autumn shorebird migration. In addition, as many as 50 pairs of Piping Plovers nest on the beaches, and there are usually a few Black-headed Gulls and Roseate Terns among the Caspian Tern colony at Havre-aux-Basques.

ATLANTIC CANADA'S TOP 100 BIRDING SITES

MARITIME QUÉBEC
Bas Saint-Laurent
1. Cacouna
2. Dégelis
3. Rimouski
4. Pointe-au-Père
5. Sainte-Flavie

The Gaspé
6. Saint-Tharcisius
7. Matane
8. Parc de la Gaspésie
9. Forillon NP
10. Percé
11. Île Bonaventure
12. Port-Daniel
13. New Carlisle–
New Richmond area
14. Îles de la Madeleine

NEW BRUNSWICK
L'Acadie
15. Madawaska
16. Campbellton
17. Bon-Ami Point, Dalhousie
18. Eel River Lagoon
19. Mount Carleton PP
20. Caraquet–Tabusintac area
21. Miscou Island
22. Miramichi Valley
23. Kouchibouguac NP
24. Shediac–Shemogue area
25. Cape Jourimain

Fundy Shore
26. Tantramar Marshes
27. Sackville
28. Mary's Point
29. Fundy NP
30. Saint John
31. Maces Bay
32. Passamaquoddy Bay
33. Grand Manan Island

Saint John River Valley
34. Kennebecasis Valley
35. Jemseg–Gagetown area
36. Fredericton
37. Mactaquac
38. Woodstock
39. Upper Saint John River Valley
40. Plaster Rock–Nictau area

PRINCE EDWARD ISLAND
North Shore
41. North Cape
42. New London Bay
43. Brackley–Covehead Marshes
44. Deroche Pond

South Shore
45. Crapaud
46. Indian River
47. Bonshaw Hills
48. Orwell–Mount Stewart area
49. Point Prim

NOVA SCOTIA
Bay of Fundy
50. Amherst Point Bird Sanctuary
51. Advocate–Parrsboro area
52. Economy–Debert area
53. Truro
54. Wolfville Ridge
55. Grand Pré–Evangeline Beach area
56. Annapolis Valley
57. Brier Island
58. Kejimkujik NP

Southern Shore
59. Yarmouth
60. Seal Island
61. Cape Sable Island
62. Crescent Beach–Cherry Hill area

Eastern Shore
63. Fall River–Mount Uniacke area
64. Halifax–Dartmouth
65. Lawrencetown Loop
66. Eastern Shore Islands

Northumberland Strait
67. Wallace Bay
68. Tatamagouche
69. Antigonish

Cape Breton Island
70. Nyanza–Baddeck area
71. Margaree Valley
72. Cape Breton Highlands NP
73. Sydney–Glace Bay area
74. Louisbourg

NEWFOUNDLAND
West Coast
75. Ramea
76. Codroy Valley
77. Stephenville

ATLANTIC CANADA
NATURAL REGIONS

Boreal Forest

Great Lakes–St. Lawrence Forest

Acadian Forest

NP=National Park
PP=Provincial Park

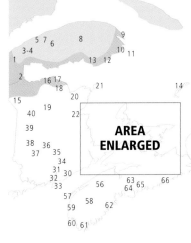

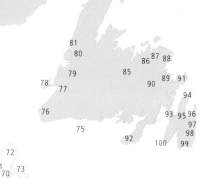

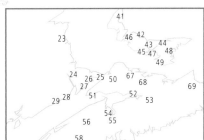

ABOUT THE SPECIES ACCOUNTS

This book gives detailed accounts of 284 species of birds that can be expected on an annual basis. Forty-one accidental species are briefly mentioned in an illustrated appendix. They can be expected to be seen again because of anticipated range expansion, migration or well-documented wandering tendencies. The order of the birds and their common and scientific names follow the American Ornithologists' Union's *Check-list of North American Birds* (7th edition, July 1998) and its supplements.

As well as discussing the identifying features of the birds, each species account attempts to bring the birds to life by describing their various character traits. Personifying a bird helps us relate to it, but the characterizations presented should not be mistaken for scientific propositions. Our limited understanding of non-human creatures, our interpretations and our assumptions restrict our ability to truly define birds. Nevertheless, we hope that a lively, engaging text will communicate scientific knowledge as smoothly and effectively as possible.

Cedar Waxing

One of the challenges of birdwatching is that many species look different in spring and summer than they do in autumn and winter. Many birds have what are generally called breeding and non-breeding plumages, and immature birds often look different from their parents. This book does not try to describe or illustrate all the different plumages of a species; instead, it focuses on the forms that are most likely to be seen in our area.

ID: It is difficult to describe the features of a bird without being able to visualize it, so this section is best used in combination with the accompanying illustrations. Where appropriate, the description is subdivided to highlight the differences between male and female birds, breeding and non-breeding birds, and immature and adult birds. The descriptions use as few technical terms as possible and favour easily understood language. Birds may not have "necklaces," "chins" or "sideburns," but these and other terms are easily understood by all readers, in spite of their scientific inaccuracy. Some of the most common anatomical features of birds are pointed out in the Glossary illustration (p. 323).

Size: The size measurement, an average length of the bird's body from bill to tail, is an approximate measurement of the bird as it is seen in nature. The size of larger birds is often

Purple Martin

given as a range, because there is variation between individuals. In addition, wingspans are given for some of the larger birds that are often seen in flight. Please note that birds with long tails often have large measurements that do not necessarily reflect "body" size.

Status: A general comment, such as "common," "uncommon" or "rare," is usually sufficient to describe the relative abundance of a species. Situations are bound to differ somewhat, because migratory pulses, seasonal changes and centres of activity tend to concentrate or disperse birds.

Habitat: The habitats we have listed describe where each species is most commonly found. In most cases, it is a generalized description, but if a bird is restricted to a specific habitat, the habitat is described precisely. Because of the freedom flight gives birds, they can turn up in almost any type of habitat. However, they will usually be found in environments that provide the specific food, water, cover and, in some cases, nesting habitat that they need to survive.

Nesting: The reproductive strategies used by different bird species vary. In each species account, we include information on nest location, nest structure, clutch size, incubation

Red-shouldered Hawk

period and parental duties. Remember that birdwatching ethics discourage the disturbance of active bird nests. If you disturb a nest, you may drive off the parents during a critical period or expose defenceless young to predators. The nesting behaviour of birds that do not nest in Atlantic Canada is not described.

Feeding: Birds spend a great deal of time foraging for food. If you know what a bird eats and where the food is found, you will have a good chance of meeting the bird you are looking for. Birds are frequently encountered while they are foraging; we hope that our description of their feeding styles and diets provides valuable identifying characteristics, as well as interesting dietary facts.

Voice: You will hear many birds, particularly songbirds, which may remain hidden from view. Memorable paraphrases of distinctive sounds will aid you in identifying a species by ear. These paraphrases only loosely resemble the call, song or sound produced by the bird. Should one of our paraphrases not work for you, feel free to make up your own—the creative exercise will reinforce your memory of the bird's sound.

INTRODUCTION

Similar Species: Easily confused species are discussed briefly. If you concentrate on the most relevant field marks, the subtle differences between species can be reduced to easily identifiable traits. You might find it useful to consult this section when finalizing your identification; knowing the most relevant field marks will shortcut the identification process. Even experienced birders can mistake one species for another.

Best Sites: If you are looking for a particular bird in Atlantic Canada, you will have more luck in some places than in others, even within the range shown on the range map. We have listed places that, besides providing a good chance of seeing a species, are easily accessible. As a result, many conservation areas and provincial and national parks are mentioned.

White-breasted Nuthatch

Range Maps: The range map for each species represents the overall range of the species in Atlantic Canada in an average year. Most birds will confine their annual movements to this range, although each year some birds wander beyond their traditional boundaries. These maps do not show differences in abundance within the range—areas of a range with good habitat will support a denser population than areas with poorer habitat. These maps also cannot show small pockets within the range where the species may actually be absent, or how the range may change from year to year. Unlike most other field guides, we have attempted to show migratory pathways—areas of the region where birds may appear while en route to nesting or winter habitat. Many of these migratory routes are "best guesses" that will likely be refined as new discoveries are made. The representations of the pathways do not distinguish high-use migration corridors from areas that are seldom used.

Range Map Symbols

summer breeding — limit of winter dispersal

year-round — winter

migration — possible breeding area

The
BIRDS

RED-THROATED LOON

Gavia stellata

The Red-throat is our smallest and lightest loon, and it is adapted to take flight with just a short takeoff effort. As a result, it can nest on smaller bodies of water than its larger, less agile relatives can. Very few people in Atlantic Canada are aware that Red-throated Loons nest beside freshwater lakes and ponds in northern Newfoundland, but adventurous summer visitors to windswept L'Anse aux Meadows can expect to see this dainty-bodied loon on its breeding territory. Elsewhere, the Red-throat is a relatively common migrant and winter resident along coasts. It is an easy bird to identify because it typically swims low in the water with its bill held high. • Red-throats are reliable meteorologists: they often become very noisy before the onset of foul weather, possibly sensing changes in barometric pressure. • The scientific name *stellata* refers to the star-like, white speckles on this bird's back in its non-breeding plumage. In Atlantic Canada, this bird may also be known as "Cape Drake" or "Cape Racer."

non-breeding

ID: slim bill points upward. *Breeding:* red throat; grey face and neck; black and white stripes from nape to back of head; plain, brownish back. *Non-breeding:* white-speckled back; white face; dark grey on crown and back of head. *In flight:* hunched back; legs trail behind tail; rapid wingbeats.
Size: *L* 60–70 cm; *W* 1.0–1.1 m.
Status: common migrant and winter resident; rare and local breeder.
Habitat: *Breeding:* small shallow lakes and ponds; often feeds at sea. *In migration* and *winter:* saltwater bays and headlands, rarely far from land.
Nesting: on the shorelines of small ponds and wetlands; nest is a mass of aquatic vegetation piled very close to the water's edge;

pair incubates 2 dark-spotted, olive eggs for up to 29 days.
Feeding: dives deeply and captures small fish; sometimes eats aquatic insects and amphibians; occasionally eats aquatic vegetation in early spring.
Voice: Mallard-like *kwuk-kwuk-kwuk-kwuk* in flight; mournful wail during courtship; distraction call is a loud *gayorwork*.
Similar Species: *Common Loon* (p. 33): larger; heavier bill; lacks white speckling on back in non-breeding plumage. *Pacific Loon:* larger; purple throat and white speckling on back in breeding plumage; all-dark back in non-breeding plumage.
Best Sites: *Summer: NF:* L'Anse aux Meadows. *In migration* and *winter: NB:* Cape Tormentine; Point Lepreau. *PEI:* North Cape. *NS:* Pinkney Point; Seaforth; Louisbourg. *NF:* Gander Bay; Biscay Bay; Cape Race. *PQ:* Pointe-au-Père; Cap-des-Rosiers (Forillon NP).

COMMON LOON
Gavia immer

Most summer cottagers and wilderness explorers recognize and delight in this loon's haunting songs and classy, black-and-white breeding plumage. These same people, however, might not recognize the silent groups of drab-coloured Common Loons that gather in sounds and bays in the shortening days of autumn. • Loons are well adapted to their aquatic lifestyle: their nearly solid bones make them less buoyant (most birds' bones are hollow), and their feet are placed well back on their bodies for underwater propulsion. Most dives are fairly shallow, but these adaptations enable loons to dive deeply. On land, however, these birds' rear-placed legs make walking seem difficult, and their heavy bodies and small wing size requires them to undertake a lengthy sprint before taking off. • The local name "Whabby," applied particularly to young birds, is probably derived from this bird's awkwardness on land.

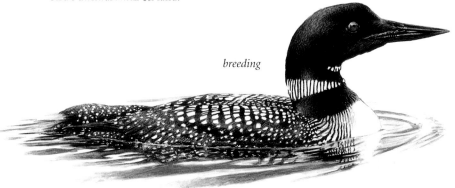

breeding

ID: *Breeding:* green-black head; stout, thick, black bill; white "necklace"; white breast and underparts; black-and-white "checkerboard" upperparts; red eyes. *Non-breeding:* sandy brown back; light underparts. *In flight:* long wings beat constantly; hunchbacked appearance; legs trail behind tail.
Size: *L* 71–89 cm; *W* 1.2–1.5 m.
Status: common migrant and winter resident; fairly common breeder.
Habitat: *Breeding:* large rivers and lakes, often with islands that provide undisturbed shorelines for nesting. *In migration* and *winter:* saltwater bays and headlands, occasionally lakes with unfrozen, open water.
Nesting: on a small island, muskrat lodge or projecting shoreline; always very near water; nest mound is built from aquatic

vegetation; pair incubates 1–3 dark-spotted olive eggs for 24–31 days.
Feeding: pursues small fish underwater to depths of 55 m; occasionally eats large, aquatic invertebrates and larval and adult amphibians.
Voice: alarm call is a quavering tremolo, often called "loon laughter"; contact call is a long but simple wailing note; breeding notes are soft, short hoots; male territorial call is an undulating, complex yodel.
Similar Species: *Red-throated Loon* (p. 32): smaller; slender bill; red throat in breeding plumage; sharply defined white face and white-spotted back in non-breeding plumage. *Pacific Loon:* smaller; dusky grey head often looks silver; dark cap extends down over eyes and is lighter than back in non-breeding plumage.
Best Sites: *NB:* Cape Tormentine; The Whistle (Grand Manan I.). *PEI:* North Cape; Cape Tryon. *NS:* Tidnish; Louisbourg. *NF:* Bellevue Beach; Biscay Bay. *PQ:* Pointe-au-Père; Barachois.

33

PIED-BILLED GREBE
Podilymbus podiceps

P ied-billed Grebes are extremely wary birds. Far more common than encounters would lead you to believe, these birds swim inconspicuously in the shallow waters of vegetated wetlands, only occasionally voicing their strange chuckle, or whinny. They build their floating nests among sparse vegetation so that they can see predators approaching from far away. When frightened by an intruder, a Pied-bill will cover its eggs and slide underwater, leaving a nest that looks like nothing more than a mat of debris. It can slowly submerge up to its head, so that only its nostrils and eyes remain above water. • The scientific name *podiceps*, which means "rump foot," refers to the way this bird's feet are located toward the back of its body. In flight, the feet extend beyond the tail and help the bird steer. • The Pied-billed Grebe, also called "Hell Diver" by fishermen, is the smallest and least colourful of our grebes.

breeding

ID: *Breeding:* all-brown body; black ring on light-coloured bill; laterally compressed "chicken bill"; black throat; very short tail; white undertail coverts; pale belly; pale eye ring. *Non-breeding:* yellow eye ring; yellow bill lacks black ring; white "chin" and throat; brownish crown.
Size: *L* 30–38 cm.
Status: uncommon migrant; uncommon local breeder; very rare in winter.
Habitat: ponds, marshes and backwaters with sparse emergent vegetation.
Nesting: among sparse vegetation in sheltered bays, ponds and marshes; floating platform nest made of wet and decaying plants is anchored to or placed among emergent vegetation; pair incubates 4–5 pale to brownish eggs for about 23 days and raises the striped young together.

Feeding: makes shallow dives and gleans the water's surface for aquatic invertebrates, small fish, adult and larval amphibians and occasionally aquatic plants.
Voice: loud, whooping call that begins quickly, then slows down: *kuk-kuk-kuk cow cow cow cowp cowp cowp.*
Similar Species: *Eared Grebe:* red eyes; black-and-white head; golden "ear" tufts and chestnut flanks in breeding plumage; seldom seen in summer. *Horned Grebe* (p. 35): red eyes; black-and-white head; golden "ear" tufts and red neck in breeding plumage; seldom seen in summer. *American Coot* (p. 113): all-black body; pale bill extends onto forehead.
Best Sites: *NB:* Eel River Lagoon; Midgic Marsh; Long Pond (Grand Manan I.); Portobello Creek. *PEI:* Crapaud; PEI NP; Deroche Pond. *NS:* Amherst Point; Missaguash Marsh; Three Fathom Harbour. *PQ:* Cacouna; Rimouski; Réserve Matane; Cap-des-Rosiers (Forillon NP).

HORNED GREBE
Podiceps auritus

Residents of Atlantic Canada rarely have a chance to see these birds in their dazzling breeding finery because Horned Grebes generally do not nest this far east. However, a visit to coastal headlands and sheltered bays in spring may reveal a few birds with rufous feathers emerging on the foreneck and underparts. At this time, most birds still sport the striking black-and-white pattern that gives them a more auk-like appearance in the cold winter months. Less sociable than loons at this time of year, Horned Grebes rarely gather in one location. • Unlike the fully webbed front toes of most swimming birds, grebe toes are individually webbed, or "lobed"—the three forward-facing toes have individual flanges ("lobes") that are not connected to the other toes. • This bird's common name and its scientific name, *auritus*, which means "eared," both refer to the golden feather tufts, or "horns," that these grebes acquire in breeding plumage. • In Atlantic Canada, all grebes are called "Spraw-Feet."

non-breeding

ID: *Breeding:* rufous neck and flanks; black head; golden "ear" tufts ("horns"); black back; white underparts; red eyes; flat crown. *Non-breeding:* lacks "ear" tufts; black upperparts; white "cheek," foreneck and underparts. *In flight:* wings beat constantly; hunchbacked appearance; legs trail behind tail.
Size: *L* 30–38 cm.
Status: locally common migrant; a few birds may remain into early winter; very rare and irregular breeder.
Habitat: *Breeding:* shallow, weedy wetlands. *In migration:* wetlands and larger lakes; inshore bays and estuaries.
Nesting: usually singly or in groups of 2–3 pairs; a floating mass of plant material is built in thick vegetation along lake edges, ponds, marshes and reservoirs; pair

incubates 4–7 pale to brownish eggs for 22–25 days and raises the young together.
Feeding: makes shallow dives and gleans the water's surface for aquatic insects, crustaceans, molluscs, small fish and adult and larval amphibians.
Voice: loud series of croaks and shrieking notes and a sharp *keark keark* during courtship; usually quiet outside the breeding season.
Similar Species: *Eared Grebe:* black neck in breeding plumage; black "cheek" and darker neck in non-breeding plumage. *Pied-billed Grebe* (p. 34): thicker, stubbier bill; mostly brown body. *Red-necked Grebe* (p. 36): larger; dark eyes; lacks "ear" tufts; white "cheek" in breeding plumage; generally louder.
Best Sites: *NB:* Cape Tormentine; Long Pond (Grand Manan I.). *PEI:* Cape Tryon; Wood Is. ferry. *NS:* Digby; Cape Sable I.; Seaforth; Glace Bay. *NF:* Blanc Sablon ferry; Branch; St. Bride's. *PQ:* Pointe-au-Père; Ste-Flavie; Forillon NP; Îles de la Madeleine.

RED-NECKED GREBE
Podiceps grisegena

I t's too bad that Red-necked Grebes rarely stray into Atlantic Canada in full breeding plumage. Their distinctive, haunting calls would enliven many springtime fishing trips and would inspire stories that even fishermen would be proud to relate. Unfortunately, most of these birds breed farther to the west and only the rather drab, winter-plumaged birds are regularly seen. These non-breeders are often mistaken for mergansers, which they superficially resemble, especially when dozing offshore. • A sociable bird, the Red-necked Grebe will join others of its kind, and other waterfowl too, in a search for small fish. Only occasionally seen out at sea, Red-necks prefer to stay close to land, especially in winter. • The scientific name *grisegena* means "grey cheek"—a distinctive field mark when this bird is in non-breeding plumage.

non-breeding

ID: *Breeding:* rusty neck; whitish "cheek"; black crown; straight, heavy bill is dark above and yellow underneath; black upperparts; light underparts; dark eyes. *Non-breeding:* greyish-white foreneck, "chin" and "cheek."
Size: *L* 43–56 cm.
Status: fairly common migrant; rare breeder; very rare winter resident.
Habitat: *Breeding:* emergent vegetation zone of lakes and ponds. *In migration:* open, deep lakes.
Nesting: usually singly, but occasionally in loosely scattered colonies; floating platform nest of aquatic vegetation is anchored to submerged plants; pair incubates 4–5 white to brownish eggs for 20–23 days.

Feeding: dives and gleans the water's surface for small fish, aquatic invertebrates and amphibians.
Voice: often-repeated, laugh-like, excited *ah-ooo ah-ooo ah-ooo ah-ah-ah-ah-ah.*
Similar Species: *Horned Grebe* (p. 35): dark "cheek" and golden "horns" in breeding plumage; red eyes, all-dark bill and bright white "cheek" in non-breeding plumage. *Pied-billed Grebe* (p. 34): thicker, stubbier bill; mostly brown body. *Mergansers* (pp. 84–86): lack combination of grey and white on head and neck, have pinkish or all-dark bills and lack distinctive hunchbacked appearance in flight.
Best Sites: *NB:* Cape Tormentine; Great Pond (Grand Manan I.). *PEI:* North Cape; Souris & Wood Is. ferries. *NS:* Tidnish; Brier I.; Port Joli Bay; Seaforth. *NF:* Ramea; Bellevue Beach; Cape Race; Biscay Bay. *PQ:* Bas St-Laurent; Cap-des-Rosiers (Forillon NP); Percé.

NORTHERN FULMAR

Fulmarus glacialis

If it looks like a gull but flies like a shear-water, then it just may be a fulmar. Look twice, because other than the stubby, yellow bill and paler plumage, the Northern Fulmar shares many physical attributes with closely related shearwaters. It can occur in a spectrum of colour "morphs"—the generally all-pale morph is most common here. • Specialized for cutting through the wild winds of open ocean expanses, fulmars are fast, skilled flyers. Slim-winged but thick-necked and bull-headed, these birds roam cooler North Atlantic waters during much of the year, returning to nesting cliffs and offshore stacks in summer. In autumn and early winter they can be the birds most commonly seen from pelagic ferries. • "Fulmar" is derived from Old Norse and means "foul gull"—when it is disturbed, this bird has a nasty habit of spewing foul-smelling fish oil. The local name "Noddy" relates to this bird's habit of sitting on the water and bobbing its head up and down in the waves as it waits for scraps of food from fishermen.

light morph

ID: short, pale yellow-tubed bill; thick neck; stubby tail; long, tapered wings; pale flash at base of primaries; many birds are intermediate between light and dark morphs. *Light morph:* whitish head and underparts; bluish-grey upperparts. *Dark morph:* deep bluish-grey throughout except for paler flight feathers. *In flight:* alternates rapid, stiff-winged flapping with graceful glides; flies low over waves.
Size: *L* 44–51 cm; *W* 1.1 m.
Status: locally common breeder; recently expanded its breeding range to include Atlantic Canada; rarely seen in winter.
Habitat: favours open ocean waters over upwellings and along the outer continental shelf; rarely approaches the coastline except in fog or storms.
Nesting: nests on sea cliffs and offshore stacks; loosely colonial; shallow nest of matted vegetation on a ledge, often covered with droppings and discarded food items; pair incubates 1 white egg for 49–53 days.
Feeding: will seize almost any edible item while swimming; makes shallow plunges beneath the water's surface; diet includes fish, squid, crustaceans (particularly copepods), invertebrates, carrion and marine fishery bycatch.
Voice: generally silent; low, quacking call may be given when competing for food.
Similar Species: *Shearwaters* (pp. 38–40): more slender, usually darker bills; more slender heads and necks. *Albatrosses:* much larger; longer, heavier bills; do not flap wings rapidly. *Gulls* (pp. 151–62): slimmer necks and bodies; slower, more consistent and less stiff wingbeats.
Best Sites: *NB:* Bay of Fundy ferry. *NS:* Seal I. *NF:* Cabot Strait; Argentia ferry; Blanc Sablon ferry; L'Anse aux Meadows; Baccalieu I.; Cape Spear; Witless Bay; Cape St. Mary's. *PQ:* Île Bonaventure.

GREATER SHEARWATER

Puffinus gravis

Many fishermen are familiar with these gregarious pirates and refer to them as "Hags" or "Bauks." Fishing boats are often mobbed by Greater Shearwaters fighting over the opportunity to grab a free meal. Sometimes they also forage in association with whales and dolphins. • Greater Shearwaters migrate to the North Atlantic for the summer months, but they do not breed here. In fact, considering their abundance here it is surprising that they breed in such a small area: Gough Island and islands in the Tristan da Cunha group in the South Atlantic. • Greater Shearwaters are most common over the outer part of the continental shelf—they tend to avoid near-shore and mid-ocean areas. However, when capelin and other small fish move to beaches to spawn, Greater Shearwaters will follow them. At such times, and in very calm or foggy weather, huge flocks may appear off headlands, especially in Newfoundland. In dead calm conditions, takeoff can only be achieved with great difficulty, and the birds are effectively grounded.

ID: brown upperparts; white underparts, except for brown belly, brown undertail coverts and incomplete brown collar; usually 1 narrow, white band at base of tail. *In flight:* straight, narrow, pointed wings; dark "wing pits" and wing linings; dark trailing edge of wings; some moulting birds have jaeger-like white wing patch.
Size: *L* 48 cm; *W* 1.1 m.
Status: common to locally abundant migrant and summer visitor from early May to October; occasionally seen well offshore from March to April and from November to early December.
Habitat: open ocean; favours cold waters; most common over the outer portion of the continental shelf; drawn inshore by weather conditions and prey abundance.

Nesting: does not nest in Atlantic Canada.
Feeding: seizes prey from the surface of the water or dives to 10 m; eats mainly small fish and squid but may also eat crustaceans.
Voice: a bleating *waaan* like a lamb.
Similar Species: *Cory's Shearwater:* lacks brown collar, belly and undertail coverts; yellow bill. *Manx Shearwater* (p. 40): darker upperparts; white belly and undertail coverts. *Albatrosses:* much larger; few, very deliberate wingbeats. *Jaegers* (pp. 148–50): wing flashes more prominent; longer tails; central tail feathers project out in flight.
Best Sites: seen from all pelagic ferries and occasionally from land. *NB:* Grand Manan I. *PEI:* East Point. *NS:* Seal I.; Cape North. *NF:* L'Anse aux Meadows; Point May (Burin); Point Verde; Cape Race. *PQ:* Île Bonaventure; Old Harry (Îles de la Madeleine).

SOOTY SHEARWATER

Puffinus griseus

Each summer, Sooty Shearwaters travel from breeding islands in the Southern Hemisphere to Atlantic Canada in numbers sometimes beyond estimate. During spring and autumn, scattered individuals are almost constantly in sight on the open ocean, and concentrations may include tens of thousands of birds. • Various sea bird families, including albatrosses, shearwaters and storm-petrels, are categorized widely as "tubenoses"—they all have external tubular nostrils and hooked bills. Their very sharp sense of smell helps them to locate areas of food abundance. • The Sooty Shearwater is most abundant along Atlantic coastlines from May through October, although a telescope may be necessary to see them because most birds forage well beyond the surf line. Large concentrations of fish can draw these birds closer to land—the popularity of schooling fish often results in multi-species feeding frenzies that include Sooties and other sea birds. Sooty Shearwaters and Greater Shearwaters dominate most mixed sea bird foraging flocks along the continental shelf. • Resident fishermen refer to Sooty Shearwaters as "Black Hags."

ID: all-dark body; slender, black bill; silvery flash on underwing linings. *In flight:* darkly streaked, white wing linings.

Size: *L* 41–46 cm.

Status: common to abundant post-breeding visitor from late April to early November; very rare to rare from December to March.

Habitat: open ocean; concentrates at upwellings and current edges along the continental shelf.

Nesting: does not nest in Atlantic Canada.

Feeding: gleans the water's surface; makes shallow dives; eats mostly capelin, squid and crustaceans, especially euphasiids; inspects passing boats, quickly forming flocks if food is available.

Voice: generally silent; occasionally utters quarrelsome calls when competing for food.

Similar Species: *Dark morph Northern Fulmar* (p. 37): thick, greenish-yellow bill; dark wing linings. *Other shearwaters* (pp. 38–40): variably pale underparts. *Immature gulls* (pp. 151–62): paler brown; heavier bills; more flapping flight.

Best Sites: seen from all pelagic ferries and occasionally from land. *NB:* Grand Manan I. *PEI:* East Point. *NS:* Brier I.; Cape North. *NF:* L'Anse aux Meadows; Point Verde; Cape Race. *PQ:* Île Bonaventure.

MANX SHEARWATER
Puffinus puffinus

You will likely have to take a pelagic ferry or visit offshore islands to observe this open-ocean bird. Its distribution is mostly European, but there are nesting colonies on islands just off the coast of Newfoundland. Most birds seen in the western Atlantic, including the birds that breed in Atlantic Canada, originate from nesting colonies off the Welsh coast, but there are a few sightings of browner birds that come from the Mediterranean Sea. • Breeding birds dig out burrows, which they may use a few years in a row, into which they lay a single egg per season. Parents may stray as far as 1000 kilometres from their nests in search of food, and they feed their nestling by regurgitation. • Large gatherings of shearwaters in Atlantic Canada almost always contain a few Manx Shearwaters. Predominantly black and white in appearance, these shearwaters sometimes get confused with jaegers when they sit on the ocean with their tails up. However, shearwaters dive more frequently and more deeply than jaegers do.

ID: dark upperparts; white underparts; white wing linings; white on throat extends to white crescent behind eye; long, slender bill with hooked tip. *In flight:* white underparts with dark wing border; white undertail coverts; stiff-winged, flap-and-glide flight pattern.
Size: *L* 30–38 cm; *W* 76–89 cm.
Status: rare to locally common from late April to mid-October; rare, but increasing, local colonial breeder from May to mid-August.
Habitat: open ocean; sometimes off headlands and rarely off beaches.
Nesting: cliffs and rock crevices on remote islands and headlands; loosely colonial; constructs burrows that are 0.5–3 m long on remote, marine islands; nest chamber may be lined with scraps of vegetation,

feathers and hair; both sexes incubate 1 white egg for 47–55 days.
Feeding: feeds on water's surface while swimming or dives after prey, sometimes from low flight; takes mostly small fish but may also take squid and crustaceans.
Voice: a range of crows, coos, croons, howls and screams repeated rapidly; a raucous, often piercing or gruff *cack-cack-cack-carr-hoo.*
Similar Species: *Greater Shearwater* (p. 38): larger; browner upperparts; brown belly and undertail coverts. *Cory's Shearwater:* larger; browner upperparts; yellow bill. *Jaegers* (p. 148–50): longer tails; central tail feathers project out in flight.
Best Sites: seen from all pelagic ferries and occasionally from land. *NB:* Grand Manan I. *NS:* Brier I.; Sydney Harbour. *NF:* L'Anse aux Meadows; Point May (Burin); Baccalieu I.; Point Verde (Cape Shore); Cape Race.

WILSON'S STORM-PETREL
Oceanites oceanicus

This long-legged storm-petrel dances over the surface of the water, feet daintily pattering as it hovers, stirring up the small shrimp, amphipods and fish that it feeds on. The outer portion of the continental shelf is where you are most likely to see the Wilson's Storm-Petrel, but it occasionally wanders close to land, coming into the Gulf of St. Lawrence and the entrance to the Bay of Fundy. Like many marine birds, the Wilson's Storm-Petrel follows fishing boats, grabbing whatever scraps of food it can. • This long-distance migrant must eat well—it travels from the Antarctic to the edge of the Arctic and back again each year. It nests in the antarctic region and around southern South America on islands and cliffs. • Wilson's Storm-Petrels can be distinguished from Leach's Storm-Petrels by their white rump patch and more swallow-like flight. • According to Greek mythology, "Oceanites" were sea nymphs that, like storm-petrels, spent their lives at sea. • Despite their small size, storm-petrels can live to be more than 20 years old.

ID: dark brown overall, with white on rump and undertail coverts; square tail. *In flight:* shallow, stiff wingbeats, suggesting a swallow; toes extend beyond end of tail.
Size: *L* 18 cm; *W* 41 cm.
Status: rare near land to locally common offshore from April to late October.
Habitat: open ocean, especially over the continental shelf, but occasionally wanders close to land along coasts.
Nesting: does not nest in Atlantic Canada.
Feeding: hovers over the water with its feet touching the surface, grabbing food items from the surface; takes shrimp, amphipods, small fish, small squid and marine worms.
Voice: usually silent; soft peeping or chattering may be heard from groups of feeding birds.
Similar Species: *Leach's Storm-Petrel* (p. 42): V-shaped white rump patch, when present; lacks white undertail coverts; longer wings; forked tail; erratic flight is more like that of a nightjar. *Shearwaters* (pp. 38–40) and *petrels:* much larger; glide much more often and rarely flap.
Best Sites: *NB:* Miscou I.; Bay of Fundy ferry. *PEI:* Souris ferry. *NS:* Maine ferries; Brier I. *NF:* Cabot Strait; Argentia ferry; Blanc Sablon ferry; L'Anse aux Meadows. *PQ:* North Shore ferries.

LEACH'S STORM-PETREL
Oceanodroma leucorhoa

Unlike many other storm-petrels, Leach's chooses not to follow fishing vessels and rarely patters or "walks" on the water's surface when feeding. The generally light-rumped subspecies found in the North Atlantic is best distinguished from other storm-petrels by its erratic, butterfly- or bat-like flight. • The Leach's Storm-Petrel nests in underground burrows, and parents visit their nest-bound young only at night—these birds' relatively large eyes help them to find their way in the dark. Domestic cats and rats introduced to nesting islands have caused dramatic declines in the success of many island-breeding colonies. The dramatic increase in the numbers of larger gulls since human colonization of Atlantic Canada has also affected breeding success. • During daylight hours these solitary birds forage far out to sea. However, Atlantic "pea-souper" fogs and raging storms may force these birds ashore, where their inability to take off from level ground renders them helpless. • These storm-petrels are known throughout Atlantic Canada as "Mother Carey's Chickens."

ID: all-dark rump or off-white rump patch that may be partially divided by 1 dark, narrow band; long forked tail. *In flight:* distinctive, erratic zigzagging flight with alternating flaps and glides; narrow, pointed wings with sharp bend at wrist.
Size: *L* 19–23 cm; *W* 48 cm.
Status: locally abundant summer visitor and breeder; uncommon to common migrant.
Habitat: open ocean; prefers upwellings and current edges.
Nesting: nests on isolated headlands and islands; colony nester; male uses feet to dig a burrow up to 1 m long in soil under rocks, grass or tree roots; nest chamber is lined with vegetation; 1 white egg is incubated by both adults over 38–46 days; young are fed by regurgitation.
Feeding: skims small fish and crustaceans, including copepods, amphipods and euphausiid shrimp from the ocean's surface while hovering; often scavenges from floating carcasses and natural animal oil slicks.
Voice: generally silent at sea; purring, chattering and trilling notes commonly given at nest site at night.
Similar Species: *Wilson's Storm-Petrel* (p. 41): smaller with pure white U-shaped rump, yellow-webbed feet and more direct flight pattern. *European Storm-Petrel*: much smaller with squared white rump and short legs. *Band-rumped Storm-Petrel*: larger with dark feet not extending beyond tail in flight. *White-faced Storm-Petrel*: pale underparts and bold black-and-white facial pattern, long webbed feet extend well beyond tail.
Best Sites: visible from pelagic ferries. *Summer: NB:* Machias Seal I.; Kent I. *PEI:* Souris ferry. *NS:* Bon Portage I.; Eastern Shore Is.; Bird Is. *NF:* Penguin Is.; Baccalieu I.; Witless Bay. *PQ:* Île Bonaventure; Île Brion (Îles de la Madeleine).

NORTHERN GANNET

Morus bassanus

Unfortunately, the Northern Gannet's spectacular feeding behaviour is often demonstrated far from the sight of land. Squadrons of birds soaring at heights of more than 30 metres above the ocean surface will suddenly arrest their flight by folding their wings back and simultaneously plunge headfirst into the ocean depths in pursuit of schooling fish. The Northern Gannet's reinforced skull has evolved to cushion the brain from diving impacts. • Northern Gannets spend most of the year feeding and roosting at sea. Only during the brief summer breeding season do they seek the stability of land to lay eggs and raise young in large sea-cliff colonies. They often mate for life, re-establishing pair bonds each year at their nest sites by indulging in elaborate face-to-face nest-duty exchange sequences that involve wing raising, tail spreading, bowing, sky pointing and preening. • "Gannet" is derived from the Anglo-Saxon (*c.* 450–1200) word "ganot," meaning "little goose." This bird was once classified taxonomically and popularly with the geese and is still known as "Solan Goose" in Europe.

ID: thick, tapered bill; long, narrow wings; pointed tail; white overall with black wing tips and feet; buffy wash on nape. *Immatures:* various stages of mottled grey, black and white.
Size: *L* 94 cm; *W* 1.8 m.
Status: locally common breeder; common offshore in migration; uncommon offshore in winter.
Habitat: roosts and feeds in coastal and open-ocean waters most of year, often seen well offshore.
Nesting: on protected mainland or island sea cliffs; male builds a tall mound of seaweed, vegetation, dirt and feathers glued together with droppings; pair shares incubation of 1 pale blue to white egg and raising of young.
Feeding: dives with closed wings to pursue prey; eats fish, including herring and mackerel, and sometimes squid; may steal from other birds or scavenge from fishing boats.
Voice: generally silent at sea or at rest but produces a low, throaty braying at the nesting colony.
Similar Species: *Snow Goose* (p. 56): shorter, pinkish bill, broader wings and long, extended neck in flight.
Best Sites: visible from pelagic ferries and off headlands in migration. *Summer: NF:* Baccalieu I.; Cape St. Mary's. *PQ:* Percé; Île Bonaventure; Bird Rocks (Îles de la Madeleine).

DOUBLE-CRESTED CORMORANT
Phalacrocorax auritus

This slick-feathered bird often appears dishevelled, and extra-close encounters typically reveal the foul stench of fish oil. A cormorant's beauty can take longer to appreciate than that of other birds, and many people refer to it scathingly as "reptilian." Cormorants are masters of the aquatic environment, however. Their long, rudder-like tails, excellent underwater vision and sealed nostrils contribute to the success of their aquatic lifestyle. In addition, the fact that their feathers are not very waterproof actually helps them during underwater dives by decreasing their buoyancy. After a bout of diving, cormorants must dry their wings, and they are often seen perched in trees with their wings partially spread. • The species name *auritus* refers to the eared tufts sported by the adults for a brief period at the start of the breeding season. • The local name "Shag" refers to a similar species found in Europe.

breeding

ID: all-black body; long, crooked neck; thin bill, hooked at tip; blue eyes. *Breeding:* throat pouch becomes intense orange-yellow; fine, black plumes trail from eyebrows. *Immature:* brown upperparts; buff throat and breast; yellowish throat patch. *In flight:* rapid wingbeats; kinked neck.
Size: *L* 66–81 cm; *W* 1.3 m.
Status: uncommon to locally common from early April to early November; rare in winter.
Habitat: large lakes and large, meandering rivers.
Nesting: colonial; on low-lying islands, often with terns and gulls, or precariously high in trees; nest platform is made of sticks, aquatic vegetation and guano; pair incubates 3–6 bluish-white eggs for 25–33 days; young are fed by regurgitation.
Feeding: long underwater dives to 9 m or more; pursues small schooling fish or, rarely,

amphibians and invertebrates; prey is grasped by the bill and brought to the surface to swallow.
Voice: generally quiet; may issue pig-like grunts or croaks, especially near nest colonies.
Similar Species: *Great Cormorant* (p. 45): larger bill and body; thicker neck; white "chin strap," head plumes and flank patches in breeding plumage; immature has white belly. *Common Loon* (p. 33): shorter neck; black bill lacks hooked tip; spotted back in breeding plumage; white underparts in non-breeding plumage. *Canada Goose* (p. 57): white "cheek"; brown overall.
Best Sites: *NB:* Bon-Ami Rocks (Dalhousie); Manawagonish (Saint John); White Horse I. (near Grand Manan I.); Oromocto. *PEI:* Ram I.; Cape Tryon. *NS:* Eastern Shore Is.; Abercrombie; Bird Is. *NF:* Traytown; Little Barrasway. *PQ:* Forillon NP; Percé; Pointe l'Est (Îles de la Madeleine).

GREAT CORMORANT

Phalacrocorax carbo

T he Great Cormorant is common throughout much of the Old World and is well established in Atlantic Canada. This cormorant relies on its superb underwater vision to detect schooling fish. Once it locates its prey, it folds its long wings tight against its body and dives down into the murky depths of the water, propelled only by its large webbed feet. Like owls, the Great Cormorant coughs up any indigestible parts of its prey in the form of a pellet. • At the nest, each chick feeds by sticking its head into the parent's open bill and lapping up the regurgitated food. The most active, robust chicks are fed first so that in times of food scarcity, only the strongest nestlings survive to fledging. • *Phalacrocorax* means "bald crow" in Latin and refers to a common European subspecies of Great Cormorant that, like our Bald Eagle, has a white head in breeding plumage. *Carbo* (also Latin) refers to the charcoal colour of this bird's plumage.

breeding

ID: all-dark bird; white "chin strap" borders yellow throat patch; thick neck; heavy bill with hooked tip. *Breeding:* white head plumes and flank patches. *Immature:* brown upperparts; white underparts; brown-streaked breast; *In flight:* flies silently in V-formation.
Size: *L* 91 cm; *W* 1.6 m.
Status: locally common breeder and migrant; locally uncommon in winter.
Habitat: shallow coastal waters; nests on rocky coastal and island cliffs; winters along sheltered bays, estuaries and jetties.
Nesting: male provides female with sticks, seaweed and other finer lining materials to build a bulky nest on a sheltered sea cliff or ledge; both adults incubate the 4–5 bluish-white eggs for 28–31 days; young are fed by regurgitation.
Feeding: a wide variety of fish are caught while diving; dives are usually within 10 m of the surface but may be to 30 m.
Voice: generally silent, except at the nest where the young keep up a noisy exchange of unmusical squawks and squeals, especially when a parent returns with food.
Similar Species: *Double-crested Cormorant* (p. 44): adult lacks white "chin strap" and flank patches and has orange throat pouch, smaller head and body and thinner neck; immature has unstreaked neck and breast.
Best Sites: *NB:* Machias Seal I.; Neguac; Cape Tormentine. *PEI:* Cape Tryon; Point Prim. *NS:* Baccaro Point; St. Margaret's Bay; Crystal Cliffs (Antigonish); Bird Is. *NF:* Cape Anguille; Cape St. Mary's. *PQ:* Forillon NP; Île Bonaventure; Île Brion & Pointe St-Pièrre (Îles de la Madeleine).

AMERICAN BITTERN

Botaurus lentiginosus

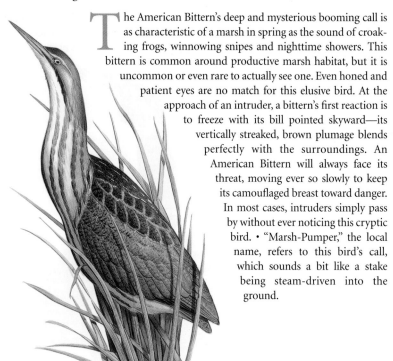

The American Bittern's deep and mysterious booming call is as characteristic of a marsh in spring as the sound of croaking frogs, winnowing snipes and nighttime showers. This bittern is common around productive marsh habitat, but it is uncommon or even rare to actually see one. Even honed and patient eyes are no match for this elusive bird. At the approach of an intruder, a bittern's first reaction is to freeze with its bill pointed skyward—its vertically streaked, brown plumage blends perfectly with the surroundings. An American Bittern will always face its threat, moving ever so slowly to keep its camouflaged breast toward danger. In most cases, intruders simply pass by without ever noticing this cryptic bird. • "Marsh-Pumper," the local name, refers to this bird's call, which sounds a bit like a stake being steam-driven into the ground.

ID: brown upperparts; brown streaking from "chin" through breast; straight, stout bill; yellow legs and feet; black outer wings; black streaks from bill down neck to shoulder; short tail.
Size: *L* 59–69 cm; *W* 1.1 m.
Status: rare to fairly common from April to late October; very rare in winter.
Habitat: marshes, wetlands and lake edges with tall, dense grasses, sedges, bulrushes and cattails.
Nesting: singly; above the waterline in dense vegetation; nest platform is made of grass, sedges and dead reeds; nest often has separate entrance and exit paths; female incubates 3–5 pale olive or buff eggs for 24–28 days.

Feeding: patient stand-and-wait predator; strikes at small fish, crayfish, amphibians, reptiles, mammals and insects.
Voice: deep, slow, resonant, repetitive *pomp-er-lunk* or *onk-a-BLONK*; most often heard in the evening or at night.
Similar Species: *Black-crowned Night-Heron* (p. 53), *Green Heron* (p. 52), *Yellow-crowned Night-Heron*, and *Least Bittern* (p. 47): juveniles lack dark streak from bill to shoulder; juvenile night-herons have white flecking on upperparts.
Best Sites: *NB:* Miramichi; Cape Jourimain; Sackville; Corbett Marsh (Fredericton). *PEI:* Crapaud; Brudenell River. *NS:* Missaguash Marsh; Ellenwood Park (Yarmouth); Hopewell Marsh; Big Glace Bay Lake. *NF:* Sandy Pond (Terra Nova NP); Long Pond (St. John's). *PQ:* St-Tharcisius; Lac des Joncs (St-Fabien).

LEAST BITTERN

Ixobrychus exilis

The Least Bittern inhabits freshwater marshes where tall, impenetrable stands of cattails conceal most of its movements. It moves about with ease, its slender body passing freely and unnoticed through dense marshland habitat. An expert climber, this bird can be seen a metre or more above water, clinging to vertical stems and walking about without getting its feet wet. • Least Bitterns are uncommon and extremely local throughout Atlantic Canada, and sightings are rare, owing in part to their secretive behaviour and solitary lifestyle. • In the Gaspé and New Brunswick the Least Bittern reaches the northern limit of its North American range. Here it pushes the boundaries of its adaptability, particularly its tolerance for chilly summer nights and rainstorms.

ID: rich buff flanks and sides; streaking on foreneck; white underparts; mostly pale bill; yellowish legs; short tail; dark primary and secondary feathers. *Male:* black crown and back. *Female and juvenile:* chestnut brown head and back; juvenile has darker streaking on breast and back. *In flight:* large, buffy shoulder patches.

Size: *L* 28–37 cm.

Status: uncommon from early May to September; a few appear into October.

Habitat: freshwater marshes with cattails and other dense emergent vegetation.

Nesting: mostly the male constructs a platform of dry plant stalks on top of bent marsh vegetation; nest site is usually well concealed within dense vegetation; pair incubates 4–5 pale green or blue eggs for 17–20 days; pair feeds the young by regurgitation.

Feeding: stabs prey with its bill; eats mostly small fish; also takes large insects, tadpoles, frogs, small snakes, leeches and crayfish; may build a hunting platform.

Voice: guttural *uh-uh-uh-oo-oo-oo-ooah* is given by the male; ticking sound is made by the female; both issue a *tut-tut* call or a *koh* alarm call.

Similar Species: *American Bittern* (p. 46): larger, with bold, brown streaking on underparts; adult has black streak from bill to shoulder. *Yellow-crowned Night-Heron* and *Black-crowned Night-Heron* (p. 53): and much larger juveniles have dark brown upperparts with white flecking. *Green Heron* (p. 52): juvenile has dark brown upperparts.

Best Sites: *NB:* Ste-Anne-de-Madawaska; Musquash Marsh; Germantown Marsh; New Horton Marsh. *NS:* Missaguash Marsh. *PQ:* Cacouna; Marais de Sacré-Coeur (Rimouski); Cap-des-Rosiers (Forillon NP).

GREAT BLUE HERON
Ardea herodias

The sight of a Great Blue Heron is always memorable. Whether you are observing this heron as it stealthily hunts or you are tracking its graceful wingbeats as it returns to a feeding site or nest, you will not fail to notice this bird's majesty. Its communal treetop nests, known as rookeries, are sensitive to human disturbances, so if you are fortunate enough to discover a colony, you should observe the birds' behaviour from a distance. • This bird is often referred to as a "crane." However, unlike a crane, which holds its neck outstretched in flight, this heron folds its neck back over its shoulders in flight like other members of its family.

breeding

ID: long, curving neck; long, dark legs; blue-grey wing coverts and back; straight, yellow bill. *Breeding:* richer colours; plumes streak from crown and throat. *In flight:* neck folds back over shoulders; legs trail behind body; slow and steady wingbeats.

Size: *L* 1.3–1.4 m; *W* 1.8 m.

Status: fairly common to locally abundant from late March to late November; very rare in winter.

Habitat: forages along the edges of rivers, lakes and marshes; also seen in fields and wet meadows.

Nesting: colonial; usually in a tree but occasionally on the ground; flimsy to elaborate stick-and-twig platform is added onto, often over years, and can be up to 1.2 m in diameter; pair incubates the 4–7 pale blue eggs for approximately 28 days.

Feeding: patient stand-and-wait predator; strikes at small fish, amphibians, small mammals, aquatic invertebrates and reptiles; rarely scavenges.

Voice: usually quiet away from the nest; occasionally a deep, harsh *frahnk frahnk frahnk* (usually during takeoff).

Similar Species: *Yellow-crowned Night-Heron* and *Black-crowned Night-Heron* (p. 53): and much smaller; shorter legs. *Sandhill Crane:* red cap; flies with neck outstretched. *Little Blue Heron:* dark overall; purplish head; lacks yellow on bill. *Tricolored Heron:* darker upperparts; white underparts.

Best Sites: *NB:* Heron I. (New Mills); Manawagonish (Saint John); Gagetown. *PEI:* New London Bay; Rustico I. *NS:* Spencer's I. (Parrsboro); Boot I. (Grand Pré); Nyanza. *NF:* Larkin Point (Codroy Valley); Notre Dame Bay. *PQ:* Cacouna; Matapédia Valley; Îles de la Madeleine.

GREAT EGRET

Ardea alba

Great Egrets were first reported in Atlantic Canada in the early 1800s, but they did not reach Newfoundland until 1928. Over the last few decades, late summer and early autumn wanderers have reached most areas of Atlantic Canada, but this species is still considered noteworthy when it does appear. Breeding hasn't been confirmed anywhere in Atlantic Canada yet. • The plumes of the Great Egret and the Snowy Egret were widely used to decorate hats in the early 20th century. An ounce of egret feathers cost as much as $32—more than an ounce of gold at that time—and, as a result, egret populations began to disappear. Some of the first conservation legislation in North America was enacted to outlaw the hunting of Great Egrets. These egrets are now recovering and expanding their range, so nesting in Atlantic Canada may occur in the future.

breeding

ID: all-white plumage; black legs; yellow bill. *Breeding:* white plumes trail from throat and rump; green skin patch between eyes and base of bill. *In flight:* neck folds back over shoulders; legs extend backward.
Size: *L* 94–104 cm; *W* 1.3 m.
Status: rare to locally common from early April to mid-October; a few may remain into early winter.
Habitat: marshes, open riverbanks, irrigation canals and lakeshores.
Nesting: 1 unconfirmed nesting record; colonial, but may nest in isolated pairs;

in a tree or tall shrub; pair builds a platform of sticks and incubates 3–5 pale blue-green eggs for 23–26 days.
Feeding: patient stand-and-wait predator; occasionally stalks slowly, stabbing at almost any small creature it can capture.
Voice: rapid, low-pitched, loud *cuk-cuk-cuk*.
Similar Species: *Snowy Egret* (p. 50): smaller; black bill; yellow feet. *Cattle Egret* (p. 51): smaller; stockier; orange bill and legs. *Little Blue Heron:* juvenile is smaller and has 2-tone bill and bluish-grey legs.
Best Sites: *NB:* St. Andrews; Long Pond (Grand Manan I.). *NS:* Yarmouth; Lawrencetown Loop. *PQ:* Cacouna; Marais de Sacré-Coeur (Rimouski); Barachois.

SNOWY EGRET
Egretta thula

The elegant, snow white plumage, bright yellow feet and black legs of the Snowy Egret are rarely seen in Atlantic Canada. This bird mainly wanders here after breeding. However, now that the Snowy Egret is becoming increasingly common in spring, it may soon expand its breeding range to include Atlantic Canada as nesting habitat is lost in New England. It does currently breed on Bon Portage Island off Nova Scotia. • By poking their feet in the muck of shallow wetlands, Snowy Egrets spook potential prey out of hiding places. Another strategy that they use is even more devious: they create shade by extending their wings over open water. When a fish is lured into the cooler shaded spot, it is promptly seized and eaten. Some paleontologists even suggest that this hunting method was one of the original functions of bird wings!

breeding

ID: white plumage; black bill and legs; bright yellow feet. *Breeding:* long plumes on throat and rump; erect crown; orange-red lores. *Juvenile:* similar to adult but with more yellow on legs. *In flight:* yellow feet are obvious.
Size: *L* 56–66 cm; *W* 1.0 m.
Status: rare from late April to October.
Habitat: open edges of rivers, lakes and marshes.
Nesting: colonial, often among other herons; in a tree or tall shrub; pair builds a platform of sticks and incubates 3–5 pale blue-green eggs for 20–24 days.
Feeding: stirs wetland muck with its feet; stands and waits; occasionally hovers and stabs; eats small fish, amphibians and invertebrates.
Voice: low croaks; bouncy *wulla-wulla-wulla* on breeding grounds.
Similar Species: *Great Egret* (p. 49): larger; yellow bill; black feet. *Cattle Egret* (p. 51): orange-yellow or pinkish legs and bill. *Little Blue Heron:* juvenile has pale, bluish-grey legs and 2-tone bill.
Best Sites: *NB:* St. Andrews; Castalia. *NS:* Bon Portage I.; Yarmouth; Three Fathom Harbour. *PQ:* Cacouna; Marais de Sacré-Coeur (Rimouski); Île Verte.

CATTLE EGRET
Bubulcus ibis

Over the last century—and without help from humans—the Cattle Egret has dispersed from Africa to inhabit every continent except Antarctica. Solitary Cattle Egrets are often seen flying through southwestern Nova Scotia and New Brunswick in spring, when there are also scattered sightings in other provinces. Larger flocks, but fewer sightings, are also recorded in autumn. Most birds seen in spring are in breeding plumage, whereas most autumn birds are juveniles.
• The Cattle Egret gets its name from its habit of following grazing animals. Unlike other egrets, its diet consists primarily of terrestrial invertebrates—it feeds on the insects and other small animals that ungulates stir up. When foraging, this egret is often seen in the company of similar-sized gulls. Like Black-headed Gulls, Cattle Egrets will sometimes follow ploughs; like Ring-billed Gulls, they occasionally scavenge at dumps.

breeding

ID: mostly white; yellow-orange bill and legs. *Breeding:* long plumes on throat and rump; buff-orange throat, rump and crown; orange-red legs and bill; purple lores. *Juvenile:* similar to adult but with black feet.
Size: *L* 48–53 cm; *W* 90–95 cm.
Status: rare to locally uncommon from late April to early December.
Habitat: agricultural fields and marshes.
Nesting: does not nest in Atlantic Canada.

Feeding: picks grasshoppers, other insects, worms, small vertebrates and spiders from fields; often associated with livestock.
Voice: generally silent.
Similar Species: *Great Egret* (p. 49): larger; black legs and feet. *Snowy Egret* (p. 50): black legs; yellow feet. *Little Blue Heron:* juvenile is more slender with pale, bluish-grey legs and 2-tone bill. *Gulls* (pp. 151–62): do not stand as erect; generally have grey mantle.
Best Sites: *NB:* St. Andrews; Saints Rest Marsh (Saint John). *NS:* New Germany; Cape Fourchu. *NF:* Kilbride. *PQ:* Marais de Sacré-Coeur & Lac à l'Anguille (Rimouski).

51

GREEN HERON

Butorides virescens

This crow-sized heron is far less conspicuous than its Great Blue cousin. The Green Heron prefers to hunt for frogs and small fish in shallow, weedy wetlands, where it often perches just above the water's surface. While hunting, Green Herons may drop small debris, such as twigs, vegetation and feathers, onto the water's surface as a form of "bait" to attract fish to within striking range. • If the light is just right, you may be fortunate enough to see a glimmer of green on the back and outer wings of this bird. Most of the time, however, this magical shine is not apparent, especially when the Green Heron stands frozen under the shade of dense marshland vegetation. • The scientific name *virescens* is Latin for "growing or becoming green," and it refers to this bird's transition from a streaky, brown juvenile to a greenish adult.

ID: stocky; green-black crown; chestnut face and neck; white foreneck and belly; blue-grey back and wings mixed with iridescent green; relatively short, green-yellow legs; bill is dark above and greenish below; short tail. *Breeding male:* bright orange legs. *Juvenile:* heavy streaks along the neck and underparts; dark brown upperparts.
Size: *L* 38–56 cm; *W* 66 cm.
Status: rare from late April to early November; local breeder.
Habitat: freshwater marshes, lakes and streams with dense shoreline or emergent vegetation.
Nesting: nests singly or in small, loose groups; male begins construction of the stick platform in a tree or shrub, usually very close to water; pair incubates 3–5 pale blue-green to green eggs for 19–21 days; young are fed by regurgitation.
Feeding: eats mostly small fish; also takes frogs, tadpoles, crayfish, aquatic and terrestrial insects, small rodents, snakes, snails and worms; stabs prey with its bill after slowly stalking or standing and waiting.
Voice: generally silent; alarm and flight call are a loud *kowp, kyow* or *skow*; aggression call is a harsh *raah*.
Similar Species: *Black-crowned Night-Heron* (p. 53): much larger juvenile has streaked face and white flecking on upperparts. *Least Bittern* (p. 47): buffy-yellow shoulder patches, sides and flanks. *American Bittern* (p. 46): larger, more tan overall; black streak from bill to shoulder.
Best Sites: *NB:* Campbellton; St-Basile; Charleston; Centreville; Saint John. *PQ:* Cacouna; Lac des Joncs (St-Fabien); Cap-des-Rosiers & Petit Gaspé (Forillon NP).

BLACK-CROWNED NIGHT-HERON

Nycticorax nycticorax

When the setting sun has sent most wetland waders to their nightly roosts, Black-crowned Night-Herons arrive to hunt the marshy waters and to voice their hoarse squawks. They patrol the shallows for prey, which they can see in the dim light with their large, light-sensitive eyes. They remain alongside water until mid-morning, when they flap off to treetop roosts. • Young night-herons are commonly seen around large cattail marshes in autumn. Because of their heavily streaked underparts, juvenile birds are easily confused with other juvenile herons and American Bitterns. • During the breeding season or in unusual weather, Black-crowned Night-Herons sometimes forage during the day. A popular hunting strategy for day-active Black-crowned Night-Herons is to sit motionless atop a few bent-over cattails. In this scenario, anything passing below the perch becomes fair game—even ducklings, small shorebirds or young muskrats. • *Nycticorax*, which means "night raven" in Greek, refers to this bird's distinctive night-time calls.

breeding

ID: black cap and back; white fore-neck, "cheek" and underparts; grey neck and wings; dull yellow legs; stout, black bill; large, red eyes. *Breeding:* 2 white plumes trail down from crown. *Juvenile:* lightly streaked underparts; brown upperparts with white flecking.
Size: *L* 58–66 cm; *W* 1.1 m.
Status: uncommon to locally abundant from early April to early November.
Habitat: shallow cattail and bulrush marshes, lakeshores and along slow rivers.
Nesting: colonial; in trees or shrubs; loose platform of twigs and sticks is lined with finer materials; male gathers the nest material, and female builds the nest; pair incubates 3–4 pale green eggs for 21–26 days.

Feeding: often at dusk; stands motionlessly and waits for prey; stabs for small fish, amphibians, aquatic invertebrates, reptiles, young birds and small mammals.
Voice: deep, guttural *quark* or *wok*, often heard as the bird takes flight.
Similar Species: *Great Blue Heron* (p. 48): much larger; longer legs; blue-grey back. *Yellow-crowned Night-Heron:* adult has white crown and "cheek" patch and white plumes on an otherwise black head; grey back; juvenile is difficult to distinguish from Black-crowned juvenile. *American Bittern* (p. 46): similar to juvenile Black-crowned Night-Heron, but bittern has black streak from bill to shoulder and is lighter tan overall.
Best Sites: *NB:* St. Jacques; Heron I. (New Mills); Inkerman; Castalia. *NS:* Missaguash Marsh; Bon Portage I.; Cape Sable I. *NF:* Ramea. *PQ:* Bas St-Laurent; Forillon NP; Percé; Port-Daniel.

GLOSSY IBIS

Plegadis falcinellus

The exotic look of the Glossy Ibis hints of its distant origins. It is most likely the same powerful trade winds that drew Christopher Columbus to North America that also guided these birds to the warm, productive Caribbean only a few centuries ago. Since the 1930s, the Glossy Ibis has quickly established stable breeding populations throughout the East Coast from its previously small, confined population in the rich coastal marshes of Florida. Sporadic breeding records in southern New Brunswick and other sightings elsewhere in Atlantic Canada suggest that this range expansion will continue northward. • The Glossy Ibis is most often seen sweeping its head back and forth through the water, skilfully using its long, sickle-shaped bill like a precision instrument to probe the marshland mud for unseen prey. Its refined form and graceful movements are similar to those of its Eurasian relative, the Sacred Ibis *(Threskiornis aethiopicus)*, which is depicted as a worshipped deity in the hieroglyphic carvings of the ancient Egyptians.

breeding

ID: long, downcurved bill; long legs; dark skin in front of brown eye is bordered by 2 pale stripes. *Breeding:* chestnut head, neck and sides; green and purple sheen on wings, tail, crown and face. *Nonbreeding:* dark grayish-brown head and neck are streaked with white. *In flight:* neck fully extended; legs trail behind tail; hunchbacked appearance; flocks fly in lines or V-formation.

Size: *L* 56–64 cm; *W* 91–94 cm.

Status: irregular in spring; occasional in autumn.

Habitat: freshwater and saltwater marshes, swamps, flooded fields and estuaries shallow enough for wading.

Nesting: only 1 confirmed nesting record; in colonies, often intermixed with egret and heron rookeries; bulky platform of marsh vegetation and sticks is built over water, on the ground or on top of tall shrubs or small trees; new material is added to nest until young fledge; 3–4 pale blue or green eggs are incubated by both sexes for approximately 21 days.

Feeding: wades through shallow water; probes and gleans for aquatic and terrestrial invertebrates; may also eat amphibian adults and larvae, snakes, leeches, crabs and small fish.

Voice: cooing accompanies billing and preening during nest relief.

Similar Species: *Double-crested Cormorant* (p. 44): much larger, with an upright gait and straight, hooked bill. *Sooty Shearwater* (p. 39): all dark, with shorter, straight bill and short, webbed feet; never seen in marshes.

Best Sites: *NB:* Manawagonish & Saints Rest Marsh (Saint John); Jemseg–Gagetown area. *PEI:* Brackley Marshes; St. Peter's Bay. *NS:* Big Glace Bay Lake; Louisbourg. *PQ:* Rimouski; Penouille (Forillon NP).

TURKEY VULTURE

Cathartes aura

Turkey Vultures are unmatched in Atlantic Canada at using updrafts and thermals—they tease lift out of the slightest pocket of rising air and patrol the skies when other soaring birds are grounded. • This bird eats carrion almost exclusively, so its bill and feet are not nearly as powerful as those of hawks and falcons, which kill live prey. The Turkey Vulture may appear grotesque with its red, featherless head, but this adaptation allows the head to remain relatively clean while it pokes through messy carcasses. • Vultures seem to have mastered the art and science of regurgitation. The ability to regurgitate meals allows parents to transport food over long distances and also enables engorged birds to repulse an attacker or to "lighten up" for an emergency takeoff. • Recent studies have shown that American vultures are most closely related to storks, not to hawks and falcons as previously thought. Molecular similarities with storks, and the shared tendency to defecate on their own legs to cool down, strongly support this taxonomic reclassification.

ID: all black; bare, red head. *Juvenile:* grey head. *In flight:* tilts side-to-side while soaring; silver grey flight feathers; black wing linings; wings are held in a shallow "V"; head appears small.

Size: *L* 66–81 cm; *W* 1.7–1.8 m.

Status: uncommon to fairly common from early April to early November; a few may remain over winter.

Habitat: usually seen flying over open country, hilltops, shorelines or roads; rarely seen over forested areas.

Nesting: in a cave crevice or among boulders; rarely a hollow stump or log; no nest material is used; female lays 2 dull white eggs on bare ground; pair incubates the eggs for up to 41 days; young are fed by regurgitation.

Feeding: entirely on carrion (mostly mammalian); not commonly seen at roadkills.

Voice: generally silent; occasionally produces a hiss or grunt if threatened.

Similar Species: *Golden Eagle* (p. 98) and *Bald Eagle* (p. 89): wings are held flat in flight; do not rock when soaring; head is more visible in flight; lack silvery grey wing linings. *Black Vulture:* rare visitor; grey head; silvery tips on otherwise black wings. *Rough-legged Hawk* (p. 97): dark morph has multibanded tail with black, subterminal tip and whitish wing linings with dark bars.

Best Sites: *NB:* Grand Manan I. *NS:* Brier I. *PQ:* Forillon NP.

SNOW GOOSE

Chen caerulescens

In spring migration, the mud flats and salt marshes of the St. Lawrence River are flecked with moving patches of white—not snowbanks, but thousands of Snow Geese of the *atlantica* subspecies. Although most birds prefer to stage around the outskirts of Québec City, some choose Île Verte and sites near Rimouski. These cackling geese can be seen in farmers' fields, fueling up on waste grain from the previous year's crops. • These birds have strong, serrated bills that are well designed to pull up the root stalks of marsh plants and to grip slippery grasses. • Snow Geese rarely associate with other geese. However, the occasional stray Ross's Goose may accompany its larger relative for protective purposes. • Snow geese pair off while they are in Atlantic Canada because the window for breeding in the Arctic is very short. • In autumn, small numbers of Snow Geese wander throughout Atlantic Canada, including several "Blue Geese" for which the species' scientific name was coined (*caerulescens* means "bluish" in Latin).

ID: white overall; black wing tips; pink feet and bill; dark "grinning patch" on bill; plumage is occasionally stained rusty red. *Blue morph:* white head and upper neck; dark blue-grey body. *Immature:* grey or dusty white plumage; dark bill and feet.
Size: *L* 71–84 cm; *W* 1.4–1.5 m.
Status: locally common migrant from late March to May; rare visitor from late September to mid-November.
Habitat: shallow wetlands, lakes and fields.

Nesting: does not nest in Atlantic Canada.
Feeding: grazes on waste grain and new sprouts; also eats aquatic vegetation, grasses, sedges and roots.
Voice: loud, nasal, constant *houk-houk* in flight.
Similar Species: *Ross's Goose:* smaller; shorter neck; lacks black "grin." *Tundra Swan* and *Mute Swan:* larger; white wing tips. *American White Pelican:* much larger bill and body.
Best Sites: *PEI:* Tryon River. *PQ:* Île Verte; Rimouski; St-Anaclet; Pointe-au-Père; Métis-sur-Mer.

CANADA GOOSE

Branta canadensis

anada Geese are among the most recognizable birds in Canada, but they are also among the least valued. In recent decades, these large, bold geese have taken up residence at urban waterfronts, picnic sites, golf courses and city parks, and today many people consider them pests. • Most of the Canada Geese found in Atlantic Canada are of the large, pale *canadensis* subspecies. A few smaller *hutchinsii* may also occur; these birds have shorter necks that often have a white ring at the base. • Many geese overwinter in more sheltered locations where food is available year-round. Pairs usually mate for life, and family groups remain together in winter, increasing the chance of survival for young birds. • Fuzzy goslings seem to compel people, especially children, to get closer. Unfortunately, Canada Goose parents can cause harm to unwelcome strangers. Hissing sounds and low, outstretched necks are signs that you should give these birds some space.

ID: long, black neck; white "chin strap"; white undertail coverts; light brown underparts; dark brown upperparts; short, black tail.
Size: *L* 55–120 cm; *W* up to 1.8 m.
Status: common to locally abundant migrant from March to May and from September to November; uncommon breeder; uncommon to locally abundant winter resident.
Habitat: lakeshores, riverbanks, ponds, farmlands and city parks.
Nesting: on islands and shorelines; usually on the ground or on a muskrat lodge; female builds a nest made of plant materials and lined with down; female incubates

3–8 white eggs for 25–28 days while the male stands guard.
Feeding: grazes on new sprouts, aquatic vegetation, grass and roots; tips up for aquatic roots and tubers.
Voice: larger subspecies have a loud, familiar *ah-honk*, often answered by other Canada Geese; smaller subspecies have a higher-pitched cackling call.
Similar Species: *Greater White-fronted Goose:* brown neck and head; lacks white "chin strap"; orange legs; white around base of bill; dark speckling on belly. *Pink-footed Goose:* brown neck and head; lacks white "chin strap"; pink legs. *Brant* (p. 58): lacks white "chin strap"; white "necklace"; black upper breast. *Snow Goose* (p. 56): blue morph has white head and upperneck.
Best Sites: common throughout.

BRANT

Branta bernicla

This cousin of the Canada Goose typically spends most of its time in saltwater environments, but in migration it passes over great expanses of land and fresh water, satisfying its hunger with freshwater plants and waste grain. • Most Brant in Atlantic Canada are of the white-bellied *hrota* race and are seen in spring and autumn, either flying low in ragged formation or congregating on shallow estuaries during migratory stopovers. • Brant populations in eastern North America declined by almost 90 percent in the 1930s, when a virulent blight killed much of their winter source of saltwater eelgrass along the Atlantic Coast. Fortunately, many birds switched to eating sea lettuce, a strategy that kept the population from disappearing altogether. Eelgrass has returned in its former abundance to some sites, and this recovery has stabilized Brant numbers. • *Branta* is derived from an Anglo-Saxon word for "burnt" or "charred," a reference to this bird's dark plumage.

ID: black neck, head and upper breast; dark upperparts; white "necklace," belly and hindquarters; black feet; pale brown sides and flanks. *Immature:* "necklace" is less conspicuous.
Size: *L* 59–70 cm; *W* 1.1–1.2 m.
Status: rare to locally common migrant from April to early June and from October to November; very rare visitor in summer and winter.
Habitat: coastal bays, estuaries, shorelines and agricultural fields.

Nesting: does not nest in Atlantic Canada.
Feeding: grazes on aquatic vegetation, preferably eelgrass, and waste grain.
Voice: deep, prolonged *c-r-r-r-uk*, with hissing.
Similar Species: *Canada Goose* (p. 57): white "chin strap"; brown upperparts and upper breast. *Greater White-fronted Goose*: brown neck and head; orange legs; white around base of bill; dark speckling on belly.
Best Sites: *NB:* Caraquet; Letete; Castalia. *PEI:* Hunter River; Brackley–Covehead area (PEI NP); Souris. *NS:* Wallace Bay; Brier I.; Gull I. (Wedgeport); Matthew's Lake; Port Williams. *PQ:* Penouille (Forillon NP).

WOOD DUCK
Aix sponsa

Few birds are forced into the adventures of life as early as Wood Ducks. Newly hatched ducklings often jump as much as 10 metres out of nest cavities in trees to follow their mother to the nearest water body. The little bundles of down are not feather light, but they bounce fairly well and seldom sustain an injury. • Landowners with a tree-lined beaver pond or other suitable wetland may attract a family of Wood Ducks by building a wooden nest box with a predator guard and lining it with sawdust. The nest box should be erected close to the wetland shoreline but at a reasonable height (usually at least 1.5 metres high). • The scientific name *sponsa* is Latin for "promised bride," suggesting that the male appears formally dressed for a wedding. This image is somewhat tarnished by the drake's propensity for illicit unions!

ID: *Male:* glossy, green head with some white streaks; crest is slicked back from crown; purple-chestnut breast is spotted with white; black-and-white shoulder slash; golden sides; dark back and hindquarters. *Female:* white teardrop-shaped eye patch; mottled, brown breast is streaked with white; brown-grey upperparts; white belly.
Size: *L* 38–53 cm.
Status: rare to locally uncommon from mid-March to late October; rare winter resident.
Habitat: *Breeding:* large beaver ponds with emergent vegetation, swamps, ponds, marshes and lakeshores with wooded edges. *Winter:* ice-free ponds and lakes.
Nesting: in a hollow or tree cavity (may be 9 m high or more); also in artificial nest boxes; usually near water; cavity is lined with down; female incubates 9–14 white to buff eggs for 25–35 days.
Feeding: gleans the water's surface and tips up for aquatic vegetation, especially duckweed, aquatic sedges and grasses; eats more fruits and nuts than other ducks and switches to a largely aquatic invertebrate diet in summer.
Voice: *Male:* ascending *ter-wee-wee.* *Female:* squeaky *woo-e-e-k.*
Similar Species: *Hooded Merganser* (p. 84): male has black head with white crest patch; slim, black bill; black-and-white breast. *Harlequin Duck* (p. 76): male is blue-grey overall, with black-and-white patches; female has unstreaked breast and white ear patch.
Best Sites: *NB:* Sackville; Portobello Creek; French Lake. *PEI:* Murray River. *NS:* Missaguash Marsh; Debert; Roseway River. *NF:* Corner Brook; Redcliffe; Bowring Park (St. John's). *PQ:* St-Anaclet; Cap-des-Rosiers (Forillon NP); Barachois.

GADWALL

Anas strepera

Male Gadwalls lack the striking plumage of most other male ducks, but they have a dignified appearance and a subtle beauty. Once you learn their field marks, the drakes are surprisingly easy to identify. Females are daintier than all but the Northern Pintail, and their white speculums are unique among North American dabbling ducks. Gadwalls pair off earlier than other dabbling ducks, sometimes as early as July of the previous year, so it is rare to find unmated adults. • Gadwalls feed equally during the day and night. Such a strategy reduces the risk of predation, because the birds avoid spending long periods of time feeding or sleeping. • Gadwall numbers have greatly increased in Atlantic Canada since the 1950s, and their breeding range has extended eastward to western Newfoundland. Most birds leave Atlantic Canada before the first snowfall—very few birds attempt to overwinter.

ID: white speculum; white belly. *Male:* mostly grey; black hindquarters; dark bill. *Female:* mottled brown overall; brown bill with orange sides.

Size: *L* 46–56 cm.

Status: uncommon to locally common from mid-April to mid-October; very rare winter resident.

Habitat: shallow wetlands, lake borders and beaver ponds.

Nesting: in tall vegetation, sometimes far from water; nest is well concealed in a scraped hollow, often with grass arching overhead; nest is made of grass and other dry vegetation and lined with down; female incubates 8–11 white eggs for 24–27 days.

Feeding: dabbles and tips up for water plants; grazes on grass and waste grain during migration; also eats aquatic invertebrates, tadpoles and small fish; one of the few dabblers to routinely dive for food.

Voice: *Male:* simple, singular *quack;* often whistles harshly. *Female:* high *kaak kaaak kak-kak-kak*, given in series and oscillating in volume.

Similar Species: *American Wigeon* (p. 62) and *Eurasian Wigeon* (p. 61): green speculums; males have distinctive head patterns; females have rufous flanks and lack black indquarters. *Other dabbling ducks* (pp. 60–68): generally lack black-and-white wing patch, black hindquarters of male Gadwall, and orange-sided bill of female.

Best Sites: *NB:* Caraquet–Tracadie area; Cape Jourimain; Sackville; Musquash Marsh. *PEI:* Indian River. *NS:* Amherst Point; Missaguash Marsh; Melbourne Lake; Lingan Bar. *PQ:* Cacouna; Barachois; Havre-aux-Basques (Îles de la Madeleine).

EURASIAN WIGEON

Anas penelope

Each year in Atlantic Canada a few birders will discover a conspicuous, chestnut-headed wigeon while scanning a flock of American Wigeons. Eurasian Wigeons are probably the most noticeable of the regularly occurring rarities to visit the Atlantic provinces. • The Eurasian Wigeons seen in Atlantic Canada are probably nothing more than misguided wanderers following their American cousins after being blown off-course while on migration from breeding sites in Scandinavia. Many Eurasian Wigeons now overwinter here with limited success. Some birds have discovered the delights of urban ponds and lakes, where human hands take away the necessity of finding limited food. • Eurasian Wigeons are not recorded breeders in North America. The increased number of sightings in spring, however, has convinced some people that there is a small breeding population somewhere in Canada, possibly in Labrador.

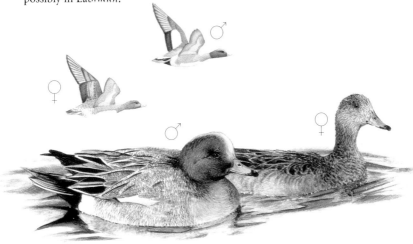

ID: *Male:* chestnut head; cream forehead; rosy breast; grey sides; black hindquarters; dark feet; black-tipped, grey-blue bill. *Female:* rufous hints on mostly brown head and breast; buffy flanks. *In flight:* large, white wing patch; dusky grey "wing pits."
Size: *L* 42–52 cm.
Status: rare migrant from early April to early July and from August to November; a few overwinter at regular sites, often close to or in large cities.
Habitat: shallow wetlands, lake edges and ponds, agricultural fields, estuaries and large rivers.
Nesting: does not nest in Atlantic Canada.

Feeding: primarily vegetarian; dabbles and grazes for grass, leaves and stems in summer and eelgrass in winter; occasionally pirates food from American Coots.
Voice: *Male:* high-pitched, 2-toned whistle. *Female:* has harsher quack than American Wigeon.
Similar Species: *American Wigeon* (p. 62): white "wing pits"; male lacks reddish-brown head; female's head is more brown. *Other dabbling ducks* (pp. 60–68): females are larger and lack white-bordered, green speculum.
Best Sites: *NB:* Caraquet; Sackville; Saint John. *PEI:* Clarke's Pond (PEI NP); Murray River. *NS:* Amherst Point; Louisbourg. *NF:* Parson's Pond; L'Anse aux Meadows; Mundy Pond & Quidi Vidi Lake (St. John's). *PQ:* Cacouna; Rimouski.

AMERICAN WIGEON

Anas americana

The male American Wigeon's piping, three-syllabled whistle sets it apart from the wetland orchestra of buzzes, quacks and ticks. • Although this bird frequently dabbles for food, nothing seems to please a wigeon more than the succulent stems and leaves of pond-bottom plants. These plants grow far too deep for a dabbling duck, however, so pirating individuals often steal from accomplished divers, such as American Coots and *Aythya* diving ducks . In contrast to most ducks, American Wigeons commonly graze on shore. • Courtship activity starts late for these wigeons, which may account for the many hybrids found in Atlantic Canada—stray Eurasian Wigeons often arrive at the same time as American Wigeons. • Because of the male's bright white crown and forehead, some people call this bird "Baldpate."

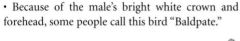

ID: large, white wing patch; cinnamon breast and sides; white belly; black-tipped, grey-blue bill; green speculum; white "wing pits." *Male:* white forehead; green swipe extends back from eye. *Female:* greyish head; brown underparts.

Size: L 46–58 cm.

Status: uncommon to locally abundant from early March to early June and from late August to October; rare to locally common breeder; rare and somewhat local in winter.

Habitat: shallow wetlands, lake edges and ponds.

Nesting: always on dry ground, often far from water; nest is well concealed in tall vegetation and is built with grass, leaves and down; female incubates 8–11 white eggs for 23–25 days.

Feeding: dabbles and tips up for aquatic leaves and the stems of pondweeds; also grazes and uproots young shoots in fields; may eat some invertebrates; occasionally pirates food from other birds.

Voice: *Male:* nasal, frequently repeated whistle: *whee WHEE wheew. Female:* soft, seldom heard quack.

Similar Species: *Gadwall* (p. 60): white speculum; lacks large, white forewing patch; male lacks green eye swipe; female has orange swipes on bill. *Eurasian Wigeon* (p. 61): grey "wing pits"; male has rufous head, cream forehead and rosy breast; lacks green eye swipe; female usually has browner head.

Best Sites: *NB:* Saint John; Portobello Creek; Jemseg–Gagetown area. *PEI:* Indian River. *NS:* Missaguash Marsh; Debert; Melbourne Lake. *NF:* Codroy Valley; St. Paul's; Quidi Vidi Lake (St. John's). *PQ:* Bas St-Laurent; Îles de la Madeleine.

AMERICAN BLACK DUCK
Anas rubripes

Male and female American Black Ducks are remarkably similar in appearance, which is unusual for waterfowl. • In recent years, the eastern expansion of the Mallard has come at the expense of this dark dabbler. A male Mallard will aggressively pursue a female American Black Duck, and if she is unable to find a mate of her own kind, she will often accept the offer. Hybrid offspring are less fertile, and they are usually unable to reproduce. Attempts to increase wooded swamp habitats, which American Black Ducks favour, have largely failed to thwart this hybridization in Atlantic Canada, because Mallards will nest almost anywhere. Fortunately, the more remote wilderness of rivers and lakes in northern Newfoundland, Québec and Labrador still attract American Black Ducks but few Mallards. • *Rubripes* means "red foot" in Latin.

ID: dark, brown-black body; light brown head and neck; bright orange feet; violet speculum. *Male:* yellow-olive bill. *Female:* dull green bill is mottled with grey or black. *In flight:* whitish underwings; dark body.
Size: *L* 51–63 cm.
Status: uncommon to locally abundant migrant from late March to late May and from August to November; uncommon to fairly common breeder and winter resident.
Habitat: *Breeding:* lakes, wetlands, rivers and agricultural areas. *Winter:* also coastal bays, salt marshes and estuaries.
Nesting: usually on the ground among clumps of dense vegetation near water; beaver ponds are preferred; female fills a shallow depression with plant material and lines it with down; female incubates 7–11 white to greenish-buff eggs for 23–33 days; second clutches are common, usually to replace lost broods.
Feeding: tips up and dabbles in shallows for the seeds and roots of pondweeds; also eats aquatic invertebrates, larval amphibians and fish eggs.
Voice: *Male:* a croak. *Female:* a loud quack.
Similar Species: *Mallard* (p. 64): white belly; blue speculum, bordered with black and white bars; female is lighter overall and has white tail. *Gadwall* (p. 60): black hindquarters; black-and-white wing patch.
Best Sites: widespread breeder; common in migration along coasts and inland.

MALLARD

Anas platyrhynchos

The male Mallard, with his iridescent, green head and chestnut breast, is the classic wild duck. Mallards can be found every day of the year in Atlantic Canada, often in flocks and always near open water. • The female's carelessness at the nest site often results in egg predation. • As well as captivating female American Black Ducks, male wild Mallards will freely hybridize with domestic ducks, which were originally derived from Mallards in Europe. Illicit unions with Northern Pintail ducks produce the most beautiful male birds imaginable. • Males moult after breeding, losing much of their extravagant plumage. This "eclipse" plumage camouflages them during the flightless period. They usually moult again into their breeding plumage by early autumn. • The scientific name *platyrhynchos* means "broad, flat bill" in Greek.

ID: dark blue speculum, bordered by white; orange feet. *Male:* glossy, green head; yellow bill; chestnut breast; white "necklace"; grey body plumage; black tail feathers curl upward. *Female:* mottled brown overall; orange bill is spattered with black.
Size: *L* 51–71 cm.
Status: rare to locally uncommon year-round; most wintering birds are descendents of domesticated releases.
Habitat: *Breeding:* lakes, wetlands, rivers, city parks, agricultural areas and sewage lagoons. *Winter:* coastal salt marshes, lagoons and estuaries.
Nesting: in tall vegetation or under a bush, often near water; nest of grass and other plant material is lined with down; female incubates 7–10 light green to white eggs for 26–30 days.
Feeding: tips up and dabbles in shallows for the seeds of sedges, willows and pondweeds; also eats aquatic invertebrates, larval amphibians and fish eggs.
Voice: *Male:* deep but quiet quacks. *Female:* loud quacks; very vocal.
Similar Species: *Northern Shoveler* (p. 66): much larger bill; male has white breast. *American Black Duck* (p. 63): darker than female Mallard; purple speculum lacks white borders. *Common Merganser* (p. 85): male lacks chestnut breast, blood red bill and white underparts.
Best Sites: *NB:* Sackville; Gagetown; Woodstock. *PEI:* Crapaud; Indian River. *NS:* Missaguash Marsh; Melbourne Lake; Sullivan's Pond (Dartmouth). *NF:* Shoal Cove East; Shoal Harbour. *PQ:* Bas St-Laurent; Îles de la Madeleine.

BLUE-WINGED TEAL
Anas discors

Blue-winged Teals are the last of the ducks to return in spring and also the last to establish pair bonds, often waiting until they are on their breeding grounds. Males defend females, but they do not establish territories. As a result, Blue-wings have more nests concentrated in a small area than any other waterfowl. • Blue-winged Teals possess a very efficient digestive system and can process food faster than any other small duck. • Despite the similarity of their names, the Green-winged Teal is not the Blue-winged Teal's closest relative. The Blue-wing is more closely related to the Cinnamon Teal *(Anas cyanoptera)* and the Northern Shoveler. All three birds have broad, flat bills, pale blue forewings and green speculums. • The scientific name *discors* is Latin for "without harmony," which might refer to this bird's call as it takes flight.

ID: *Male:* blue-grey head; white crescent on face; black-spotted breast and sides. *Female:* mottled brown overall. *In flight:* blue forewing patch; green speculum.

Size: *L* 36–41 cm.

Status: fairly common to common from early April to mid-May and from late August to late October; rare to uncommon breeder; very few remain into winter.

Habitat: shallow lake edges and wetlands; prefers areas of short but dense emergent vegetation.

Nesting: in grass along shorelines and in meadows; nest is built with grass and considerable amounts of down; female incubates 8–13 white eggs (may be tinged with olive) for 23–27 days.

Feeding: gleans the water's surface for sedge and grass seeds, pondweeds, duckweeds and aquatic invertebrates.

Voice: *Male:* soft *keck-keck-keck*. *Female:* soft quacks.

Similar Species: *Green-winged Teal* (p. 68): female has smaller bill, black-and-green speculum and lacks blue forewing patch. *Northern Shoveler* (p. 66): female has much larger bill with paler base; male has green head and lacks spotting on body. *Harlequin Duck* (p. 76): male is blue-grey overall with many black-and-white patches; female is plain brown with no wing patches.

Best Sites: breeders can be found in less exposed wetlands.

65

NORTHERN SHOVELER

Anas clypeata

The initial reaction upon seeing this bird for the first time is often, "Wow, look at the big honker on that Mallard!" A closer look, however, reveals a completely different bird altogether: the Northern Shoveler. The Shoveler, in fact, is closely related to the teals, and has the same kind of surface-skimming feeding behaviour. An extra large, spoon-like bill allows this handsome duck to strain small invertebrates from the water column and from the bottoms of ponds. Shovelers eat much smaller organisms than do most other waterfowl, and their intestines are elongated to prolong the digestion of these hard-bodied invertebrates. • During the breeding season, male Shovelers fiercely defend small feeding territories. However, they are remarkably sociable in migration and on their wintering grounds. • The scientific name *clypeata* is Latin for "furnished with a shield." The male's reddish belly patch appears shield-shaped when seen in flight from below.

ID: large, spatulate bill; blue forewing patch; green speculum. *Male:* green head; white breast; chestnut sides. *Female:* mottled brown overall; orange-tinged bill.

Size: *L* 46–51 cm.

Status: uncommon to fairly common from late March to early June and from September to early November; locally uncommon breeder; very rare winter resident.

Habitat: shallow marshes, bogs and lakes with muddy bottoms and emergent vegetation, usually in open and semi-open areas.

Nesting: in a shallow hollow on dry ground, usually within 50 m of water; female builds the nest with dry grass and down and incubates 10–12 pale greenish-buff eggs for 21–28 days.

Feeding: dabbles in shallow and often muddy water; strains out plant and animal matter, especially aquatic crustaceans, insect larvae and seeds; rarely tips up.

Voice: generally quiet; occasionally a raspy chuckle or quack; most often heard during spring courtship.

Similar Species: *Mallard* (p. 64): blue speculum, bordered by white; lacks pale blue forewing; male has chestnut breast and white flanks. *Blue-winged Teal* (p. 65): much smaller bill; smaller overall; male has spotted breast and sides.

Best Sites: *NB:* Sackville; Saint's Rest Marsh (Saint John); Portobello Creek; Gagetown. *PEI:* Indian River; Covehead. *NS:* Amherst Point; Missaguash Marsh; West Lawrencetown. *NF:* Codroy Valley; Stephenville; St. Paul's. *PQ:* Cap-des-Rosiers (Forillon NP); Barachois.

NORTHERN PINTAIL

Anas acuta

The male Northern Pintail's beauty and style are unsurpassed by most of Atlantic Canada's water birds. This drake's trademark is his long, tapering tail feathers, which are easily seen in flight and point skyward when he dabbles. In Atlantic Canada, only the male Long-tailed Duck shares this pintail feature. • Spring-flooded agricultural fields tend to attract the largest Northern Pintail flocks. Migrating Pintails are often seen in flocks that have almost twice as many males as females. This ratio is probably the result of summer predation on females at the fairly open ground nesting sites. • Although this widespread duck appears to be declining overall across its range in other parts of North America, it has fared somewhat better in Atlantic Canada. The main breeding population is in northern Newfoundland, but other breeding birds are scattered across all five provinces.

ID: long, slender neck; dark, glossy bill. *Male:* chocolate brown head; long, tapering tail feathers; white of breast extends up sides of neck; dusty grey body plumage; black-and-white hindquarters. *Female:* mottled, light brown overall. *In flight:* slender body; brownish speculum with white trailing edge.
Size: *Male: L* 64–76 cm. *Female: L* 51–56 cm.
Status: fairly common to common from early April to late May and from late August to early November; locally common breeder; rare winter resident.
Habitat: *Breeding:* shallow wetlands, fields and lake edges. *Winter:* flooded fields, coastal salt marshes, lagoons and estuaries.
Nesting: in a small depression of vegetation; nest of grass, leaves and moss is

lined with down; female incubates 6–12 greenish-buff eggs for 22–25 days.
Feeding: diet is more varied than that of other dabbling ducks; tips up and dabbles in shallows for the seeds of sedges, willows and pondweeds; also eats aquatic invertebrates and larval amphibians; eats waste grain in agricultural areas during migration.
Voice: *Male:* soft, whistling call. *Female:* rough quack.
Similar Species: male is distinctive. *Mallard* (p. 64) and *Gadwall* (p. 60): females are chunkier, usually with dark or 2-toned bills, and lack tapering tail and long, slender neck. *Blue-winged Teal* (p. 65): female is smaller; green speculum; blue forewing patch. *Long-tailed Duck* (p. 80): head is not uniformly dark; all-dark wings.
Best Sites: most nesting sites are in northern and western NF; found mostly along coasts in migration.

GREEN-WINGED TEAL

Anas crecca

When intruders cause Green-winged Teals to rocket up from wetlands, these small ducks circle quickly overhead in small, tight-flying flocks. They return to the water only when the threat has departed. Green-wings are among the most speedy and manoeuvrable of waterfowl. A predator's only hope of catching a healthy teal is to snatch it from the water or from a nest. Although females go to great lengths to conceal their nests among upland grasses and brush, there are always a few nests that are discovered by hungry predators. • Most Green-wings in Atlantic Canada are of the *carolinensis* subspecies. During migration, however, keen birders can find a few obvious European *crecca* and even the occasional Asian *nimia*. • Weighing less than half a kilogram, Green-winged Teals are the smallest of Atlantic Canada's dabbling ducks. They often loiter on ponds and marshy wetlands until cold winter weather freezes the water's surface.

ID: small bill; green-and-black speculum. *Male:* chestnut head; green swipe extends back from eye; white shoulder slash; creamy breast is spotted with black; pale grey sides. *Female:* mottled, brown overall; light belly.

Size: *L* 30–41 cm.

Status: uncommon to common from late March to mid-May and from late August to early November; rare to uncommon breeder; rare winter resident.

Habitat: *Breeding:* shallow lakes, wetlands, beaver ponds and meandering rivers.

Winter: coastal wetlands, estuaries and shallow bays.

Nesting: well concealed in tall vegetation; nest is built of grass and leaves and is lined with down; female incubates 6–14 cream to pale buff eggs for 20–24 days.

Feeding: dabbles in the shallows, particularly on mud flats, for aquatic invertebrates, larval amphibians, marsh plant seeds and pondweeds.

Voice: *Male:* crisp whistle. *Female:* soft quack.

Similar Species: *American Wigeon* (p. 62): male lacks white shoulder slash and chestnut head. *Blue-winged Teal* (p. 65): female has blue forewing patch.

Best Sites: abundant in migration, especially along coasts.

REDHEAD

Aythya americana

T he Redhead has only recently begun nesting in Atlantic Canada. Its usual breeding habitat is farther west. In Atlantic Canada, the Redhead first colonized southwestern New Brunswick and gradually made its way to western Newfoundland. The efforts of the Canadian Wildlife Service and Ducks Unlimited Canada to provide duck-nesting and -feeding habitats are partly responsible for this recent nesting success. • Female Redheads usually incubate their eggs and brood their young as other ducks do, but they occasionally lay their eggs in the nests of other ducks. Blue-winged Teals, Gadwalls, Ring-necked Ducks and Lesser Scaups have been victims of Redhead egg dumping, otherwise known as "brood parasitism." • The Redhead is a diving duck, but it will occasionally feed on the surface of a wetland like a dabbler. In Atlantic Canada it usually shuns salt water.

ID: blue-grey, black-tipped bill. *Male:* rounded, red head; black breast and hindquarters; grey back and sides. *Female:* dark brown overall; light "chin" and "cheek" patches.
Size: *L* 46–56 cm.
Status: rare from April to mid-May and from September to mid-December; rare but increasing local breeder.
Habitat: large, shallow, well-vegetated wetlands, ponds and lakes; less often bays and rivers.
Nesting: usually in shallow water, sometimes on dry ground; deep basket nest of reeds and grass is lined with fine white down and suspended over water at the base of emergent vegetation; female incubates 9–14 eggs for 23–29 days; female may lay eggs in other ducks' nests.

Feeding: dives to depths of 3 m; primarily eats aquatic vegetation, especially pond-weeds, duckweeds and the leaves and stems of plants; occasionally eats aquatic invertebrates.
Voice: generally quiet. *Male:* cat-like meow in courtship. *Female:* rolling *kurr-kurr-kurr; squak* when alarmed.
Similar Species: *Canvasback:* clean, white back; bill extends onto forehead. *Ring-necked Duck* (p. 70): female has more prominent, white eye ring, white ring on bill and peaked head. *Tufted Duck* (p. 71): female has darker, more angular head; prominent white wing bar. *Lesser Scaup* (p. 73) and *Greater Scaup* (p. 72): male has dark head and whiter sides; female has more white at base of bill; prominent, white wing bar.
Best Sites: *NB:* Middle I. (lower Saint John River); Fredericton. *PEI:* Indian River; Deroche Pond. *NS:* Amherst Point; Missaguash Marsh; Wallace Bay. *NF:* Codroy Valley. *PQ:* Barachois.

69

RING-NECKED DUCK
Aythya collaris

The Ring-necked Duck is a fairly common nesting species throughout Atlantic Canada, and it appears to be expanding its range. Small, shy groups are often seen floating on boreal forest bogs, sedge-meadow wetlands and tree-edged beaver ponds. These birds rarely allow a close approach, and nests are rarely discovered until after the young are out on the water. • Ring-necks prefer to feed in shallow waters where they can reach aquatic plants, snails, aquatic insects and clams. Although Ring-necks are diving ducks, like scaups and Redheads, they behave more like dabbling ducks, frequently up-ending for food, hiding their young in dense vegetation and taking flight directly from the water. • The common name is derived from the scientific name *collaris*, which resulted from an English ornithologist looking at an indistinct cinnamon collar on a museum specimen.

ID: *Male:* angular, dark purple head; black breast, back and hindquarters; white shoulder slash; grey sides; blue-grey bill with black and white bands at tip; thin, white border around base of bill. *Female:* dark brown overall; white eye ring; dark bill with black and white bands at tip; pale crescent on front of face.
Size: *L* 36–46 cm.
Status: uncommon to common from mid-March to late May; fairly common from mid-September to early November; rare to fairly common breeder; occasional winter resident.
Habitat: reservoirs, shallow wooded ponds, swamps, marshes and sloughs with emergent vegetation.

Nesting: frequently over water on floating islands or hummocks, rarely on a shoreline; bulky nest of grass and moss is lined with down; female incubates 8–10 olive tan eggs for 25–29 days.
Feeding: dives underwater for aquatic vegetation, including seeds, tubers and pondweed leaves; also eats aquatic invertebrates and molluscs.
Voice: seldom heard. *Male:* low-pitched, hissing whistle. *Female:* growling *churr.*
Similar Species: *Tufted Duck* (p. 71): shows broad, white wing stripe in flight; male usually has noticeable crest and white flanks; female has smaller dark tip on bill. *Lesser Scaup* (p. 73) and *Greater Scaup* (p. 72): both lack white ring near tip of bill; male lacks black back; female lacks eye ring. *Redhead* (p. 69): female has less prominent eye ring; rounded rather than peaked head; less white on front of face.
Best Sites: common nester on small ponds and lakes.

TUFTED DUCK
Aythya fuligula

You are watching a raft of diving ducks but there is one pair that you can't quite figure out. The male looks like a Ring-necked Duck, but he lacks the white stripe across the bill, and he appears to have a long tuft trailing down the back of his head. Wasn't that a scaup-like wing bar in flight? Could it be a Tufted Duck? Indeed, it could, because this European relative of the scaups occasionally ventures into North American waters. The first sighting in North America was in 1911 in Alaska. Since then, there have been several sightings in British Columbia, but Atlantic Canada is now the best place to see this recent immigrant. • Look for this bird in winter and spring when open fresh water is in short supply. The Tufted Duck can also be seen in coastal bays and estuaries, especially in Nova Scotia and Newfoundland, and in freshwater habitat. • This bird's species name, *fuligula*, refers to the male's sooty upperparts in breeding plumage.

ID: *Male:* long, loose tuft on head; dark, iridescent purple head and neck; black back, wings, rump and breast; pure white flanks and belly; black mark on tip of bill. *Female:* short, brown tuft; dark brown head, back and wings; reddish-brown breast; pale grey-brown flanks; white belly; black mark on tip of bill; many have scaup-like facial patch.
Size: *L* 43 cm.
Status: rare, local visitor from late October to early April.
Habitat: freshwater lakes and ponds before they freeze up; saltwater bays and estuaries in mid-winter; also in city harbours.

Nesting: does not nest in Atlantic Canada.
Feeding: dives for plants, crustaceans, molluscs and aquatic insects.
Voice: usually silent in winter; male's courtship call is a duckling-like, peeping whistle; female utters a low, growling *err-err*.
Similar Species: *Ring-necked Duck* (p. 70): white band on bill; no tuft; male has grey flanks; female has white streak trailing behind eye; lacks white wing bar. *Greater Scaup* (p. 72) and *Lesser Scaup* (p. 73): lack tuft; males' backs and wings are greyer; females have more extensive white patch at base of bill.
Best Sites: *NB:* Courtenay Bay (Saint John). *NS:* Halifax Harbour. *NF:* Conception Bay; Quidi Vidi Lake (St. John's).

GREATER SCAUP
Aythya marila

Greater Scaups in large rafts are seen alongside Long-tailed Ducks, Common Eiders, scoters and Common Goldeneyes during autumn migration and into the winter months, when they seem to share the mollusc beds with these sea ducks. Later on, they switch back to a more traditional *Aythya* diet. • Greater Scaups are abundant throughout much of Atlantic Canada in migration, and they can be confused with Lesser Scaups, which are less common but growing in number. Look for the rounder (not peaked), greenish head of the Greater Scaup to distinguish it from its Lesser relative. As Lesser Scaups continue prospecting in Atlantic Canada, there is a possibility that more hybrids will appear; some hybrids have already started to turn up in Newfoundland. • Greater Scaups nest primarily on the open tundra of the Labrador coast, but breeding birds can also be found scattered throughout all five provinces most years.

ID: rounded head; golden eyes. *Male:* iridescent, dark green head; black breast; white belly and flanks; light grey back; dark hindquarters; blue, black-tipped bill. *Female:* brown overall; well-defined white patch at base of bill. *In flight:* white flash through wing extends well onto primary feathers.
Size: *L* 41–48 cm.
Status: uncommon to abundant migrant from late February to May and from September to November; rare to locally common breeder; uncommon to locally common winter resident.
Habitat: *Breeding:* ponds and small lakes on open tundra; fens or bogs. *In migration:* lakes, large marshes and reservoirs, usually far from shore; occasionally gravel pits and small urban ponds. *Winter:* shallow inlets and estuaries.

Nesting: on a grass- or sedge-covered shoreline; female lines a shallow depression with dry vegetation and down; may nest in small, loose colonies; female incubates 5–11 olive-buff eggs for 24–28 days.
Feeding: dives underwater, to greater depths than other *Aythya* ducks, for aquatic invertebrates and vegetation; fresh-water molluscs are favoured in winter.
Voice: generally quiet in migration; alarm call is a deep *scaup.* *Male:* a 3-note whistle and a soft *wah-hooo. Female:* a subtle growl.
Similar Species: *Lesser Scaup* (p. 73): fractionally smaller; shorter, white wing flash in flight; slightly smaller bill; male has peaked, purplish head; female usually has peaked head. *Tufted Duck* (p. 71) and *Ring-necked Duck* (p. 70): white ring near tip of bill; male has black. *Redhead* (p. 69): female has less white at base of bill; male has red head and darker sides.
Best Sites: *Summer: NB:* Grassy I. (lower Saint John River). *PEI:* Indian River. *NF:* L'Anse aux Meadows; Cape Race. *PQ:* Pointe de l'Est (Îles de la Madeleine). *Winter:* almost always on salt water.

LESSER SCAUP

Aythya affinis

The male Lesser Scaup and his close relative, the male Greater Scaup, portray the colour pattern of an Oreo cookie: they are black at both ends and dark in the middle. • Lesser Scaups are most at home among the boreal lakes to the west, but some birds wander to all parts of Atlantic Canada. These scaups have nested in maritime Québec and New Brunswick. Birds can be found in the other Atlantic provinces in summer and may breed there as well. • These light ducks leap up neatly before diving underwater, where they propel themselves with powerful strokes of their feet. • The scientific name *affinis* is Latin for "adjacent" or "allied"—a reference to this scaup's close association with other diving ducks. "Scaup" may refer to a preferred winter food (shellfish beds are called "scalps" in Scotland), or it may be a phonetic interpretation of one of this bird's calls.

ID: yellow eyes. *Male:* dark, purplish head is peaked; black breast and hindquarters; dusty white sides; greyish back; blue-grey, black-tipped bill. *Female:* dark brown overall; well-defined white patch at base of bill.

Size: *L* 38–46 cm.

Status: rare to uncommon migrant from mid-March to mid-May and from late August to early November; rare breeder; rare winter resident.

Habitat: *Breeding:* woodland and tundra ponds, wetlands and lake edges with grassy margins. *In migration:* lakes, large marshes and rivers.

Nesting: in tall, concealing vegetation, generally close to water and occasionally on an island; nest hollow is built of grass and lined with down; female incubates 8–14 olive-buff eggs for about 21–27 days; usually nests later than other ducks.

Feeding: dives underwater for aquatic invertebrates, mostly molluscs, amphipods, insect larvae; occasionally takes aquatic vegetation.

Voice: alarm call is a deep *scaup. Male:* soft *whee-oooh* in courtship. *Female:* purring *kwah.*

Similar Species: *Greater Scaup* (p. 72): slightly larger bill; longer white wing flash; rounded head; male has greenish head. *Tufted Duck* (p. 71) and *Ring-necked Duck* (p. 70): male has white shoulder slash and black back; female has white-ringed bill. *Redhead* (p. 69): female has less white at base of bill; male has red head and darker sides.

Best Sites: *NB:* Cape Brule; Tracadie; Long Pond (Grand Manan I.). *PEI:* Long Pond (PEI NP). *NS:* La Have River. *NF:* Parson's Pond; Middle Arm (Carmanville). *PQ:* Cacouna; Rimouski; Cap-des-Rosiers (Forillon NP).

KING EIDER

Somateria spectabilis

If you want to travel to see a spectacular bird, the dazzling King Eider is worth the effort: the male boasts no fewer than six bold colours on his magnificent head and bill. • King Eiders do not breed in Atlantic Canada, but in migration or winter, birders going on cold excursions may be rewarded by a glimpse of this impressive duck. It is not surprising that this bird's favoured wintering sites receive visits from many birders each year. • King Eiders are equipped with some of the finest insulation in the bird world (eider down), so they are well adapted for loafing on ice floes and taking extended deep dives into frigid arctic water. Taking a dip in the surf off coastal headlands and coming up with a gizzard full of mussels must seem like a perfect vacation to this northerner!

ID: *Male:* blue crown; green "cheek"; orange nasal disc; red bill; black wings; white neck, breast, back, upperwing patches and flank patches. *Female:* mottled, rich rufous-brown overall; black bill extends into nasal shield; sides have V-shaped markings. *Immature male:* dark overall; white breast; yellow-orange bill resembles female's bill.
Size: *L* 48–64 cm; *W* 89–102 cm.
Status: rare migrant; rare to locally uncommon winter visitor.
Habitat: surf lines and beyond off coastal headlands, often farther from shore than Common Eiders and scoters.
Nesting: does not nest in Atlantic Canada.

Feeding: dives primarily for aquatic molluscs; may dive to more than 45 m; also takes small insects, crustaceans, echinoderms and some vegetation, especially in summer.
Voice: *Male:* soft cooing sounds in courtship. *Female:* low, twanging clucks.
Similar Species: *Common Eider* (p. 75): first-winter male has larger, greyer bill; female has evenly barred sides; feathering on sides of long, droopy bill extend to nostril; immature has white streaking on back. *Female scoters* (pp. 77–79): more bulbous bills; lack nasal shield; more patchy colours on heads; solid brown plumages.
Best Sites *NB:* Point Lepreau; Indian Point (St. Andrews). *PEI:* North Cape; Cape Tryon. *NS:* Cow Bay. *NF:* St. Anthony; Point La Haye; Cape St. Mary's; Cape Race. *PQ:* Ste-Flavie; Cap Gaspé.

COMMON EIDER
Somateria mollissima

Floating leisurely in rafts of thousands, Common Eiders regularly veil the frigid winter waters of the Atlantic Coast. Like scoters, these hefty birds are well adapted for living in cold, northern seas. Their high metabolic rate and dense down feathers facilitate their almost entirely marine lifestyle. Long periods of inactivity are punctuated by frantic bouts of feeding or short flights to a nearby area, usually situated close to coastal headlands. • During the breeding season, female eiders pluck downy feathers from their own bodies to provide insulation and camouflage for their eggs. For centuries, people have prized eider down for its superior insulative properties, and down-gathering still goes on in parts of Québec and Newfoundland.

ID: *Male:* smoothly sloping forehead; black-and-white overall; green tinge on nape and nasal shield. *Female:* grey to rusty brown overall; barred breast, flanks and back; grey bill and nasal shield. *Immature male:* dark head and body; white streaking on back. *In flight:* flies close to the water's surface with its head lowered.
Size: *L* 58–68 cm; *W* 88–106 cm.
Status: locally abundant winter resident; locally common breeder.
Habitat: shallow coastal waters in all seasons; occasionally seen on large freshwater lakes. *Breeding:* rocky shorelines, islands or tundra in close proximity to water.
Nesting: colonial; in a shallow depression on a rocky shelf; nest is lined with plant material and large quantities of down; female incubates 3–6 olive grey eggs for 24–25 days.
Feeding: molluscs, especially blue mussels, pried from ocean depths are swallowed whole; may dive deeper than 45 m; crustaceans, echinoderms, insects and plant material are also taken when they are available.
Voice: *Male:* raucous, moaning *he-ho-ha-ho* or *a-o-waa-a-o-waa;* courtship calls are *ah-oo* and *k'doo. Female:* mallard-like *wak-wak-wak-wak-wak;* angry *wh-r-r-r-r;* courtship call is *aw-aw-aw.*
Similar Species: male is distinctive. *American Black Duck* (p. 63): some look similar to female in poor light; much smaller bill; purple speculum; white underwing coverts. *Scoters* (pp. 77–79): lack barring of female and white back and breast of male. *King Eider* (p. 74): male has colourful, blocky head; female has long nasal shield; immature male has yellow-orange bill and lacks white streaking on back.
Best Sites: *Summer: NB:* West Quaco; Deer I. *NS:* Spencer's I. (Parrsboro); Eastern Shore Is.; Canso. *NF:* L'Anse aux Meadows; Penguin Is. *PQ:* Îles Razades (Trois Pistoles); Bicquette I.; Île Brion (Îles de la Madeleine). *Winter:* always on salt water.

HARLEQUIN DUCK

Histrionicus histrionicus

The Harlequin Duck is a widespread nesting species in the Gaspé and northern Newfoundland, but elsewhere it is a local migrant and winter resident. Eastern Harlequin populations have dwindled to approximately a thousand birds, initially as a result of overhunting, but more recently because of a serious decline in fish stocks. • Most Harlequins are seen close to shore in spring and autumn. Although their stay is usually brief, their startling appearance never fails to excite and impress fortunate onlookers. A few birds linger at favoured locations over winter, riding the rough, storm-swept waters of the Atlantic Ocean. • The Harlequin Duck's favourite breeding habitat is tumbling coastal mountain streams. • This bird's distinctive mouse-like call has given it the local name of "Sea Mouse." Some people also refer to Harlequins as "Lords and Ladies."

ID: small, rounded duck; blocky head; short bill; raises and lowers its tail while swimming. *Male:* grey-blue body; chestnut sides; white spots and stripes outlined in black on head, neck and flanks. *Female:* dusky brown overall; light underparts; 2–3 light patches on head.

Size: *L* 36–48 cm.

Status: locally rare from March to early May and from September to November; very local breeder; locally uncommon to common winter resident.

Habitat: *Breeding:* mountain streams and occasionally offshore islets. *Winter:* coastal headlands and bays.

Nesting: on the ground, in bushy vegetation or rock recesses by fast-flowing streams; female incubates 4–7 creamy eggs for 28–29 days.

Feeding: dabbles and dives for aquatic invertebrates in rivers and crustaceans and molluscs in freshwater lakes; often searches river bottoms, probing rock crevices for invertebrates and fish eggs.

Voice: a high-pitched whistle on the breeding grounds; generally silent outside breeding season.

Similar Species: male is distinctive. *Bufflehead* (p. 81): smaller; never found on fast-flowing water; female lacks white between eye and bill. *Surf Scoter* (p. 77): female has bulbous bill. *White-winged Scoter* (p. 78): female has white wing patch and bulbous bill.

Best Sites: *Summer: NB:* Charlo River. *NF:* Western Brook (Gros Morne NP); L'Anse aux Meadows. *PQ:* Ste-Anne-des-Monts; Île Bonaventure; Port-Daniel. *In migration* and *winter: NS:* Cherry Hill; Ingonish. *NF:* L'Anse aux Meadows; Point La Haye; Golden Bay (Cape St. Mary's). *PQ:* Pointe-au-Père; Bic; Pointe St-Pierre (Îles de la Madeleine).

SURF SCOTER

Melanitta perspicillata

Surfing is hardly a favoured activity in the frigid waters of the North Atlantic. However, there is nothing that rafts of Surf Scoters like more than riding wave crests and diving through the breaking surf to reach their food. When spring storms whip up whitecaps, Surf Scoters rest comfortably among the crashing waves. These scoters are most often seen in migration, when tired flocks settle upon open water in large, dark rafts. They spend their winters just beyond the breaking surf on the Atlantic Coast. • Small numbers of Surf Scoters nest in northern Québec and Labrador. Unfortunately, this region is fairly inaccessible, and this bird is very secretive during the nesting season. • The scientific name *Melanitta* means "black duck"; *perspicillata* is Latin for "spectacular," which refers to this bird's colourful, bulbous bill. The white patches on the adult male's head are the reason for its popular nickname "Skunk Head."

ID: large, stocky duck; large bill; sloping forehead. *Male:* black overall; white on forehead and back of neck; orange bill and legs; black spot, outlined in white, at base of bill. *Female:* brown overall; dark grey bill; 2 whitish patches on sides of head.
Size: *L* 43–53 cm.
Status: common to locally abundant migrant from mid-April to late May and from August to November; rare breeder; locally common to abundant winter resident.
Habitat: along the coast, along headlands and in both sheltered and windswept bays; occasionally visits freshwater lakes and even city ponds.
Nesting: in a shallow scrape under bushes, often well away from open water; nest is lined with down; female incubates 5–9 buff-coloured eggs for 28–30 days.
Feeding: dives underwater to depths of 9 m; eats mostly molluscs; also takes aquatic insect larvae, crustaceans and some aquatic vegetation; rafts of scoters typically gather together and dive for food in a synchronized wave.
Voice: generally quiet; infrequently utters low, harsh croaks. *Male:* occasionally gives a low, clear whistle. *Female:* guttural *krraak krraak*.
Similar Species: *White-winged Scoter* (p. 78): white wing patches; male lacks white on forehead and nape. *Black Scoter* (p. 79): male is all black; female has well-defined pale "cheek."
Best Sites: *Summer:* most common in northern and northeastern PQ and interior Labrador. *Winter:* almost always on salt water.

WHITE-WINGED SCOTER

Melanitta fusca

While White-winged Scoters scoot across Atlantic Canada's lakes and shorelines, their flapping wings reveal a key identifying feature: the white inner-wing patches that strike a sharp contrast with the bird's otherwise black plumage. • The White-winged Scoter is the largest of the three scoters in Atlantic Canada. Scoters have small wings relative to the weight of their bodies, so they require long stretches of water for takeoff. • The name "scoter" may be derived from the way this bird scoots across the water's surface. Scooting can be a means of travelling quickly from one foraging site to another. The name "coot" has also been applied to all three species of scoter because of their superficial resemblance to this totally unrelated species.

ID: stocky, all-dark duck; large, bulbous bill; sloping forehead; base of bill is fully feathered. *Male:* black overall; white patch below eye. *Female:* brown overall; grey-brown bill; 2 whitish patches on sides of head. *In flight:* white wing patches.
Size: *L* 48–61 cm.
Status: common year-round; rare breeder.
Habitat: *Breeding:* northern lakes, muskeg wetlands and slow-flowing rivers. *Winter:* coastal bays and estuaries.
Nesting: not confirmed in Atlantic Canada, although breeding is suspected in northern NF; among bushes very near shorelines; in a shallow scrape lined with

sticks, leaves, grass and down; often well concealed; female incubates 9–14 pinkish eggs for up to 28 days.
Feeding: deep, underwater dives last up to 1 minute; eats mostly molluscs; may also take crustaceans, aquatic insects and some small fish.
Voice: courting pair produces guttural and harsh noises, between a *crook* and a quack.
Similar Species: *Surf Scoter* (p. 77): lacks white wing patches; male has white forehead and nape. *Black Scoter* (p. 79): lacks white patches in wings and around eyes. *American Coot* (p. 113): whitish bill and nasal shield; lacks white patches on wings and around red eyes.
Best Sites: *In migration:* common throughout. *Winter:* almost always on salt water.

BLACK SCOTER
Melanitta nigra

B lack Scoters of the *americana* subspecies take their time during migration. Some Black Scoters begin to travel south from their breeding grounds in northern Québec and Labrador as early as August. The majority of birds arrive at their wintering grounds through late September and October, just as the first snows start to blanket the region. Favourite winter sites include Cherry Hill, Nova Scotia and Golden Bay, Newfoundland. • While floating on the water's surface, Black Scoters tend to hold their heads high, unlike other scoters, which tend to look downward. The male is the only North American duck that is uniformly black. • Of the three species of scoters, the Black Scoter is the least common, which belies its earlier designation as Common Scoter, the name still given to the European subspecies, *nigra*. On occasion, however, large flocks may be seen off the coast of all five Atlantic provinces. Some birds winter in flocks at favoured locations.

ID: *Male:* black overall; large, yellow knob on bill. *Female:* light "cheek"; dark cap; brown overall; dark grey bill.

Size: L 43–53 cm.

Status: uncommon from mid-April to May; rare to locally common from mid-August to early November; locally uncommon in winter.

Habitat: mainly on salt water. *Breeding:* large, deep lakes, large rivers and coastal lagoons.

Nesting: in a depression on the ground lined with grass and down, usually near the water's edge; the female incubates 6–10 light to pinkish-buff eggs for 27–31 days.

Feeding: dives underwater; eats molluscs and aquatic insect larvae; occasionally eats aquatic vegetation and small fish.

Voice: generally quiet; occasionally an unusual *cour-loo*; wings whistle in flight.

Similar Species: *White-winged Scoter* (p. 78): white wing patches; male has white slash below eyes. *Surf Scoter* (p. 77): male has white on head; female has 2 whitish patches on sides of head.

Best Sites: *NB:* Bon-Ami Point (Dalhousie); Grande-Anse (Shepody Bay); Point Lepreau. *PEI:* Point Prim. *NS:* Crescent Beach; Cherry Hill; Seaforth. *NF:* Chance Cove; Golden Bay; Biscay Bay. *PQ:* Bas St-Laurent; New Carlisle.

LONG-TAILED DUCK
Clangula hyemalis

Although they are probably the most numerous arctic-breeding ducks in the world, Long-tailed Ducks tend to remain offshore, limiting observers to brief glimpses of their winter finery and long, slender tail feathers. Their closest breeding sites are along coastal Labrador and at Brador, Québec. As a result, they are rarely seen in summer. In migration, large numbers of Long-tailed Ducks join Common Eiders, scoters and other diving ducks by the surf line. Birds that stay for the winter are often seen in the company of Horned Grebes. • The breeding and non-breeding plumages are like photo-negatives of each other: the breeding plumage is mostly dark with white highlights; the non-breeding plumage is mostly white with dark patches. • Until recently, this duck was officially called "Oldsquaw," and many people still use that name.

breeding

non-breeding

ID: *Breeding male:* dark head with white eye patch; dark neck and upperparts; white belly; dark bill; long, dark central tail feathers. *Breeding female:* short tail feathers; grey bill; dark crown, throat patch, wings and back; white underparts. *Non-breeding male:* pale head with dark patch; pale neck and belly; dark breast; long white patches on back; pink bill with dark base; long, dark central tail feathers. *Non-breeding female:* similar, but generally lighter, especially on head.
Size: *L* 43–51 cm.
Status: locally common from November to late April; common migrant in May and October; very rare breeder.
Habitat: *Breeding:* tundra wetlands and coastal islands. *In migration* and *winter:*
coastal waters and occasionally large, deep lakes.
Nesting: on dry ground near water; depression in the ground, usually partly concealed by vegetation or rocks, is lined with plant material and down; female incubates 5–11 olive grey to olive buff eggs for 24–29 days; young birds join other broods and can fly within 40 days.
Feeding: dives for molluscs, crustaceans and aquatic insects; occasionally eats roots and young shoots; may also take some small fish.
Voice: courtship call, an *owl-owl-owlet*, is rarely heard outside the breeding range.
Similar Species: *Northern Pintail* (p. 67): thin, white line extending up sides of neck; grey sides.
Best Sites: *In migration* and *winter:* common, especially in maritime PQ and northern NF; always on salt water.

80

BUFFLEHEAD
Bucephala albeola

The scarcity of Buffleheads in some areas and their relative abundance in others may seem random, but it isn't. They are common where tidal bays are constricted. Here, there is relatively shallow water with a regular turnover of food, which is exactly what a small diving duck requires in winter. • Buffleheads are small goldeneyes with a taste for adventure. They are hyperactive, spending as much time chasing each other as they do feeding. Rarely do you see a raft of Buffleheads at rest—it's just not their nature. Activity intensifies as spring approaches. Courtship takes place on the wintering grounds, and there is always plenty of competition for mates. • This bird's common name refers to its large head, which is similar in shape to that of a buffalo. The scientific name *Bucephala* also relates to the shape of this bird's head—it means "ox-headed" in Greek. *Albeola* is Latin for "white," a reference to the male's plumage.

ID: very small, rounded duck; white speculum; short, grey bill; short neck. *Male:* white wedge on back of head; head is otherwise iridescent dark green or purple, usually appearing black; dark back; white neck and underparts. *Female:* dark brown head; white, oval ear patch; light brown sides.

Size: *L* 33–38 cm.

Status: common to locally abundant from late October to early May; rare at other times.

Habitat: open water of lakes, large ponds and rivers, coastal bays and estuaries.

Nesting: does not nest in Atlantic Canada.

Feeding: dives for aquatic invertebrates; water boatmen, and mayfly and damselfly larvae are taken in summer; molluscs (particularly snails) and crustaceans are favoured in winter; also eats some small fish and pondweeds.

Voice: *Male:* growling call. *Female:* harsh quack.

Similar Species: *Hooded Merganser* (p. 84): white crest is outlined in black. *Harlequin Duck* (p. 76): female has several light spots on head. *Common Goldeneye* (p. 82) and *Barrow's Goldeneye* (p. 83): males are larger and have white patch between eyes and bill. *Other diving ducks* (pp. 69–87): females are much larger.

Best Sites: *NB:* Long Pond (Grand Manan I.). *PEI:* Long Pond (PEI NP); Deroche Pond. *NS:* Annapolis Royal; Bass River. *NF:* Traytown. *PQ:* Forillon NP; Port-Daniel; Grosse-Île (Îles de la Madeleine).

COMMON GOLDENEYE

Bucephala clangula

The courtship display of the male Common Goldeneye looks much like an avian slapstick routine, although to the bird itself it is surely a serious matter. The male performs a number of odd postures and vocalizations, often to apparently disinterested females. In one common routine, he arches his puffy, irridescent head backward until his forehead seems to touch his back. Then he catapults his neck forward like a coiled spring while producing a seemingly painful *peent* sound. • Common Goldeneyes are widespread but local breeders throughout Atlantic Canada, except in mainland Nova Scotia. After hatching, ducklings remain in the nest for one to three days before jumping out of the tree cavity, often falling a long distance to the ground below. • Common Goldeneyes are frequently called "Whistlers," because the wind whistles through their wings when they fly.

ID: steep forehead with peaked crown; black wings with large, white patches; golden eyes. *Male:* dark, iridescent green head; round, white "cheek" patch; dark bill; dark back; white sides and belly. *Female:* chocolate brown head; grey-brown body plumage; dark bill, tipped with yellow in spring and summer.

Size: *L* 41–51 cm.

Status: common to locally abundant from mid-October to mid-April; locally common breeder.

Habitat: *Breeding:* marshes, ponds, lakes and rivers. *In migration* and *winter:* open water of bays and estuaries; occasionally freshwater lakes before they freeze up.

Nesting: in a tree cavity; will use nest boxes; often close to water but occasionally quite far from it; cavity is lined with wood chips and down; female incubates 6–10 blue-green eggs for 28–32 days; 2 females may each lay a full clutch in the same nest if cavities are in short supply.

Feeding: dives for crustaceans, molluscs and aquatic insect larvae; may also eat tubers, leeches, frogs and small fish.

Voice: *Male:* a nasal *peent* and a hoarse *kraaagh. Female:* harsh croak.

Similar Species: *Barrow's Goldeneye* (p. 83): male has large, white, crescent-shaped "cheek" patch and purplish head; female has more orange on bill and more steeply sloped forehead.

Best Sites: *Summer:* widespread. *Winter:* mostly at or near the coast.

BARROW'S GOLDENEYE
Bucephala islandica

The Barrow's Goldeneye population in Atlantic Canada may be small, but this bird appears to be expanding its breeding range in eastern Newfoundland and the Gaspé. Any birder will tell you that it is hard to forget the first meeting with a Barrow's Goldeneye. It may be only black and white, but it has style! Look for it in shallow water with strong tidal rips. • Like the Common Goldeneye, the Barrow's has an amusing foraging style: after taking a deep dive for food, it pops back up to the surface like a colourful cork. The Barrow's Goldeneye also indulges in the same series of acrobatic courtship displays as its less showy cousin. • This diving duck bears the name of Sir John Barrow, a 19th century secretary to the British Admiralty who was committed to finding the Northwest Passage.

ID: medium-sized, rounded duck; short bill; steep forehead. *Male:* dark purple head; white crescent on "cheek"; white underparts; dark back and wings with white spotting. *Female:* chocolate brown head; black tip on yellow bill in spring and summer; grey-brown body plumage.

Size: *L* 41–51 cm.

Status: rare to locally common from late October to mid-April; locally uncommon breeder.

Habitat: *Breeding:* streams and ponds just below the treeline. *In migration and winter:* open lakes, rivers, ponds and lagoons until they freeze up, then saltwater bays and estuaries.

Nesting: close to or on the ground, in tree hollows or holes in rocks; female incubates

6–12, sometimes more, creamy buff eggs for 26–30 days.

Feeding: dives for molluscs and crustaceans.

Voice: generally silent. *Male:* "mewing" call in spring. *Female:* hoarse croaks in spring.

Similar Species: *Common Goldeneye* (p. 82): slightly smaller with less angled head; male has small, round, white "cheek" patch and greenish head; female has darker bill without black tip.

Best Sites: *Summer: NF:* Western Brook (Gros Morne NP); Portland Creek; Hawkes Bay; Notre Dame Bay. *In migration and winter: NB:* Bon-Ami Point (Dalhousie); Shediac. *PEI:* Oyster Bed Bridge; Tracadie Bay. *NS:* Pugwash; Annapolis Royal; Louisbourg. *NF:* Deer Lake; St. Paul's; Traytown. *PQ:* Bas St-Laurent; Dégelis; Gaspé Bay.

HOODED MERGANSER

Lophodytes cucullatus

Most of the time, the male Hooded Merganser holds his crest flat to avoid the attention of predators, but in moments of arousal or agitation he quickly unfolds his brilliant crest to attract a mate or signal approaching danger. He displays his full range of colours and athletic abilities in elaborate, late-winter courtship displays and chases. It is important that he put on an impressive display, because there are usually twice as many males as there are females. • Hoodies are commonest in southern New Brunswick and Nova Scotia and throughout Prince Edward Island wherever woodlands occur near waterways. They are difficult to find in summer. • All mergansers have thin bills with small, tooth-like serrations to help the birds keep a firm grasp on slippery prey. The smallest of the mergansers, Hoodies have a more diverse diet than their larger relatives. They add crustaceans, insects and even acorns to the usual diet of fish.

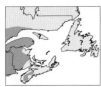

ID: slim body; crested head; dark, thin, pointed bill. *Male:* black head and back; bold, white crest is outlined in black; white breast with 2 black slashes; rusty sides. *Female:* dusky brown body; shaggy, reddish-brown crest. *In flight:* small, white wing patches.

Size: *L* 41–48 cm.

Status: rare to locally uncommon from late March to mid-May; locally common from mid-September to November; rare and very local breeder; a few regularly overwinter.

Habitat: forest-edged ponds, beaver ponds, wetlands, lakes and rivers; occasionally at estuaries in winter.

Nesting: usually in a tree cavity 4–12 m high; may also use nest boxes; cavity is lined with leaves, grass and down; female incubates 10–12 white eggs for 29–33 days;

some females may lay their eggs in other birds' nests, including nests of other species.

Feeding: very diverse diet; dives for small fish, caddisfly and dragonfly larvae, snails, amphibians and crayfish.

Voice: low grunts and croaks. *Male:* frog-like *crrrrooo* in courtship display. *Female:* generally quiet; occasionally a harsh *gak* or a croaking *croo-croo-crook.*

Similar Species: *Bufflehead* (p. 81): male lacks black outline to crest and 2 black breast and shoulder slashes. *Red-breasted Merganser* (p. 86) and *Common Merganser* (p. 85): females have much longer, orange bill and grey back. *Other small diving ducks* (pp. 69–87): females lack crest.

Best Sites: *Summer: NB:* Nepisquit River (Campbellton); St. George; Portobello Creek. *NS:* Wallace Bay; Caledonia–Harmony area. *NF:* Redcliffe. *PQ:* Dégelis. *In migration: NB:* Eel River Lagoon; Black River (Kouchibouguac NP); Portobello Creek. *PEI:* Deroche Pond. *NS:* Mersey River. *NF:* Grand Codroy Estuary. *PQ:* Forillon NP.

COMMON MERGANSER

Mergus merganser

After a laboured takeoff, the Common Merganser flies arrow-straight, low over the water, making broad, sweeping turns to follow the meanderings of rivers and lake shorelines. • This duck is very social, and it often gathers in large groups over winter and in migration. Any source of open water with a fish-filled shoal may support many Common Mergansers in winter. • Rafts of these skilled divers build up along the coast and on lakes in late February and March when the ice breaks up. At first, males may outnumber females. After mating, the male's part in the rearing of young is complete, and the female departs to find a nest site along a freshwater stream. • The *americanus* subspecies is the most widespread and abundant merganser in North America. Two subspecies also occur in Europe and Asia, where it is called "Goosander."

ID: large, elongated body. *Male:* glossy, green head without crest; blood red bill and feet; white body plumage; black stripe on back; dark eyes. *Female:* rusty neck and crested head; clean white "chin" and breast; orange bill; grey body; orangish eyes. *In flight:* shallow wingbeats; body is compressed and arrow-like.

Size: *L* 56–69 cm.

Status: uncommon to common from late September to late April; rare to common breeder.

Habitat: *Breeding:* large rivers and deep lakes. Winter: also coastal bays and estuaries.

Nesting: often in a tree cavity 4.5–6 m high; occasionally on the ground, under a bush or log, on a cliff ledge or in a large nest box; usually not far from water; female incubates 8–11 pale buff eggs for 30–35 days.

Feeding: dives to 9 m for small fish, usually trout and young salmon; young birds eat surface insects and aquatic invertebrates before switching to small fish.

Voice: *Male:* harsh *uig-a*, like a guitar twang. *Female:* harsh *karr karr*.

Similar Species: *Red-breasted Merganser* (p. 86): male has shaggy, green crest and spotted, red breast; female lacks cleanly defined white throat. *Mallard* (p. 64): male has chestnut breast and yellow bill. *Common Goldeneye* (p. 82): male has white "cheek" patch and stubby, dark bill. *Red-throated Loon* (p. 32): pale, uptilted bill; lacks crest. *Red-necked Grebe* (p. 36): yellow bill; white "cheeks"; more white in wing.

Best Sites: *Summer:* freshwater lakes and rivers. *Winter:* usually at estuaries.

RED-BREASTED MERGANSER

Mergus serrator

Its glossy, slicked-back crest and wild red eyes give the Red-breasted Merganser the disheveled, wave-bashed look of an adrenalized windsurfer or windswept pirate. This bird was formerly called "Sawbill" and "Sea-Robin." It's a good thing that bird names have been standardized—who knows what we would be calling this bird now. Sports fishermen have a number of derogatory nicknames for this accomplished diver because they consider it a fierce competitor for young salmon and trout. In fact, many mergansers catch as many "coarse" fish as they do salmonids. • The Red-breast's lack of dependence on trees enables it to nest where related hole-nesting species can't. Shortly after their mates have begun incubating, males fly off to join large offshore rafts for the rest of summer. At this time, a brief moult makes the males largely indistinguishable from their female counterparts.

ID: large, elongated body; red eyes; thin, orange, serrated bill; shaggy, slicked-back head crest. *Male:* green head; light rusty breast is spotted with black; white collar; grey sides; black-and-white shoulders. *Female:* grey-brown overall; reddish head; white "chin," foreneck and breast. *In flight:* white wing patch crossed by 2 narrow, black bars.

Size: *L* 48–66 cm.

Status: uncommon to locally abundant migrant from late March to May and from October to November; common winter resident; uncommon to locally common breeder.

Habitat: lakes and large rivers, especially those with rocky shorelines and islands.

Nesting: usually on a rocky island or shoreline; on the ground, well concealed under bushes or in dense vegetation; female builds a nest lined with down and incubates 7–10 olive buff eggs for 29–35 days.

Feeding: dives underwater for small fish; also eats aquatic invertebrates, fish eggs and crustaceans.

Voice: generally quiet. *Male:* cat-like *yeow* during courtship and feeding. *Female:* harsh *kho-kha.*

Similar Species: *Common Merganser* (p. 85): female's rusty foreneck contrasts against white "chin" and breast; male has clean, white breast and lacks head crest. *Red-necked Grebe* (p. 36): yellow bill; white "cheeks"; plain-coloured back; lacks crest; more white in wing.

Best Sites: *Summer:* usually near coast. *Winter:* almost always on salt water.

RUDDY DUCK

Oxyura jamaicensis

Clowns of the wetlands, male Ruddy Ducks display energetic courtship behaviour with comedic enthusiasm. The small males vigorously pump their bright blue bills, almost touching their breasts. The *plap, plap, plap-plap-plap* of the display increases in speed to its hilarious climax: a spasmodic jerk and a sputter. But even clowns need a rest. In late summer Ruddies blend into the crowd, their white "cheeks" the only sign that they were the stars of the show. • In contrast to their springtime exuberance, Ruddies are the epitome of decorum in winter. They spend hours with their heads tucked into their back feathers, their tails flattened against the water. At this time of year, they keep flights to a minimum. Takeoff requires full use of a Ruddy Duck's legs and wings, so diving is a preferred option to avoid predators.

breeding

non-breeding

ID: large bill and head; short neck; long, stiff tail feathers (often cocked up). *Breeding male:* white "cheek"; chestnut red body; blue bill; black tail and crown. *Female:* brown overall; dark "cheek" stripe; darker crown and back. *Non-breeding male:* like female but with white "cheek."

Size: *L* 38–41 cm.

Status: uncommon migrant from April to early June and from late September to mid-November; rare to locally uncommon breeder; occasional winter resident.

Habitat: *Breeding:* shallow marshes with dense emergent vegetation and muddy bottoms. *In migration* and *winter:* sewage lagoons and open, shallow water.

Nesting: in cattails, bulrushes or other emergent vegetation; female suspends a woven platform nest over water; may use

an abandoned duck or coot nest, muskrat lodge or exposed log; female incubates 5–10 rough, whitish eggs for 23–26 days; is an occasional brood parasite.

Feeding: dives to the bottom of wetlands for the seeds of pondweeds, sedges and bulrushes and for the leafy parts of aquatic plants; also eats a few aquatic invertebrates.

Voice: *Male:* courtship display is *chuck-chuck-chuck-chur-r-r-r. Female:* generally silent.

Similar Species: *Horned Grebe* (p. 35): breeding adults have yellow tufts rather than white "cheeks"; dark, pointed bill; stubby tail; white in wing. *Pied-billed Grebe* (p. 34): non-breeding birds have all-brown plumage; pale, stubby bill. *Other diving ducks* (pp. 69–86): females lack long, stiff tail and dark facial stripe.

Best Sites: *NB:* Sackville; Saint John; Long Pond (Grand Manan I.); French Lake. *PEI:* Indian River; Long Pond (PEI NP); Deroche Pond. *NS:* Missaguash Marsh; Amherst Point. *PQ:* Forillon NP.

OSPREY

Pandion haliaetus

The Osprey is unique in many ways. It is the only species in its family, and unlike other such birds, it is found on every continent except Antarctica. Most fish-eating birds land on water and dive for their food like cormorants or enter it head-first like gannets. An Osprey takes the middle ground. It hovers far above the water and hurls itself in a perilous headfirst dive toward a flash of silver or a slowly moving shadow. An instant before striking the water, the Osprey rights itself and thrusts its feet forward to grasp its slippery prey. It may even disappear under the water momentarily. • An Osprey's feet are specialized to prevent its catch from making a squirmy escape. Two toes face forward, two face backward, and the toes have sharp spines to help it clamp tightly onto the slipperiest of fish.

ID: dark brown upperparts; white underparts; dark eye line; light crown; yellow eyes. *Male:* all-white throat. *Female:* fine, dark "necklace." *In flight:* long wings are held in a shallow "M"; dark wrist patches; brown and white banded tail.
Size: *L* 56–64 cm; *W* 1.7–1.8 m.
Status: uncommon to fairly common from late March to late October; a few birds occasionally linger into winter.
Habitat: lakes and slow-flowing rivers and streams; estuaries and bays in migration.
Nesting: on treetops, usually near water; also on specially made platforms, utility poles or towers up to 30 m high; massive stick nest is reused over many years; pair incubates 2–4 eggs for about 38 days; both adults feed the young, but the male hunts more.
Feeding: dramatic, feet-first dives into the water; "coarse" fish and flounders, averaging 1 kg, make up almost all of the diet.
Voice: series of melodious ascending whistles: *chewk-chewk-chewk*; also an often-heard *kip-kip-kip*.
Similar Species: *Bald Eagle* (p. 89): larger; holds its wings straighter while soaring; adult has clean white head and tail on otherwise dark body; immatures lack white underparts and dark wrist patches. *Rough-legged Hawk* (p. 97): smaller; hovers with wings in an open "V"; light phase has whitish wing linings and light tail band.
Best Sites: *NB:* Cape Jourimain; St. Andrews. *PEI:* Alberton. *NS:* Brier I. *NF:* Stephenville Crossing. *PQ:* Penouille; Port-Daniel.

BALD EAGLE

Haliaeetus leucocephalus

The Bald Eagle can't compete with the Golden Eagle in strength of talon and character, but legends persist that endow it with a mystical quality that is difficult to dispute. • Bald Eagles feed mostly on fish and scavenged carrion. Sometimes a Bald Eagle will steal food from an Osprey. • Pairs perform spectacular aerial displays. The most impressive display involves flying to a great height, locking talons and tumbling perilously toward the earth. The birds break off at the last second before they crash into the ground. • Bald Eagles generally mate for life. Pair bonds are renewed each year by adding new sticks and branches to their massive nests, which are the largest of any North American bird.

immature

ID: white head and tail on otherwise dark brown body; yellow bill and feet. *1st-year:* dark over-all, with dark bill and some white in underwings. *2nd-year:* has dark "bib" and white in underwings. *3rd-year:* mostly white plumage, with yellow at base of bill and yellow eyes. *4th-year:* light head with dark facial streak, variable pale and dark plumage, yellow bill and paler eyes. *In flight:* broad wings are held flat.
Size: *L* 76–109 cm; *W* 1.7–2.4 m.
Status: uncommon to locally common resident; winter numbers may be augmented by birds moving south from northern PQ and Labrador.
Habitat: sea coasts, estuaries, large lakes and rivers.
Nesting: usually in trees bordering lakes or large rivers but may be far from water; huge stick nest, up to 4.5 m across, is often reused for many years; pair incubates 1–3 white eggs for 34–36 days; young remain in the nest until they can fly.
Feeding: water birds, small mammals and fish captured at the water's surface; frequently feeds on carrion, ranging from fish to birds and mammals.
Voice: thin, weak squeal or gull-like cackle: *kleek-kik-kik-kik* or *kah-kah-kah*.
Similar Species: adult is distinctive. *Golden Eagle* (p. 98): adult is dark overall, except for golden nape; tail may appear faintly banded with white; immature has prominent white patch on each wing and at base of tail. *Osprey* (p. 88): like 4th-year Bald Eagle but has M-shaped wings in flight, dark wrist patches and dark bill. *Hawks* (pp. 90–97): much smaller with varying patterns on head, underparts, underwings and tail.
Best Sites: almost always along the coast, but they will overwinter inland. *NS:* Bay of Fundy; Cape Breton; Gaspereau Lake Wolfville. *NF:* anywhere.

NORTHERN HARRIER
Circus cyaneus

The Northern Harrier may be the easiest raptor to identify on the wing, because no other mid-sized hawk routinely flies with its wings slightly angled upward. This bird cruises low over fields, meadows and marshes, grazing the tops of long grasses and cattails, relying on sudden surprise attacks to capture its prey. Although the harrier has excellent vision, its owl-like, parabolic facial disc allows it to hunt easily by sound as well. • The Northern Harrier was once known as the "Marsh Hawk" in North America, and it is still called the "Hen Harrier" in Europe. Britain's Royal Air Force was so impressed by this bird's manoeuvrability that it named its Harrier aircraft after this hawk. • The perilous courtship flight of the Northern Harrier is a spring event worth seeing. The pale-coloured male climbs almost vertically in flight and then stalls, sending himself into a reckless dive toward solid ground and saves himself at the last second with an flight course that sends him skyward again.

ID: long wings and tail; white rump; black wing tips. *Male:* blue-grey to silvery-grey upperparts; white underparts; indistinct tail bands, except for 1 dark subterminal band. *Female:* dark brown upperparts; streaky brown-and-buff underparts. *Immature:* rich reddish-brown plumage; dark tail bands; streaked breast, sides and flanks.
Size: *L* 41–61 cm; *W* 1.1–1.2 m.
Status: fairly common from late March to May and common from September to early November; widespread but uncommon breeder; locally rare winter resident.
Habitat: open country, including fields, wet meadows, cattail marshes, bogs and croplands.
Nesting: on the ground, often on a slightly raised mound, usually in grass, cattails or tall vegetation; shallow depression or platform nest is lined with grass, sticks

and cattails; female incubates 4–6 bluish-white eggs for 30–32 days.
Feeding: hunts in low, rising and falling flights, often skimming the tops of vegetation; eats small mammals, birds, amphibians, reptiles and some invertebrates.
Voice: most vocal near the nest and during courtship, but generally quiet; high-pitched *ke-ke-ke-ke-ke-ke* near the nest.
Similar Species: *Rough-legged Hawk* (p. 97): broader wings; dark wrist patches; black tail with wide, white base; dark belly. *Red-tailed Hawk* (p. 96): lacks white rump and long, narrow tail. *Turkey Vulture* (p. 55): much larger and darker; wings held in more closed "V"; silver-grey wing coverts; lacks white rump.
Best Sites: *In migration* and *summer:* widespread in open areas. *NB:* Tantramar Marshes; Grand Manan I. *PEI:* Wood Is. *NS:* Missaguash Marsh; Chebogue Point. *NF:* Cow Head; Cape Freels. *PQ:* St-Fabien-sur-Mer; Gaspé Bay.

SHARP-SHINNED HAWK

Accipiter striatus

After a successful hunt, the small Sharp-shinned Hawk usually perches on a favourite "pluck-ing post," grasping its meal in its razor-sharp talons. Sharpies prey almost exclusively on small birds, such as chickadees, finches, sparrows and even robins, chasing them in high-speed pursuits. • Most people never see a Sharpie nest, because the birds are very tight sitters. Disturb one, however, and you will feel the occupants' wrath. These birds are feisty defenders of their nest and young. • When delivering food to his nestlings, a male Sharp-shinned Hawk is cautious around his mate—she is typically one-third larger than he is and notoriously short-tempered. • "Accipiters," named after their genus, are woodland hawks. Their short, rounded wings, long, rudder-like tails and flap-and-glide flight pattern give them the manoeuvrability necessary to negotiate a maze of forest foliage at high speed.

ID: short, rounded wings; long, straight, heavily barred, square-tipped tail; dark barring on pale underwings; blue-grey back; red horizontal bars on under-parts; red eyes. *Immature:* brown overall; yellow eyes; vertical, brown streaking on breast and belly. *In flight:* flap-and-glide flyer, but very agile in wooded areas.
Size: *Male: L* 25–30 cm; *W* 51–61 cm. *Female: L* 30–36 cm; *W* 61–71 cm.
Status: common migrant from mid-March to early May and from late August to mid-November; fairly common breeder; uncommon winter resident in cities.
Habitat: dense to semi-open forests and large woodlots; occasionally along rivers; favours bogs and dense, moist coniferous forests.
Nesting: in a conifer; usually builds a new stick nest each year (about 60 cm across);

might remodel an abandoned crow nest; female incubates 4–5 eggs for 34–35 days; male feeds the female during incubation.
Feeding: pursues small birds through forests; rarely takes small mammals, amphibians and insects.
Voice: silent, except during the breeding season when an intense and often repeated *kik-kik-kik-kik* can be heard.
Similar Species: *Cooper's Hawk* (p. 92): larger; tail tip is more rounded and has broader terminal band. *American Kestrel* (p. 99): long, pointed wings; 1 dark "tear streak" and 1 dark "sideburn"; typically seen in open country. *Merlin* (p. 100): pointed wings; rapid wingbeats; 1 dark "tear streak"; brown streaking on buff underparts; dark eyes; usually more obvious and darker tail bands.
Best Sites: most often observed in migra-tion or at winter feeders. *NB:* Fundy NP; Hartland. *PEI:* Wood Is. *NS:* Brier I.; Halifax–Dartmouth. *NF:* Long Point (Port au Port); St. John's. *PQ:* Rimouski.

COOPER'S HAWK

Accipiter cooperii

Larger and heavier than the Sharp-shinned Hawk, the Cooper's Hawk glides silently along forest clearings, using surprise and speed snatch its prey from mid-air. Females have the size and bulk of male Goshawks and can seize and decapitate birds as large as Ruffed Grouse, which they sometimes pursue on the ground like overweight roadrunners. • These birds are now protected by law, and the use of DDT has been banned throughout North America. As a result, Cooper's Hawks are increasing in numbers, and they are extending their range into all parts of Atlantic Canada. • This forest hawk bears the name of William Cooper, one of the many hunters who supplied English and American ornithologists with bird specimens for museum collections during the early 19th century.

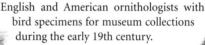

ID: short, rounded wings; long, straight, heavily barred, rounded tail; dark barring on pale undertail and underwings; squarish head; blue-grey back; red horizontal barring on underparts; red eyes; white terminal tail band. *Immature:* brown overall; dark eyes; vertical, brown streaks on breast and belly. *In flight:* flap-and-glide flyer.

Size: *Male: L* 38–43 cm; *W* 69–81 cm. *Female: L* 43–48 cm; *W* 81–94 cm.

Status: rare to uncommon migrant from late March to late April and from September to late October; rare breeder; rare winter resident.

Habitat: mixed woodlands, riparian woodlands and woodlots, and increasingly urban gardens with feeders.

Nesting: nest of sticks and twigs is built 6–20 m high in the crotch of a deciduous or coniferous tree; often near a stream or pond; might reuse an abandoned crow nest; female incubates 3–5 bluish-white eggs for 34–36 days; male feeds the female during incubation.

Feeding: pursues prey in flight through forests; eats mostly songbirds, squirrels and chipmunks; uses plucking post or nest for eating.

Voice: fast, woodpecker-like *cac-cac-cac-cac.*

Similar Species: *Sharp-shinned Hawk* (p. 91): smaller; less rounded tail tip; thinner terminal tail band. *American Kestrel* (p. 99): smaller; long, pointed wings; 1 dark "tear streak" and 1 dark "sideburn"; typically seen in open country. *Merlin* (p. 100): smaller; pointed wings; rapid wingbeats; 1 dark "tear streak"; brown streaking on buff underparts; dark eyes; usually more obvious and darker tail bands.

Best Sites: *Summer* and *in migration: PEI:* Bonshaw Hills. *NB:* Saint John; Long Pond (Grand Manan I.). *NS:* Brier I.; Kejimkujik NP; Seal I.; Hopewell. *PQ:* St-Fabien-sur-Mer; Ste-Anne-des-Monts; Cap Gaspé.

NORTHERN GOSHAWK
Accipiter gentilis

Northern Goshawks are agile, powerful predators capable of negotiating lightning-fast turns through dense forest cover. They are as ferocious when defending their nest sites as they are when capturing prey. Unfortunate souls who wander too close to a goshawk nest can be assaulted with an almost deafening, squawking dive-bomb attack. • Northern Goshawks require extensive areas of forest in which to hunt and raise their families. The clearing of forests for agricultural and residential development has caused goshawk populations to decline significantly throughout their range in Northern Europe, Asia and parts of North America. • The Latin *gentilis* obviously does not mean "gentle," but it does have a connection to the closely related "gentile." This hawk was used by the upper classes for falconry.

ID: rounded wings; long, banded tail with 1 white terminal band; white eyebrow; dark crown; blue-grey back; fine, grey, vertical streaking on pale breast and belly; grey barring on pale undertail and underwings; red eyes. *Immature:* brown overall; brown, vertical streaking on whitish breast and belly; brown barring on pale undertail and underwings; greyish-yellow eyes.
Size: *Male:* L 53–58 cm; W 1.0–1.1 m. *Female:* L 58–64 cm; W 1.1–1.2 m.
Status: rare to uncommon year-round; very elusive in summer.
Habitat: *Breeding:* mature coniferous, deciduous and mixed woodlands. *In migration* and *winter:* forest edges, semi-open parklands and farmlands.
Nesting: in deep woods; male builds a large, bulky stick platform in the crotch of a deciduous or coniferous tree, usually 8–25 m high; nest is often reused for several years;

female incubates 2–4 bluish-white eggs for 35–36 days; male feeds the female during incubation.
Feeding: low foraging flights through the forest; feeds primarily on large songbirds, grouse, rabbits and squirrels.
Voice: silent, except during the breeding season when adults utter a loud, shrill and fast *kak-kak-kak-kak*.
Similar Species: *Cooper's Hawk* (p. 92) and *Sharp-shinned Hawk* (p. 91): smaller; adults have reddish breast bars and lack white eyebrow stripe; immatures are smaller and have yellow eyes, which become more orange with age. *Buteos* (pp. 94–97): shorter tails; broader wings; grey or brown eyes. *Gyrfalcon* (p. 101): more pointed wings; dark eyes; often has dark "tear streak."
Best Sites: widespread; rarely observed except in migration or winter. *NB:* Mount Carleton; Perth-Andover. *PEI:* Bonshaw Hills. *NS:* Brier I.; Chéticamp River. *NF:* L'Anse aux Meadows; White Hills (St. John's). *PQ:* Dégelis; Cap Gaspé.

93

RED-SHOULDERED HAWK

Buteo lineatus

The Red-shouldered Hawk's breeding range extends just to the south and west of New Brunswick and Nova Scotia, so it is not surprising that more birds are turning up in these provinces. On occasion, they even breed here. This hawk is a bird of wetter habitats than the closely related Broad-winged and Red-tailed Hawks. • In migration, Red-shouldered Hawks can be found gathering with other buteos at coastal headlands. Here they wait for ideal weather conditions to attempt the tricky crossing to the other side of the Bay of Fundy. Positioning yourself at a headland on either side of the Bay of Fundy offers you the best chance of success when looking for Red-shouldered Hawks.

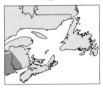

ID: chestnut red shoulders on otherwise dark brown upperparts; reddish underwing linings; narrow, white bars on dark tail; barred, reddish breast and belly; reddish undertail coverts. *Immature:* large, brown streaks on white underparts; whitish undertail coverts. *In flight:* light and dark barring on underside of flight feathers and tail; white crescents at base of primaries.

Size: *L* 48 cm; *W* 1.0 m.

Status: locally uncommon from late September to early November; rare from early April to mid-May; rare and very local breeder; extremely rare in winter.

Habitat: mature deciduous and mixed forests, wooded riparian areas, swampy woodlands and large, mature woodlots.

Nesting: both sexes assemble a bulky nest of sticks and twigs, usually 5–25 m high in the crotch of a decidious tree; nest is often reused; female incubates 2–4 darkly blotched, bluish-white eggs for about 33 days; both adults raise the young.

Feeding: small mammals, birds, reptiles and amphibians are usually detected from a fence post, tree or telephone pole and caught after a swooping attack; may catch prey flushed by low flight.

Voice: a repeated series of high *key-ah* notes.

Similar Species: *Broad-winged Hawk* (p. 95): lacks reddish shoulders; wings are broader, more whitish and dark-edged underneath; wide, white tail bands. *Red-tailed Hawk* (p. 96): lacks barring in tail and light "windows" at base of primaries.

Best Sites: *In migration: NB:* Hopewell; Chignecto Campground (Fundy NP); Long Eddy Point (Grand Manan I.); Portobello Creek; Mactaquac; Woodstock. *NS:* Brier I. *PQ:* Matane.

BROAD-WINGED HAWK
Buteo platypterus

The generally shy and secretive Broad-winged Hawk prefers different habitat than most other buteos. Shunning the open fields and forest clearings favoured by the Red-tailed Hawk, it secludes itself in dense, often wet forests. In this habitat, its short, broad wings and highly flexible tail help it to manoeuver in the heavy growth. • Most hunting is done from a high perch with a good view. The Broad-winged Hawk may be so attached to its perch that it will return to the perch after being flushed to resume its vigilant search for a meal. • At the end of the nesting season, "kettles" of buteos and other hawks spiral up from their forest retreats, testing thermals for the opportunity to head south. Broad-wings are often the most numerous species in these flocks. They overwinter in South America, so they have far to go.

light morph

light morph

ID: broad, black and white tail bands; broad wings with pointed tips; heavily barred, rufous brown breast; dark brown upperparts. *Immature:* dark brown streaks on white breast, belly and sides; buff and dark brown tail bands. *In flight:* pale underwings are outlined with dark trim.
Size: *L* 36–48 cm; *W* 81–99 cm.
Status: common to abundant migrant from September to early October with some stragglers into November; fairly common breeder; uncommon migrant from early April to mid-May.
Habitat: *Breeding:* dense, mixed and deciduous forests and woodlots. *In migration:* escarpments and shorelines; also uses riparian and deciduous forests and woodland edges.

Nesting: usually in a deciduous tree, often near water; bulky stick nest is built in a crotch 7–12 m high; usually builds a new nest each year; mostly female incubates 2–4 brown-spotted, whitish eggs for 28–31 days; both adults raise the young.
Feeding: swoops from a perch for small mammals, amphibians, insects and young birds; often seen hunting from roadside telephone poles in northern areas.
Voice: high-pitched, whistled *peeeo-wee-ee*; generally silent in migration.
Similar Species: *Other buteos* (pp. 94–97): lack broad banding on tail and dark-edged, broad wings with pointed tips. *Accipiters* (pp. 91–93): long, narrow tails with less distinct banding.
Best Sites: *Summer* and *in migration: NB:* Campbellton; Alma; Grand Manan I.; Woodstock. *PEI:* Bonshaw Hills. *NS:* Tatamagouche; Brier I.; Tusket; Hopewell. *PQ:* St-Fabien-sur-Mer; Lac des Joncs (St-Fabien); Parc de la Gaspésie.

RED-TAILED HAWK

Buteo jamaicensis

The Red-tailed Hawk is the most commonly seen hawk in Atlantic Canada, and it can be seen every month of the year. An afternoon drive through the countryside in the Maritime provinces often reveals resident Red-tails perching on exposed tree limbs, on fence posts or on utility poles overlooking open fields and roadsides. • During spring courtship, excited Red-tailed Hawks dive at each other, sometimes locking talons and tumbling through the air together before breaking off to avoid crashing to the ground. Perhaps they are auditioning for the role of eagles! • This hawk's tail does not obtain its brick red coloration until the bird matures into a breeding adult. Most eastern birds are pale morphs, in contrast to western North America, where dark morphs are more common.

ID: red tail; dark upperparts with some white highlights; dark brown band of streaks across belly. *Immature:* very variable; lacks red tail; generally darker; band of streaks on belly. *In flight:* fan-shaped tail; white or occasionally tawny brown underside and underwing linings; dark leading edge on underside of wing; light underwing flight feathers have faint barring.
Size: *Male: L* 46–58 cm; *W* 1.2–1.5 m. *Female: L* 51–64 cm; *W* 1.2–1.5 m.
Status: common to abundant year-round in suitable habitat.
Habitat: open country with some trees; roadsides, fields, woodlots, hedgerows, mixed forests and moist woodlands.
Nesting: in woodlands adjacent to open habitat; usually in a deciduous tree; rarely on cliffs or in conifers; bulky stick nest is usually added to each year; pair incubates

2–4 brown-blotched, whitish eggs for 28–35 days; male brings food to the female and young.
Feeding: scans for food while perched or soaring; drops to capture prey; rarely stalks prey on foot; eats voles, mice, rabbits, chipmunks, birds, amphibians and reptiles; rarely takes large insects.
Voice: powerful, descending scream: *keeearrrr.*
Similar Species: *Rough-legged Hawk* (p. 97): white tail base; dark wrist patches on underwings; broad, dark terminal tail band. *Broad-winged Hawk* (p. 95): broadly banded tail; broader wings with pointed tips; lacks dark belt. *Red-shouldered Hawk* (p. 94): reddish wing linings and underparts; reddish shoulders.
Best Sites: common in farmlands and open woods. *NB:* Alma; Southwest Head (Grand Manan I.). *PEI:* East Point. *NS:* Wentworth Valley; Gaspereau Lake; Argyle–Wedgeport area. *NF:* Codroy Valley; Burin Peninsula. *PQ:* Pointe-au-Père; Bic.

ROUGH-LEGGED HAWK

Buteo lagopus

While hunting, the Rough-legged Hawk often "wind-hovers" to scan the ground below, flapping to maintain a stationary position while facing upwind. This ability is unique among the hawks of Atlantic Canada. • There are roughly equal numbers of light and dark morphs of Rough-legged Hawks, although most of the dark-plumaged birds call Labrador home. • When voles and northern lemmings are in short supply, Rough-legs will swallow their pride, gather reinforcements and head southwest in hopes of catching mice. • Summer is usually the only time of year that you hear a Rough-leg call, and many people are startled to hear what sounds like a kitten voicing its indignation. • The name *lagopus*, meaning "hare's foot," refers to this bird's distinctive feathered legs, which are an adaptation for survival in cold climates.

light morph

ID: white tail base with 1 wide, dark subterminal band; dark brown upperparts; light flight feathers; legs are feathered to toes. *Light morph:* wide, dark abdominal "belt"; darkly streaked breast and head; dark wrist patches; light underwing linings. *Dark morph:* dark wing linings, head and underparts. *Immature:* lighter streaking on breast; bold belly band; buff leg feathers. *In flight:* frequently hovers; most birds show dark wrist patches.
Size: *L* 48–61 cm; *W* 1.2–1.4 m.
Status: irregularly rare to common visitor from mid-September to mid-May; locally uncommon breeder.
Habitat: *Breeding:* coastal tundra; requires an elevated natural or artificial ledge for nesting. *In migration* and *winter:* tundra, fields, meadows, open bogs and agricultural croplands.

Nesting: in a large stick nest on an elevated structure; nests are reused over many years; mostly female incubates 3–4 bluish-white eggs with brown and violet blotches for 28–31 days; both adults raise the young.
Feeding: soars and hovers while searching for prey; usually eats small rodents; occasionally eats birds, amphibians and large insects.
Voice: alarm call is a cat-like *kee-eer*, usually dropping at the end.
Similar Species: *Other buteos* (pp. 94–96): rarely hover; adults lack dark wrist patches and white tail base. *Northern Harrier* (p. 90): facial disc; lacks dark wrist patches and dark belly band; longer, thinner tail lacks broad, dark subterminal band.
Best Sites: *Summer: NB:* Mount Carleton. *NF:* L'Anse aux Meadows. *In migration* and *winter:* widespread. *NB:* Cape Jourimain; Tantramar Marshes. *PEI:* Mount Stewart. *NS:* Pinkney Point; Cape North. *NF:* Grand Codroy Estuary; Pistolet Bay; Cape Race. *PQ:* Île Verte; St-Fabien-sur-Mer.

GOLDEN EAGLE

Aquila chrysaetos

Golden Eagles embody the wonder and wildness of the North American landscape. Unfortunately, because they were perceived as threats to livestock in the past, bounties were offered encouraging the shooting and poisoning of Golden Eagles. Birds in Atlantic Canada mostly escaped this slaughter, because they nest in the remote mountain areas where people and livestock are largely absent. • Few people ever forget the sight of a Golden Eagle soaring overhead—the average wingspan of an adult is just short of 3 metres! Although the adult is uniformly coloured except for its tawny head, the immature has a white patch in the centre of each wing and at the base of the tail. These patches distinguish it from the smaller immature Bald Eagle.

immature

ID: very large; all brown, with golden tint to neck and head; brown eyes; dark bill; brown tail has greyish-white bands; yellow feet; legs are fully feathered. *Immature:* white tail base; white patch at base of underwing primary feathers. *In flight:* relatively short neck; long tail; long, large, rectangular wings.
Size: *L* 76–102 cm; *W* 2.0–2.3 m.
Status: rare migrant from late March to late April and from late September through early November; very rare local breeder and winter resident.
Habitat: *Breeding:* open and semi-open areas close to cliff faces, often along lakeshores or wide river canyons. *In migration:* along escarpments and lake shorelines. *Winter:* semi-open woodlands and fields.
Nesting: usually on a cliff near open foraging areas; infrequently in trees; huge nest of sticks, branches and roots measures up to 3 m across; often reuses a nest site for many years; nest might become stained from droppings; mostly the female incubates 1–3 brown-marked, whitish to buff eggs for 41–45 days; both adults raise the young.
Feeding: swoops on prey from a soaring flight; eats hares, grouse, ptarmigan, rodents, foxes and occasionally young ungulates; often eats carrion.
Voice: generally quiet; rarely a short bark.
Similar Species: *Bald Eagle* (p. 89): longer neck; shorter tail; immature lacks distinct, white underwing patches and tail base. *Turkey Vulture* (p. 55): naked, pink head; pale flight feathers; dark wing linings. *Dark-morph Rough-legged Hawk* (p. 97): pale flight feathers.
Best Sites: *NB:* Mount Carleton. *NS:* Gaspereau Lake; Chéticamp; Pleasant Bay. *PQ:* Rimouski; St-Fabien-sur-Mer; Réserve Matane; Parc de la Gaspésie; Chic-Chocs; Île Bonaventure; Forillon NP.

AMERICAN KESTREL

Falco sparverius

The American Kestrel is the smallest and most widespread of Atlantic Canada's falcons. It hunts small mammals in open areas. Its numbers probably skyrocketed when the first settlers started to clear land and plant crops, triggering an invasion of small rodents. The kestrel's eyesight is phenomenal and its response to such a proliferation of prey was likely immediate. Few rodents escape this hunter's vigilance—a kestrel will hover in the wind and patiently wait until the right opportunity presents itself, when it dives to the ground. • The American Kestrel's small size allows it to nest in the shelter of tree cavities, which helps protect defenceless young kestrels from hungry predators. Kestrels that take advantage of nest boxes may also take advantage of the House Sparrows, Starlings and urban rodents that city living offers.

ID: 2 distinctive facial stripes. *Male:* rusty back; blue-grey wings; blue-grey crown with rusty cap; lightly spotted underparts. *Female:* rusty back, wings and breast streaking. *In flight:* frequently hovers; long, rusty tail; buoyant, indirect flight style.
Size: *L* 19–20 cm; *W* 51–61 cm.
Status: common from late March to late October; rare to locally common breeder, rare to uncommon winter resident.
Habitat: open fields, riparian woodlands, woodlots, forest edges, bogs, roadside ditches, grassy highway medians, grasslands and croplands.
Nesting: in a cavity in a standing dead tree (usually an abandoned woodpecker or flicker cavity); may use a nest box; incubates 4–6 brown- and grey-spotted, white to pale brown eggs for 29–30 days; both adults raise the young.

Feeding: swoops from a perch (a tree, fenceline, post, road sign or power line) or from a hovering position; eats mostly insects and some small rodents, birds, reptiles and amphibians.
Voice: loud, often repeated, shrill *killy-killy-killy* when excited; female's voice is lower pitched.
Similar Species: *Merlin* (p. 100): only 1 facial stripe; less colourful; does not hover; flight is more powerful and direct. *Sharp-shinned Hawk* (p. 91): short, rounded wings; reddish barring on underparts; lacks facial stripes; flap-and-glide flight pattern.
Best Sites: *Summer* and *in migration:* common in farmlands and open areas; sometimes stages at headlands in migration. *NB:* Sackville; St. Stephen. *PEI:* North Cape; Montague. *NS:* Brier I.; Ingonish. *NF:* Codroy Valley; Lobster Cove Head (Gros Morne NP); Cape St. Mary's. *PQ:* Matane; Penouille.

MERLIN

Falco columbarius

The Merlin is a lethal, fast-flying killing machine. Its sleek body, long, narrow tail and pointed wings are well designed for high-speed song-bird pursuits. • Many individuals regularly pursue small shorebirds. The first indication of a Merlin's presence is often the frenzied takeoff of all the shorebirds in the immediate area. These shorebird pursuits are likely at Mary's Point in New Brunswick, Sunday Point in Nova Scotia and Saint Paul's in Newfoundland. • Most Merlins migrate to Central and South America each autumn, but a few remain over winter. Wintering birds capitalize on the abundance of small songbirds that are attracted to suburban ornamental shrubs and backyard feeders. • The Merlin was formerly known as "Pigeon Hawk," and the scientific name *columbarius* comes from the Latin for "pigeon," which it somewhat resembles in flight.

ID: banded tail; heavily streaked underparts; 1 indistinct facial stripe; long, narrow wings and tail. *Male:* blue-grey back and crown; rusty leg feathers. *Female:* brown back and crown. *In flight:* very rapid, shallow wingbeats.

Size: *L* 25–30 cm; *W* 58–66 cm.

Status: rare to uncommon from late March to early October; rare but increasingly seen in winter.

Habitat: *Breeding:* forests and plantations adjacent to open hunting grounds; sometimes found in suburban areas. *In migration:* open fields and lakeshores.

Nesting: in coniferous or deciduous trees, crevices or cliffs; usually reuses abandoned raptor, crow, jay or squirrel nests; mostly the female incubates 4–5 whitish eggs, marked with reddish-brown, for 28–32 days; male feeds the female away from the nest; both adults raise the young.

Feeding: overtakes smaller birds in flight; also eats rodents and large insects, such as grasshoppers and dragonflies; may also take bats.

Voice: loud, noisy, cackling cry: *kek-kek-kek-kek-kek* or *ki-ki-ki-ki*; calls in flight or while perched, often around the nest.

Similar Species: *American Kestrel* (p. 99): 2 facial stripes; more colourful; less direct flight style; often hovers. *Peregrine Falcon* (p. 102): larger; well-marked, dark "helmet"; pale, unmarked upper breast; black flecking on light underparts. *Sharp-shinned Hawk* (p. 91) and *Cooper's Hawk* (p. 92): short, rounded wings; reddish barring on breast and belly. *Rock Dove* (p. 174): larger; broader wings in flight; shorter tail; often glides with its wings held in a "V." *Mourning Dove* (p. 175): sleeker and more elongated; pointed tail; uniform colour.

Best Sites: *NB:* Mary's Point; Southwest Head (Grand Manan I.). *PEI:* North Cape. *NS:* Cape Split; Evangeline Beach; Ingonish. *NF:* Stephenville Crossing; Long Point (Port au Port); St. John's; Cape Race. *PQ:* Bas St-Laurent; Penouille.

GYRFALCON

Falco rusticolus

The Gyrfalcon was, and in some places still is, the falcon used for falconry by kings, and it is, indeed, a king among falcons. • Watching a Gyrfalcon in flight is like watching an expertly piloted fighter plane. Cruising at low speed, it looks for potential targets and then reacts with lightning speed. Unlike the Peregrine Falcon, the Gyrfalcon rarely swoops down from above with its wings closed—it prefers to outfly its prey, often launching a surprise attack from below. Even Dovekies flying low over water are not safe from this falcon's relentless pursuit. • If you want to see Gyrfalcons of all three colour morphs at work and play, take a winter trip to Newfoundland's northern headlands, where the birds regularly hang out. • During its time in the Arctic, the Gyrfalcon feeds mostly on ptarmigans and hares.

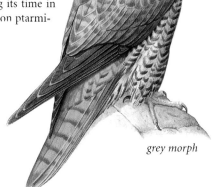

grey morph

white morph

ID: long tail extends beyond wing tips when bird is perched; tail may be barred or unbarred. *Grey morph:* dark grey upperparts; streaking on white underparts. *Brown morph:* dark brown upperparts; streaking on white underparts. *White morph:* pure white head, breast and rump; white back and wings have dark flecking and barring. *Immature:* darker and more heavily streaked than adult; grey (rather than yellow) feet and cere.
Size: *Male: L* 51–56 cm; *W* 1.2–1.3 m. *Female: L* 56–64 cm; *W* 1.3–1.4 m.
Status: very rare from mid-October to mid-April.
Habitat: open and semi-open areas, including tundra marshes, fields and open wetlands where prey concentrate.
Nesting: does not nest in Atlantic Canada, except in extreme northern Labrador.

Feeding: locates prey from an elevated perch or by flying low over the ground; takes prey in mid-air or chases it down; eats mostly birds, especially waterfowl, shorebirds and ptarmigans; takes Rock Doves in southern areas; also takes small mammals.
Voice: loud, harsh *kak-kak-kak*.
Similar Species: *Peregrine Falcon* (p. 102): prominent dark "helmet"; shorter tail; adults have unstreaked upper breast and throat. *Northern Goshawk* (p. 93): deceptively similar at times to grey morph; prominent white eyebrow; dark cap; rounded wings in flight; greyer underparts with finer streaking; unstreaked white undertail coverts; eyes are red (adult) or pale yellow (immature).
Best Sites: *NB:* Bon-Ami Point (Dalhousie); Dark Harbour (Grand Manan I.). *NS:* Cape Sable I. *NF:* L'Anse aux Meadows; St. Anthony; White Hills (St. John's); Bear Cove Head (Renews). *PQ:* Bas St-Laurent; Forillon NP.

PEREGRINE FALCON

Falco peregrinus

No bird elicits more admiration than a hunting Peregrine Falcon in full flight, and nothing causes more panic in a tightly packed flock of ducks or shorebirds. Every twist and turn the flock makes is matched by the Peregrine until it finds a weaker or less experienced bird. As it reaches its top speed (it can dive at 360 kilometres per hour), the Peregrine clenches its feet and then strikes its prey with a lethal blow that will often send both falcon and prey tumbling. • The Peregrine's awesome speed and hunting skills were little defence against the pesticide DDT, which caused contaminated birds to lay eggs with thin shells. Captive-bred *anatum* Peregrines have been released into wild habitats in Atlantic Canada with some success, and wild birds of both the *tundrius* and *anatum* races have persisted along the coast of Labrador.

immature

ID: blue-grey back; prominent, dark "helmet"; light underparts with dark, fine spotting and flecking. *Immature:* brown where adult is blue-grey; heavier breast streaks; grey (rather than yellow) feet and cere. *In flight:* pointed wings; long, narrow, dark-banded tail.

Size: *Male: L* 38–43 cm; *W* 94–109 cm. *Female: L* 43–48 cm; *W* 1.1–1.2 m.

Status: uncommon migrant from late August to mid-October; rare migrant from late March to early May; locally rare breeder; rare winter resident.

Habitat: lakeshores, river valleys, river mouths, urban areas and open fields.

Nesting: usually on rocky cliffs or cutbanks; may use skyscraper ledges; no material is added, but the nest is littered with prey remains, leaves and grass; nest sites are often reused; mostly the female incubates 3–4 eggs for 32–34 days.

Feeding: high-speed, diving stoops; strikes birds with clenched feet in mid-air; prey is consumed on a nearby perch; pigeons, waterfowl, shorebirds, flickers, ptarmigans and larger songbirds are the primary prey; rarely takes small mammals or carrion.

Voice: loud, harsh, continuous *cack-cack-cack-cack-cack* near the nest site.

Similar Species: *Gyrfalcon* (p. 101): larger; lacks dark "helmet"; longer tail. *Merlin* (p. 100): smaller; lacks prominent dark "helmet"; heavily streaked breast and belly.

Best Sites: *Summer* and *in migration: NB:* Mary's Point; Saint John. *PEI:* Orby Head; East Point. *NS:* Evangeline Beach; Pinkney Point; Cape Sable I.; Louisbourg. *NF:* St. Paul's; Point May; St. John's; Cape St. Mary's. *PQ:* Bas St-Laurent; Forillon NP.

GRAY PARTRIDGE

Perdix perdix

Gray Partridges, like other seed-eating birds, regularly swallow small bits of gravel. These small stones accumulate in the gizzard and help to crush the hard grain and other seeds that these birds feed on. • When flushed, Gray Partridges burst suddenly from cover, flapping furiously and then gliding to a safe haven nearby. • During cold weather, Gray Partridges huddle together in a circle with each bird facing outward, ready to burst into flight. In extreme conditions they will dig into snowbanks for protection, much like Ruffed Grouse and ptarmigans. • These birds, also known as "Hungarian Partridges" or "Huns," were first introduced to two sites in Nova Scotia from Czechoslovakia in 1926. Other releases within the province took place from 1927 to 1934. A similar series of introductions occurred in Prince Edward Island. • In recent years, populations have declined. These birds are now concentrated in fewer locations.

ID: small, rounded body; short tail with chestnut brown outer feathers; chestnut brown barring on flanks; orange-brown face and throat; grey breast; mottled brown back; bare, yellowish legs. *Male:* chestnut brown patch on white belly. *Female:* no belly patch; paler.
Size: *L* 28–36 cm.
Status: rare to locally uncommon year-round resident.
Habitat: grassy and weedy fields and agricultural croplands; generally absent from alfalfa fields.
Nesting: in hayfields, pastures and grassy fencelines and field margins; on the ground in a scratched-out depression lined with grass; female incubates 15–17 olive-coloured eggs for 23–25 days; after young leave the nest, the male helps care for the brood until the following spring.
Feeding: at dawn and dusk in summer; throughout the day during winter; gleans the ground for waste agricultural grains and seeds; may also eat leaves and large insects; often seen feeding on manure piles in winter.
Voice: at dawn and dusk; sounds like a rusty gate hinge: *kee-uck* or *scirl;* call is *kuta-kut-kut-kut* when excited.
Similar Species: *Ruffed Grouse* (p. 105): lacks rusty face and outer tail feathers. *Chukar:* black border around cream throat patch; bold black bars on flanks; red bill and legs.
Best Sites: *PEI:* New London; Kensington; Bonshaw Hills; Mount Stewart. *NS:* Economy–Glenholme area; Canning–Wolfville area.

RING-NECKED PHEASANT

Phasianus colchicus

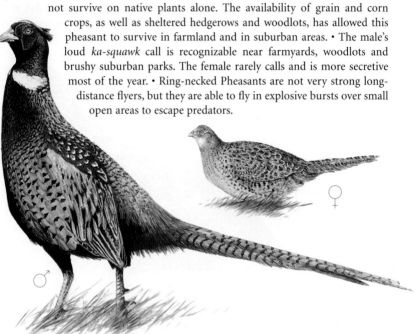

The spectacular Ring-necked Pheasant was first introduced to Nova Scotia in 1856, not as a gamebird for hunters but because of its beauty. This first introduction failed, but later releases in this and the other Atlantic provinces were more successful. • Cold, snowy winters are a problem for this bird. Unlike native grouse, the Ring-necked Pheasant does not have feathered legs and feet, and it cannot survive on native plants alone. The availability of grain and corn crops, as well as sheltered hedgerows and woodlots, has allowed this pheasant to survive in farmland and in suburban areas. • The male's loud *ka-squawk* call is recognizable near farmyards, woodlots and brushy suburban parks. The female rarely calls and is more secretive most of the year. • Ring-necked Pheasants are not very strong long-distance flyers, but they are able to fly in explosive bursts over small open areas to escape predators.

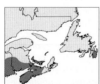

ID: large; long, barred tail; unfeathered legs. *Male:* green head; white collar; bronze underparts; naked, red face patch. *Female:* mottled brown overall; light underparts.
Size: *Male: L* 76–91 cm. *Female: L* 51–66 cm.
Status: rare to locally common year-round resident.
Habitat: *Breeding:* grasslands, grassy ditches, hayfields and grassy or weedy fields, fencelines, crop margins and woodlot margins. *In migration:* grain and corn fields in autumn. *Winter:* woodlots, cattail marshes and shrubby areas close to crops.
Nesting: on the ground, among grass or sparse vegetation or next to a log or other natural debris; in a slight depression lined with grass and leaves; female incubates 10–12 olive-buff eggs for 23–28 days; male takes no part in parental duties.
Feeding: *Summer:* gleans the ground and vegetation for weed seeds, grains, legumes and insects. *Winter:* eats mostly seeds, corn kernels and buds.
Voice: *Male:* loud, raspy, rooster-like crowing: *ka-squawk*; whirring of the wings, mostly just before sunrise.
Similar Species: male is distinctive. *Other grouse-like birds* (pp. 103–08): generally smaller; shorter tails.
Best Sites: *NB:* Sackville; Woodstock; Florenceville. *PEI:* Kensington; Stanhope; Souris. *NS:* Amherst; Wallace Bay; Annapolis Valley; Yarmouth; Liverpool.

RUFFED GROUSE

Bonasa umbellus

Puzzled by the sound of a two-stroke motorcycle or lawnmower engine starting up and stalling in the woods? Actually, what you are hearing is the sound of a "drumming" Ruffed Grouse. Each spring, and occasionally in autumn, the male Ruffed Grouse proclaims his territory. He struts along a fallen log with his tail fanned and his neck feathers ruffed, beating the air with accelerating wingstrokes. • The Ruffed Grouse's preference for birch stands has earned it the name of "Birch Partridge." However, it is quite cosmopolitan in its choice of habitats—it may even wander into towns sometimes. • Populations of Ruffed Grouse seem to fluctuate over a ten-year cycle, and many predators show population fluctuations that closely follow Ruffed Grouse trends. • During winter, scales grow out along the sides of this bird's toes, providing the Ruffed Grouse with temporary snowshoes. • In extreme conditions, birds will bury themselves in snowbanks to escape chilly winds and persistent predators.

grey morph

ID: small head crest; mottled grey-brown overall; black feathers on sides of lower neck (visible when fluffed out in courtship displays); grey- or reddish-barred tail has broad, dark subterminal band and white tip. *Female:* incomplete subterminal tail band.
Size: *L* 38–48 cm.
Status: common year-round resident.
Habitat: deciduous and mixed forests and riparian woodlands; in many areas it favours young second-growth stands with birch and poplar.
Nesting: in a shallow depression among leaf litter; often beside boulders, under logs or at the base of a tree; female incubates 9–12 buff-coloured eggs for 23–25 days.
Feeding: gleans from the ground and vegetation; omnivorous diet includes seeds, buds, flowers, berries, catkins, leaves, insects, and snails; may take small frogs.
Voice: *Male:* uses his wings to produce a hollow, drumming courtship display of accelerating, deep booms. *Female:* clucks and "hisses" around her chicks.
Similar Species: *Spruce Grouse* (p. 106): dark tail lacks barring and white tip; lacks head crest; male has red combs above eyes. *Sharp-tailed Grouse:* lacks fan-shaped tail and black feathers on lower neck. *Willow Ptarmigan* (p. 107): breeding birds show white on wings and legs; non-breeding birds are all white.
Best Sites: extremely widespread in open broadleaf and mixed woods with birch.

SPRUCE GROUSE

Falcipennis canadensis

The forest-dwelling Spruce Grouse trusts its camouflaged plumage to conceal it from view in its dark, damp year-round home. The Northern Goshawk is its most common predator, but the Spruce Grouse must also be wary of many mammalian carnivores. Despite its many predators, this grouse often allows people to approach to within a few metres, which is the reason it is often called "Fool Hen." • Spruce Grouse are most conspicuous in late April and early May, when females issue their vehement calls and strutting males magically appear in open areas along trails, roads and campgrounds. • The Spruce Grouse's deep call is nearly undetectable to the human ear. However, displaying males attract attention as they transform from their usual dull camouflage to become red-eyebrowed, puff-necked, fan-tailed splendours.

grey morph

ID: black, unbarred tail with chestnut brown tip; mottled grey, brown and black overall; feathered legs. *Male:* red comb over eye; black throat, neck and breast; white-tipped undertail, lower neck and belly feathers. *Female:* barred, mottled underparts.
Size: *L* 33–41 cm.
Status: locally uncommon year-round resident; introduced to the island of NF and steadily extending its breeding range beyond the introduction sites.
Habitat: conifer-dominated forests and scrubby, often poorly drained, upland cover; sometimes disperses into deciduous forests.
Nesting: on the forest floor; in a well-hidden, shallow scrape lined with a few grasses and needles; female incubates 4–10 buff eggs, blotched and spotted with brown and chestnut, for up to 21 days.
Feeding: live buds and needles of spruce, pine and fir trees; also eats berries, seeds and occasionally insects in summer.
Voice: very low, guttural *krrrk krrrk krrrk*.
Similar Species: *Ruffed Grouse* (p. 105): head is crested; tail has broad, dark subterminal band and white tip; lacks black throat and breast. *Willow Ptarmigan* (p. 107): breeding birds show white on wings and legs. *Sharp-tailed Grouse*: thinner, sharper tail; white throat; yellow eye combs.
Best Sites: *NB:* Kouchibouguac NP; UNB Woodlot (Fredericton). *NS:* Chignecto Game Sanctuary; Jeremy Bay (Kejimkujik NP); Cape Breton Highlands NP. *NF:* Beothuk PP; Buchans; Glover's Harbour–Point Leamington area.

WILLOW PTARMIGAN

Lagopus lagopus

To meet a Willow Ptarmigan in Atlantic Canada, you must be willing to travel to the island of Newfoundland, where they are widespread in open barrens and low growth, or go to the remote communities of Labrador or northern Québec. The best time to see ptarmigans is from mid-June to early July. At this time, excited males strut about noisily voicing their bizarre clucking calls and urging you to *go back.* • In some years, Willow Ptarmigans are seen in high densities. In other years, you should consider yourself lucky if you find a few widely scattered individuals. Like many arctic animals, ptarmigans experience significant cyclical fluctuations in their numbers. • The Latin *lagopus* refers to this bird's heavily feathered feet, which act just like snowshoes in deep snow.

breeding

ID: black outer tail feathers; short, rounded wings; black bill. *Spring male:* red comb above eye; deep chestnut brown head and neck; dark upper breast and back; otherwise mostly white. *Breeding male:* red comb; mottled brown and black overall; white wings, belly, legs and under-tail coverts. *Breeding female:* mottled brown and black; white wings. *Non-breeding:* white overall.
Size: *L* 35–43 cm.
Status: very rare to abundant year-round resident; abundance varies between years.
Habitat: arctic or alpine tundra and a variety of open habitats where willow, alder and birch are found; birds move toward the lowlands and coasts in harsh winters.
Nesting: on tundra and barrens; in a shallow scrape lined with grass, leaves, moss and feathers; usually on a raised hummock

or a raised ridge; female incubates 5–14 eggs for about 22 days; young leave the nest with their mother within a few hours of hatching.
Feeding: gleans vegetation and foliage for buds, flowers, leaves and small branches of willow, alder and birch shrubs; eats insects in summer; eats berries in autumn.
Voice: loud, crackling *go-back go-back go-back.*
Similar Species: *Rock Ptarmigan* (p. 108): non-breeding male has prominent black eye line and thicker red eye comb; female is virtually indistinguishable from non-breeding female Willow Ptarmigan. *Spruce Grouse* (p. 106): lacks white on wings. *Ruffed Grouse* (p. 105): crested head; lacks white on wings.
Best Sites: *NF:* Corner Brook; Lookout Hills & James Callaghan Trail (Gros Morne NP); L'Anse aux Meadows; Carmanville; Bonavista; Chance Cove; Cape Shore; St. Shott's; Cape Race.

ROCK PTARMIGAN
Lagopus mutus

In spring, Rock Ptarmigans explode into the air with whirring wings and a woodpecker-like rattle. These birds are strong flyers—they can fly for as far as 1.5 kilometres before needing to alight. As a result, they occasionally appear on coastal headlands away from their Newfoundland breeding range. • Ptarmigans quietly graze among the rock rubble looking for weed seeds or anything else edible. In winter, their diet consists mostly of the twigs, buds and seeds that they can find above the snow. • Males moult later than females in spring, when the cocks can be quite conspicuous in their white plumage. • Newfoundlanders call older male Willow Ptarmigans "Rockers" because they maintain a winter territory amid large boulders, which has caused confusion between these two species in historical records.

breeding

ID: *Breeding:* red eyebrow (more prominent on male than female); mottled, brownish-grey plumage; white wings; white, feathered legs and feet; black bill; female has very little white in summer and has more barring. *Non-breeding:* white plumage; male has red eyebrow and black eye stripe.

Size: *L* 36 cm.

Status: rare to locally uncommon year-round resident in northern NF; very rare vagrant elsewhere, usually at coastal headlands and offshore islands.

Habitat: *Breeding:* dry, open, rock-strewn subalpine mountaintops or arctic and alpine headlands; in rocks and boulders mixed with shrubby areas and sedge meadows. *Winter:* may remain in summer habitat, use lower slopes or may move into shrubby areas in broken forest.

Nesting: on ground in a rocky area; shallow depression lined with moss, lichen, grass and feathers; female incubates 7–9 buff eggs with dark markings for about 21 days; the young remain with the female throughout summer.

Feeding: picks at vegetation while walking; in winter, may follow herds of caribou to feed where the animals have scraped away the snow; mostly vegetarian diet includes buds, catkins, leaves, flowers, berries, seeds and sometimes insects and snails.

Voice: both sexes give clucking notes. *Male:* a croaking, throaty rattle followed by a hissing *krrrr-karrrr wsshhh* while displaying.

Similar Species: *Willow Ptarmigan* (p. 107): females are very difficult to distinguish in winter; females are browner in summer; male's breeding plumage is more reddish; male's non-breeding plumage lacks black eye stripe.

Best Sites: *NF:* Serpentine Tablelands; Lookout Hills & Gros Morne (Gros Morne NP); L'Anse aux Meadows.

YELLOW RAIL

Coturnicops noveboracensis

Rails are masters at slipping through tightly packed stands of low marsh vegetation with their laterally compressed bodies. Their large feet, which distribute their weight and help them to rest atop thin mats of floating plant material, add to their strange appearance. • The Yellow Rail might be the most challenging breeding bird to find in Atlantic Canada because it is quite rare and very cryptic. Initially regarded as a rare vagrant, the Yellow Rail has been found in several New Brunswick marshes and may well nest each year in similar habitats in maritime Québec and Nova Scotia. • The Yellow Rail mystified early residents who heard its unmistakable call in spring, which sounds like dry bones being clicked together. • Rails may have gotten their name because they look "as thin as a rail." The Latin *Coturnicops* refers to the Yellow Rail's superficial resemblance to Old World migratory quails of the genus *Coturnix*.

ID: short, pale bill; black and tawny stripes on upperparts (black stripes have fine, white barring); broad, dark line through eye; white throat and belly. *Juvenile:* darker overall; pattern on upperparts extends onto breast, sides and flanks. *In flight:* white trailing edge on inner wing.
Size: *L* 17–19 cm.
Status: rare and extremely local in most of Atlantic Canada to locally uncommon in southern NB from mid-May to August; rarely seen in migration from August to late October.
Habitat: sedge marshes and wet sedge meadows.

Nesting: on the ground or low over water, hidden by overhanging plants; shallow cup nest is made of grass or sedges; female incubates 8–10 eggs for up to 18 days.
Feeding: picks food from the ground and aquatic vegetation; eats mostly snails, aquatic insects, spiders and possibly earthworms; occasionally eats seeds.
Voice: like 2 bones or small stones clicking together: *tik, tik, tik-tik-tik*.
Similar Species: *Sora* (p. 111): lacks stripes on back and white patches on wings; breeding birds have black face and throat and bright yellow bill; distinctly different call. *Virginia Rail* (p. 110): larger; long, reddish bill; lacks stripes on back and white patches in wings; rusty breast; grey face.
Best Sites: *NB:* Midgic & Jolicure Marshes (Sackville); Grand Lake Meadows. *NS:* Amherst Point; Seal I. *PQ:* Barachois.

VIRGINIA RAIL

Rallus limicola

The best way to meet a Virginia Rail is to sit alongside a wetland marsh in mainland Atlantic Canada in spring, clap your hands three or four times to imitate this bird's *kidick* calls and wait patiently. If you are lucky, a Virginia Rail will reveal itself for a brief instant, but on most occasions you will only hear this elusive bird. • When pursued by an intruder or predator, a rail will almost always attempt to scurry away through dense, concealing vegetation, rather than risk exposure in a fluttering getaway flight. • The Virginia Rail and its relative the Sora are often found living in the same marshes. The secret of their successful coexistence is found in their microhabitat preferences and distinct diets. The Virginia Rail typically favours dry watersides of marshes and feeds on invertebrates; the Sora prefers waterfront property and eats plants and seeds. Both birds occasionally attempt to overwinter in our region, usually with limited success.

ID: long, down-curved, reddish bill; grey face; rusty breast; barred flanks; chestnut brown wing patch; very short tail. *Immature:* much darker overall; light bill.
Size: *L* 23–28 cm.
Status: uncommon to locally fairly common from early May to mid-September; some birds attempt to overwinter.
Habitat: freshwater wetlands, especially cattail and bulrush marshes.
Nesting: concealed in emergent vegetation, usually suspended just over the water; loose basket nest is made of coarse grass, cattail stems or sedges; pair incubates 5–13 spotted, pale buff eggs for up to 20 days.
Feeding: probes into soft substrates and gleans vegetation for invertebrates,

including beetles, snails, spiders, earthworms, insect larvae and nymphs; also eats some pondweeds and seeds.
Voice: call is an often-repeated, telegraph-like *kidick, kidick*; also "oinks" and croaks.
Similar Species: *King Rail:* much larger; dark legs; lacks reddish bill and grey face; juvenile is mostly pale grey. *Sora* (p. 111): short, yellow bill; black face and throat. *Yellow Rail* (p. 109): short, pale yellowish bill; black-and-tawny striped back; white trailing edges of wings are seen in flight.
Best Sites: *NB:* Sackville; Hazen Creek (Saint John); Portobello Creek; Corbett Marsh (Fredericton). *PEI:* Deroche Pond; Mount Stewart. *NS:* Amherst Point; Missaguash Marsh. *NF:* Codroy Valley. *PQ:* Rimouski; St-Fabien; Petit Gaspé; Barachois; Îles de la Madeleine.

SORA

Porzana carolina

The small Sora is the commonest and most widespread member of its family in Atlantic Canada. It has two main calls: a clear, whistled *coo-wee* that is easy to imitate and a strange, descending whinny. Its elusive habits and preference for dense marshlands force most would-be observers to settle for a quick look. However, if you venture out alone or with suitably silent partners on a calm, clear night in appropriate habitat, your chances of observing this bird are greatly increased. • Even though its feet are not webbed or lobed, the Sora swims quite well over short distances. It is also a strong long-distance flyer. • Hardier than many suspect, Soras sometimes overwinter here, often sharing their soggy habitats with Common Snipes.

breeding

ID: short, yellow bill; black face, throat and fore-neck; grey neck and breast; long, greenish legs. *Immature:* no black on face; buffier with paler underparts; bill is more greenish.

Size: *L* 20–25 cm.

Status: uncommon to common from mid-April to early November; some birds attempt to overwinter.

Habitat: wetlands with abundant emergent cattails, bulrushes, sedges and grasses.

Nesting: usually over water, but occasionally in a wet meadow under concealing vegetation; well-built basket nest is made of grass and aquatic vegetation; pair incubates 10–12 eggs for 18–20 days.

Feeding: gleans and probes for seeds, plants, aquatic insects and molluscs.

Voice: usual note is a clear, 2-note *coo-wee*; alarm call is a sharp *keek*; courtship song begins *or-Ah or-Ah*, descending quickly in a series of maniacal *weee-weee-weee* notes.

Similar Species: *Virginia Rail* (p. 110): larger; long, downcurved bill; chestnut brown wing patch; rufous breast. *Yellow Rail* (p. 109): streaked back; tawny upperparts; white throat; white trailing edges of wings are seen in flight; most likely confused with immatures in autumn migration.

Best Sites: *NB:* Strawberry Marsh (Newcastle); Sackville; Hazen Creek (Saint John). *PEI:* Deroche Pond; Mount Stewart. *NS:* Missaguash Marsh; Canning; Hopewell Marsh. *NF:* Cape Anguille; Long Pond (St. John's); Cuslett. *PQ:* Bas St-Laurent; Lac Cap Vert (Îles de la Madeleine).

COMMON MOORHEN

Gallinula chloropus

The Common Moorhen is a curious-looking creature that appears to have been assembled from bits and pieces left over from other birds: it has the bill of a chicken, the body of a duck and the long legs and large feet of a small heron. It strolls around a wetland with its head bobbing back and forth in synchrony with its legs, producing a comical, chugging stride. Its swimming style perpetuates the head bobbing and accentuates the white undertail coverts. • Fiercely argumentative when nesting, Moorhens, formerly known as "Florida Gallinules," somewhat moderate their bombastic tendencies in migration when they will feed with American Coots, grebes and ducks. The responsibilities of parenthood do not end when the young hatch—both parents feed and shelter juveniles until they are capable of feeding themselves and flying on their own.

breeding

ID: reddish forehead shield; yellow-tipped bill; grey-black body; white streak on sides and flanks; long, yellow legs. *Breeding:* brighter bill and forehead shield. *Juvenile:* paler plumage; duller legs and bill; white throat.
Size: *L* 30–38 cm.
Status: rare to locally uncommon breeder from late May to mid-October; migrants appear from April through May, and from October through November; some birds attempt to overwinter in milder areas of NB and NS.
Habitat: freshwater marshes, ponds, lakes and sewage lagoons; never found on salt water.
Nesting: pair builds a platform nest or a wide, shallow cup of bulrushes, cattails and reeds in shallow water or along a shoreline; often built with a ramp leading to the water; pair incubates 6–17 buffy, finely speckled eggs for 19–22 days.
Feeding: eats mostly aquatic vegetation, berries, fruits, tadpoles, insects, snails and worms; may take carrion and eggs.
Voice: noisy in summer; various sounds include chicken-like clucks, screams, squeaks and a loud *cup*; courting males give a harsh *ticket-ticket-ticket*.
Similar Species: *American Coot* (p. 113): white bill and forehead shield; lacks white streak on flanks. *Scoters* (pp. 77–79): larger; bulbous bills have different colour patterns.
Best Sites: *NB:* Hillsborough; New Horton Marsh; Red Head Marsh (Saint John). *PEI:* Mount Stewart. *NS:* Amherst Point; Caledonia–Harmony area; Seal I.; Three Fathom Harbour. *PQ:* Rimouski; Matane; Petit Gaspé.

AMERICAN COOT
Fulica americana

The American Coot behaves much like both a duck and a grebe. Like a duck, it dives and dabbles in the water and also grazes confidently on land. Like the most accomplished grebe, it swims about skillfully with its lobed feet. • Outside the breeding season, American Coots gather together in large groups. They squabble constantly during the breeding season, not just among themselves but also with any water bird that has the audacity to intrude upon their patch of waterfront property. • A male American Coot often swims with his head down and his bill thrust forward to show off his white forehead shield to the females. • Coots are colloquially known as "Mud Hens," and few birders realize that they are not a species of duck.

ID: grey-black, duck-like bird; white, chicken-like bill with dark ring around tip; reddish spot on white forehead shield; long, green-yellow legs; lobed toes; red eyes. *Immature:* lighter body colour; darker bill and legs; lacks prominent forehead shield. **Size:** *L* 33–41 cm.

Status: uncommon to abundant migrant from early April to mid-May and from September to mid-November; rare to locally uncommon breeder; a few may overwinter.

Habitat: *Breeding:* shallow marshes, ponds and wetlands with open water and emergent vegetation. *In migration* and *winter:* large, coastal lakes and bays, both salt and fresh water; urban ponds and golf courses.

Nesting: in emergent vegetation; floating nest built by the pair is usually made of cattails and grass; pair incubates 8–12 buffy white, brown-spotted eggs for 21–25 days; regularly produces 2 broods in a season.

Feeding: eats aquatic vegetation, insects, snails, crayfish, worms, tadpoles and fish; gleans the water's surface; sometimes dives, tips up or even grazes on land; may steal food from ducks, although Gadwalls and American Wigeons sometimes steal from American Coots.

Voice: calls frequently in summer, day and night: *kuk-kuk-kuk-kuk-kuk*; also grunts.

Similar Species: *Scoters* (pp. 77–79): shape and colours of bill are different; females are brown, not black. *Grebes* (pp. 34–36): lack white forehead shield and all-dark plumage. *Common Moorhen* (p. 112): reddish forehead shield; yellow-tipped bill; white streak on flanks.

Best Sites: *NB:* Midgic Marsh; Saints Rest Marsh (Saint John). *PEI:* St. Peter's Bay. *NS:* Amherst Point; Missaguash Marsh; River John; Seal I. *PQ:* Bas St-Laurent; Barachois; Lac Cap Vert & Fatima (Îles de la Madeleine).

BLACK-BELLIED PLOVER

Pluvialis squatarola

The Black-bellied Plover's black-and-white breeding plumage is seen briefly in spring as birds race northward to make full use of the short arctic summer. After nesting is completed, adults in faded plumage begin to appear along Atlantic coastlines in August. They are followed by juveniles in brighter, gold-flecked dress in September and October. Black-bellies choose a variety of wet habitats in autumn migration, such as intertidal mud flats and beaches, as well as drier habitats, such as grassland pools and farmlands. • Black-bellied Plovers are the most widespread of the larger plovers and are found in the greatest variety of habitats. • A Black-bellied Plover forages for small invertebrates with a robin-like run-and-stop technique. It frequently pauses to lift its head for a reassuring scan of its surroundings. • Most plovers have three toes, but the Black-belly has a fourth toe high on its leg, like most sandpipers.

breeding

ID: short, black bill; long, black legs. *Breeding:* black face, breast, belly and flanks; white undertail coverts; white stripe leading from crown down to collar, neck and sides of breast; mottled black-and-white back. *Non-breeding:* mottled grey-brown upperparts; lightly streaked, pale underparts. *In flight:* black "wing pits"; whitish rump; white wing linings.
Size: *L* 27–33 cm.
Status: rare to locally abundant migrant from mid-April to early June and from late July to late November; a few birds may remain in summer; small numbers overwinter in NS and NF.
Habitat: ploughed fields, meadows, shores and mud flats along the edges of coastal bays and estuaries, inland marshes, lagoons, lakes and farmlands.
Nesting: does not nest in Atlantic Canada.
Feeding: run-and-stop foraging technique; eats insects on fields, molluscs and crustaceans along seashores.
Voice: rich, plaintive, 3-syllable whistle: *pee-oo-ee.*
Similar Species: *American Golden-Plover* (p. 116): upperparts are mottled with gold; black undertail coverts in breeding plumage; lacks black "wing pits." *European Golden-Plover* (p. 115): upperparts mottled with gold; white border between wings and black belly; lacks black "wing pits." *Red Knot* (p. 129): non-breeding birds have longer bills, shorter legs and lack black "wing pits."
Best Sites: along coasts and on farmlands.

EUROPEAN GOLDEN-PLOVER
Pluvialis apricaria

breeding

Also known as the Greater Golden-Plover and the Eurasian Golden-Plover, this bird's distribution is mostly European—Iceland, the Faeroes, Scotland, northern Europe and northwestern Asia comprise much of its breeding range. It is irregularly seen as far west as Newfoundland, and it may occasionally stray to other parts of Atlantic Canada as well. The European Golden-Plover is most likely to be seen in spring, when it moults out of its striking breeding plumage. • The European Golden-Plover is generally stockier than the American Golden-Plover, and it has a shorter bill. It is also more regular in spring than its close cousin, which chooses an interior route north. Birds that arrive in Atlantic Canada have been blown off course while heading from western Africa to their subarctic breeding grounds. • The species name, *apricaria,* is derived from the Latin word "apricus," meaning "sunny."

ID: relatively stocky body; short, black bill. *Breeding:* mottled, golden upperparts; black face and underparts; white band separates mottled upperparts from black underparts; white underwing coverts. *Non-breeding:* mottled, golden upperparts and breast; cream eyebrow and throat; white belly and underwing coverts.
Size: *L* 28 cm.
Status: rare to irregularly fairly common spring migrant from early April to late May.
Habitat: freshwater and brackish wetlands; farm fields and grassy headlands.
Nesting: does not nest in Atlantic Canada.
Feeding: run-and-stop foraging technique; feeds on earthworms, molluscs, snails,

slugs, insects and their larvae and some vegetation.
Voice: calls include a plaintive *tlui* and a soft piping *wheep wheep;* flight song is a repeated *perPEEoo;* generally gives lower and simpler calls than the American Golden-Plover.
Similar Species: *American Golden-Plover* (p. 116): in breeding plumage, black on belly extends to mottled, golden plumage (white band does not extend this far down); non-breeding plumage is greyer overall with white eyebrow; greyish underwing coverts. *Black-bellied Plover* (p. 114): upperparts lack yellow colouring; black "wing pits." *Sandpipers* (pp. 130–39): lack combination of mottled, golden upperparts and black belly.
Best Sites: *NF:* L'Anse aux Meadows; Cape Bonavista; Kilbride; Cape Race; St. Shott's.

AMERICAN GOLDEN-PLOVER

Pluvialis dominica

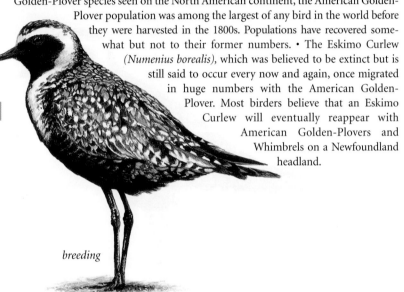

I n late summer, adult American Golden-Plovers with varying amounts of black on their bellies and sides gather and make their first, relatively short journey to stage in Atlantic Canada. Here they fatten up before heading across the western Atlantic to Brazil. Juveniles with somewhat brighter, but sometimes less golden, feathers follow and can be seen in Atlantic Canada well into December. • One of three Golden-Plover species seen on the North American continent, the American Golden-Plover population was among the largest of any bird in the world before they were harvested in the 1800s. Populations have recovered somewhat but not to their former numbers. • The Eskimo Curlew *(Numenius borealis)*, which was believed to be extinct but is still said to occur every now and again, once migrated in huge numbers with the American Golden-Plover. Most birders believe that an Eskimo Curlew will eventually reappear with American Golden-Plovers and Whimbrels on a Newfoundland headland.

breeding

ID: straight, black bill; long, black legs. *Breeding:* black face and underparts; S-shaped, white stripe from forehead down to shoulders; dark upperparts are speckled with gold and white. *Non-breeding:* broad, pale eyebrow; dark streaking on pale neck and underparts; much less gold on upperparts; early autumn arrivals still have blackish blotches on underparts. *Juveniles:* somewhat brighter than adults, with white forehead. *In flight:* grey "wing pits."
Size: *L* 25–38 cm.
Status: rare migrant from early April to May; common to abundant migrant from early August to November.
Habitat: cultivated fields, meadows, shores and mud flats along the edges of coastal bays, estuaries, marshes and lagoons; occasionally mountain barrens in autumn.
Nesting: not known to nest in Atlantic Canada.
Feeding: run-and-stop foraging technique; snatches insects, molluscs and crustaceans; seeds and berries are also taken by birds visiting inland and mountain habitats.
Voice: soft, melodious whistle: *quee, quee-dle.*
Similar Species: *Black-bellied Plover* (p. 114): white undertail coverts; whitish crown; lacks gold speckling on upperparts; conspicuous black "wing pits." *European Golden-Plover* (p. 115): white undertail coverts; white area between black belly and golden-brown upperparts; white underwings. *Buff-breasted Sandpiper* (p. 139): longer, finer bill; lacks black on underparts; flashy, white wing linings.
Best Sites: along coasts and on farmlands, mainly at headlands and estuaries.

SEMIPALMATED PLOVER

Charadrius semipalmatus

In Atlantic Canada, especially in Newfoundland, these small, active plovers have to be carefully identified. Piping Plovers and Common Ringed Plovers may also be present, the former in summer and the latter in autumn. Even in good light there can be confusion identifying birds from sight, but each species has a different flight call. • Spring migration is a brief affair, with most birds seen along the coast in mid-May. In late summer and autumn, it seems that wherever you look along the shorelines there are groups of plovers stopping and starting as they comb the beaches, mud flats and shore margins for food. Adults are the first to appear in early July, followed in late August by the first juveniles. New arrivals continue to appear until mid-November. • The scientific name *semipalmatus* refers to the partial webbing between the toes of this plover. The webbing may give its feet more surface area when it walks on soft substrates.

breeding

ID: *Breeding:* dark brown back; white breast with 1 black, horizontal band; long, orange legs; stubby, orange, black-tipped bill; white patch above bill; white throat and collar; black band across forehead. *Non-breeding:* duller; mostly dark bill. *Juvenile:* dark legs and bill; more indistinct, brown bands.
Size: *L* 18 cm.
Status: rare to common migrant in May and early June and from late July to mid-November; uncommon to common breeder.
Habitat: *Breeding:* sand and gravel bars along shorelines. *In migration:* sandy beaches, shorelines, river edges and mud flats.
Nesting: on sand or gravel, usually near extensive salt or brackish marshes; in a depression sparsely lined with vegetation;

pair incubates 4 creamy buff eggs, cryptically marked at the larger end, for 23–25 days.
Feeding: run-and-stop feeding, usually on shorelines and beaches; eats crustaceans, worms and insects.
Voice: crisp, high-pitched, 2-part, rising whistle: *tu-wee.*
Similar Species: *Killdeer* (p. 119): larger; 2 black bands across breast. *Common Ringed Plover:* broader black breastband; different call. *Piping Plover* (p. 118): lacks dark band through eyes; narrower breast band, incomplete in females and most males; much lighter upperparts.
Best Sites: *Summer: NB:* Waterside; Grand Manan I. *PEI:* New London Bay; Maximeville. *NS:* Brule–River John area; Cook's Beach. *NF:* St. Paul's; Pistolet Bay; Notre Dame Bay. *PQ:* Havre-aux-Basques & Grosse Île (Îles de la Madeleine). *In migration:* mud flats and sandy beaches.

PIPING PLOVER

Charadrius melodus

A master of illusion, the Piping Plover is hardly noticeable when it settles on shorelines and beaches. Its pale, sand-coloured plumage is the perfect camouflage against a sandy beach. As well, the dark bands across its forehead and neckline resemble scattered pebbles or strips of washed-up vegetation at the tide line and just below the dunes. The only way to find a Piping Plover is to watch for one of its characteristic short runs. • This plover's cryptic plumage has done little to protect it from wetland drainage, increased predation and disturbance by humans. As a listed endangered species it has legislative protection, but these laws are patchily enforced anywhere but on national park beaches. • The species name *melodus* refers to this bird's clear, whistled call.

breeding

ID: pale, sandy upperparts; white underparts; orange legs. *Breeding:* black-tipped, orange bill; black forehead band; black "necklace" (usually incomplete, especially on females). *Non-breeding* and *juvenile:* no breast or forehead band; all-black bill.

Size: *L* 18–19 cm.

Status: locally uncommon from mid-March to late September; a few may remain into November; rare local breeder.

Habitat: *Breeding:* sandy beaches backed by dunes and close to shallow tidal flats. *In migration:* sandbars, beaches and mud flats, rarely away from the coast.

Nesting: on bare sand along an open shoreline; in a shallow scrape that is sometimes lined with pebbles and tiny shells; pair incubates 4 pale buff eggs, blotched with dark brown and black, for 26–28 days.

Feeding: run-and-stop feeding; eats worms and insects; almost all its food is taken from the ground.

Voice: clear, whistled melody: *peep peep peep-lo.*

Similar Species: *Semipalmated Plover* (p. 117): dark band over eye; much darker upperparts. *Killdeer* (p. 119): larger; 2 breast bands; much darker upperparts.

Best Sites: *NB:* Tracadie–Miscou area; Kouchibouguac NP. *PEI:* PEI NP; Brudenell River. *NS:* southwest beaches. *NF:* Grand Bay West; Cheeseman PP; Flat I. (St. George's); Lumsden–Cape Freels area. *PQ:* Îles de la Madeleine.

KILLDEER

Charadrius vociferus

The ubiquitous Killdeer is often the first shorebird a birdwatcher will learn to identify. Its boisterous *kill-dee-dee* calls rarely fail to catch the attention of most people passing through its wide variety of nesting environments. • Many sitting birds remain tight on the nest, confident that their disruptive coloration will render them virtually invisible. If you happen to wander too close to a Killdeer nest, however, the parent will try to lure you away, issuing loud alarm calls, feigning a broken wing and exposing its rufous rump. Most predators swallow the bait and are led far enough away for the parent to suddenly recover from its life-threatening injury and fly off, sounding its piercing calls. Smaller plovers have similar distraction displays but the Killdeer's broken wing act is by far the gold medal winner. • The scientific name *vociferus* aptly describes this vocal bird, but double-check all calls in spring—at this time of year the Killdeer is often imitated by frisky Starlings.

ID: long, dark yellow legs; white upperparts with 2 black breast bands; brown back; white face patch above bill; black forehead band; rusty rump. *Immature:* downy; only 1 breast band.

Size: *L* 23–28 cm.

Status: common to abundant from mid-March to late October; a few remain until December and some overwinter when winters are mild.

Habitat: open ground, fields, lakeshores, sandy beaches, mud flats, gravel stream beds, wet meadows and grasslands; in urban areas, parks and open ground, often at a distance from water.

Nesting: on open ground; in a shallow, usually unlined depression; pair incubates 4 eggs for 24–28 days; occasionally raises 2 broods.

Feeding: run-and-stop feeder; eats mostly insects; also takes spiders, snails, earthworms and marine invertebrates.

Voice: loud and distinctive *kill-dee kill-dee kill-deer* and variations, including *deer-deer*.

Similar Species: *Semipalmated Plover* (p. 117): smaller; only 1 breast band. *Piping Plover* (p. 118): smaller; lighter upperparts; 1 breast band.

Best Sites: suburban sites, open areas and mud flats.

GREATER YELLOWLEGS

Tringa melanoleuca

A number of medium-sized shorebirds known as "tattlers," a name derived from the same root as "tattle-tale," perform the role of lookout among mixed flocks of shorebirds. In Atlantic Canada, the task has fallen to the Greater Yellowlegs, a bird with a sense of vigilance and a far-carrying, three-note descending whistle. • Mixed flocks of Greater Yellowlegs and Lesser Yellowlegs are found throughout the Atlantic provinces during migration. It's relatively easy to distinguish between the two species if viewing conditions are good. It's quite another matter when mists roll in and relative sizes are skewed, but even then it helps to remember that the Lesser Yellowlegs utters a higher one- or two-note whistle. • Greater Yellowlegs nest in parts of Cape Breton and Newfoundland, primarily among wet bogs and fens. Even before you are close to the nest, you will be bombarded with angry, high-pitched calls from atop a black spruce or tamarack.

breeding

ID: long, bright yellow legs; 2-tone dark bill is slightly upturned toward tip and is noticeably longer than head width. *Breeding:* brown-black back and upperwing; fine, dense, dark streaking on head and neck; dark barring on breast often extends onto belly; subtle, dark eye line; light lores. *Non-breeding:* grey overall; fine streaks on breast; clear belly. *Juvenile:* warmer brown upperparts, spotted with pale buff notches; clear, brown streaks on breast, flanks and undertail.
Size: *L* 33–38 cm.
Status: common to very common from late April to mid-May and common to locally abundant from mid-July to October; rare local breeder; rare in early winter.
Habitat: *Breeding:* bogs, alluvial wetlands, sedge meadows, fens and beaver ponds. *In migration:* almost all wetlands, even in cities.

Nesting: in a depression on a dry mound; usually on a ridge near open bogs or natural openings in muskeg; never far from water; well-hidden nest is sparsely lined with leaves, moss and grass; female incubates 4 dark buff, heavily marked eggs for about 23 days.
Feeding: usually wades in water over its knees; primarily eats aquatic invertebrates, but will also eat small fish; occasionally snatches prey from the water's surface.
Voice: quick, whistled series of *tew-tew-tew*, usually 3 notes but sometimes 4.
Similar Species: *Lesser Yellowlegs* (p. 121): smaller; straight bill is not noticeably longer than width of head; call is generally a pair of higher notes: *tew-tew*. *Willet* (p. 123): white wing bars; heavier bill; distinctive, clear *pill-will-willet* call.
Best Sites: *Summer: NS:* Cape Breton Highlands NP. *NF:* Tablelands (Gros Morne NP). *In migration:* in any wetland sites, along the coast and inland.

LESSER YELLOWLEGS

Tringa flavipes

Some birders still find it a challenge to distinguish Lesser Yellowlegs and Greater Yellowlegs in the field. However, with practice you will notice that the Lesser's bill is finer, straighter and not noticeably longer than the width of its head, that the Greaters will stray into deeper water and even swim at times, and that the species' calls are different. If you are still puzzled at the bird's identity, don't despair—simply write "yellowlegs spp." in your field notes and try again next time. • Visits by Lesser Yellowlegs are relatively brief in spring because most birds are heading for muskeg country west of Atlantic Canada, but a few Greater Yellowlegs can be anticipated throughout summer. The autumn migration period for both species is lengthy, and Lesser Yellowlegs can be seen from early July to mid-October. A few birds linger into November with their hardier cousins.

breeding

ID: bright yellow legs; all-dark bill is not noticeably longer than width of head. *Breeding:* brown-black back and upperwing; fine, dense, dark streaking on head, neck and breast; lacks barring on belly; subtle, dark eye line; *Non-breeding:* similar, but grey overall.

Size: *L* 25–28 cm.

Status: uncommon to locally common from mid-April to late May; common to abundant from early July to mid-October; rare in June and in late October and November.

Habitat: *Breeding:* grassy ponds and open forests. *In migration:* shorelines of lakes, rivers, marshes and ponds, mud flats and beaches.

Nesting: does not nest in Atlantic Canada.

Feeding: snatches prey from the water's surface; frequently wades in shallow water; primarily eats aquatic invertebrates, but will also take small fish and tadpoles.

Voice: typically a high-pitched pair of *tew* notes.

Similar Species: *Greater Yellowlegs* (p. 120): larger; bill is slightly upturned toward tip and noticeably longer than width of head; *tew* call is usually given in a series of 3 notes. *Solitary Sandpiper* (p. 122): white eye ring; darker upperparts; paler bill; greenish legs. *Willet* (p. 123): much bulkier; black-and-white wings; heavier bill.

Best Sites: coastal wetlands and mud flats.

SOLITARY SANDPIPER

Tringa solitaria

Most of the time the Solitary Sandpiper is true to its name, seen alone, bobbing its body like a spirited dancer as it forages for insects along stream courses and lake shores. Solitary Sandpipers are also very aggressive when feeding or protecting the nest site, so breeding pairs are rarely in close proximity. Once in a while, however, especially during migration, a lucky observer may happen upon a small group of Solitary Sandpipers. • In spring, birds pass through Atlantic Canada mostly in May. Autumn migration is much more prolonged, with the first birds turning up in mid-July and the majority of juveniles arriving from mid-August to early October. • The Solitary Sandpiper's nesting strategy remained a mystery until 1903, when someone peered into what he thought was a robin's nest, but found a sandpiper instead. Once sandpiper chicks break out of their eggs, they are ready to run, hide and feed on their own.

breeding

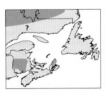

ID: white eye ring; short, green legs; dark yellowish bill with black tip; brown-grey spotted back; white lores; brown-grey head, neck and breast have fine white streaks; dark upper tail feathers with black-and-white barring on sides. *In flight:* dark underwings.

Size: *L* 19–23 cm.

Status: uncommon from May to early October; rare in late April and mid-October.

Habitat: *Breeding:* heavily forested wetlands, bogs, fens and streams. *In migration:* wet meadows, sewage lagoons, muddy ponds, sedge wetlands, beaver ponds and wooded streams.

Nesting: in a spruce tree in a bog or in muskeg; will use the abandoned nest of a thrush, blackbird or other songbird; pair incubates 4 eggs for 23–24 days.

Feeding: stalks shorelines, picking up aquatic invertebrates, such as water boatmen and damselfly nymphs; also gleans for terrestrial invertebrates; occasionally stirs the water with its foot to spook out prey.

Voice: high, thin *peet-wheet* or *wheat wheat wheat* during summer.

Similar Species: *Lesser Yellowlegs* (p. 121): no eye ring; longer, bright yellow legs. *Spotted Sandpiper* (p. 124): incomplete eye ring; spotted breast in breeding plumage; orange, black-tipped bill.

Best Sites: *NB:* Newcastle; Cold Brook; Eel Lake (Grand Manan I.). *PEI:* Dalvay. *NS:* Cape Sable I., Cape Breton Highlands NP. *PQ:* Cacouna, Lac à l'Anguille (Rimouski).

WILLET

Catoptrophorus semipalmatus

A resting Willet gives the impression of being a rather overweight, under-active yellowlegs. The moment it takes flight, however, its black-and-white wings add sudden colour while it calls out a loud, rhythmic *will-will willet, will-will-willet.* The bright, bold flashes of the Willet's wings may alert other shore-birds to imminent danger. These flashes may also double as a means of intimidating predators during the bird's dive-bombing defence of its young. • In spring, most Willets head straight to their nest sites on coastal salt marshes to establish territories that are fiercely defended throughout the early summer. Where there are several pairs, they parcel out the area and take turns scolding and dive-bombing potential predators of all sizes. Once young are out of the nest, aggressive tendencies subside and feeding parties form.

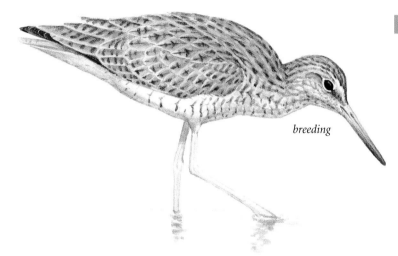

breeding

ID: plump; heavy, straight, black bill; light throat and belly. *Breeding:* dark streaking and barring overall. *In flight:* black-and-white wing pattern.
Size: *L* 36–41 cm.
Status: rare to locally common visitor from mid-April to early October; some birds linger into November.
Habitat: *Breeding:* wet fields and salt marshes along the coast and very rarely by inland marshes, lakes and ponds. *In migration:* coastal salt marshes, mud flats, sand-bars and shorelines.
Nesting: on ground; well hidden among low bushes in fields or bushy pastures; shallow depression with a lining of leaves and dry grasses; pair incubates 4 olive or buff, heavily spotted eggs for 22 days.
Feeding: feeds by probing muddy areas; also gleans the ground for insects; occasionally eats shoots and seeds.
Voice: loud, rolling *will-will willet, will-will-willet.*
Similar Species: *Marbled Godwit* and *Hudsonian Godwit* (p. 127): much longer, pinkish-yellow bill with dark, slightly upturned tip; larger body; lacks black-and-white wing pattern. *Greater Yellowlegs* (p. 120): long, yellow legs; slightly upturned bill; lacks black-and-white wing pattern.
Best Sites: *Summer: NB:* Gulf Shore. *PEI:* PEI NP. *NS:* Tatamagouche; southwest marshes; Cape Breton. *NF:* Grand Codroy Estuary; Flat I. (St. George's). *PQ:* Gaspé Bay; Îles de la Madeleine.

123

SPOTTED SANDPIPER

Actitis macularia

A widespread breeder in Atlantic Canada, the Spotted Sandpiper is the sandpiper most frequently encountered away from the coast throughout summer. • It wasn't until 1972 that the unexpected truths about the Spotted Sandpiper's breeding activities were realized. Female Spotted Sandpipers defend territories and mate with more than one male in a single breeding season. Males tend the nests and eggs. This unusual nesting behaviour, known as polyandry, is found in about one percent of all bird species. • Although its breast spots aren't noticeable from a distance, the Spottie's stiff-winged, quivering flight pattern and tendency to burst from the shore are easily recognizable. Like the Solitary Sandpiper, it is also known for its continuous teetering behaviour as it forages.

breeding

ID: teeters continuously. *Breeding:* white underparts are heavily spotted; yellow-orange, black-tipped bill; yellow-orange legs; white eyebrow. *Non-breeding* and *juvenile:* pure white breast, foreneck and throat; brown bill; dull yellow legs. *In flight:* flies close to the water's surface with very rapid, shallow wingbeats; white upperwing stripe.

Size: *L* 18–20 cm.

Status: common from late April to late September; a few stragglers in October and November; extremely rare in December.

Habitat: shorelines, gravel beaches, ponds, marshes, drainage ditches, rivers, streams, swamps and sewage lagoons; occasionally seen in cultivated fields.

Nesting: usually near water; often under overhanging vegetation among logs or under bushes; in a shallow depression lined with grass; male almost exclusively incubates the 4 creamy buff, heavily blotched and spotted eggs and raises the young.

Feeding: picks and gleans along shorelines for terrestrial and aquatic invertebrates; also snatches flying insects from the air.

Voice: sharp, crisp *eat-wheat, eat-wheat, wheat-wheat-wheat-wheat.*

Similar Species: *Solitary Sandpiper* (p. 122): complete eye ring; lacks spotting on breast; yellowish bill with dark tip. *Other sandpipers* (pp. 120–39): mostly black bills and legs; lack spotting on breast.

Best Sites: rivers, lakeshores and coasts; often nests in urban areas.

UPLAND SANDPIPER

Bartramia longicauda

In spring, Upland Sandpipers are occasionally seen perched atop tall fence posts belting out airy "wolf-whistle" courtship tunes. Excited males will launch into the air to perform courtship flight displays, combining song with shallow, fluttering wingbeats. At the height of the breeding season, however, these large-eyed, inland shorebirds are rarely seen, remaining hidden in the tall grass of abandoned fields and ungrazed pastures. • Twice each year, these wide-ranging shorebirds make the incredible journey between Canada and South America without jet propulsion or inflight movies. • In Atlantic Canada this bird nests only in limited areas of New Brunswick and Prince Edward Island where grassland habitat persists. Elsewhere, it is a rare bird indeed, seen only briefly in migration.

ID: small head; long neck; large, dark eyes; yellow legs; mottled brownish upperparts; lightly streaked breast, sides and flanks; white belly and undertail coverts; bill is about as long as head. *In flight:* looks like miniature curlew but with straight bill; may issue courtship song while flying.

Size: *L* 28–32 cm.

Status: rare to uncommon from mid-April to late September; occasionally seen on offshore islands as late as mid-November.

Habitat: hayfields, ungrazed pastures, grassy meadows, abandoned fields, natural grasslands and airports.

Nesting: in dense grass or along a wetland; in a depression, usually with grass arching overtop; pair incubates 4 pale eggs, lightly spotted with reddish-brown, for 22–27 days; both adults tend the young.

Feeding: gleans the ground for insects, especially grasshoppers and beetles.

Voice: courtship song is an airy, whistled *whip-whee-ee you*; alarm call is *quip-ip-ip*.

Similar Species: *Willet* (p. 123): longer, heavier bill; dark greenish legs; black-and-white wings in flight. *Buff-breasted Sandpiper* (p. 139): buffer; shorter neck; larger head; daintier bill; lacks streaking on "cheek" and foreneck. *Pectoral Sandpiper* (p. 135): abrupt end to streaking on breast; smaller eyes; shorter neck; usually seen in flocks.

Best Sites: *NB:* Pointe Sapin; Coal Branch; Sackville; Salisbury; Musquash Marsh; Fredericton. *PEI:* Kensington; Montague. *NS:* Pubnico. *PQ:* Mont-Joli; Percé.

WHIMBREL

Numenius phaeopus

Whimbrels do not nest in Atlantic Canada, yet they are plentiful in autumn migration as they gather on the crowberry barrens of Newfoundland. Here, they gorge on berries before they fly to rocky islets or isolated headlands to roost for the night. • The tendency of Whimbrels and their closely related cousins to travel in large, loyal flocks was their undoing when people started hunting them commercially. Both the Whimbrel and Eskimo Curlew *(N. borealis)* suffered devastating losses to their populations during the commercial hunts of the late 1800s. • Most birds seen are of the North American subspecies *hudsonicus.* However, there have been a number of autumn sightings of the white-rumped Eurasian *phaeopus* in Nova Scotia and Newfoundland and one or two spring sightings of the very similar, Iceland-nesting *islandicus.* • *Numenius* is from the Greek for "new moon," and it refers to the curved shape of this bird's bill.

ID: long, down-curved bill; striped crown; dark eye line; mottled brown body; long legs. *In flight:* dark underwings.

Size: *L* 45 cm.

Status: rare migrant from late April to early June and common to locally abundant from early July to late October; rare in summer and early winter.

Habitat: coastal headlands, sandy beaches, sand dunes, farmlands, airports and flooded fields.

Nesting: does not nest in Atlantic Canada.

Feeding: probes and pecks for invertebrates in mud or vegetation; also eats enormous amounts of berries in autumn.

Voice: incoming flocks can be heard uttering a distinctive, and easily imitated, rippling *bibibibibibibi* long before they come into sight.

Similar Species: *Upland Sandpiper* (p. 125): smaller; straight bill; lacks head markings; lighter back; yellowish legs. *Long-billed Curlew:* much larger overall; much longer bill; lacks bold striping on head and through eye. *Eskimo Curlew:* unbarred primaries; pale cinnamon wing linings; shorter, slightly straighter bill; darker upperparts.

Best Sites: usually on crowberry barrens, but also at estuaries and mud flats.

HUDSONIAN GODWIT

Limosa haemastica

The Hudsonian Godwit's non-stop voyage to South America is fueled solely by fat reserves that are built up on its north-coast staging grounds prior to departure. Fortunately, not all of these godwits fly south in early autumn. Birders who are scouting the shores of Atlantic Canada from mid-July to early October are able to enjoy the sight of small parties of these long-billed, long-legged shorebirds wading out beyond their smaller relatives. • When Hudsonian Godwits take to the wing, their broad white wing bars and two-tone tail give them an extra touch of class. It is worth checking out the wing linings, which are black in Hudsonian Godwits. A few Black-tailed Godwits, most of them fresh-plumaged juveniles with white wing linings, appear in Atlantic Canada each year.

non-breeding

ID: long, yellow-orange bill with dark, slightly upturned tip; white rump; black tail; long, black-blue legs. *Breeding:* heavily barred, chestnut red underparts; dark greyish upperparts; male is more brightly coloured. *Non-breeding:* greyish upperparts; whitish underparts may show a few short, black bars. *Juvenile:* dark brown upperparts, fringed pale buff; well-marked scapulars and tertials; underparts faintly washed with brownish-buff. *In flight:* white rump; black "wing pits" and wing linings.
Size: *L* 36–40 cm.
Status: rare migrant in June; uncommon to locally common migrant from mid-July to early November.
Habitat: flooded fields, marshes, mud flats and shorelines.

Nesting: does not nest in Atlantic Canada.
Feeding: probes deeply into water or mud; walks into deeper water than most shorebirds but rarely swims; eats insects and other invertebrates; also picks earthworms from ploughed fields.
Voice: usually quiet in migration; sometimes a sharp, rising *god-WIT!*
Similar Species: *Marbled Godwit:* larger; mottled brown overall; lacks white rump. *Greater Yellowlegs* (p. 120): shorter, all-dark bill; bright yellow legs; lacks white rump. *Short-billed Dowitcher* (p. 140) and *Long-billed Dowitcher:* smaller; straight, all-dark bills; yellow-green legs; mottled brown-black upperparts in breeding plumage.
Best Sites: *NB:* Miscou Harbour; Gulf Shore; Grand-Anse (Shepody Bay). *PEI:* PEI NP. *NS:* Northumberland Strait; southwest marshes; Big Glace Bay Lake. *NF:* west coast; L'Anse-au-Loup (Burin). *PQ:* Île Verte, Lac Cap Vert (Îles de la Madeleine).

RUDDY TURNSTONE

Arenaria interpres

The name "Turnstone" is appropriate for this bird, which uses its bill to flip over pebbles, shells and washed-up vegetation to expose hidden invertebrates. Its short, stubby, slightly upturned bill is an ideal utensil for this unusual foraging style. • These birds' painted faces and eye-catching, black-and-red backs set them apart from the salmon-bellied Red Knots and the multitudes of little brown-and-white sandpipers. Stocky and with heavier bills than most of their companions, Ruddies walk with a comical, rolling gait and sometimes tilt sideways to counteract the influence of strong winds. • Ruddy Turnstones are truly long-distance migrants. The majority head southeast from their arctic summer homes and eventually find their way to the seaweed-covered rocks and pebble-strewn shorelines of Atlantic Canada. They are particularly common along the northwest coast of Newfoundland, where flocks of several hundred birds are not unknown. A few overwinter at places like Harbour Grace and Louisbourg.

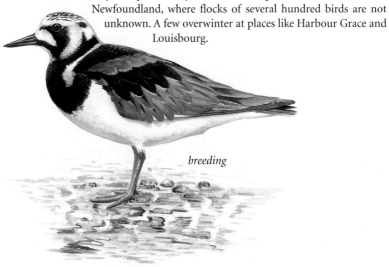

breeding

ID: white belly; black "bib" curves up to shoulder; stout, black, slightly upturned bill; orange-red legs. *Breeding:* ruddy upperparts (female is slightly paler); white face; black collar; dark, streaky crown. *Non-breeding:* brownish upperparts and face.
Size: *L* 24 cm.
Status: uncommon migrant in May and common to locally abundant from mid-July to early November; some may remain in summer and winter.
Habitat: shorelines, especially wave-washed rocks with plenty of seaweed, reservoirs, marshes and lagoons; also in cultivated fields.

Nesting: does not nest in Atlantic Canada.
Feeding: probes under and flips rocks, weeds and shells for food items; picks, digs and probes for invertebrates from the soil or mud; also eats crabs, barnacles, fish heads, berries, seeds, spiders and carrion.
Voice: clear staccato, rattling *cut-a-cut* alarm call and lower repeated contact notes.
Similar Species: *Other sandpipers* (pp. 120–39): all lack the Turnstone's bold patterning and flashy wing markings in flight. *Plovers* (pp. 114–19): equally bold plumage but in significantly different patterns; more inconspicuous wing bars.
Best Sites: wetland sites, especially rocky shorelines.

RED KNOT

Calidris canutus

For a brief period from mid-April to late May, the normally drab and undemonstrative Red Knots become veritable shorebird superstars in their bright rufous dress. They seem to sense their importance and alternately probe and preen, poke and pose as if every camera lens were focused on them, which they might well be. • In autumn and winter, much greater numbers of drab, grey-and-white Red Knots are more difficult to distinguish from the other migrating shorebirds, because they blend perfectly with open sandy beaches. Not all birds patrol the shorelines—a significant number of Red Knots seem to find the company of Black-bellied Plovers on farm fields and shingle bars. • The name "Knot" and the Latin *canutus* are references to King Canute, who is reputed to have spent his time watching the tide come in on the shores of The Wash in England, where this species is equally common.

breeding

ID: chunky, round body; greenish legs. *Breeding:* rusty face, breast and underparts; brown, black and buff upperparts. *Non-breeding:* pale grey upperparts; white underparts with some faint streaking on upper breast; faint barring on rump. *Juvenile:* buffy wash on breast; scaly-looking back. *In flight:* white wing stripe.
Size: *L* 27 cm.
Status: rare to uncommon migrant from mid-April to early June and uncommon to locally common from mid-July to early November; a few overwinter.
Habitat: shorelines, marshes, mud flats and ploughed fields.
Nesting: does not nest in Atlantic Canada.
Feeding: gleans shorelines for insects, crustaceans and molluscs; probes soft substrates, creating lines of small holes.

Voice: usually silent; low, monosyllabic *knut* reminiscent of its name.
Similar Species: *Long-billed Dowitcher* and *Short-billed Dowitcher* (p. 140): much longer bills (at least 1½ times longer than width of head); barring under tail and on flanks; white "V" on rump and tail and on trailing edge of wings. *Buff-breasted Sandpiper* (p. 139): finer, shorter bill; light buff in colour; dark flecking on sides. *Other peeps* (pp. 130-38) smaller; most have black legs; only *Sanderling* (p. 130) and *Curlew Sandpiper* show reddish coloration on the undersides in breeding plumage.
Best Sites: *NB:* Gulf Shore; Grand-Anse (Shepody Bay). *PEI:* PEI NP. *NS:* Grand Pré; southwest beaches; Martinique. *NF:* west coast; Cape Freels; Spaniard's Bay. *PQ:* Cacouna, Pointe-au-Père, Penouille, Havre-aux-Basques (Îles de la Madeleine).

SANDERLING

Calidris alba

A stroll along a sandy beach is often made more memorable by the spectacle of tiny Sanderlings running in the waves. Their well-known habit of chasing waves has a simple purpose: to snatch washed-up aquatic invertebrates before the next wave rolls into shore. Sanderlings are also expert tweakers of marine worms and other soft-bodied critters just below the surface of mud flats. • When sprinting on the beach while foraging, a Sanderling moves so fast on its dark legs that it appears to glide across the sand. When resting, it will often tuck one leg up to preserve body heat. It seeks the company of other sandpipers, plovers and turnstones for the same reason. • This sandpiper is one of the world's most widespread birds. It breeds across the Arctic in Alaska, Canada and Russia, and it spends winter running up and down sandy shorelines in North America, South America, Asia, Africa and Australia.

breeding

ID: straight, black bill; black legs; striking, white wing bar and pale rump. *Breeding:* dark spotting or mottling on rusty head and breast. *Non-breeding:* white underparts; pale grey upperparts; black shoulder patch (often concealed).

Size: *L* 18–22 cm.

Status: fairly common migrant from early April to mid-June; common to abundant from early July to early November; some overwinter.

Habitat: sandy and muddy shorelines, cobble and pebble beaches, spits, lakeshores, marshes and reservoirs.

Nesting: does not nest in Atlantic Canada.

Feeding: gleans shorelines for insects, crustaceans and molluscs; probes repeatedly, creating a line of small holes in the sand or mud.

Voice: flight call is a sharp *kip*, easily distinguishable from other sandpipers' call.

Similar Species: *Dunlin* (p. 137): larger and taller; darker; slightly downcurved bill. *Red Knot* (p. 129): larger; grey-barred, whitish rump; breeding adult has unstreaked, reddish belly. *Least Sandpiper* (p. 132): smaller and darker; yellowish legs; lacks rufous breast in breeding plumage. *Western Sandpiper* and *Semipalmated Sandpiper* (p. 131): lack rufous breast in breeding plumage; sandy upperparts in non-breeding plumage.

Best Sites: sand flats and sandy beaches.

SEMIPALMATED SANDPIPER
Calidris pusilla

In Atlantic Canada, if it's a small shorebird and part of a massed throng of similarly sized birds, as many as 500,000 at a time, it's most likely to be a Least Sandpiper or a Semipalmated Sandpiper. See pale legs and it's a Least; see dark legs and it's a Semi. • Each spring and autumn, large numbers of Semis touch down in Atlantic Canada, pecking and probing in mechanized fury to replenish body fat for the remainder of their long journey. Semipalmated Sandpipers fly almost the entire length of the Americas during migration, so their staging sites must provide ample food sources. Several sites around the Bay of Fundy and elsewhere are being designated as Hemispheric Migratory Shorebird Reserves.

non-breeding

breeding

ID: short, straight, black bill; black legs. *Breeding:* mottled upperparts; slight tinge of rufous on ear patch, crown and scapulars; faint streaks on upper breast and flanks. *Non-breeding:* white eyebrow; grey-brown upperparts; white underparts with light brown wash on sides of upper breast. *Juvenile:* much like breeding adults but with smudgier markings on upper breast; often washed warm buff; white line above eye; dark brown lores and ear coverts. *In flight:* narrow, white wing stripe; white rump is split by 1 black line.
Size: *L* 14–18 cm.
Status: uncommon to common migrant from the end of April to mid-June; common to abundant migrant from early July to early November; very rare in winter.

Habitat: coastal mud flats, beaches and shorelines, spits and pond shores.
Nesting: does not nest in Atlantic Canada.
Feeding: probes soft substrates and gleans for aquatic insects and crustaceans.
Voice: flight call is a harsh *cherk*; sometimes a longer *chirrup* or chittering alarm call.
Similar Species: *Least Sandpiper* (p. 132): yellowish legs; darker upperparts; immatures have distinctive white "V" on back. *Western Sandpiper:* longer, slightly downcurved bill; bright rufous wash on crown and ear patch, sometimes on back. *White-rumped Sandpiper* (p. 133): larger; white rump; folded wings extend beyond tail. *Baird's Sandpiper* (p. 134): larger; longer bill; folded wings extend beyond tail.
Best Sites: tidal flats around the Bay of Fundy and Atlantic coasts.

LEAST SANDPIPER

Calidris minutilla

The Least Sandpiper is the smallest North American shorebird. Like most other "peeps," it migrates almost the entire length of the globe twice each year, from the Arctic to the southern tip of South America and back again. A few save time and travel by regularly nesting in northern Newfoundland and sometimes other Atlantic provinces. • Birds that travel to the Arctic begin moving south as early as the first week of July, so these birds are some of the first migrants to arrive back in Atlantic Canada. • Least Sandpipers are much more likely to be found along tidal channels on salt marshes, where their high-pitched, mouse-like calls are very distinctive. A few will even supply a shortened version of their towering song flight, replete with a high-pitched, rolling trill. • The genus name *Calidris* is a Greek word meaning "a grey-speckled sandpiper." Not surprisingly, *minutilla* translates as "tiniest."

breeding

ID: *Breeding:* black bill; yellowish legs; dark, mottled back; buff-brown breast, head and nape; prominent white "V" on back; light breast streaking. *Non-breeding:* much duller; often lacks back stripes; prominent, streaked, brown breast band. *Juvenile:* similar to breeding adult, but with faintly streaked breast.

Size: *L* 13–17 cm.

Status: rare to common migrant from mid-April to early June and from early July to October; fairly common breeder; a few may remain into November.

Habitat: *Breeding:* coastal tundra, sedge or grass bogs and marshes. *In migration:* sandy beaches, lakeshores, ditches, sewage lagoons, mud flats and wetland edges.

Nesting: on a grassy or moss hummock surrounded by wet ground; in a shallow depression lined with grass, leaves and moss; pair incubates 4 brown-blotched, pale buff eggs.

Feeding: probes or pecks for insects, crustaceans, small molluscs and occasionally seeds.

Voice: high-pitched *kreee.*

Similar Species: *Semipalmated Sandpiper* (p. 131): black legs; lighter upperparts; tinge of rufous on crown, ear patch and scapulars. *Western Sandpiper:* slightly larger; black legs; lighter breast wash in all plumages; rufous patches on crown, ear and scapulars in breeding plumage.

Best Sites: often with Semipalmated Sandpipers on tidal flats but also along tidal channels.

WHITE-RUMPED SANDPIPER

Calidris fuscicollis

In the first snows of mid-October on the northwest coast of Newfoundland, a flock of "peeps" that have rested up after an over-water flight from Québec or Labrador start to stir. Small, brownish heads emerge from hiding, back feathers are ruffled, wings are stretched and, almost without warning, the birds take flight and flash pure white rumps. They are White-rumped Sandpipers and they are on migration to the southern reaches of South America. They make the journey in a few long, non-stop flights, sometimes lasting 60 hours at a time. • This bird's white rump might serve as a visual signal to alert other birds when danger threatens. Flocks of White-rumped Sandpipers may also collectively rush at a predator and then suddenly scatter in its face. • The scientific name *fuscicollis* means "brown neck," a characteristic that this bird shares with many of its close relatives.

breeding

ID: wings extend well beyond tail; black legs; black bill. *Breeding:* mottled brown and rufous upperparts; streaked breast and flanks. *Non-breeding:* mottled grey upperparts; white eyebrow. *Immature:* black upperparts, edged with white, chestnut and buff. *In flight:* white rump, dark tail, indistinct wing bar.

Size: *L* 18–20 cm.

Status: rare migrant from late April to early June; common to locally abundant from late July until mid-November; a few may remain into December and try to overwinter.

Habitat: shorelines, lakeshores, flooded meadows, roadside ditches and, sometimes early in winter, street puddles.

Nesting: does not nest in Atlantic Canada.

Feeding: gleans the ground and shorelines for insects, crustaceans and molluscs.

Voice: flight call is a characteristic, squeal-like *tzeet*, higher than any other "peep."

Similar Species: *Baird's Sandpiper* (p. 134): lacks clean white rump; breast streaking does not extend onto flanks. *Stilt Sandpiper* (p. 138) and *Curlew Sandpiper*: much longer legs trail beyond tail in flight.

Best Sites: along the coasts of NF; sometimes seen in ditches and in urban areas.

BAIRD'S SANDPIPER
Calidris bairdii

L ike its *Calidris* relatives, this modest-looking shorebird has extraordinary migratory habits—it flies twice annually between South America and the Arctic. In spring and autumn, most birds take the interior route, but in late summer a few break tradition and head east with Semipalmated Sandpipers and White-rumped Sandpipers. Birds travelling with Semis are more likely to appear around the Bay of Fundy, while those with White-rumps test the identification skills of birders in Newfoundland and Cape Breton. • Adults start appearing in July and are difficult to distinguish unless they are with smaller relatives. After a few weeks of accumulating fat reserves on their breeding grounds, the juveniles head south and those that arrive in Atlantic Canada in late August to October are in much fresher plumage and are easier to identify than the adults. • Spencer Fullerton Baird, a director of the Smithsonian Institute in the 19th century, organized several natural history expeditions across North America. Elliott Coues named this bird in recognition of Baird's efforts.

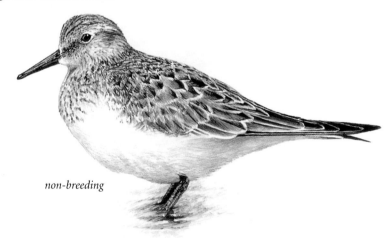

non-breeding

ID: folded wings extend beyond tail; black legs and bill; faint, buff-brown breast speckling. *Breeding:* black, diamond-like patterns on back and wing coverts. *Juvenile:* brighter and browner; scaly appearance to back.

Size: *L* 18–19 cm.

Status: rare to uncommon migrant from late July to early October; extremely rare migrant in mid-May.

Habitat: sandy beaches, mud flats, wetland edges and meadows.

Nesting: does not nest in Atlantic Canada.

Feeding: gleans aquatic invertebrates, especially larval flies; also eats beetles and grasshoppers; rarely probes.

Voice: soft, rolling *kriit kriit*.

Similar Species: "scaly" back is fairly distinctive. *White-rumped Sandpiper* (p. 133): breast streaking extends onto flanks; head and back are more streaked. *Pectoral Sandpiper* (p. 135): dark breast ends abruptly at edge of white belly. *Least Sandpiper* (p. 132): smaller; yellowish legs. *Western Sandpiper* and *Sanderling* (p. 130): lack streaked, grey-buff breast. *Semipalmated Sandpiper* (p. 131): smaller; shorter bill.

Best Sites: *NB:* Long Pond (Grand Manan I.). *PEI:* Brackley Marshes. *NS:* New Harbour (Canso). *NF:* St. Paul's; Eddies Cove East; L'Anse aux Meadows, Chance Cove.

PECTORAL SANDPIPER

Calidris melanotos

This widespread traveller may be found in Siberia as well as the Canadian Arctic, and its epic, annual migrations include destinations such as South America, Australia or New Zealand. In spring, most Pectoral Sandpipers take an interior route through Ontario, but after the brief arctic summer has passed, many adults and then juveniles head out to the Atlantic Coast to fatten up for the long flight south. Peak numbers occur from mid-August to late October, and the birds are almost always found in pastures and cord grass flats, which provide both food and cover for these grass-loving shorebirds. Flocks are worth checking for Buff-breasted Sandpipers and Baird's Sandpipers. • Unlike most sandpipers, the Pectoral exhibits sexual dimorphism—the females are only two-thirds the size of the males. Males also use "leks" to perform spectacular displays. When agitated, the male will inflate the air sacs in his neck, causing his feathers to rise.

ID: brown breast streaks end at edge of white belly; white undertail coverts; black bill with slightly down-curved tip; long, yellow legs; mottled upperparts; may have faintly rusty, dark crown and back; folded wings extend beyond tail. *Juvenile:* less spotting on breast; broader, white feather edges on back form 2 white "V"s.
Size: *L* 23 cm (female is slightly smaller).
Status: fairly common to locally common migrant from late July to late-October; some linger to late November; rare to locally uncommon migrant from mid-April to mid-May.
Habitat: almost always freshwater and saltwater marshes and pastures; very rarely shorelines, ditches and sewage outlets.

Nesting: does not nest in Atlantic Canada.
Feeding: probes and pecks for small insects (mainly flies, but also beetles and some grasshoppers); may also take small molluscs, amphipods, berries, seeds, moss, algae and some plant material; some birds feed on fish scraps in fishing harbours in Cape Breton and NF.
Voice: sharp, short, low and distinctive *krrick krrick*.
Similar Species: *Other peeps* (pp.129–38): lack well-defined, dark "bib" and yellow legs. *Ruff:* male is larger and more heavily marked on upperparts and underparts; usually yellow legs; female has all-dark bill, indistinct "bib" and greenish or straw legs. *Buff-breasted Sandpiper* (p. 139): paler; no "bib"; flashy white underwings.
Best Sites: usually in salt marshes but sometimes at sewage lagoons and in pastures.

PURPLE SANDPIPER

Calidris maritima

The Purple Sandpiper is chunky and has no flashy colours or ringing calls to applaud. However, you have to admire it anyway. Unlike most shorebirds, which prefer shallow marshy areas, sand beaches or mud flats, Purple Sandpipers have chosen to live on the edge. They are content to forage perilously close to crashing waves along rocky headlands, piers and breakwaters. They also expertly navigate their way across rugged, slippery rocks while foraging for crustaceans, molluscs and insect larvae. • Purple Sandpipers overwinter in good numbers all along the Atlantic Coast, where small parties take up residence each year and are generally left to themselves. They are so well camouflaged among the rocks that they become visible only when a wave breaks and temporarily dislodges them. • The name "purple" was given to this sandpiper for the purplish iridescence that is occasionally observed on its shoulders.

non-breeding

ID: long, slightly drooping, black-tipped bill with orange-yellow base; orange-yellow legs; dull streaking on breast and flanks. *Non-breeding:* unstreaked, grey head, neck and upper breast; grey spots on white belly. *Juvenile:* streaking on head; chestnut brown, white and buff feather edgings on upperparts.
Size: *L* 23 cm.
Status: rare to locally common from late October to mid-May; occasionally seen in summer.

Habitat: sand and gravel beaches, rocky shorelines, piers and breakwaters.
Nesting: does not nest in Atlantic Canada.
Feeding: food is found visually and is snatched while moving over rocks and sand; eats mostly molluscs, insects, crustaceans and other invertebrates; also eats a variety of plant material
Voice: call is a soft *prrt-prrt*.
Similar Species: *Other peeps* (pp. 129–38)*:* all lack unstreaked, grey hood in winter, bicoloured bill and yellow-orange legs.
Best Sites: widespread in late autumn and winter; overwinters locally, mostly on the eastern coasts.

DUNLIN

Calidris alpina

In Atlantic Canada, Dunlins are usually among late-arriving flocks of sandpipers. Spring sightings of birds in breeding plumage are rare because the adults take a direct northern route to the Arctic through the interior of the continent. However, in autumn juvenile Dunlins form tight flocks that rarely include other species and head to the coasts. Birds that choose the East Coast have plenty of sites where they can gather and fatten up before flying to the southeastern US. Unlike many of their shorebird relatives, few Dunlins ever cross the equator. • Dunlins are fairly distinct in their breeding attire: their black bellies and legs make them look as though they have been wading belly-deep in puddles of ink.
• This bird was originally called "Dunling" (meaning "a small, brown bird"), but with the passage of time, the "g" was dropped.

breeding

ID: slightly down-curved, black bill; black legs. *Breeding:* black belly; streaked white neck and underparts; rusty wings, back and crown. *Non-breeding:* pale grey underparts; brownish-grey upperparts; light brown streaking on breast and nape. *Juvenile:* buffy on head and breast; mantle and scapulars fringed chestnut and white, with whitish "V" on back; blackish-brown lines on flanks and belly sides. *In flight:* white wing stripe.
Size: *L* 19–23 cm.
Status: rare to uncommon migrant from mid-April to late May and from late July to November; a few overwinter.
Habitat: shorelines, beaches, mud flats and the shores of ponds, marshes and lakes;
occasionally seen in pastures and sewage lagoons.
Nesting: does not nest in Atlantic Canada.
Feeding: gleans and probes mud flats for crustaceans, worms, molluscs and insects.
Voice: flight call is a grating *cheezp* or *treezp.*
Similar Species: black belly in breeding plumage is distinctive. *Western Sandpiper* and *Semipalmated Sandpiper* (p. 131): smaller; non-breeding plumage is browner overall; female bill tips are less down-curved. *Least Sandpiper* (p. 132): smaller; darker upperparts; yellowish legs. *Sanderling* (p. 130): paler; straight bill; usually seen running in the surf. *Stilt Sandpiper* (p. 138): larger; longer bill; yellowish-green legs.
Best Sites: often in drier locations than other small sandpipers.

STILT SANDPIPER

Calidris himantopus

With the silhouette of a small Lesser Yellowlegs and the foraging behaviour of a dowitcher, the Stilt Sandpiper is easily overlooked by birders. Named for its relatively long legs, this shorebird prefers to feed in shallow water, where it digs like a dowitcher, often dunking its head completely underwater. Moving on tall "stilts," this sandpiper will also wade into deep water up to its breast in search of a meal. To snag freshwater shrimp, insect larvae or tiny minnows from just below the water's surface, it may occasionally sweep its bill from side to side. • Individualists for the most part, Stilt Sandpipers rarely gather in flocks. Most of the birds that make it to Atlantic Canada from mid-July to late October are drab post-breeding adults, but every once in a while a smartly attired juvenile hangs around between mid-August and the end of September.

non-breeding

ID: long, greenish legs; long bill droops slightly at end. *Breeding:* chestnut red ear patch; white eyebrow; striped crown; streaked neck; barred underparts. *Non-breeding:* less conspicuous, white eyebrow; dirty white neck and breast; white belly; dark brownish-grey upperparts. *Juvenile:* dark brown upperparts, fringed rufous or light buff; throat and breast with buff wash; faintly streaked, white belly. *In flight:* white rump; legs trail behind tail; no wing stripe.
Size: *L* 20–23 cm.
Status: rare migrant from May to June; rare to uncommon migrant from mid-July to late October.
Habitat: shores of bays, estuaries, reservoirs, lakes, ponds and marshes.

Nesting: does not nest in Atlantic Canada.
Feeding: probes deeply in shallow water; eats mostly invertebrates; occasionally picks insects from the water's surface or the ground; also eats seeds, roots and leaves.
Voice: soft, rattling *querp* or *kirr* in flight; clearer *whu*.
Similar Species: *Yellowlegs* (pp. 120–21): straight bill; yellow legs; lack red ear patch of breeding adults, chestnut mantle of juvenile or blotchy back feathers of non-breeding adult. *Curlew Sandpiper:* bill has more obvious curve; black legs; paler grey upperparts in non-breeding plumage. *Dunlin* (p. 137): shorter, black legs; dark rump; whitish wing bar.
Best Sites: *NB:* Tracadie, Castalia. *PEI:* Dalvay. *NS:* Lawrencetown Loop; Three Fathom Harbour. *PQ:* Cacouna; Havreaux-Basques (Îles de la Madeleine).

BUFF-BREASTED SANDPIPER

Tryngites subruficollis

Shy in behaviour and humble in appearance, the Buff-breasted Sandpiper nevertheless exudes class if you care to take a closer look. Buff-breasts are rarely seen in spring and summer, but from late August through September it is worth checking every sandspit, barren headland or coastal field to look for them. • When feeding, this subtly coloured bird stands motionless, blending beautifully into a backdrop of furrowed cultivated fields, sandbars or cured, grassy pastures. Only when it catches sight of moving prey does it become visible, making a short, forward sprint to snatch a fresh meal. • Most adult Buff-breasts migrate through the centre of the continent, so most birds in Atlantic Canada are juveniles heading south for the first time. Perhaps this explains why they choose the company of foraging Pectoral Sandpipers, Black-bellied Plovers and American Golden-Plovers.

ID: buffy, unpatterned face and foreneck; large, dark eyes; very thin, straight, black bill; buff underparts; small spots on crown, hindneck, breast, sides and flanks; "scaled" look to back and upperwings; yellow legs. *In flight:* pure white underwings; no wing stripe.
Size: *L* 19–21 cm.
Status: rare to uncommon migrant from mid-August to late September; extremely rare migrant from mid-May to mid-June.
Habitat: cultivated and flooded fields; shorelines, sandspits and salt marshes.
Nesting: does not nest in Atlantic Canada.

Feeding: gleans the ground and shorelines for insects, spiders and small crustaceans; may eat seeds.
Similar Species: *Upland Sandpiper* (p. 125): more boldly streaked on breast; longer neck; smaller head; larger bill; streaking on "cheek" and foreneck. *Pectoral Sandpiper* (p. 135): greyer brown on back and breast; white on belly; white ovals at side of tail. *Ruff:* larger and heavier; sloping forehead; markings less tidy; greener legs; white ovals at side of tail.
Best Sites: *NB:* Miscou I. *PEI:* Brackley Marshes. *NS:* Grand Pré; Cook's Beach; Chebogue Point; New Harbour (Canso); Morien Bar. *NF:* St. Paul's; L'Anse aux Meadows; Cape Freels; L'Anse-au-Loup; Cape St. Mary's.

SHORT-BILLED DOWITCHER

Limnodromus griseus

Long before autumn foliage erupts into its full splendour, flocks of Short-billed Dowitchers arrive from Hudson Bay and northern Québec. These plump shorebirds are usually seen in the largest concentrations during the protracted autumn migration, which begins as soon as early July and ends in mid-October. They spread out on the mud flats, marshes and beaches of Atlantic Canada. Short-bills are seen in small numbers during spring migration. • Dowitchers tend to be stockier than most shorebirds, and they generally avoid venturing into deep water. While foraging along shorelines, these birds "stitch" up and down into the mud with a sewing-machine-like rhythm. Their performance is not only fascinating to watch, it is also very helpful for long-range field identification. • Distinguishing between the Short-billed Dowitcher and the Long-billed Dowitcher *(L. scolopaceus)* is a difficult task for any birder, but it can be done with practice, a good eye and a good ear.

breeding

ID: straight, long, dark bill; white eyebrow; chunky body; yellow-green legs. *Breeding:* white belly; dark spotting on reddish-buff neck and upper breast; prominent dark barring on white sides and flanks. *Non-breeding:* dirty grey upperparts; dirty white underparts. *Juvenile:* chestnut-edged crown and back; barred or striped tertials; unstreaked and unspotted underparts. *In flight:* white wedge on rump and lower back.

Size: *L* 28–30 cm.

Status: common to locally abundant from early July to mid-October; uncommon migrant in May; very rare in summer and winter.

Habitat: mud flats, shorelines, pondsides and marshes.

Nesting: does not nest in Atlantic Canada.

Feeding: aquatic invertebrates, including insects, molluscs, crustaceans and worms; may feed on seeds, aquatic plants and grasses; wades in shallow water or on mud, probing deeply into the substrate with a rapid drilling motion.

Voice: generally silent; flight call is a mellow, repeated *tututu, toodulu* or *toodu.*

Similar Species: *Long-billed Dowitcher:* black-and-white barring on red flanks in breeding plumage; dark spotting on neck and upper breast; alarm call is high-pitched *keek. Red Knot* (p. 129): much shorter bill; unmarked, red breast in breeding plumage; non-breeding birds lack barring on tail and white wedge on back in flight. *Common Snipe* (p. 141): heavy streaking on neck and breast; bicoloured bill; light median stripe on crown; shorter legs.

Best Sites: widespread in autumn migration; less common in spring, usually on mud flats and estuaries.

COMMON SNIPE

Gallinago gallinago

We've all heard it—that eerie, hollow winnowing sound that seems to fill the sky overhead. UFOs, possibly, some new radio-controlled toy, perhaps, or some huge flying insect spawned in a dank, dark bog? Not at all, it's just courting male Common Snipes putting on an act for females in the swampy areas below. These birds' specialized outer tail feathers vibrate rapidly in the air as they perform daring, headfirst dives high above their marshland habitat. Snipes display most actively in the early morning, but evening performances are not uncommon. Outside the courtship season, this well-camouflaged bird becomes shy and secretive. The best times to see it in the open are in the twilight hours or in autumn when birds gather at the mouths of small streams where food is plentiful.

ID: long, sturdy, bicoloured bill; relatively short legs; heavily striped head, back, neck and breast; dark eye stripe; dark barring on sides and flanks; unmarked white belly. *In flight:* quick zigzags as it takes off.

Size: *L* 27–29 cm.

Status: fairly common to common from late March to mid-November; a few may overwinter near open water, often in sewage runoff and ditches.

Habitat: cattail and bulrush marshes, sedge meadows, poorly drained floodplains, bogs and fens; willow and red osier dogwood tangles.

Nesting: usually in dry grass, often under vegetation; nest is made of grass, moss and leaves; female incubates 4 olive buff to brown eggs, marked with dark brown, for about 20 days; both parents raise the young, often splitting the brood.

Feeding: probes soft substrates for larvae, earthworms and other soft-bodied invertebrates; also eats molluscs, crustaceans, spiders, small amphibians and some seeds.

Voice: eerie, accelerating courtship song is produced in flight: *woo-woo-woo-woo-woo-woo*; often sings *wheat wheat wheat* from an elevated perch; alarm call is a nasal *scaip*.

Similar Species: *Short-billed Dowitcher* (p. 140) and *Long-billed Dowitcher:* lack heavy striping on head, back, neck and breast; longer legs; all-dark bills; usually seen in flocks. *American Woodcock* (p. 142): unmarked buff underparts; yellowish bill; light bars on black crown and hindneck.

Best Sites: widespread.

141

AMERICAN WOODCOCK

Scolopax minor

This resident of moist woodlands and damp thickets usually goes about its business in a quiet and reclusive manner. The American Woodcock's behaviour usually mirrors its cryptic and inconspicuous attire. During courtship, however, the male Woodcock reveals his true character. Just before dawn or just after sunset, he struts provocatively in an open woodland clearing or a brushy, abandoned field, while calling out a series of loud *peeent* notes. He twitters through the air in a circular flight display, and then, with wings partly folded, he plummets to the ground in the zigzag pattern of a falling leaf. • They may be hard to find, but the portly, chestnut-coloured American Woodcocks are out there rooting around while you're resting in bed.

ID: very long, sturdy bill; very short legs; large head; short neck; chunky body; large, dark eyes; buff, unmarked underparts; light-coloured bars on black crown and hindneck. *In flight:* rounded wings; makes a twittering sound when flushed from cover.

Size: *L* 27–29 cm.

Status: fairly common to common breeder from March to early November; a few may overwinter near open water.

Habitat: moist woodlands and brushy thickets adjacent to grassy clearings or abandoned fields.

Nesting: on the ground in woods or overgrown fields; female digs a scrape and lines it with dead leaves and other debris; female incubates 4 brown- and grey-blotched, pinkish-buff eggs for 20–22 days; female tends the young.

Feeding: probes in soft, moist or wet soil for earthworms and insect larvae; also takes spiders, snails, millipedes and some plant material, including seeds, sedges and grasses.

Voice: nasal *peent*; during courtship dance male produces high-pitched, twittering, whistling sounds.

Similar Species: *Common Snipe* (p. 141): heavily striped head, back, neck and breast; dark barring on sides and flanks. *Short-billed Dowitcher* (p. 140): all-dark bill; longer legs; lacks light-coloured barring on dark crown and hindneck; usually seen in flocks.

Best Sites: widespread; rare in NF, mostly in alder swales and damp broadleaf forests with open glades.

WILSON'S PHALAROPE

Phalaropus tricolor

The Wilson's Phalarope is the only phalarope that breeds in Atlantic Canada, and it is the only one likely to be seen away from salt water. A few pairs have colonized the southern shore of the St. Lawrence River in Québec, several sites in southern New Brunswick and a few sites in Nova Scotia and Prince Edward Island. They betray their presence with a fluttering flight and a most unshorebird-like series of croaks and grunts. • Not only are phalaropes among the most colourful of the shorebirds, but they are also among the most unusual. Phalaropes practise an uncommon mating strategy known as polyandry: each female mates with several duller-plumaged males, often producing a clutch of eggs with each mate. After laying a clutch, the female often abandons her mate, leaving him to incubate the eggs and tend the precocial young.

breeding

ID: dark, needle-like bill; light underparts; black legs. *Breeding female:* very sharp colours; grey cap; chestnut brown on sides of neck; black eye line extends down side of neck and onto back. *Breeding male:* duller overall; dark cap. *Non-breeding:* all-grey upperparts; white eyebrow and grey eye line; white underparts; dark yellowish or greenish legs. *Juvenile:* dark brown upperparts, with scaly look; buffy sides of breast; pinkish-yellow legs.
Size: *L* 22–24 cm.
Status: rare to locally uncommon migrant from mid-May to mid-June; rare breeder; uncommon migrant from early August to October; a few birds linger into November.
Habitat: *Breeding:* freshwater coastal marshes, cattail marshes and grass or sedge margins of sewage lagoons. *In migration:* also mud flats, lakeshores and brackish estuaries; hardly ever on salt water.
Nesting: often near water; well concealed in a depression lined with grass and other

vegetation; male incubates 4 brown-blotched, buff eggs for 18–27 days; male rears the young.
Feeding: whirls in tight circles in shallow or deep water to stir up prey, then picks aquatic insects, worms and small crustaceans; makes short jabs on land to pick up invertebrates in open areas.
Voice: deep, grunting *work work* or *wu wu wu*, usually given on the breeding grounds.
Similar Species: *Red-necked Phalarope* (p. 144): rufous stripe down side of neck in breeding plumage; dark nape and line behind eye in winter. *Red Phalarope* (p. 145): all-reddish underparts in breeding plumage; dark nape and broad, dark line behind eye in winter; rarely seen inland. *Peeps* (pp.129–38): less conspicuous facial markings; mainly streaked underparts.
Best Sites: *NB:* Gulf Shore; Jolicure Marsh; Sackville; Saints Rest Marsh (Saint John); Jemseg–Gagetown area; Grassy I. *PEI:* Royalty Point; PEI NP. *NS:* Amherst Point. *PQ:* Cacouna; Lac à l'Anguille (Rimouski); Barachois; Chandler.

RED-NECKED PHALAROPE

Phalaropus lobatus

The only way to guarantee seeing phalaropes in Atlantic Canada is to be taken for a ride—a saltwater boat ride, to be precise. The open seas far from land are the place to find these tiny shorebirds. They may seem out of place here, but this is where they feel at home for most of the year. Zipping about in tight flocks, they feed where there are ocean upwellings. They spin and whirl about in tight circles, stirring up tiny crustaceans, molluscs and other aquatic invertebrates. As prey funnel toward the water's surface, these birds daintily pluck them with their needle-like bills. Although all pelagic ferries offer chances to see phalaropes, the waters off Grand Manan Island and in Passamaquoddy Bay claim the greatest numbers of Red-necked Phalaropes. • "Phalarope" is the Greek word for "coot's foot." Like coots and grebes, phalaropes have individually webbed, or lobed, toes, a feature that makes them proficient swimmers.

breeding

ID: thin, black bill; long, grey legs; lobed toes. *Breeding female:* chestnut stripe on neck and throat; white "chin"; blue-black head; white belly; 2 rusty-buff stripes on each upperwing. *Breeding male:* white eyebrow; less intense colours than female. *Non-breeding:* white underparts; dark nape; broad, dark band from eye to ear; whitish stripes on blue-grey upperparts. *Juvenile:* buff-and-black upperparts; white underparts.
Size: *L* 18 cm.
Status: common to abundant migrant offshore from late April to early June and from late June to late November; rare along coasts and very rare inland.
Habitat: well out to sea, off headlands and around areas of ocean upwellings in the Bay of Fundy.

Nesting: does not nest in Atlantic Canada.
Feeding: highly social at sea, often in huge concentrations; whirls in tight circles in shallow or deep water, picking insects, small crustaceans and small molluscs from the water; on land, makes short jabs to pick up insects.
Voice: often noisy in migration; soft *krit krit krit.*
Similar Species: *Wilson's Phalarope* (p. 143): female has grey cap and black eye line extending down side of neck and onto back in breeding plumage; dark cap in non-breeding plumage. *Red Phalarope* (p. 145): all-red underparts in breeding plumage; lacks white stripes on upperwing in non-breeding plumage. *Peeps* (pp. 129–38): less pronounced head markings; mainly streaked underparts.
Best Sites: from pelagic ferries. *NB:* Miscou I., Passamaquoddy Bay. *NS:* Port Hebert; Cape Sambro; Cape North. *NF:* L'Anse aux Meadows, Cape Race. *PQ:* Cap Gaspé (Forillon NP), Îles de la Madeleine.

RED PHALAROPE
Phalaropus fulicaria

The Red Phalarope sports its reddish breeding plumage for a short period in spring. Unfortunately, at this time most birds are far from land or are heading to their arctic breeding grounds. This bird's dull autumn wardrobe reveals why it is known as the Grey Phalarope in other parts of the world. Outside of the breeding season, there is little to make this bird stand out from its similar-looking relative, the Red-necked Phalarope. Still, the Red Phalarope's heavier bill, larger size and plain, blue-grey upperparts usually provide sufficient clues for sharp-eyed birders to distinguish between these two species in the field. • In mid-May to early June, and again from early July to late September, huge numbers of these birds concentrate at upwellings in the Bay of Fundy, with Red Phalaropes much more common than Red-necks off Digby Neck and Brier Island.

breeding

ID: *Breeding female:* chestnut red neck and underparts; white face; black crown and forehead; black-tipped, yellow bill. *Breeding male:* mottled brown crown; duller face and underparts. *Non-breeding:* white head, throat and underparts; blue-grey upperparts; mostly dark bill; black nape; broad, dark patch extends from eye to ear. *Juvenile:* like non-breeding adult, but is buff-coloured overall; dark streaking on upperparts.
Size: *L* 22 cm.
Status: common to abundant at sea from April to early June, and from early July to November at sea and close to land in the Bay of Fundy; very rare migrant on land from late August to late October.
Habitat: lakes, large wetlands and sewage lagoons.

Nesting: does not nest in Atlantic Canada.
Feeding: small crustaceans, molluscs, insects and other invertebrates; rarely takes vegetation or small fish; gleans from the water's surface, usually while swimming in tight, spinning circles.
Voice: calls include a shrill, high-pitched *wit* or *creep* and a low *clink clink.*
Similar Species: *Red-necked Phalarope* (p. 144): breeding birds lack all-red underparts; non-breeding birds have pale white stripes on upperwing. *Wilson's Phalarope* (p. 143): breeding birds lack all-red underparts; non-breeding birds lack dark mask. *Peeps* (pp. 129–38): less conspicuous facial markings; mainly streaked underparts.
Best Sites: from pelagic ferries. *NB:* Miscou I., Passamaquoddy Bay. *NS:* Seal I., Cape Sable I., Hartlen Point. *NF:* L'Anse aux Meadows; Cape Race. *PQ:* Îles de la Madeleine.

GREAT SKUA

Stercorarius skua

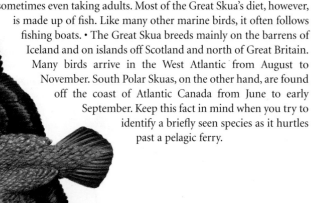

This fast, powerful flyer is also called "Sea Hawk," because some of its habits resemble those of birds of prey. Like falcons, it catches small birds in the air; it also raids breeding colonies of smaller sea birds, pillaging eggs and chicks and sometimes even taking adults. Most of the Great Skua's diet, however, is made up of fish. Like many other marine birds, it often follows fishing boats. • The Great Skua breeds mainly on the barrens of Iceland and on islands off Scotland and north of Great Britain. Many birds arrive in the West Atlantic from August to November. South Polar Skuas, on the other hand, are found off the coast of Atlantic Canada from June to early September. Keep this fact in mind when you try to identify a briefly seen species as it hurtles past a pelagic ferry.

ID: dark brown upperparts with pale streaking; pale brown underparts; dark, hooked beak. *In flight:* white patch on upper wing.
Size: *L* 56 cm; *W* 1.4 m.
Status: rare visitor from mid-August to October, sometimes into November and early December.
Habitat: open ocean, usually far from shore; occasionally scavenges on land.
Nesting: does not nest in Atlantic Canada.
Feeding: picks up items from the water's surface while swimming or in flight; preys on smaller birds and may pirate food from larger birds, especially Herring Gulls and

shearwaters; diet consists of fish, small mammals, carrion and the eggs, chicks and adults of other birds.
Voice: generally silent; may give a short *hek* call or a series of nasal *pyeh* notes.
Similar Species: *South Polar Skua* (p. 147): dark morph lacks streaking on upperparts and is more grey-brown; light morph has paler head and underparts; more likely to be seen in summer. *Jaegers* (pp. 148–50): smaller; dark morph adults are darker; light morph adults have pale necks and dark heads.
Best Sites: *NB:* Bay of Fundy. *PEI:* Souris ferry. *NS:* Maine ferries; Brier I. *NF:* L'Anse aux Meadows; Cape Bonavista; Cape Race; St. Shott's. *PQ:* St. Lawrence ferries; Cap Gaspé.

SOUTH POLAR SKUA

Stercorarius maccormicki

The South Polar Skua is the smallest of the skuas. It breeds in the Antarctic and "overwinters" in our region from May to September. The South Polar Skua and the Antarctic Skua *(S. antarctica)* were previously considered different races of the same species, but although their breeding ranges around Antarctica overlap, the two birds generally do not interbreed. • Like its close relatives, the South Polar Skua is aggressive in pursuit of a meal. It will sometimes attack shearwaters or gulls, shaking them violently with its bill until they give up their catch. • *Stercorarius* refers to this bird's habit of eating offal. In the Old World, the term "skua" also refers to birds that we refer to in North America as "jaegers." "Skua" is derived from an Old Norse word meaning "predatory gull."

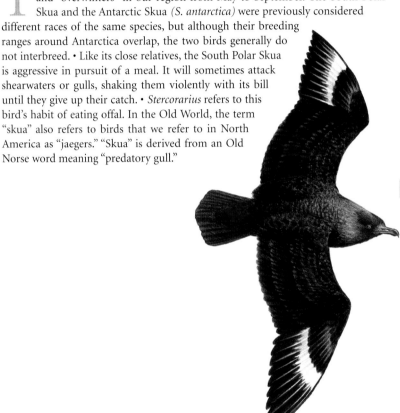

ID: white wing flash; dark, hooked bill. *Dark morph:* dark grey-brown overall; yellowish nape. *Light morph:* pale body; dark wings with pale streaking.

Size: *L* 53 cm; *W* 1.3 m.

Status: rare to locally uncommon from late May to mid-September.

Habitat: open ocean and large bays, occasionally inshore.

Nesting: does not nest in Atlantic Canada.

Feeding: catches items from the water's surface or dives into water from flight;

scavenges around fishing boats; raids breeding colonies; robs other birds; diet consists mostly of fish; sometimes eats carrion and the eggs and young of other birds.

Voice: generally silent; may give a weak, gull-like *scoo-ah*.

Similar Species: *Great Skua* (p. 146): all plumages have more reddish tone; more likely in autumn. *Jaegers* (pp. 148–50): wings broader and more rounded; tails shorter and broader.

Best Sites: *NB:* Grand Manan I. ferry; Bay of Fundy ferry. *NS:* Brier I. *NF:* Cabot Strait; Argentia ferry; Cape Shore; Cape Race.

POMARINE JAEGER
Stercorarius pomarinus

Jaegers are powerful, swift predators that seem to be forged from the moulds of gulls, terns and hawks. Most of their lives are spent in the air, although they occasionally rest on the ocean's surface. They seek the solid footing of land only during the nesting season. • Late summer and early autumn are the best seasons for observing Pomarine Jaegers on pelagic ferry routes and off headlands, especially in Newfoundland. • Most novice birders differentiate the three jaeger species based on the shape and length of their central tail feathers. This comparison applies only to adult jaegers. Knowing the subtleties of plumage, wingbeat rhythm and wing breadth is most important in making an accurate identification. Pomarines appear larger and heavier than other jaegers and usually have darker underparts.

dark morph

light morph

ID: long, central tail feathers. *Light morph:* dark cap; dark, mottled breast band, sides and flanks; dark vent. *Dark morph:* dark body except for white in wing. *Juvenile:* central tail feathers extend just past tail; variable dark barring on underwings and underparts; lacks black cap. *In flight:* wings are wide at base of body; powerful, steady wingbeats; white flash at base of underwing primaries.
Size: *L* 51–58 cm; *W* 1.2 m.
Status: uncommon to locally common offshore migrant from late April until early November, with most birds appearing inshore in late summer.
Habitat: open ocean; moves inshore in fog or after storms and is rarely found on land.
Nesting: does not nest in Atlantic Canada.

Feeding: snatches fish from the ocean surface while in flight; chases down small birds; may also take small mammals and nestlings; pirates food from gulls; may scavenge at landfills.
Voice: generally silent; may give a sharp *which-yew,* a squealing *weak-weak* or a squeaky whistled note in migration.
Similar Species: *Parasitic Jaeger* (p. 149): long, thin, pointed tail; lacks mottled sides and flanks; short, sharpened tail streamers; immatures have barred underparts. *Long-tailed Jaeger* (p. 150): very long, thin pointed tail streamers; lacks very dark vent and dark, mottled breast band, sides and flanks; juvenile has stubby, spoon-shaped tail streamers and solid dark markings on throat and upper breast.
Best Sites: *NB:* Grand Manan I. ferry. *PEI:* North Cape; Souris ferry. *NS:* Brier I.; Seal I.; Cape North. *NF:* widespread, especially on eastern coast and ferry routes. *PQ:* Cap Gaspé; Îles de la Madeleine.

PARASITIC JAEGER
Stercorarius parasiticus

Although "jaeger" is a German word for "hunter," "parasitic" more aptly describes this bird's foraging tactics. Parasitic Jaegers harrass and intimidate terns and gulls until they regurgitate their partially digested meals. A few jaegers target alcids returning to their nests with food in their bills—as soon as the food is ejected, these aerial pirates snatch it out of mid-air or pick it from the water's surface in a swooping dive. Less than 25 percent of chases are successful, and many Parasitic Jaegers are content to find their own food. • The Parasitic Jaeger is the most numerous jaeger in the world. It is the most commonly seen jaeger in Atlantic Canada—they usually outnumber other jaegers by as much as 10 to 1, and they are more widespread close to shore.

light morph

ID: long, pointed, dark wings; slightly longer, pointed central tail feathers; brown upperparts; dark cap; light underwing tips. *Light morph:* white underparts; white to cream-coloured collar; light brown neck band. *Dark morph:* all-brown underparts and collar. *Juvenile:* barred underparts; central tail feather extends just past tail.
Size: *L* 38–53 cm; *W* 91 cm.
Status: common to locally abundant offshore migrant from early May to early November, with rather more seen inshore from late July to mid-September.
Habitat: open ocean, usually appearing close to land only in fog or after storms.
Nesting: does not nest in Atlantic Canada.

Feeding: pirates, scavenges and hunts for food; often pirates food from terns, small gulls and alcids.
Voice: generally silent; may make shrill calls while migrating.
Similar Species: *Pomarine Jaeger* (p. 148): adult has shorter, blunt and twisted central tail feathers; dark mottled sides and flanks; white on upperwing primaries. *Long-tailed Jaeger* (p. 150): much smaller; adult has much longer, pointed central tail feathers; lacks dark neck band.
Best Sites: *NB:* Grand Manan I. ferry. *PEI:* North Cape; Souris ferry. *NS:* Maine ferries; Brier I.; Cape North. *NF:* widespread, especially on eastern coast and ferry routes. *PQ:* L'Anse-au-Lard (Rimouski); Îles de la Madeleine.

LONG-TAILED JAEGER

Stercorarius longicaudus

The graceful, buoyant flight of the Long-tailed Jaeger is a rare sight in most of Atlantic Canada, yet there are places where sightings are almost guaranteed. This jaeger is a regular migrant off the coasts of Newfoundland and Labrador, where it is sometimes common. Few birds come close enough to shore to identify them with certainty, but seasoned observers are able to use a combination of build and plumage to distinguish these jaegers from the commoner species. • In migration, Long-tails hunt for fish over ocean waters and are less inclined than their close relatives to pirate food from gulls. They prefer to harass immature Black-legged Kittiwakes and Arctic Terns. • *Stercorarius* is Latin for "pertaining to dung"—a misleading reference to this bird's diet, which may include carrion and putrid food waste, but never excrement. This misconception is also the reason for its Newfoundland name "Dung-Bird."

ID: long, twinned tail feathers; dark cap; clean white throat and belly; yellow collar; grey upperparts; dark flight feathers. *Subadult:* dark "necklace"; dark barring on sides, flanks and rump. *Juvenile:* dark "chin" and throat; dark barring on sides, flanks and rump; mottled underwing linings; brown upperparts; short, rounded tail streamers.
Size: *L* 51–58 cm; *W* 1.0 m.
Status: rare to locally uncommon migrant from early May to mid-September, perhaps later well offshore.

Habitat: open ocean, usually well offshore except in fog or after storms.
Nesting: does not nest in Atlantic Canada.
Feeding: eats mainly fish, which are sometimes pirated from other birds.
Voice: generally silent; may make shrill calls while migrating.
Similar Species: *Pomarine Jaeger* (p. 148): adult has shorter, spoon-shaped central tail feathers; dark, mottled breast band, sides and flanks; more white on upperwing primaries; very dark vent. *Parasitic Jaeger* (p. 149): adult has much shorter central tail feathers; dark neck band.
Best Sites: *NB:* Miscou I. *PEI:* Souris ferry. *NS:* Maine ferries. *NF:* Cape Norman; L'Anse aux Meadows; Cape Shore. *PQ:* Îles de la Madeleine.

150

LAUGHING GULL

Larus atricilla

In the late 19th century, high commercial demand for egg collections and feathers resulted in the extirpation of the Laughing Gull as a breeding species in many parts of its East Coast range. It is now limited to a small colony on Machias Seal Island, New Brunswick, and a few pioneering birds elsewhere. Today, East Coast populations are gradually assuming their former abundance, and the Laughing Gull may soon return to Atlantic Canada on a more regular basis. Although this gull may appear in any month of the year, May, June, August and September support the most sightings. • The Latin name *atricilla* refers to a black band present only on the tails of immature birds, while the laughing call explains its common name.

breeding

ID: *Breeding:* black head; broken, white eye ring; red bill. *Non-breeding:* white head with some pale grey bands; black bill. *3rd-year:* white neck and underparts; dark grey back; black-tipped wings; black legs. *Immature:* variable, brown-to-grey and white overall.

Size: *L* 38–43 cm; *W* 1.0 m.

Status: extremely rare visitor from April to October, with a few birds remaining until mid-December.

Habitat: offshore islands, coastal shorelines and less often lakes and rivers.

Nesting: very rare as a nesting species in Atlantic Canada; usually in small colonies; nest of grass and weeds is built on the ground; the pair incubates 2–3 buffy-olive eggs, spotted and blotched with brown, for 20–23 days.

Feeding: omnivorous; gleans insects, small molluscs, crustaceans, spiders and small fish from the ground or water while flying, wading, walking or swimming; may steal food from other birds; may eat the eggs and nestlings of other birds.

Voice: loud, high pitched laughing call: *ha-ha-ha-ha-ha-ha.*

Similar Species: *Franklin's Gull:* smaller overall; red legs; shorter, slimmer bill; non-breeding adult has black mask. *Black-headed Gull* (p. 152) and *Bonaparte's Gull* (p. 153): orange or reddish legs; slimmer bill; lighter mantle; white wedge on upper leading edge of wing; black "hood" on breeding adult does not extend over nape. *Little Gull:* paler mantle; reddish legs; dainty black bill; no eye ring; lacks black wing tips.

Best Sites: *NB:* Machias Seal I. *PQ:* New Carlisle–New Richmond area.

BLACK-HEADED GULL

Larus ridibundus

Black-headed Gulls are a regular, and increasing, attraction for birdwatchers in Atlantic Canada. Several birds can be found cavorting with large gatherings of Bonaparte's Gulls in autumn, and numbers increase after their small relatives leave. The often raucous concentrations of gulls in southern Newfoundland's harbours and field roosts often have a small number of these wanderers. • The Black-headed Gull is a relative newcomer to Canada. The first sighting in North America was recorded in the 1920s. Small nesting colonies have been established on islands off the coast of Newfoundland and Québec, and there may be other nests in Nova Scotia. • In North America, there are many gulls with black heads. Ironically, the Black-headed Gull has a chocolate-brown head, which can easily be mistaken for black in the misty conditions that sometimes envelop Atlantic Canada's coasts.

breeding

non-breeding

ID: white underparts; grey mantle; red feet and legs. *Breeding:* red bill; dark brown "hood" appears blackish and does not extend onto nape; broken, white eye ring. *Non-breeding:* dark ear patch; white cap; red bill. *Immature:* pale legs; white mottling on "hood" in summer; dark tail band; black-tipped, yellow bill; brown on wing in winter. *In flight:* white upper forewing wedge; black wing tips; dark underwing primaries.
Size: *L* 36–41 cm; *W* 1.0 m.
Status: rare to uncommon visitor from early April to May; locally rare breeder; many remain through the winter.
Habitat: coastal marshes, lakeshores and offshore islets.
Nesting: on offshore islets and coastal marshes; in colonies; on ground or on low vegetation and made of local plant materials;

pair incubates 2–4 brown-spotted and blotched, darker brown eggs for 22–24 days.
Feeding: gleans insects, small molluscs, crustaceans, spiders and small fish from the ground or the water's surface; often catches insects in flight; may also take seeds and berries; may steal food from other birds.
Voice: high-pitched *craah*.
Similar Species: *Bonaparte's Gull* (p. 153): smaller overall; black bill; mostly white underwing primaries; black "hood" on breeding adult extends onto upper nape. *Laughing Gull* (p. 151): lack white leading edge of wing; black "hood" on breeding adult extends over nape; non-breeding Franklin's adult has black face mask and bill.
Best Sites: *Summer: NF:* Flat I. (St. George's); Stephenville Crossing; Ladle Cove (Carmanville); Cape Freels. *PQ:* Havre-aux-Basques (Îles de la Madeleine). *In migration* and *winter:* more widespread, especially in Halifax–Dartmouth, NS, and Conception Bay and St. John's, NF.

BONAPARTE'S GULL

Larus philadelphia

The graceful, reserved Bonaparte's Gull is nothing like its larger, aggressive relatives that fight over food scraps. Delicate in plumage and behaviour, this small gull avoids landfills. It prefers to dine on flying insects or from the water's surface. Bonaparte's Gulls raise their soft, scratchy voices in excitement only when they spy a school of fish, an abundance of euphausiid shrimps or a swarm of aerial insects. • The Bonaparte's Gull takes advantage of local food supplies in autumn migration. Huge flocks of these gulls, often numbering several thousands of birds, gather in places like Head Harbour Passage, New Brunswick, to feast on swarms of euphausiids. These small crustaceans are an essential food source for the rest of the birds' long journey south. • In years when mild winter weather prevails, many Bonaparte's Gulls will remain until November, but even these birds move out of Atlantic Canada well before year's end.

non-breeding

breeding

ID: black bill; grey mantle; white underparts. *Breeding:* black head; incomplete, white eye ring. *Non-breeding:* white head; dark ear patch. *In flight:* white forewing wedge; black wing tips.
Size: *L* 30–36 cm; *W* 84 cm.
Status: rather uncommon migrant from early April to late May and common to locally abundant migrant from late July through November; very rare winter visitor.
Habitat: *In migration:* offshore upwellings, coastal mud flats, estuaries and salt marshes, occasionally lakeshores.
Nesting: not known to nest in Atlantic Canada.
Feeding: dabbles and tips up for aquatic invertebrates, small fish and tadpoles while swimming; gleans the ground for terrestrial invertebrates; also captures insects in the air.
Voice: scratchy, soft *ear ear* while feeding, when they can be very noisy.
Similar Species: *Franklin's Gull:* lacks white upper forewing wedge; breeding adult has orange bill; non-breeding adult has black face mask. *Little Gull:* daintier bill; adult has white wing tips; breeding adult's black "hood" extends over nape; non-breeding adult has white cap. *Black-headed Gull* (p. 152): larger overall; larger, red bill; dark underwing primaries; breeding adult has brownish "hood." *Sabine's Gull:* large black, white and grey triangles on upperwings; yellow-tipped dark bill; almost always offshore.
Best Sites: *NB:* Charlo River; Tracadie; Deer I. *PEI:* PEI NP; Charlottetown; Souris; Wood Is. *NS:* Wallace Bay; Canso Causeway. *NF:* L'Anse aux Meadows. *PQ:* Île Bonaventure; Barachois.

MEW GULL

Larus canus

This petite and delicate gull is the smallest of the typical "white-headed" gulls. Adults in breeding plumage are seldom seen here—these birds usually breed in western Canada and Alaska. Most of the Mew Gulls seen in Atlantic Canada in winter are of the slightly larger European subspecies *canus*, although smaller *brachyrhynchus* individuals may also be seen. Immatures are more problematic to identify, but Europeans, who call this bird the "Common Gull," refer to its neater looks, smaller bill and darker terminal tail band. The large eyes and single, subterminal white patch in the black wing tip makes the adult an easy gull to identify. • The soft "mewing" call for which this gull was named is a pleasant change from the usual screeches of other gulls. Unfortunately, this call is mostly used on the breeding grounds. • *Larus* is Latin for "gull," and *canus* is Latin for "greyish-white."

breeding

non-breeding

ID: dainty; small, thin bill; wings extend beyond tail at rest; rapid walking stride. *Non-breeding:* greenish-yellow bill (variable) with dark smudge on lower mandible; medium grey back; minimal to extensive dusky streaking or clouding on head, neck and upper breast; noticeable single white area on black wing tips; pale green-yellow legs and feet. *1st-winter:* dingy grey-brown with greyish back; dark-tipped pink bill; slightly darker brown outer primaries; broad, blackish terminal tail band.

Size: *L* 38–46 cm.

Status: rare and local visitor from October to mid-April.

Habitat: mostly harbours and freshwater lakes close to the coast.

Nesting: does not nest in Atlantic Canada.

Feeding: opportunistic; captures fish, crustaceans and other invertebrates by plunging to the water's surface, plucking from wave-wash or picking from the ground; normally avoids garbage dumps but will scavenge at sewage outlets in harbours.

Voice: members of flocks at feeding or roosting sites utter a high-pitched cough, *queeoh!*; not particularly vocal in Atlantic Canada.

Similar Species: *Ring-billed Gull* (p. 155): paler grey above with distinct black-ringed, yellow bill; pale eyes; black ring around bill; lacks eye-catching single white wing tip area; less dusky-headed in winter. *California Gull:* much larger; red and black marks on lower mandible of yellowish or dull blue-grey bill; lacks Mew Gull wing tip pattern.

Best Sites: *NS:* Halifax–Dartmouth. *NF:* Quidi Vidi Lake; St. John's Harbour.

RING-BILLED GULL
Larus delawarensis

Although this bird nests locally in Atlantic Canada, it wanders almost everywhere and has picked up many of the bad habits associated with its larger relatives. Its numbers have greatly increased over recent years, and its tolerance for humans has made it a part of our everyday lives. Ring-bills will join Herring Gulls to scavenge our litter or foul the windshields of our automobiles! Some people think that Ring-billed Gulls have become pests; many parks, beaches, golf courses and even fast-food restaurant parking lots are often inundated with marauding gulls looking for food handouts. Few species, however, have fared as well as Ring-bills in the face of human development, which is something to appreciate, if not to enjoy.

non-breeding

breeding

ID: *Breeding:* white head; yellow bill and legs; black ring around bill tip; pale grey mantle; yellow eyes; white underparts. *Non-breeding:* brown mottling on head. *Immature:* grey back; brown wings and breast. *In flight:* black wing tips with few white spots.

Size: *L* 46–51 cm; *W* 1.2 m (male is slightly larger).

Status: common to locally abundant migrant and year-round resident; most common from August to mid-October; locally uncommon to common breeder.

Habitat: *Breeding:* sparsely vegetated islands, open beaches, breakwaters and dredge-spoil areas. *In migration* and *winter:* lakes, rivers, landfills, golf courses, fields, parks and garbage dumps.

Nesting: colonial; in a shallow scrape on the ground lined with plants, debris, grass and sticks; pair incubates 2–4 brown-blotched, grey to olive eggs for 23–28 days.

Feeding: gleans the ground for garbage, spiders, insects, rodents, earthworms, grubs and some waste grain; scavenges for carrion; surface-tips for aquatic invertebrates and fish.

Voice: high-pitched *kakakaka-akakaka*; also a low, laughing *yook-yook-yook*.

Similar Species: *Herring* (p. 156), *Glaucous* (p. 159) and *Iceland* (p. 157) *gulls:* larger; adults have pinkish legs, lack bill ring and have red spot near tip of lower mandible. *Mew Gull* (p. 154): adults have less black on wing tips, dark eyes, darker mantles and lack bill ring. *Lesser Black-backed Gull* (p. 158) and *Great Black-backed Gull* (p. 160): larger; much darker mantle; much less white on wing tips; lack bill ring; immatures much larger, with heavier, all-dark bills.

Best Sites: *Summer: NB:* Acadie coast; Grand Lake. *PEI:* O'Leary; New London Bay; Murray Harbour. *NF:* Larkin Point (Codroy Valley); Stephenville; St. Paul's; Hawkes Bay; Ladle Cove. *PQ:* Rimouski; Îles Razades (Trois Pistoles). *In migration:* widespread. *Winter:* urban areas.

155

HERRING GULL

Larus argentatus

G ull nest sites are never far from a steady food source. It is rare to walk anywhere along a coastal path without seeing and hearing nesting gulls on the cliff ledges below. Herring Gulls often nest comfortably in large colonies, sometimes terrorizing Black-legged Kittiwakes or terns. However, sometimes a pair will choose a site kilometres from any other gulls. • Like many gulls, Herrings have a small red spot on their lower mandible that serves as a target for nestling young. When a downy chick pecks at the lower mandible, the parent recognizes the cue and regurgitates its meal. Many juveniles continue to beg for food well into winter, with varied success depending on their parents' disposition.

breeding

non-breeding

ID: large gull; yellow bill; red spot on lower mandible; light eyes; light grey mantle; pink legs. *Breeding:* white head; white underparts. *Non-breeding:* white head and nape are washed with brown. *Immature:* mottled brown overall. *In flight:* white-spotted, black wing tips.
Size: L 58–66 cm; W 1.2 m.
Status: abundant migrant and locally abundant visitor from October to early April; common to locally abundant breeder from April to September.
Habitat: *Breeding:* undisturbed islands, peninsulas and cliffs. *In migration:* large lakes, wetlands, rivers, landfills and urban areas.
Nesting: singly or colonially; often nests with other gulls, pelicans and cormorants; on open beaches and islands; on the ground in a shallow scrape lined with

plants and sticks; pair incubates 3 darkly blotched, olive to buff eggs for 31–32 days.
Feeding: surface-tips for aquatic invertebrates and fish; gleans the ground for insects and worms; scavenges dead fish and garbage at landfills; eats other birds' eggs and young.
Voice: loud, bugle-like *kleew-kleew*; also an alarmed *kak-kak-kak*.
Similar Species: *Ring-billed Gull* (p. 155): smaller; black bill ring; yellow legs; immatures have much greyer back and pinkish bill. *Glaucous Gull* (p. 159) and *Iceland Gull* (p. 157): paler mantle; lack black in wings; immatures generally whiter or paler buff. *Lesser Black-backed Gull* (p. 158) and *Great Black-backed Gull* (p. 160): much darker mantle; immatures more discretely marked with brown.
Best Sites: *Summer:* nesting colonies along all coasts and at some inland sites. *Winter:* abundant at urban sites, lakes and bays; at garbage dumps, harbours and near fast-food restaurants.

ICELAND GULL

Larus glaucoides

The pale Iceland Gull can be seen in Atlantic Canada each winter in moderate numbers. It is usually among large flocks of wintering Great Black-backed Gulls and Herring Gulls. • The Iceland Gull spends much of its time searching for schools of fish over icy, open waters. When fishing proves unrewarding, this opportunistic gull has no qualms about digging through a landfill or scavenging in a fishing harbour for food. Human onlookers might think that the dirty brown head and breast streaking of some birds is a result of its filthy scavenging habits, but in truth these are natural markings of their non-breeding plumage. • The Iceland Gull comes in two slightly different forms in Atlantic Canada. Many birds have grey in their wing tips and are considered to be of the *kumlieni* subspecies, whereas others have pure white wing tips, suggesting that they are birds of the *glaucoides* subspecies that nests on Baffin Island and other arctic islands.

non-breeding

ID: *Breeding:* relatively short, yellow bill with red spot on lower mandible; rounded head; yellow eyes; dark eye ring; white wing tips with some dark grey; pink legs; white underparts; pale grey mantle. *Non-breeding:* head and breast streaked with brown. *Immature:* dark eyes, black bill and various plumages with varying amounts of grey on upperparts and brown flecking over entire body.
Size: *L* 56 cm; *W* 1.4 m.
Status: uncommon to locally abundant visitor from October to May.

Habitat: harbours and open water on large lakes and rivers, rarely far from the coast.
Nesting: does not nest in Atlantic Canada.
Feeding: eats mostly fish; may also take crustaceans, molluscs, carrion, seeds; scavenges at landfills and in fishing harbours.
Voice: high, screechy calls, much less bugling than other large gulls.
Similar Species: *Herring Gull* (p. 156): black wing tips; darker mantle. *Glaucous Gull* (p. 159): longer, heavier bill; pure white wing tips. *Ring-billed Gull* (p. 155): smaller; dark ring on yellow bill; yellow legs. *Lesser Black-backed Gull* (p. 158) and *Great Black-backed Gull* (p. 160): darker mantle; black wing tips; Lesser has yellow legs.
Best Sites: *Winter:* widespread in maritime NF and PQ; more local in NB, PEI and NS.

LESSER BLACK-BACKED GULL
Larus fuscus

Equipped with long wings for long-distance flights, small numbers of Lesser Black-backed Gulls leave their familiar European and Icelandic surroundings each autumn to make their way to North America. Most of these gulls settle along the East Coast in winter, and it is sometimes a challenge to pick them out in a huge flock of roosting gulls. However, most birds are much daintier and longer-winged than their bulky neighbours. • The Lesser Black-backed Gull is a European nesting species. However, the increasing number of sightings in Atlantic Canada outside of winter suggests that this immigrant may soon be applying for Canadian status, much like some of its smaller relatives. Some Lesser Black-backed Gulls have already been found paired with Herring Gulls, which indicates we may be in for even more puzzling hybrids.

non-breeding

non-breeding

ID: *Breeding:* dark grey *(graellsii)* or black *(fuscus)* mantle; mostly black wing tips; yellow bill with red spot on lower mandible; yellow eyes; yellow legs; white head and underparts. *Non-breeding:* head and neck streaked with brown. *Immature:* dark or light eyes; black or pale bill with black tip; various plumages with varying amounts of grey on upperparts and brown flecking over entire body.
Size: *L* 53 cm; *W* 1.4 m.
Status: rare to uncommon visitor from September to late April; very rare summer resident.
Habitat: harbours, open areas, landfills and open water on large lakes.

Nesting: not known to nest in Atlantic Canada.
Feeding: eats mostly fish, crustaceans, molluscs, insects, small rodents, carrion and seeds; scavenges for garbage.
Voice: screechy call is like a lower-pitched version of the Herring Gull's.
Similar Species: *Herring Gull* (p. 156): lighter mantle; pink legs. *Glaucous Gull* (p. 159) and *Iceland Gull* (p. 157): pale grey mantle; white or grey wing tips; pink legs. *Ring-billed Gull* (p. 155): smaller; dark ring on yellow bill; paler mantle. *Great Black-backed Gull* (p. 160): much larger; black mantle; heavier bill; pale pinkish legs.
Best Sites: *NB:* Bay of Fundy ferry. *NS:* Halifax Harbour. *NF:* Rocky Harbour; Quidi Vidi Lake; St. John's Harbour; Bay Bulls.

GLAUCOUS GULL

Larus hyperboreus

The Glaucous Gull is our largest gull. Endowed with great powers of observation and an almost fanatical need to wander, it traditionally fished for its meals or stole food from smaller gulls or even fast-flying Gyrfalcons. Some birds even perfected a hunting technique that allowed them to catch alcids trapped in narrow channels in winter ice. More recently, however, wintering Glaucous Gulls have traded the rigours of hunting for the job of defending plots of garbage at various landfills or following fishing boats for easy pickings. • Immatures are more difficult to identify than adults. Fortunately, they are light enough to be easily distinguished from other immature gulls, and most birds have a distinctive pale pink bill with a dark tip. These young gulls will often linger well into the summer before drifting north again, and they are more likely to stray from traditional wintering sites. • The scientific name *hyperboreus* means "of the far north."

non-breeding

non-breeding

ID: *Breeding:* relatively long, heavy, yellow bill with red spot on lower mandible; pure white wing tips; flattened crown profile; yellow eyes; pink legs; white underparts; very pale grey mantle. *Non-breeding:* head, neck and breast are streaked with brown. *Immature:* dark eyes; pale, black-tipped bill; various plumages have varying amounts of brown flecking on body.
Size: *L* 69 cm; *W* 1.5 m.
Status: rare to locally uncommon visitor from early November through May; exceptionally rare visitor from June to early July.
Habitat: harbours, slob ice, landfills and open water on large lakes and bays.

Nesting: does not nest in Atlantic Canada.
Feeding: predator, pirate and scavenger; eats mostly fish, crustaceans, molluscs and some seeds; feeds on carrion and at landfills.
Voice: high, screechy calls similar to Herring Gull's *kak-kak-kak*.
Similar Species: *Iceland Gull* (p. 157): smaller; slightly darker mantle; grey on wing tips. *Herring Gull* (p. 156): slightly smaller; black wing tips; much darker mantle. *Great Black-backed Gull* (p. 160): same size; darker in all plumages; young birds have all-dark bills.
Best Sites: *NB:* Cape Tormentine. *PEI:* North Rustico. *NS:* Halifax Harbour. *NF:* Corner Brook; Gros Morne NP; L'Anse aux Meadows; Quidi Vidi Lake; Bay Bulls. *PQ:* Bas St-Laurent; Forillon NP.

GREAT BLACK-BACKED GULL

Larus marinus

The Great Black-backed Gull's commanding size and bold, aggressive disposition enables it to dominate other gulls, ensuring that it has first dibs at food, whether it is fresh fish or a meal from a landfill. No other gull species, with the exception of the Glaucous Gull, is equipped to dispute ownership with this domineering gull. • Great Black-backed Gulls do not tolerate Herring Gulls around their nest sites. As a result, terns, which often suffer high mortality during the breeding season because of Herring Gulls, benefit considerably from the presence of this unwitting ally. • Although the Great Black-backed Gull prefers to nest in colonies throughout most of its range, a few isolated pairs may nest away from other gulls. • The Great Black-backed Gull is a "four-year gull," meaning that it goes through various plumage stages until its fourth winter, when it develops its refined adult plumage. Most immature gulls have dark streaking, spotting or mottling, which helps them to avoid detection by predators.

breeding

ID: very large gull; all white except for grey underwings and black mantle; pale pinkish legs; light-coloured eyes; large, yellow bill with red spot on lower mandible. *Non- breeding:* may have faintly streaked nape. *Immature:* variable, mottled grey-brown, white and black; black bill or black-tipped, pale bill.
Size: *L* 76 cm; *W* 1.6 m.
Status: common year-round resident, with populations augmented in winter.
Habitat: *Breeding:* rocky islands and cliffs; rarely on beaches. *Winter:* harbours, bays, landfills and open water on large lakes.

Nesting: usually colonial, but also breeds in isolated pairs; on islands, cliff tops or beaches; pair builds a mound of vegetation and debris on the ground, often near rocks; pair incubates 2–3 brown-blotched, olive to buff eggs for 27–28 days.
Feeding: opportunistic feeder; eats fish, eggs, birds, small mammals, berries, carrion, molluscs, crustaceans, insects and other invertebrates; scavenges at landfills; finds food by flying, swimming, or walking.
Voice: a harsh *kyow*.
Similar Species: *Glaucous Gull* (p. 159): same size but paler plumage. *Other gulls* (pp. 151–62): smaller; most lack black mantle.
Best Sites: *Summer:* coastal nesting colonies. *Winter:* abundant in urban areas, lakes and bays; often visits garbage dumps and harbours.

BLACK-LEGGED KITTIWAKE

Rissa tridactyla

The Black-legged Kittiwake is more closely associated with the marine environment than any other gull, coming ashore only to breed in noisy, cliff-ledge colonies. After leaving their nests in August, swirling flocks of black-and-white patterned juvenile kittiwakes head out to sea to find food and endure the attention of piratical jaegers and skuas. Some Black-legged Kittiwakes retreat to coastal harbours where weather conditions are less brutal, but most birds cling fiercely to their pelagic natures. Even during the most violent storms, Black-legged Kittiwakes will remain in open water, floating among massive swells. They are able to spend most of their lives in saltwater environments because they have developed glands above their eyes that enable them to extract and secrete excess salt from their bodies. • The name "kittiwake" comes from the call this bird makes at nesting colonies. People from Newfoundland are fond of calling it "Tickle-Ace."

1st winter

non-breeding

breeding

ID: *Breeding:* black legs; grey mantle; white underparts; white head; yellow bill. *Non-breeding:* grey nape; dark grey smudge behind eye. *Immature:* black bill; wide, black half-collar; dark ear patch. *In flight:* adult has solid black triangular wing tips; immature has black "M" on upper forewing from wing tip to wing tip and black terminal tail band.

Size: *L* 41–46 cm; *W* 91 cm.

Status: uncommon to locally abundant breeder from late April to late August; rare to locally common inshore until mid-October; rare in winter.

Habitat: open ocean, sometimes open water in bays and estuaries; rare in harbours and very rare inland on large lakes.

Nesting: in large colonies, usually on cliff ledges; neat cup of seaweed, grass and moss, added to each summer; pair incubates 1–3 spotted and blotched greenish- or bluish-buff eggs for 25–30 days.

Feeding: small fish are preferred; also takes crustaceans, insects and molluscs; dips to the water's surface to snatch prey; may plunge under the water's surface or glean from the surface while swimming.

Voice: calls *kitti-waaak* and *kekekek.*

Similar Species: *Franklin's, Laughing* (p. 151), *Bonaparte's* (p. 153), *Black-headed* (p. 152) and *Little gulls:* lack combination of black legs, yellow bill, grey nape and solid black triangular wing tips.

Best Sites: *Summer: NB:* Deer I. *NS:* Bird Is.; Gabarus Bay. *NF:* Baccalieu I.; Witless Bay; Cape St. Mary's. *PQ:* Forillon NP; Percé; Île Bonaventure; Bird Rocks & Île Brion (Îles de la Madeleine). *In migration* and *winter:* widespread.

IVORY GULL

Pagophila eburnea

This dainty gull is easy to differentiate from other gulls by its snowy white appearance, black legs and two-tone bill. Immature birds are also distinctive, with a blackish facial patch and black markings on the wings and tail. The Ivory Gull's tern-like call and flight also distinguish it from other small gulls. • The Ivory Gull rarely ventures far from drifting pack ice. It feeds on fish, as well as the droppings of large polar bears, whales, walruses and seals! It is best known, however, for its preference for seal meat. Birders in northern Newfoundland will even willingly part with cash to obtain enough of a carcass to attract a flock of these predominantly offshore gulls. • Ivory Gulls are found in Atlantic Canada in winter only, when they travel down to the coast of Labrador, Newfoundland and the Gaspé from their breeding grounds in northern Canada and Greenland. • The genus name *Pagophila* means "frost lover" in Greek; *eburnia* means "ivory-coloured."

ID: pure white plumage; black legs; grey, yellow-tipped bill.
Size: *L* 40–43 cm; *W* 1.1–1.2 m.
Status: rare to irregularly common visitor from late November to mid-March, occasionally into April.
Habitat: consolidated pack ice, drift ice, and the ice edge; occasionally ventures into harbours.

Nesting: does not nest in Atlantic Canada.
Feeding: catches fish on the water's surface or makes shallow dives; also takes marine invertebrates, dung and carrion, especially seal meat.
Voice: a harsh, tern-like *keeuur.*
Similar Species: none.
Best Sites: *NB:* Cape Tormentine. *NS:* Canso; North Sydney. *NF:* L'Anse aux Meadows; St. Anthony. *PQ:* Pointe-au-Père; Ste-Anne-des-Monts.

CASPIAN TERN

Sterna caspia

In size and habits, the mighty Caspian Tern bridges the gulf between smaller terns and raucous gulls. It is the largest tern in North America, and its wingbeats are slower and more gull-like than those of most other terns. Because of this gull-like flight, many birders confuse it with a gull until its raucous call gives it away. This tern's distinctive, heavy, red-orange bill and forked tail also give away its true identity. • Caspian Terns are often seen with gulls on shoreline sandbars and mud flats during migration or in the breeding season, when they nest in colonies on exposed islands or protected beaches. In Atlantic Canada, most Caspian Terns nest in colonies with other terns and sometimes gulls. • A Caspian Tern foraging for alewife and other small schooling fish often impresses observers. Foraging high over open waters, this tern hovers, then folds its wings suddenly, plunging headfirst toward its target. • This tern was first collected from the Caspian Sea, hence its name.

breeding

ID: *Breeding:* black cap; heavy, red-orange bill with faint black tip; light grey mantle; black legs; shallowly forked tail; white underparts; long, frosty, pointed wings; dark grey on underside of outer primaries. *Non-breeding:* black cap, streaked with white.

Size: *L* 48–58 cm; *W* 1.3–1.4 m.

Status: rare local breeder from late April to late August; uncommon from early September to mid-October.

Habitat: *Breeding:* usually on small offshore islands. *In migration:* saltwater bays, estuaries, wetlands and shorelines of large lakes and rivers.

Nesting: in a shallow scrape on bare sand, lightly vegetated soil or gravel; nest is sparsely lined with vegetation, rocks or twigs; pair incubates 1–3 brown- or black-spotted, pale buff eggs for 20–22 days.

Feeding: hovers over water and plunges headfirst after small fish, tadpoles and aquatic invertebrates; also feeds by swimming and gleaning at the water's surface.

Voice: low, harsh *ca-arr*; loud *kraa-uh*; juveniles answer with a high-pitched whistle.

Similar Species: *Common Tern* (p. 165) and *Arctic Tern* (p. 166): much smaller; daintier bills; lack obvious dark triangle in wing.

Best Sites: *Summer: NF:* Grand Bay West; L'Anse aux Meadows; Penguin Is.; Deadman's Bay. *PQ:* Havre-aux-Maisons (Îles de la Madeleine). *In migration:* more widespread, especially on the north shore of PEI and the coasts of NF.

ROSEATE TERN
Sterna dougallii

The Roseate Tern can be found worldwide. In Canada, it is considered an endangered species. Fortunately, there are a number of stable colonies in Nova Scotia and Îles de la Madeleine, plus a few pairs and smaller colonies elsewhere. • The Roseate Tern often nests in colonies with other terns. It scrapes out a shallow depression for a nest, usually in dense vegetation, but it may build its nest in such human-made structures as tires or wooden boxes. • If you think that you see three terns looking after the same brood, this just may be the case. Unmated birds sometimes try to help out with the parental duties of a nesting pair. Quite often these helpers are driven off by the parents, but occasionally they are welcomed with open wings to form trios or quartets. • This tern was named for the very faint pink tone on its breast in breeding plumage.

breeding

ID: *Breeding:* black crown and nape; grey upperparts; white underparts; faint pink tone on breast; black bill; red-orange legs. *Non-breeding:* white breast; black cap extends forward only to eye. *In flight:* long, deeply forked tail; relatively short, straight wings are narrow; quick, stiff wingbeats.

Size: *L* 31–34 cm; *W* 70 cm.

Status: rare and local colonial breeder from mid-May to late July; rare migrant from mid-July to early September.

Habitat: sandy or rocky islands; often in protected bays and estuaries; usually close to shallow water for feeding.

Nesting: colonially with other terns; on ground under cover of vegetation, rocks, driftwood or human-made structures; 1–4 cream eggs, blotched with brown, are laid in a shallow scrape and incubated by both parents for 21–26 days.

Feeding: flies low over water and then dives to capture prey; takes mostly small fish and sometimes crustaceans, molluscs and insects.

Voice: sharp *keek* given in flight or soft plover-like *chi-vik* given in flight.

Similar Species: *Caspian Tern* (p. 163) and *Royal Tern:* larger; long, thick, all-red bills; black legs. *Forster's, Arctic* (p. 166) and *Common* (p. 165) *terns:* dark wing tips visible in flight; lack rosy wash on breast. *Gulls* (pp. 151–62): either lack black cap or black cap extends well below eye.

Best Sites: *NB:* Machias Seal I. *NS:* Brier I.; southwest coast; St. Margaret's Bay; Fox I. (Lawrencetown Loop); New Harbour (Canso); Sable I. *PQ:* Îles de la Madeleine.

COMMON TERN

Sterna hirundo

C ommon Terns patrol the shorelines of coastal bays, estuaries, lakes and rivers in spring and autumn. In summer, they settle in large nesting colonies, usually on islands or sandbars. Males and females perform aerial courtship dances. For most pairs, the nesting season commences when the female accepts her suitor's gracious fish offerings. • Tern colonies are noisy and chaotic, and they are often close to noisier gull colonies. Should an intruder approach a tern nest, the parent will dive repeatedly, often defecating on the offender. Needless to say, it is best to keep a respectful distance from nesting terns, and from all nesting birds, for that matter. • Terns are effortless flyers, and they are some of the most impressive long-distance migrants. Recently, a Common Tern banded in Great Britain was recovered in Australia.

breeding

ID: *Breeding:* black cap; thin, red, black-tipped bill; red legs; white rump; white tail with grey outer edges; white underparts. *Non-breeding:* black nape; lacks black cap. *In flight:* shallowly forked tail; long, pointed wings; dark grey wedge near lighter grey upperwing tips.
Size: *L* 33–41 cm; *W* 76 cm.
Status: common migrant and breeder from April to mid-December; may be very abundant locally in autumn.
Habitat: *Breeding:* natural and human-made islands, breakwaters and beaches. *In migration:* large lakes, open wetlands and slow-moving rivers.
Nesting: primarily colonial; usually on islands with non-vegetated, open areas; in a small scrape lined sparsely with pebbles,

vegetation or shells; pair incubates 1–3 variably marked eggs for up to 27 days.
Feeding: hovers over the water and plunges headfirst after small fish and aquatic invertebrates.
Voice: high-pitched, drawn-out *keee-are* is most commonly heard at colonies but also in foraging flights.
Similar Species: *Arctic Tern* (p. 166): all-red bill; deeply forked tail; upper primaries lack dark grey wedge; greyer underparts; rare in migration. *Roseate Tern* (p. 164): all-dark bill; all-white wings; sometimes rosy tinge on underparts. *Caspian Tern* (p. 163): much larger overall; much heavier, red-orange bill; very dark primary underwing patch.
Best Sites: *Summer:* some large colonies at South Kouchibouguac Dune in NB; isolated pairs farther north. *In migration:* widespread.

165

ARCTIC TERN
Sterna paradisaea

The Arctic Terns that nest in Atlantic Canada make annual round-trip migrations to foreign lands and oceans that include South America, Antarctica, Europe, Africa and the Indian Ocean. In some years, an Arctic Tern might fly a distance of 32,000 kilometres! Because this tern experiences long hours of daylight while on its northern nesting grounds and long days of sunlight on its non-breeding grounds, an Arctic Tern probably experiences more daylight in an average year than most living creatures. • The Arctic Tern is more common than the Common Tern in northern parts of Atlantic Canada. The Arctic Tern is also more likely to nest in isolated pairs than its less demonstrative relative. An Arctic Tern will follow through with its threats, and it is not afraid to voice them—it is even able to scream while holding a small fish in its bill! • Most tern sightings outside the breeding season are of Arctic Terns from more northerly colonies.

breeding

ID: *Breeding:* blood red bill and legs; black cap and nape; short neck; white "cheek"; grey underparts; long, white, forked tail extends to wing tips when perched. *Immature* and *non-breeding:* white underparts; black band through eyes and across nape; black bill. *In flight:* appears neckless; deeply forked tail; even grey wings with thin, dark, trailing underwing edge.
Size: *L* 36–43 cm; *W* 74–84 cm.
Status: locally uncommon migrant from late April to mid-June; uncommon breeder from early May to late August; rare from September to early November.

Habitat: *Breeding:* marshy tundra, sand and gravel bars, sandspits, barren islands, beaches and rocky shorelines. *In migration:* large lakes, rivers and wetlands.
Nesting: colonial; on sand, gravel, rock or marshy tundra; in a shallow, generally unlined scrape; pair incubates 2–3 black- and brown-blotched, pale olive to buff eggs for 20–24 days.
Feeding: dives into the water from a stationary hover; preys on small fish and aquatic invertebrates.
Voice: harsh, high-pitched *kee kahr!*
Similar Species: *Common Tern* (p. 165): black-tipped bill; dark grey wedge on upper primaries; whiter underparts. *Roseate Tern* (p. 164): all-black bill; pure white wings; sometimes light rosy tinge on breast.
Best Sites: widespread.

BLACK TERN

Chlidonias niger

Wheeling about in foraging flights, Black Terns pick small minnows from the water's surface or catch flying insects in mid-air. Even in stiff winds, these acrobats slice through the sky with grace. Black Terns are frail birds in many ways, but they have dominion over the winds. When they leave their freshwater breeding sites in August and September, they head for warmer foreign waters. • Black Terns are finicky nesters, refusing to return to nesting areas that show slight changes in water level or in the density of emergent vegetation. This selectiveness has contributed to a significant decline in this bird's population over recent decades in other parts of Canada. Commitment to restore and protect valuable wetland habitat in Atlantic Canada has helped this bird to colonize areas provided for waterfowl, first in New Brunswick and more recently in other parts of Atlantic Canada. • In order to spell this tern's genus name correctly, one must misspell *chelidonias*, the Greek word for "swallow."

breeding

ID: *Breeding:* black head and underparts; grey back, tail and wings; white undertail coverts; black bill; reddish-black legs. *Non-breeding:* white underparts and forehead; moulting autumn birds may be mottled with brown. *In flight:* long, pointed wings; shallowly forked tail.

Size: *L* 23–25 cm; *W* 61 cm.

Status: locally uncommon migrant and breeder from mid-May to mid-September; a few may remain into October.

Habitat: shallow freshwater cattail marshes, wetlands, lake edges and sewage ponds with emergent vegetation.

Nesting: loosely colonial; nest of dead plant material is built on floating vegetation, a muddy mound or a muskrat house; pair incubates 3 darkly blotched, olive to pale buff eggs for 21–22 days.

Feeding: snatches insects from the air, from tall grass and from the water's surface; also eats small fish.

Voice: greeting call is a shrill, metallic *kik-kik-kik-kik-kik*; typical alarm call is *kreea*.

Similar Species: *Other terns* (pp. 163–66): all are light in colour, not dark.

Best Sites: *NB:* Belledune–Jacquet River area; French & Timber Lakes; Portobello Creek; Gagetown. *PEI:* New London Bay. *NS:* Missaguash Marsh; Seal I.; Three Fathom Harbour. *NF:* L'Anse aux Meadows. *PQ:* Ste-Flavie.

DOVEKIE

Alle alle

The name "Dovekie" means "little diver" in Anglo-Saxon. Like other members of the alcid family, Dovekies are designed to capture fish by underwater pursuit. They have small wings, webbed feet and sleek, waterproofed plumage. In general, the best time to look for alcids along coastlines is during late autumn and winter storms, when the birds must seek refuge close to shore. • Many arctic animals rely on the Dovekie for food, including Gyrfalcons, arctic foxes, gulls, large fish and even whales. Despite heavy predation and the fact that each pair lays only one egg per year, Dovekies remain abundant. • The Dovekie can be found in large concentrations on the Grand Banks and the Scotian Shelf and along the shores of Newfoundland in winter. • This bird is also called "Little Auk" in Great Britain and "Bullbird" in Newfoundland. Bay Bulls in Newfoundland was, in fact, named for this bird, which sometimes overwinters in the harbour in large numbers.

non-breeding

ID: stocky body; stubby bill; black upperparts, with some white on back and on trailing edge of wings; white underparts.
Breeding: black neck and breast. *Non-breeding:* white throat and breast; black "collar"; black rump.
Size: *L* 21 cm.
Status: common to locally abundant from late October to April; extremely rare in summer.
Habitat: often very far from land; sometimes around pack ice; prefers colder waters.

Nesting: does not nest in Atlantic Canada.
Feeding: dives and swims underwater; most dives are relatively shallow; feeds mostly on small crustaceans, including calanoid copepods, amphipods and euphausiids; may also take fish, molluscs, marine worms and algae.
Voice: generally silent.
Similar Species: *Other alcids* (pp. 169–73): larger; longer necks and bills.
Best Sites: *NB:* The Whistle (Grand Manan I.). *PEI:* Souris ferry. *NS:* Cape Sable I. *NF:* widespread. *PQ:* L'Anse-au-Lard; Pointe-au-Père; Forillon NP; Île Bonaventure; Pointe St-Pierre (Îles de la Madeleine).

COMMON MURRE

Uria aalge

Common Murres nest in huge, tightly packed colonies on coastal cliffs, stacks and off-shore islands. Some sites support tens of thousands of birds. In winter, Common Murres may travel far out into the open Atlantic, disappearing from shore altogether. However, sudden midwinter visits by large numbers of birds to breeding rocks suggests that many Common Murres also overwinter fairly close to shore.
• Many water birds share the countershading pattern of this murre. From above, the bird's dark back blends with the steely sea; from below, predators and prey may be slow to notice this bird's light-coloured underbelly against the shimmering surface of the water. • Although many murres die in inshore fishing nets, the greatest losses are a result of unintentional oil spills and intentional cleaning of tanks at sea, neither of which has ever been adequately policed.

breeding

ID: deep, sooty-brown upperparts; white underparts; slender black bill. *Breeding:* dark brown neck. *Non-breeding:* white neck, "chin" and lower face.
Size: *L* 41–44 cm.
Status: common to locally abundant year-round resident; resident populations may be augmented from late September to late April.
Habitat: *Breeding:* on offshore islands, islets and rocks. *Foraging:* on open ocean from just beyond the surf zone to far offshore; father-and-chick pairs sometimes visit estuaries from July to early September.
Nesting: highly colonial; on bare rock or a flat rocky surface close to water; 1 variably marked and coloured egg is incubated by parents over 28–37 days; incubating adults are often within touching range in tightly packed colonies numbering up to tens of thousands.

Feeding: dives from the water's surface for fish; also takes squid, marine worms and crustaceans.
Voice: adults utter a low, harsh *murrr*; dependent juvenile gives a high-pitched, quavering whistle: *FEED-me-now, feed-me-now, feed-me-now!*
Similar Species: *Thick-billed Murre* (p. 170) and *Razorbill* (p. 171): slightly larger; black on wings and back; white stripe on bill. *Dovekie* (p. 168): much smaller; small, stubby bill; black-and-white plumage. *Scoters* (pp. 77–79): much bulkier; heavy, duck-like bills; shorter necks. *Common Loon* (p. 33): much larger overall; larger head; white underparts are not visible when floating. *Horned Grebe* (p. 35): smaller; longer neck; red eyes.
Best Sites: *Summer: NB:* Machias Seal I. *NS:* Bird Is. *NF:* Cape Bonavista; Baccalieu I.; Witless Bay; Cape St. Mary's. *In migration and winter:* widespread. *PQ:* Cap Gaspé; Percé; Île Bonaventure; Bird Rocks (Îles de la Madeleine).

THICK-BILLED MURRE

Uria lomvia

The Thick-billed Murre is one of the deepest-diving birds. It regularly dives to 100 metres, and it occasionally even dives to below 200 metres. Sometimes it remains underwater for more than three minutes at a time! It steers and propels itself with its wings while it chases after marine fish and invertebrates. • The Thick-billed Murre is one of the most abundant marine birds in the Northern Hemisphere. Breeding pairs pack themselves into suitable breeding areas, nesting in large colonies that can include up to one million birds. They often nest shoulder to shoulder on the rocky cliffs of their nest sites. The largest colonies in North America are along the Labrador coast and in the eastern Arctic, but there are also smaller colonies in Newfoundland and Îles de la Madeleine.

breeding

ID: *Breeding:* black upperparts; white underparts; short, thick, black bill. *Non-breeding:* white "chin" and throat.

Size: *L* 46 cm.

Status: rare to locally uncommon colonial breeder from mid-April to August; uncommon to locally abundant from October to April.

Habitat: along coastal and continental shelf waters, usually farther offshore than Common Murres; harbours and coastal bays in winter.

Nesting: in colonies on cliff ledges; 1 pale egg with variable dark markings is laid on bare rock and incubated by both parents for 30–35 days.

Feeding: dives deeply for fish, crustaceans and occasionally marine worms and squid.

Voice: guttural calls range from a faint *urr* to a loud *aargh*.

Similar Species: *Common Murre* (p. 169): streaked flanks; chocolate-brown upperparts; more white on head and neck in non-breeding plumage. *Razorbill* (p. 171): thicker bill with vertical white line; more white on head and neck in non-breeding plumage. *Dovekie* (p. 168): much smaller; thick neck; very short bill.

Best Sites: *Summer: NF:* Witless Bay; Cape St. Mary's. *PQ:* Île Bonaventure; Bird Rocks (Îles de la Madeleine). *In migration* and *winter:* more widespread, especially in NF.

RAZORBILL
Alca torda

This bird's sharp bill is well adapted for capturing slippery fish. As the Razorbill "flies" underwater with its powerful wings, it may catch several fish in its large mouth in a single dive. One of the larger species of alcids, the Razorbill also routinely supplements its captures with fish pirated from other birds. • Like other alcids, the Razorbill moults all of its feathers at once, rendering it flightless at sea for a few weeks following the breeding season. • The Newfoundland name "Tinker" probably refers to this bird's habit of standing upright with its head held back like a deep thinker. This behaviour can easily be seen at the nesting ledge. • The Razorbill is believed to be the closest living relative of the extinct Great Auk *(Penguinus impennis)*, which had a colony at Grand Funk off the coast of Newfoundland.

breeding

ID: black upper-parts; white under-parts; tall, laterally compressed bill with 1 vertical white line; horizontal white line along top of bill; white trailing edge of wings. *Breeding:* black extends down neck. *Non-breeding:* white "cheek" and throat.
Size: *L* 43 cm.
Status: fairly common migrant from late September to early December and from March to April; locally uncommon breeder from late April to August; rare from mid-December to mid-April.
Habitat: concentrates over offshore shoals and ledges; nests on cliffs or rocky shore-lines and on islands.
Nesting: colonial; on a ledge or crevice of a cliff or in an abandoned burrow; usually

no nest material but sometimes a collection of pebbles and grass; pair incubates 1 pale egg with brown markings for 32–39 days.
Feeding: dives to 9 m for small fish, small crustaceans and marine worms; may steal fish from other auks.
Voice: generally silent; sometimes produces a grunting *urrr* call.
Similar Species: *Common Murre* (p. 169), *Thick-billed Murre* (p. 170) and *Black Guillemot* (p. 172): thinner bills lack vertical white line. *Dovekie* (p. 168): much smaller; short bill. *Shearwaters* (pp. 38–40): thinner bills; generally have brown or grey plumage instead of black.
Best Sites: *Summer: NB:* Machias Seal I. *NS:* Bird Is. *NF:* Cape Bonavista; Witless Bay; Cape St. Mary's; Cape Pine. *PQ:* Cap Bon-Ami; Percé; Île Bonaventure; Bird Rocks & Île Brion (Îles de la Madeleine). *In migration* and *winter:* widespread.

BLACK GUILLEMOT

Cepphus grylle

This is the alcid that you are most likely to see from shore. The Black Guillemot prefers feeding in shallower water than many other alcids. In its shallow dives it sometimes turns over rocks along the sea floor in search of prey. • This bird's common name is appropriate only during the breeding season—in winter its plumage is primarily white. In most of its North American range, the Black Guillemot is also known as "Sea Pigeon" because of its winter plumage and pigeon-like flight. • Alcid eggs are more conical in shape than the eggs of many other birds. Whereas elliptical eggs would likely roll off a rock ledge if set in motion, an alcid's eggs are more inclined to roll around in a circle, avoiding potential disaster.

breeding

ID: thin, black bill; reddish legs and feet; white under-wing in flight. *Breeding:* black overall with large, white wing patch. *Non-breeding:* white overall, with some black on back, wings and tail.
Size: *L* 33 cm.
Status: common breeder from mid-April to August; uncommon to locally abundant from September to early April.
Habitat: usually close to shore in relatively shallow water; sometimes far offshore; may feed on freshwater lakes near coast.
Nesting: may nest singly or in small colonies; along rocky shores, low cliffs and sometimes beaches; nest may be a scrape or a thin layer of pebbles or debris; pair incubates 1–2 pale eggs with dark spots for 23–39 days.
Feeding: may dive to 30 m but usually only to 9 m; feeds primarily on fish and crustaceans but will also take molluscs, insects, marine worms and some vegetation.
Voice: a drawn-out, high-pitched *see-oo* or *swweeeeeer.*
Similar Species: *Other alcids* (pp. 168–73): lack distinctive white wing patch; darker upperparts in non-breeding plumage.
Best Sites: nesting colonies are wide-spread, especially along the Gulf Shore of PQ and the Atlantic coasts of NS and NF.

ATLANTIC PUFFIN

Fratercula arctica

This sea bird is easily recognized by its colourful yellow, orange and grey bill. • When it brings food back to its young, the Atlantic Puffin can line up more than a dozen small fish crosswise in its bill. Its round tongue and the slight serrations on its upper mandible may help this puffin keep its hoard in place. Nonetheless, great skill must be required to continue to capture fish without losing all previous catches! • When the nestling is about 40 days old, the parents abandon it in the nest burrow. Following a week of fasting, the nestling ventures out to the ocean, fully capable of feeding itself. • This bird was previously known as "Common Puffin"; other names for it include "Sea Parrot," "Labrador Auk" and "Hatchet-Bill."

breeding

ID: *Breeding:* orange bill with triangular grey patch, bordered by yellow, at base of bill; white face; black crown, nape and upperparts; white underparts; orange legs. *Non-breeding:* grey bill base lacks yellow border; grey face.
Size: *L* 32 cm.
Status: locally common migrant from late August to late October; rare to locally abundant breeder from late April to mid-August; rare to locally uncommon from November to mid-April.
Habitat: *Breeding:* inaccessible coastal cliffs and offshore islands with turf; coastal and offshore waters. *In migration* and *winter:* open ocean, occasionally inshore.

Nesting: colonial; in burrows or in crevices among rocks; nest chamber lined with grass and feathers; pair incubates 1 white egg with dark markings for 39–42 days.
Feeding: dives to 15 m and sometimes even 60 m; takes small fish, crustaceans, molluscs and marine worms.
Voice: usually silent; may give a low, growling *arrr* at breeding sites.
Similar Species: *Dovekie* (p. 168): smaller; tiny bill; black head on breeding adults; black-and-white head pattern on non-breeding birds.
Best Sites: *NB:* Machias Seal I. *NS:* Pearl I.; Tusket; Bird Is. *NF:* L'Anse aux Meadows; Penguin Is.; Cape Bonavista; Cape Spear; Witless Bay; Cape St. Mary's; Cape Pine. *PQ:* Île Bonaventure; Bird Rocks & Île Brion (Îles de la Madeleine).

ROCK DOVE

Columba livia

R ock Doves were likely domesticated from Eurasian birds in about 4500 BC, as a source of meat. Since their domestication, these doves have been used as message couriers (both Caesar and Napoleon used them), as scientific subjects and even as pets. Much of our understanding of bird migration, endocrinology and sensory perception derives from experiments involving Rock Doves. • Introduced to North America in the 17th century, Rock Doves have settled wherever cities, towns, farms and grain elevators are found. Most birds seem content to nest on buildings or farm houses, but "wilder" members of this species occasionally nest in crevices on tall cliffs, which were this dove's original nest sites. • No other "wild" bird varies as much in coloration. This variability is the result of semi-domestication and extensive inbreeding.

ID: colour is highly variable (iridescent blue-grey, red, white or tan); usually has white rump and orange feet; dark-tipped tail. *In flight:* holds its wings in deep "V" while gliding.

Size: *L* 31–33 cm (male is usually larger).

Status: locally abundant year-round resident.

Habitat: urban areas, railway yards, agricultural areas; high cliffs provide a more natural habitat for some.

Nesting: on ledges of barns, cliffs, bridges, buildings and towers; flimsy nest of sticks, grass and assorted vegetation; pair incubates 2 eggs for 16–19 days; pair feeds the young "pigeon milk"; may raise broods year-round.

Feeding: gleans the ground for waste grain, seeds and fruits; occasionally eats insects.

Voice: soft, cooing *coorrr-coorrr-coorrr.*

Similar Species: *Mourning Dove* (p. 175): smaller; slimmer; pale brown plumage; long tail and wings. *Merlin* (p. 100): not as heavy bodied; longer tail; does not hold its wings in a "V"; wings do not clap on takeoff.

Best Sites: found everywhere except heavily forested areas and barren uplands.

MOURNING DOVE

Zenaida macroura

The soft coos of the Mourning Dove filter through Atlantic Canada's broken woodlands, farmlands and suburban parks and gardens. They are often confused with the sounds of a hooting owl. • Despite its fragile look, the Mourning Dove is a swift, direct flyer whose wings often whistle as it cuts through the air at high speed. • In Atlantic Canada, the largest concentrations of breeding Mourning Doves are among the abundance of open habitats, weed seeds and waste grain found in the Bas Saint-Laurent, Québec, and valleys of the Saint John River, New Brunswick. In recent decades, birdfeeders and cropland grain elsewhere have provided a food source for an increased number of wintering doves. • Juveniles have shorter tail feathers than adults. They are more likely to disperse to the parts of Nova Scotia and Newfoundland where Mourning Doves don't nest. • This bird's common name reflects its sad song. *Zenaida* honours Zenaide, Princess of Naples, the wife of Charles Lucien Bonaparte (the zoologist nephew of the French emperor).

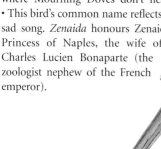

ID: buffy, grey-brown plumage; small head; long, white-trimmed, tapering tail; sleek body; dark, shiny patch below ear; dull red legs; dark bill; pale rosy underparts; black spots on upperwing.

Size: *L* 28–33 cm.

Status: common to abundant year-round resident in parts Atlantic Canada; less common breeding species but common migrant elsewhere, with some birds overwintering.

Habitat: open or riparian woodlands, woodlots, forest edges, agricultural and suburban areas and open parks; has benefited from human-induced habitat change.

Nesting: occasionally on the ground or in the fork of a shrub or tree; female builds a fragile, shallow platform nest from twigs supplied by the male; pair incubates 2 white eggs for 14 days; young are fed "pigeon milk."

Feeding: gleans the ground and vegetation for seeds; visits feeders.

Voice: soft, slow *oh-woe-woe-woe.*

Similar Species: *Rock Dove* (p. 174): stockier; white rump; shorter tail; iridescent neck. *Yellow-billed Cuckoo* (p. 177) and *Black-billed Cuckoo* (p. 176): curved bill; long tail with broad, rounded tip; brown upperparts; white underparts.

Best Sites: *Summer* and *in migration:* widespread in farmlands and open areas. *Winter:* at feeders and in sheltered areas.

BLACK-BILLED CUCKOO
Coccyzus erythropthalmus

Shrubby field edges, hedgerows, tangled riparian thickets and abandoned, over-grown fields provide elusive Black-billed Cuckoos with their preferred nesting haunts. Although they can be fairly common where they are found, Black-billed Cuckoos remain enigmatic to many would-be observers. They quietly hop, flit and skulk through low, dense deciduous vegetation in their ultra-secretive search for sustenance. Only when vegetation is in full bloom will males issue their loud, long, irregular calls, advertising to females that it is time to nest. After raising their young in a rather fragile nest, Black-billed Cuckoos promptly return to their covert lives. • The Black-billed Cuckoo is one of few birds that thrives on hairy caterpillars, particularly tent caterpillars. There is even evidence to suggest that Black-billed Cuckoo populations increase when a caterpillar infestation occurs. • This cuckoo is reluctant to fly more than a short distance during nesting, but it will migrate as far as northwestern South America to avoid the North American winter.

ID: brown upperparts; white underparts; long, white-spotted undertail; downcurved, dark bill; reddish eye ring. *Immature:* buff eye ring; may have buff tinge on throat and undertail coverts.

Size: *L* 28–33 cm.

Status: rare to irregularly fairly common breeder from mid-May to late July; birds move to the coast from mid-September to late October.

Habitat: dense second-growth woodlands, shrubby areas and thickets; often in tangled riparian areas and abandoned farmlands with low deciduous vegetation and adjacent open areas.

Nesting: in a shrub or small deciduous tree; flimsy nest of twigs is lined with grass and other vegetation; occasionally lays eggs in other birds' nests; pair incubates 2–5 blue-green, occasionally mottled eggs for 10–14 days.

Feeding: gleans hairy caterpillars from leaves, branches and trunks; also eats other insects and berries.

Voice: fast, repeated *cu-cu-cu* or *cu-cu-cu-cu-cu*; also a series of *ca*, *cow* and *coo* notes.

Similar Species: *Mourning Dove* (p. 175): short, straight bill; pointed, triangular tail; buffy, grey-brown plumage; black spots on upperwing. *Yellow-billed Cuckoo* (p. 177): yellow bill; rufous tinge to primaries; larger, more prominent, white undertail spots; lacks red eye ring.

Best Sites: *NB:* widespread. *PEI:* Carleton. *NS:* Truro; Granville Ferry; Seal I.; Whycocomagh. *NF:* Ramea. *PQ:* Rivière-du-Loup; Carleton–New Richmond area.

YELLOW-BILLED CUCKOO
Coccyzus americanus

Most of the time the Yellow-billed Cuckoo skilfully negotiates its tangled home in silence, relying on obscurity for survival. For a short period during nesting, however, the male cuckoo tempts fate, issuing a barrage of loud, rhythmic courtship calls. Some people have suggested that this species has a propensity for calling on dark, cloudy days in late spring and early summer. It is even called "Rain Crow" in some parts of its North American range. • In Atlantic Canada, the Yellow-billed Cuckoo is a rare sight unless you happen to live in southwestern New Brunswick, where a few pairs may breed each year. • In addition to consuming large quantities of hairy caterpillars, Yellow-billed Cuckoos feast on wild berries, young frogs and newts, small bird eggs and a variety of insects, including beetles, grasshoppers and cicadas. • Unlike distantly related Eurasian cuckoos, which lay their eggs only in other birds' nests, neither of the North American cuckoos is considered to be an "obligate nest parasite."

ID: olive-brown upperparts; white underparts; down-curved bill with black upper mandible and yellow lower mandible; yellow eye ring; long tail with large white spots on underside; rufous tinge to primaries.

Size: *L* 28–33 cm.

Status: rare breeder in southwestern NB from early May to August; sometimes locally uncommon along coastlines from mid-September to early November.

Habitat: semi-open deciduous habitats; dense tangles and thickets at the edges of orchards, urban parks, agricultural fields and roadways; some woodlots.

Nesting: on a horizontal branch in a deciduous shrub or small tree, within 2 m of the ground; builds a flimsy platform of twigs

lined with roots and grass; pair incubates 3–4 pale bluish-green eggs for 9–11 days.

Feeding: gleans insect larvae, especially hairy caterpillars, from deciduous vegetation; also eats berries, small fruits, small amphibians and occasionally the eggs of small birds.

Voice: long series of deep, hollow *kuks*, slowing near the end: *kuk-kuk-kuk-kuk kuk kop kow kowlp kowlp*.

Similar Species: *Mourning Dove* (p. 175): short, straight bill; pointed, triangular tail; buffy to grey-brown plumage; black spots on upperwing. *Black-billed Cuckoo* (p. 176): all-black bill; lacks rufous tinge to primaries; less prominent, white undertail spots; red rather than yellow eye ring; immatures have buff eye ring and may have buff wash on throat and undertail coverts.

Best Sites: *In migration: NB:* St. Stephen; St. Andrews; Grand Manan I. *NS:* Seal I. *NF:* Cape Ray; Argentia; Blackhead (Cape Spear); Cape Race; Ramea.

GREAT HORNED OWL

Bubo virginianus

This formidable, primarily nocturnal hunter uses its acute hearing and powerful vision to hunt a wide variety of prey. Almost any small creature that moves is fair game for the Great Horned Owl. This owl has a poorly developed sense of smell, which might explain, why it is the only consistent predator of skunks. • The familiar *hoo-hoo-hoooo hoo-hoo* that resounds through woodlands, suburban parks and farmyards is the call of these adaptable and superbly camouflaged owls. Great Horned Owls often begin their courtship as early as January, at which time their hooting calls make them quite conspicuous. Males initiate the calling sequences and females reply, usually at a higher pitch. By February and March, females are already incubating eggs. The pair continue to feed the young, both in and out of the nest, well into autumn. • The large eyes of owls are fixed in place, so to look up, down or to the side, they must move their entire heads.

ID: yellow eyes; tall "ear" tufts are set wide apart on head; fine, horizontal barring on breast; facial disc is outlined in black and is often rusty orange in colour; white "chin"; heavily mottled grey, brown and black upperparts; overall plumage varies from light grey to dark brown.
Size: *L* 46–64 cm; *W* 91–152 cm.
Status: fairly common to common year-round resident.
Habitat: fragmented forests, agricultural areas, woodlots, meadows, riparian woodlands, wooded suburban parks and the wooded edges of landfills and town dumps; absent from the interior of large areas of continuous forest.
Nesting: in the abandoned stick nest of another bird; may also nest on cliffs; adds little or no material to the nest; mostly the female incubates 2–3 dull whitish eggs for 28–35 days; the pair continue to feed their young well into autumn.
Feeding: mostly nocturnal but also hunts at dusk or by day in winter; usually swoops from a perch; eats small mammals, birds, snakes, amphibians and even fish.
Voice: 4–6 deep hoots during the breeding season: *hoo-hoo-hoooo hoo-hoo* or *eat-my-food, I'll-eat you*; male gives higher-pitched hoots.
Similar Species: *Long-eared Owl* (p. 182): smaller; thinner; vertical breast streaks; "ear" tufts are close together. *Eastern Screech-Owl:* much smaller; vertical breast streaks. *Short-eared Owl* (p. 183) and *Barred Owl* (p. 181): no "ear" tufts.
Best Sites: common throughout in mixed and conifer woodlands, often in suburban sites and sometimes in urban parks.

SNOWY OWL
Nyctea scandiaca

When the mercury drops and the landscape hardens in winter's icy grip, ghostly white Snowy Owls may appear on fence posts, utility poles, fields and shorelines throughout Atlantic Canada. Most of the birds we see are immatures, which are forced to wander much farther south and east than adults in times of prey shortage. Snow cover is not a prerequisite for a Snowy Owl visit—many of these birds perch conspicuously on earth-tone fields and coastal spits. • Feathered to the toes, a Snowy Owl can remain active at low temperatures that often send other owls to the woods for shelter. Unlike most owls, Snowies will often fly over open water to catch wintering alcids or small gulls feeding in narrow channels among winter ice. • Snowy Owls are annual visitors to Atlantic Canada, but their numbers can fluctuate quite dramatically. When lemming and vole populations in the Arctic crash, large numbers of Snowy Owls venture south in search of food.

ID: predominantly white; yellow eyes; black bill and talons; no "ear" tufts. *Male:* almost entirely white, with very little dark flecking. *Female:* prominent dark barring or flecking on breast and upperparts. *Immature:* heavier barring than adult female.

Size: *L* 51–69 cm; *W* 1.4–1.7 m (female is noticeably larger).

Status: irregular; rare to locally common winter visitor from mid-October to early May; a few birds may linger into midsummer at coastal sites.

Habitat: open country, including croplands, meadows, airports, coastal spits and shorelines; often perches on fence posts, buildings and utility poles.

Nesting: does not nest in Atlantic Canada.

Feeding: swoops from a perch, often punching through the snow to take mice, voles, grouse, hares, weasels and rarely songbirds, sea birds and water birds.

Voice: quiet in winter.

Similar Species: no other owl is largely white and lacks "ear" tufts.

Best Sites: *NB:* Tantramar Marshes. *PEI:* Rustico I.; East Point. *NS:* Advocate; Hartlen's Point. *NF:* L'Anse aux Meadows; St. Anthony; Cape Bonavista; White Hills (St. John's); Cape Race. *PQ:* Pointe-au-Père; Ste-Flavie; Gaspé Bay; Percé; Îles de la Madeleine.

NORTHERN HAWK OWL
Surnia ulula

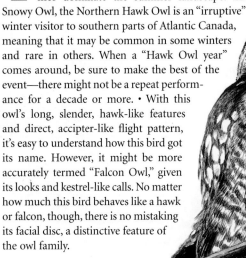

The Northern Hawk Owl resides in the northern boreal forest of the Gaspé, northern New Brunswick and Newfoundland, where treed bogs and black-flies dominate the summer landscape. Like the Snowy Owl, the Northern Hawk Owl is an "irruptive" winter visitor to southern parts of Atlantic Canada, meaning that it may be common in some winters and rare in others. When a "Hawk Owl year" comes around, be sure to make the best of the event—there might not be a repeat performance for a decade or more. • With this owl's long, slender, hawk-like features and direct, accipiter-like flight pattern, it's easy to understand how this bird got its name. However, it might be more accurately termed "Falcon Owl," given its looks and kestrel-like calls. No matter how much this bird behaves like a hawk or falcon, though, there is no mistaking its facial disc, a distinctive feature of the owl family.

ID: long tail; no "ear" tufts; fine horizontal barring on underparts; white facial disc is bordered with black; pale bill; yellow eyes; white-spotted forehead.
Size: *L* 38–43 cm; *W* 80–90 cm.
Status: rare to uncommon nesting species in northern parts of Atlantic Canada; rare winter visitor.
Habitat: black spruce bogs and muskegs, old burns and tree-bordered clearings.
Nesting: in an abandoned woodpecker cavity or an abandoned nest; adds no lining to the nest; female incubates 5–7 whitish eggs for 25–30 days.

Feeding: swoops from a perch; eats mostly voles, mice and birds; also eats some large insects in summer.
Voice: usually quiet; whistled, purring breeding trill; call is an accipiter-like *kee-kee-kee*.
Similar Species: *Boreal* (p. 184), *Northern Saw-whet* (p. 185) and *Short-eared* (p. 183) *owls:* much shorter tails; vertical breast streaks. *Merlin* (p. 100): smaller; shorter tail; lacks facial disc.
Best Sites: *NB:* Miscou I.; Miramichi; Fundy NP; McGowans Corner–Jemseg area. *NS:* Cape Split; Cape North. *NF:* Corner Brook; Gros Morne NP; Daniel's Harbour; Cape Norman. *PQ:* Parc de la Gaspésie.

BARRED OWL

Strix varia

Each spring, the memorable sound of courting Barred Owls echoes through our forests: *Who cooks for you? Who cooks for you all?* The escalating laughs, hoots and gargling howls reinforce the bond between pairs. They tend to be more vocal during early evening or early morning when the moon is full and the air is calm. At the height of courtship and when they are raising their young, a pair of Barred Owls may continue to call well into daylight hours. • Barred Owls are usually most active between 12 AM and 4 AM, when the forest floor rustles with the movements of mice, voles and shrews. These birds' eyesight in darkness is 100 times as keen as that of humans, and they are able to locate prey using sound alone. During the nesting season, Barred Owls may hunt actively day and night. • Barred Owls have relatively weak talons, and they mainly prey on smaller animals, such as voles. Nonetheless, they sometimes take small birds and even smaller owls.

ID: dark eyes; horizontal barring around neck and upper breast; vertical streaking on belly; light-coloured bill; no "ear" tufts; dark grey-brown mottled plumage.
Size: *L* 43–61 cm; *W* 1.0–1.3 m (female is slightly larger).
Status: uncommon year-round resident.
Habitat: mature coniferous and mixed-wood forests, especially in dense stands near swamps, streams and lakes.
Nesting: in a natural tree cavity, broken treetop or abandoned stick nest; adds very little to the nest; female incubates 2–3 white eggs for 28–33 days; male feeds the incubating female.

Feeding: nocturnal; swoops from a perch to pounce on prey; eats mostly mice, voles and squirrels; also eats amphibians and smaller birds.
Voice: most characteristic of all the owls; loud, hooting, rhythmic, laughing call is heard mostly in spring but also throughout the year: *Who cooks for you? Who cooks for you all?*
Similar Species: *Northern Hawk Owl* (p. 180): yellow eyes; finely barred underparts. *Great Horned Owl* (p. 178): "ear" tufts; light-coloured eyes. *Short-eared Owl* (p. 183): yellow eyes; lacks horizontal barring on upper breast.
Best Sites: widespread in woodlands at the bottom of slopes; occasionally in larger urban parks with wet areas.

LONG-EARED OWL
Asio otus

Long-eared Owls are widespread and probably fairly common throughout much of the Maritime provinces. Most residents often overlook these birds, however, because of their cryptic plumage and reclusive habits. Only at dusk do these owls emerge from their secret hideouts to prey upon the small creatures of the night. Long-eared Owls are most noticeable during the winter months in Nova Scotia and southern parts of New Brunswick, where they roost in woodlots, hedgerows or isolated tree groves. They usually roost in groups, sometimes with Short-eared Owls.
• To scare off an intruder, the Long-eared Owl expands its air sacs, puffs its feathers and spreads its wings. To hide from an intruder, it takes the opposite approach—it flattens its feathers and compresses itself into a long, thin vertical form. • All owls, as well as many other birds, including herons, gulls, crows and hawks, regurgitate "pellets." A pellet consists of the indigestible parts of the bird's prey, compressed into an elongated ball. The feathers, fur and bones that make up pellets are interesting to analyze, because they reveal what the animal has eaten.

ID: long "ear" tufts are relatively close-set; slim body; vertical belly markings; rusty brown facial disc; mottled, brown plumage; yellow eyes; white around bill.
Size: L 33–41 cm; W 91–120 cm.
Status: uncommon to locally common migrant and winter visitor from September to April; rare to locally uncommon breeder.
Habitat: *Breeding:* dense coniferous, mixed and riparian forests and areas with tall shrubs. *Winter:* woodlots, dense riparian woodlands and hedgerows; isolated tree groves in meadows, fields, cemeteries, farmyards or parks.
Nesting: sometimes in loose colonies; often in an abandoned hawk or crow nest; female incubates 2–6 white eggs for 26–28 days; male feeds the incubating female.

Feeding: nocturnal; flies low, pouncing on prey from the air; eats mostly voles and mice, occasionally eats shrews, moles, small rabbits, small birds and amphibians.
Voice: breeding call is a low, soft, ghostly *quoo-quoo*; alarm call is *weck-weck-weck*; also issues various shrieks, hisses, whistles, barks, hoots and dove-like coos.
Similar Species: *Great Horned Owl* (p. 178): much larger; "ear" tufts are set farther apart; stout body; rounder face. *Short-eared Owl* (p. 183): lacks long "ear" tufts; nests on the ground. *Eastern Screech-Owl:* much shorter, stout body; shorter, wider-set "ear" tufts.
Best Sites: *Summer* and *in migration: NB:* St. Jacques; Inkerman; Miscou I.; McAdam; Plaster Rock. *PEI:* Morell. *NS:* Grand Pré; Wolfville Ridge; Roseway River; Hopewell; French Mountain (Cape Breton Highlands NP). *PQ:* Grande-Entrée (Îles de la Madeleine).

SHORT-EARED OWL

Asio flammeus

Like the Snowy Owl, the Short-eared Owl lacks conspicuous "ear" tufts and fills the open areas left unoccupied by forest-dwelling owls. It can be surprisingly difficult to locate, especially during the breeding season, when females sit tightly on their ground nests. • In spring, pairs perform visually dramatic courtship dances. Courting pairs fly together, and the male claps his relatively long wings together on each downstroke as he periodically performs short dives. Short-eared Owls do not "hoot" like forest-dwelling owls because visual displays are a more effective means of communication in open environments. • As with many other predators, Short-eared Owl populations increase and decline over many years in response to dramatic fluctuations in prey availability. Cold weather and decreases in small mammal populations occasionally force large numbers of these owls, especially immatures, to become temporary nomads, often sending them to areas well outside their breeding range. • Short-ears often form colonial winter roosts on the ground in meadows and ditches.

ID: yellow eyes set in black sockets; heavy vertical streaking on buff belly; straw-coloured upperparts; short "ear" tufts are inconspicuous. *In flight:* dark wrist crescents; deep wingbeats; long wings.
Size: *L* 33–43 cm; *W* 1.0–1.2 m (female is slightly larger).
Status: uncommon to locally fairly common migrant and winter visitor from early October to April; rare to uncommon breeder from April to September.
Habitat: open areas, including grasslands, wet meadows, marshes, fields, airports, forest clearings, muskeg and open bogs.
Nesting: on wet ground in open areas; a slight depression is sparsely lined with grass; female incubates 4–7 white eggs for 24–37 days; male feeds the incubating female.
Feeding: forages while flying low over marshes, wet meadows and tall vegetation; pounces on prey from the air; eats mostly voles and other small rodents; also takes insects, small birds and amphibians.
Voice: generally quiet; produces a soft *toot-toot-toot* during the breeding season; also squeals and barks like a small dog.
Similar Species: *Long-eared Owl* (p. 182) and *Great Horned Owl* (p. 178): long "ear" tufts; rarely hunt during the day. *Barred Owl* (p. 181): dark eyes; horizontal barring on upper breast; nocturnal hunter.
Best Sites: *Summer:* coastal marshes and dunes. *In migration* and *winter:* more widespread, often in interior fields and farmlands.

BOREAL OWL
Aegolius funereus

The Boreal Owl routinely ranks in the top five of the most desired species to see, according to birdwatcher surveys across North America. Because of the Boreal Owl's remote habitat and nocturnal habits, ornithologists have yet to uncover many aspects of its ecology and behaviour. • This small owl is known to be well adapted to snowy forest environments—it is quite capable of locating and catching prey that lives beneath the snow. In winter, the Boreal Owl may depart from its secretive, nocturnal summertime activities in dense forest to visit more open woodlands and even suburban gardens. It may even roost in bird feeders or nest boxes! • Unfledged young leave the confines of their nest hole after a month and climb tree trunks by using their claws and bill.

ID: small; rounded head; whitish face with dark border; white spots on black forehead; yellowish bill; vertical, rusty streaks on underparts; white-spotted, brown upperparts; black eyebrow; short tail. *Immature:* brown underparts; brown face with white between eyes.
Size: *L* 23–31 cm; *W* 55–74 cm.
Status: rare breeder from mid-March to August; locally uncommon migrant and winter visitor outside breeding range from September to March.
Habitat: *Breeding:* mature coniferous and mixed forests. *In migration* and *winter:* more open woodlands, suburban gardens and parklands; coastal scrub, especially on headlands and islands.
Nesting: in an abandoned woodpecker cavity or natural hollow in a tree; lines the

cavity with a few feathers; female incubates 4–6 white eggs for 26–32 days; male feeds the incubating female.
Feeding: swoops from a perch for voles, mice, shrews, flying squirrels and insects; often plunges through the snow to catch prey in winter; may cache food.
Voice: rapid, accelerating, continuous whistle: *whew-whew-whew-whew-whew-whew;* easily imitated.
Similar Species: *Northern Saw-whet Owl* (p. 185): adult has dark bill, white forehead streaking and lacks dark, vertical eyebrow; immature has reddish underparts. *Northern Hawk Owl* (p. 180): much longer tail; fine horizontal barring on underparts.
Best Sites: *Summer* and *in migration: NB:* Miscou I.; Pointe Sapin. *NS:* Hopewell; Cape North. *NF:* Big Brook & Ochre Hill (Terra Nova NP). *PQ:* Pointe-au-Père; Réserve Matane; Parc de la Gaspésie; Cap Gaspé; Grosse Île (Îles de la Madeleine).

NORTHERN SAW-WHET OWL

Aegolius acadicus

The Northern Saw-whet Owl's call, for which it was named, can be uttered for several minutes. The call is difficult to locate when the calling bird rotates its head to mask its location. • This tiny owl is an opportunistic hunter, taking whatever it can, whenever it can. If temperatures are below freezing and prey is abundant, this small owl may choose to catch more than it can eat in a single sitting. The extra food is usually stored in trees, where it quickly freezes. When hunting efforts fail, a hungry Saw-whet will return to thaw out its frozen cache by "incubating" the food as if it were a clutch of eggs! • Predation by larger owls is relatively common, and martens are a major problem where they occur. • Saw-whets take readily to nest boxes, and young can be very noisy until they leave the nest. The young become cannibals if food supplies are scarce. • The scientific name *acadicus* is Latin for "from Acadia," the region where this bird was first collected.

ID: small body; large, rounded head; light, unbordered facial disc; dark bill; vertical, rusty streaks on underparts; brown, white-spotted upperparts; white-streaked forehead; short tail. *Immature:* white patch between eyes; rich brown head and breast; buff-brown belly.

Size: *L* 18–23 cm; *W* 43–55 cm.

Status: rare to uncommon year-round resident; rare to locally uncommon migrant and winter visitor from mid-October to late March.

Habitat: *Breeding:* pure and mixed coniferous and deciduous forests; wooded city parks and ravines. *In migration* and *winter:* coastal scrub on headlands and islands; suburban parklands and gardens.

Nesting: in an abandoned woodpecker cavity or natural hollow in a tree; female incubates 5–6 white eggs for 27–29 days; male feeds the incubating female.

Feeding: swoops from a perch; eats mostly mice and voles; also eats larger insects, songbirds, shrews, moles and occasionally amphibians; may cache food.

Voice: whistled, evenly spaced notes are repeated about 100 times per minute: *whew-whew-whew-whew...*; continuous and easily imitated.

Similar Species: *Boreal Owl* (p. 184): adult has light-coloured bill, white spotting on black forehead, dark vertical eyebrow and dark border to facial disc; immature has dark chocolate brown breast. *Northern Hawk Owl* (p. 180): much longer tail; fine horizontal barring on underparts; white spotting on black forehead.

Best Sites: *Summer* and *in migration: NB:* widespread. *PEI:* Crapaud; East Point. *NS:* Debert; Jeremy Bay (Kejimkujik NP); Roseway River; Sackville–Fall River area; Hopewell. *PQ:* Rimouski; Lac des Joncs (St-Fabien).

COMMON NIGHTHAWK

Chordeiles minor

Each May and June, the male Common Nighthawk flies high above forest clearings, lakeshores and often townsites, gaining elevation in preparation for the climax of his noisy aerial dance. From a great height, the male will dive swiftly. Then he thrusts his wings forward in a final braking action as he strains to pull out of the steep dive. This quick thrust of the wings produces a deep, hollow *vroom* that attracts female nighthawks. • Like other members of the nightjar family, the Common Nighthawk is adapted for catching insects in mid-air: its gaping mouth is surrounded by feather shafts that funnel insects into its mouth. • Nighthawks are generally less nocturnal than other nightjars, but they still spend most of the daylight hours resting on a tree limb or on the ground. They sit along the length of tree branches, rather than across the branch the way most perched birds do.

ID: cryptic, mottled plumage; barred underparts. *Male:* white throat. *Female:* buff throat. *In flight:* bold white patches on long, pointed wings; shallowly forked, barred tail; flight is erratic.
Size: *L* 22–25 cm.
Status: uncommon spring migrant and breeder from May to August; fairly common to locally common autumn migrant from mid-August to early September; a few may remain into October.
Habitat: *Breeding:* in forest openings as well as burns, bogs, rocky outcroppings, gravel rooftops and sometimes fields with sparse cover or bare patches. *In migration:* any place where large numbers of flying insects can be found; usually roosts in trees, often near water.
Nesting: on bare ground; no nest is built; female incubates 2 well-camouflaged eggs for about 19 days; both adults feed the young.
Feeding: primarily at dawn or dusk, but will also feed during the day and night; may fly around street lights at night to catch prey attracted to the lights; catches insects in flight, often high in the air; eats mosquitoes, blackflies, midges, beetles, flying ants, moths and other flying insects.
Voice: frequently repeated, nasal *peent peent*; also makes a deep, hollow *vroom* with its wings during courtship flight.
Similar Species: *Whip-poor-will* (p. 187): less common; lacks white wrist patches; shorter, rounder wings; rounded tail.
Best Sites: in urban areas and close to water.

WHIP-POOR-WILL
Caprimulgus vociferus

This nocturnal hunter fills the late evening with the sound of its own name: *whip-poor-will*. Although it is heard throughout many of the open woodlands within its range, this cryptic bird is rarely seen. Because of its camouflaged plumage, sleepy daytime habits and secretive nesting behaviour, a hopeful observer must literally stumble upon it. Only occasionally is a Whip-poor-will seen roosting on an exposed tree branch or alongside a quiet road. • The Whip-poor-will is a member of the nightjar, or "goatsucker," family. During the days of Aristotle, there was a widely believed superstition that these birds would suck milk from the udders of female goats, causing the goats to go blind! • Within days of hatching, young Whip-poor-wills scurry away from their nest in search of protective cover. Until the young are able to fly (about 20 days after hatching), the parents feed them regurgitated insects.

ID: mottled, brown-grey overall with black flecking; reddish tinge on rounded wings; black throat; long, rounded tail. *Male:* white "necklace"; white outer tail feathers. *Female:* buff "necklace."
Size: *L* 23–25 cm; *W* 41–49 cm.
Status: locally rare breeder from mid-May to September; rare to uncommon migrant.
Habitat: ungrazed woodlands with open glades; woodland edges; small woodlots in migration.
Nesting: on ground, sometimes in dry leaf litter; mostly female incubates 2 brown-and grey-blotched, dull white eggs for 19–21 days; both adults raise the young.

Feeding: almost entirely nocturnal; catches insects in flight, often high in the air; eats mosquitoes, blackflies, midges, beetles, flying ants, and other flying insects; particularly partial to moths.
Voice: far-carrying and frequently repeated *whip-poor-will*, accented on the last syllable; most often uttered at dusk and through the night.
Similar Species: *Common Nighthawk* (p. 186): less rufous in plumage; longer, pointed wings with white bar; squared tail with white bar.
Best Sites: *NB:* Edmundston; Belledune–Jacquet River area; Miramichi; Cap St. Louis; Sackville; UNB Woodlot (Fredericton); Pennfield Ridge. *NS:* Kejimkujik NP; Seal I; Roseway River; Ohio River; Lake Echo. *PQ:* Penouille (Forillon NP).

CHIMNEY SWIFT

Chaetura pelagica

Chimney Swifts feed, drink, bathe, collect nesting material and even mate while in flight! Only the business of nesting and rest keep these birds off their wings. • Chimney Swifts are most conspicuous as they forage on warm summer evenings and during autumn migration, when huge flocks migrate south alongside large numbers of Common Nighthawks. • Chimney Swift populations appear to be declining throughout eastern North America, but the cause of this decline is unclear. Perhaps the answer lies on this bird's wintering grounds in South America. • These swifts once relied on natural tree cavities and woodpecker excavations for roosting and nesting, but they have adapted to living in brick chimneys. Several small towns in the Annapolis Valley of Nova Scotia and elsewhere boast the presence of nesting and roosting Chimney Swifts.

ID: brown overall; slim body and long, thin, pointed wings; squared tail. *In flight:* rapid wingbeats; boomerang-shaped profile; erratic flight pattern.

Size: *L* 11–14 cm; *W* 30–32 cm.

Status: common migrant from early May to early June and from mid-August to mid-September; a few may remain into early October; fairly common breeder from May to August.

Habitat: forages over cities and towns; roosts and nests in chimneys, and sometimes tree cavities in more remote areas.

Nesting: often colonial; nests deep in the interior of a chimney or tree cavity, or in the attic of an abandoned building; pair fixes a half-saucer nest of short, dead twigs to a vertical wall with saliva; pair incubates 4–5 white eggs for 19–21 days; both adults feed the young.

Feeding: flying insects are swallowed whole during continuous flight.

Voice: rapid, chattering call is given in flight: *chitter-chitter-chitter*; also gives a rapid series of *chip* notes.

Similar Species: *Swallows* (pp. 216–21): broader, shorter wings; smoother flight pattern; most have forked or notched tail.

Best Sites: abundant at traditional nighttime roosts, usually in chimney stacks.

RUBY-THROATED HUMMINGBIRD
Archilochus colubris

Ruby-throated Hummingbirds span the ecological gap between birds and bees—they feed on the sweet, energy-rich nectar that flowers provide and pollinate the flowers in the process. Many avid gardeners and birders have long understood the nature of this codependence and have planted native nectar-producing plants in their yards. Even non-gardeners can attract hummingbirds by maintaining a clean sugarwater feeder in a safe location. • Hummingbirds are briefly capable of achieving speeds of up to 100 kilometres per hour and are among the few birds that are able to fly vertically and in reverse. In straight-ahead flight, they beat their wings up to 80 times per second, and their hearts can beat up to 1200 times per minute. • Each year, Ruby-throated Hummingbirds migrate across the Gulf of Mexico—an incredible, non-stop journey of more than 800 kilometres.

ID: tiny; long bill; iridescent green back; light underparts; dark tail. *Male:* ruby red throat; black "chin." *Female* and *immature:* fine, dark throat streaking.
Size: *L* 9.0–9.5 cm.
Status: common migrant from mid-August to mid-September; a few may remain, usually at feeders, into late October; fairly common breeder from mid-May to early August.
Habitat: open, mixed woodlands, wetlands, orchards, tree-lined meadows, flower gardens and backyards with trees and feeders.
Nesting: on a horizontal tree limb; tiny, deep cup nest of plant down and fibres is held together with spider silk; lichens and leaves are pasted on the exterior walls; female incubates 2 white eggs for 13–16 days; female feeds the young.
Feeding: uses its long bill and tongue to probe blooming flowers and sugar-sweetened water from feeders; also eats small insects and spiders.
Voice: most noticeable is the soft buzzing of the wings while in flight; also produces a loud *chick* and high squeaks.
Similar Species: *Rufous Hummingbird:* hummingbirds in early winter are most likely to be of this species; exceptionally rare; male has red on flanks and back; female has red-spotted throat and reddish flanks.
Best Sites: often visits sugarwater feeders.

BELTED KINGFISHER

Ceryle alcyon

Many of Atlantic Canada's lakes, rivers, streams, marshes and beaver ponds are closely monitored by the boisterous Belted Kingfisher. Never far from water, this bird is often found uttering its distinctive, rattling call while perched on a bare branch that extends out over a productive pool. With a precise headfirst dive, the Belted Kingfisher can catch fish at depths of up to 60 centimetres or snag a frog immersed in only a few centimetres of water. • During the breeding season, a pair of kingfishers will typically take turns excavating the nest burrow. They use their bills to chip away at an exposed sandbank, and then they kick loose material with their feet to excavate the tunnel. Female kingfishers have the traditional female reproductive role for birds, but, like phalaropes, they are more colourful than their mates. • Alcyon (Halcyone) was the daughter of the wind god in Greek mythology; she and her husband were transformed into kingfishers.

ID: bluish upper-parts; shaggy crest; blue-grey breast band; white collar; long, straight bill; short legs; white underwings; small white patch near eye. *Male:* no "belt." *Female:* rust-coloured "belt" (occasionally incomplete).
Size: *L* 28–36 cm.
Status: common breeder from early April through late August; fairly common migrant from September to late October; sometimes overwinters at favoured sites along the coast.
Habitat: rivers, large streams, lakes, marshes and beaver ponds, especially near exposed soil banks, gravel pits or bluffs; occasionally feeds in brackish or salt water.
Nesting: in a cavity at the end of an earth or soft rock burrow, often up to 2 m deep, dug by the pair with their bills and claws; pair incubates 6–7 eggs for 22–24 days; both adults feed the young.
Feeding: dives headfirst, either from a perch or from hovering flight; eats mostly small fish, aquatic invertebrates and tadpoles.
Voice: fast, repetitive, cackling rattle, a little like a teacup shaking on a saucer.
Similar Species: *Blue Jay* (p. 212): more intensely blue; smaller bill and head; behaves in a completely different fashion.
Best Sites: near bodies of water; wintering birds are always close to open fresh water at coasts.

YELLOW-BELLIED SAPSUCKER

Sphyrapicus varius

Yellow-bellied Sapsuckers are conspicuous in May, when they perform their characteristic courting rituals. Their drumming differs from that of other woodpeckers—it consists of a loud roll with clearly separated taps at the end, like a motor running out of gas. • Lines of parallel "wells" freshly drilled in tree bark are a sure sign that a Yellow-bellied Sapsucker is nearby. A pair may drill a number of sites within their forest territory. As the wells fill with sweet, sticky sap, they attract insects. These birds then make their rounds eating both the trapped bugs and the pooled sap. Yellow-bellied Sapsuckers don't actually suck sap; they lap it up with a tongue that resembles a paintbrush. This variation of the typical woodpecker foraging strategy has proven to be quite successful for the Yellow-bellied Sapsucker.

ID: black "bib"; red forecrown; black-and-white face, back, wings and tail; large, white wing patch; yellow wash on lower breast and belly. *Male:* red "chin." *Female:* white "chin." *Juvenile:* brownish overall, but with large, clearly defined wing patches.

Size: *L* 18–20 cm.

Status: fairly common to common migrant and breeder from mid-April to mid-October; a few immatures may attempt to overwinter, but they are rarely seen after December.

Habitat: deciduous and mixed forests, especially dry, second-growth birch and aspen woodlands.

Nesting: in a cavity; usually in a live poplar or birch tree with heart rot; usually lines the cavity with wood chips; pair incubates 5–6 white eggs for 12–13 days.

Feeding: hammers on trees for insects; drills "wells" in live trees where it collects sap and trapped insects; also flycatches for insects.

Voice: nasal, cat-like meow; territorial and courtship hammering has a distinctive 2-speed quality; soft *vee-ooo* when alarmed.

Similar Species: *Red-headed Woodpecker:* juvenile lacks white patch on wing. *Downy Woodpecker* (p. 192) and *Hairy Woodpecker* (p. 193): lack large, white wing patch and red forecrown; red nape; white back. *Black-backed Woodpecker* (p. 195) and *Three-toed Woodpecker* (p. 194): lack white wing patch; yellow forecrown.

Best Sites: deciduous woods and woodlots dominated by white birch and aspen.

DOWNY WOODPECKER

Picoides pubescens

A regular patron of backyard suet feeders, this small and widely common bird is often the first woodpecker a novice birdwatcher will identify with confidence. Once you become familiar with this bird's dainty appearance, it won't be long before you recognize it by its soft taps and the brisk staccato calls that filter through your neighbourhood. These encounters are not all confusion free, however, because the larger, closely related Hairy Woodpecker looks remarkably similar.
• Like other members of the woodpecker family, the Downy has evolved a number of features that help to cushion the repeated shocks of a lifetime of hammering. These characteristics include a strong bill, strong neck muscles, a flexible, reinforced skull, and a brain that is tightly packed in its protective cranium. Another feature that Downies share with other woodpeckers is feathered nostrils, which serve to filter out the sawdust it produces when hammering.

ID: clear white belly and back; black wings are barred with white; black eye line and crown; short, stubby bill; mostly black tail; white outer tail feathers are spotted with black. *Male:* small red patch on back of head. *Female:* no red patch.
Size: *L* 15–18 cm.
Status: common to locally abundant year-round resident.
Habitat: all wooded environments, especially deciduous and mixed forests and areas with tall deciduous shrubs; most common where birch trees are widespread.
Nesting: pair excavates a cavity in a dying or decaying trunk or limb and lines it with wood chips; excavation lasts more than 2 weeks; pair incubates 4–5 white eggs for 11–13 days; both parents feed the young.

Feeding: forages on trunks and branches, often in saplings and shrubs; chips and probes for insect eggs, cocoons, larvae and adults; also eats nuts and seeds.
Voice: long, unbroken trill; calls are a sharp *pik* or *ki-ki-ki* or whiny *queek queek;* drums more than the Hairy Woodpecker and at a higher pitch, usually on smaller trees and dead branches.
Similar Species: *Hairy Woodpecker* (p. 193): larger; bill is as long as head is wide; no spots on white outer tail feathers. *Yellow-bellied Sapsucker* (p. 191): large white wing patch; red forecrown; lacks red nape and clean, white back. *Black-backed Woodpecker* (p. 195) and *Three-toed Woodpecker* (p. 194): larger; yellow forecrown; black barring on white back and sides.
Best Sites: common to abundant in open broadleaf and mixed woodlands, especially in birch stands; many birds move to feeders in winter.

HAIRY WOODPECKER

Picoides villosus

A second or third look is often required to confirm the identity of the Hairy Woodpecker, because to uneducated eyes it is often confused with its smaller cousin, the Downy Woodpecker. A convenient way to learn to distinguish one bird from the other is by watching for these woodpeckers at a backyard feeder. It is not uncommon to see both birds vying for food, and the Hairy is larger and more aggressive. • The secret to woodpeckers' feeding success is hidden in their skulls. Most woodpeckers have very long tongues—in some cases more than four times the length of the bill—made possible by twin structures that wrap around the perimeter of the skull. These structures store the tongue in much the same way that a measuring tape is stored in its case. In addition to being long and manoeuvrable, the tip of the tongue is sticky with saliva and is finely barbed to help seize reluctant wood-boring insects.

ID: pure white belly; black wings are spotted with white; black "cheek" and crown; bill is about as long as head is wide; black tail with unspotted, white outer feathers. *Male:* small red patch on back of head. *Female:* no red patch. *Juvenile:* more indistinct patterning, with brown instead of black.
Size: *L* 19–24 cm.
Status: uncommon to fairly common year-round resident.
Habitat: deciduous and mixed forests, usually in denser, more mature stands with conifers.
Nesting: pair excavates a nest site in a live or decaying tree trunk or limb; excavation lasts more than 2 weeks; lines the cavity with wood chips; pair incubates 4–5 white eggs for 12–14 days; both adults feed the young.

Feeding: forages on tree trunks and branches; chips, hammers and probes bark for insect eggs, cocoons, larvae and adults; also eats nuts, fruit and seeds; attracted to feeders with suet, especially in winter.
Voice: loud, sharp call: *peek peek*; long, unbroken trill: *keek-ik-ik-ik-ik-ik*; drums less regularly and at a lower pitch than Downy Woodpecker, always on tree trunks and large branches.
Similar Species: *Downy Woodpecker* (p. 192): smaller; shorter bill; dark spots on white outer tail feathers. *Yellow-bellied Sapsucker* (p. 191): large, white wing patch; red forecrown; lacks red nape and clean, white back. *Black-backed Woodpecker* (p. 195) and *Three-toed Woodpecker* (p. 194): yellow forecrown; black barring on white back and sides.
Best Sites: conifer and mixed forests; a few birds move to feeders in winter.

THREE-TOED WOODPECKER
Picoides tridactylus

The Three-toed Woodpecker is a quiet, inconspicuous bird. Although it may seem rare throughout much of its range, it is often fairly common in areas where standing dead trees are infested with wood-boring beetle larvae. • During the breeding season, this woodpecker builds its nest in rotting trees and snags. In winter, it is more likely to be seen in open areas and in scrubby coastal growth. • While foraging, the Three-toed Woodpecker chisels off large flakes of bark from old or dying conifers, exposing the red inner surface of the trunk. Eventually the trees take on a distinct reddish look and are skirted with bark fragments. • Both the Three-toed Woodpecker and the Black-backed Woodpecker have three toes rather than the usual four.

ID: inconspicuous, black-and-white barring down centre of back; white underparts; black barring on sides; predominantly black head with 2 narrow white stripes; black tail with black-spotted white outer tail feathers; 3 toes. *Male:* yellow crown. *Female:* black crown with occasional white spotting.
Size: *L* 21–24 cm.
Status: rare to uncommon year-round resident; irruptive, especially in winter.
Habitat: *Breeding:* spruce and fir forests, bogs and disturbed areas. *Winter:* coastal scrub.
Nesting: excavates a cavity, usually in a dead or dying conifer trunk; excavation can take up to 12 days; pair incubates 3–4 white eggs for 12–14 days; both adults feed the young.

Feeding: chips away bark to expose larval and adult wood-boring insects; occasionally eats berries and sap.
Voice: call is a low *pik* or *teek*; drumming is a prolonged series of short bursts; nestlings and fledglings are noisier than most woodpecker young.
Similar Species: *Black-backed Woodpecker* (p. 195): solid black back; unspotted, white outer tail feathers. *Hairy Woodpecker* (p. 193): clean white back; lacks dark barring on sides. *Yellow-bellied Sapsucker* (p. 191): large white wing patch; red forecrown; black "bib"; yellow-tinged underparts.
Best Sites: *NB:* Edmundston; Riley Brook–Nictau area. *PEI:* Summerside. *NS:* Lake Ainslie; Cape Breton Highlands NP. *NF:* Barachois Pond PP; Gros Morne NP; Ochre Hill (Terra Nova NP). *PQ:* Rimouski; Neigette; Parc de la Gaspésie.

BLACK-BACKED WOODPECKER

Picoides arcticus

E ven experienced naturalists can have difficulty finding the elusive, semi-nomadic Black-backed Woodpecker in remote, uninhabited tracts of boreal forest. Only during the brief courtship season does the male Black-backed Woodpecker advertise his presence by drumming on the top of a broken, standing dead tree or "snag." • This reclusive bird is most active in recently burned forest patches where wood-boring beetles thrive under the charred bark of spruce, pine and fir trees. When it forages on blackened tree trunks, its black-backed form can be difficult to spot, especially from a distance. • In years when food is scarce, this bird often moves beyond its normal breeding range, occasionally showing up in woodlots where it may, over several days or even weeks, totally strip a dead or dying tree in search of larvae. Sighting records suggest that large, irruptive southern invasions of Black-backed Woodpeckers and Three-toed Woodpeckers occur at six- to eight-year intervals. • The scientific name *arcticus* reflects this bird's largely northern distribution.

ID: solid black back; white underparts; black barring on sides; predominantly black head with white line below eye; black "moustache" stripe; 3 toes; black tail with pure white outer tail feathers. *Male:* yellow crown. *Female:* black crown.
Size: *L* 23–25 cm.
Status: uncommon to locally fairly common year-round resident; irruptive, especially in winter.
Habitat: coniferous forests, especially burned-over sites with many standing dead trees.
Nesting: excavates a cavity in a dead or dying conifer trunk or limb; excavation can take up to 12 days; pair incubates 4 white eggs for 12–14 days; both adults feed the young.
Feeding: chisels away bark flakes to expose larval and adult wood-boring insects; may eat some nuts and fruits.
Voice: call is a low *kik*; drumming is a prolonged series of short bursts.
Similar Species: *Three-toed Woodpecker* (p. 194): white back with black horizontal barring or spots; black spots on white outer tail feathers. *Hairy Woodpecker* (p. 193): clean white back; lacks dark barring on sides. *Yellow-bellied Sapsucker* (p. 191): black-and-whitish back; large white wing patch; red forecrown; black "bib"; yellow-tinged underparts.
Best Sites: mainly in flooded softwoods, especially black spruce, but also in coastal tuckamore thickets and timberline forests.

NORTHERN FLICKER

Colaptes auratus

Unlike most woodpeckers, the Northern Flicker spends much of its time on the ground, feeding on ants and other insects. It appears almost robin-like as it hops about in grassy meadows and fields and along forest clearings. • Like many woodpeckers, the Northern Flicker has zygodactyl feet—each foot has two toes pointing forward and two toes pointing backward. Stiff tail feathers help to prop up woodpeckers' bodies while they scale trees and excavate cavities. Flickers are often seen bathing in dusty depressions. The dust particles absorb oils and bacteria that are harmful to the birds' feathers. To clean even more thoroughly, flickers will squish captured ants and then preen themselves with the remains (ants produce formic acid, which can kill small parasites on the flicker's skin and feathers).

ID: brown, barred back and wings; spotted buff to whitish underparts; black "bib"; yellow underwings and undertail; white rump; long bill; brownish to buff face; grey crown. *Male:* black "moustache" stripe; red nape crescent. *Female:* no "moustache." **Size:** *L* 32–33 cm.

Status: abundant migrant and breeder from April to late October; rare to locally uncommon visitor from November to March.

Habitat: *Breeding:* open deciduous, mixed and coniferous woodlands and forest edges, fields, meadows, beaver ponds and other wetlands. *In migration* and *winter:* coastal vegetation, offshore islands and urban gardens.

Nesting: pair excavates a cavity in a dead or dying deciduous tree; excavation lasts for about 2 weeks; also uses nest boxes; lines the cavity with wood chips; pair incubates 5–8 white eggs for 11–16 days; both adults feed the young.

Feeding: forages on the ground for ants and other terrestrial insects; also eats berries and nuts; probes bark; occasionally flycatches; readily visits feeders for suet, seeds and berries.

Voice: loud, laughing, rapid *kick-kick-kick-kick-kick-kick; woika-woika-woika* issued during courtship.

Similar Species: *Red-bellied Woodpecker:* pattern on back is black and white; more red on head; dark underwings.

Best Sites: *Summer:* open woods and forest edges; suburban woodlots. *In migration:* local along coasts. *Winter:* at feeders.

PILEATED WOODPECKER

Dryocopus pileatus

With its flaming red crest, swooping flight and maniacal call, this impressive deep-forest dweller can stop hikers in their tracks. Using its powerful, dagger-shaped bill and stubborn determination, the Pileated Woodpecker chisels out uniquely shaped rectangular cavities in its unending search for grubs and ants. These cavities are often the first indication that a breeding pair is resident in an area. • These magnificent birds are not encountered with much frequency in other parts of eastern Canada. A pair of breeding Pileated Woodpeckers generally requires more than 40 hectares of mature forest to set-tle. In Atlantic Canada, the patchwork of woodlots and small towns limits the availability of continuous habitat, requiring Pileated Woodpeckers to show themselves more. They are often seen flying over urban areas. • As a primary cavity nester, the Pileated Woodpecker plays an important role in forest ecosystems. Other birds and even mammals depend on the activities of this woodpecker—ducks, small falcons, owls and even flying squirrels are frequent nesters in abandoned Pileated Woodpecker cavities.

ID: predominantly black; white wing linings; flaming red crest; yellow eyes; stout, dark bill; white stripe running from bill to shoulder; white "chin." *Male:* red "moustache"; red crest extends from forehead. *Female:* no red "moustache"; red crest starts on crown.
Size: *L* 41–48 cm.
Status: uncommon to locally common year-round resident.
Habitat: extensive tracts of mature deciduous, mixed or coniferous forest; some occur in riparian woodlands or woodlots in suburban and agricultural areas.

Nesting: pair excavates a cavity in a dead or dying tree trunk; excavation can take 3–6 weeks; lines the cavity with wood chips; pair incubates 4 white eggs for 15–18 days; both adults feed the young.
Feeding: hammers the base of rotting trees, creating fist-sized or larger, rectangular holes; eats carpenter ants, wood-boring beetle larvae, berries and nuts.
Voice: loud, fast, laughing, rolling *woika-woika-woika-woika;* long series of *kuk* notes; loud, resonant drumming; sounds similar to, but much louder than, the Northern Flicker.
Similar Species: *Other woodpeckers* (pp. 191–96): much smaller. *American Crow* (p. 213) and *Common Raven* (p. 214): lack white underwings and flaming red crest.
Best Sites: mixed mature woods and suburban woodlots; visits feeders in winter.

197

OLIVE-SIDED FLYCATCHER

Contopus cooperi

An early morning drive along any road in Atlantic Canada's boreal forests often reveals a most curious and incessant wild call: *Quick-three-beers! Quick-three-beers!* This interpretation of the male Olive-sided Flycatcher's courtship song may seem silly, but it is surprisingly accurate. Once nesting has begun, this flycatcher quickly changes its tune to an equally enthusiastic, but less memorable, territorial *pip-pip-pip*. Like other "tyrant flycatchers," Olive-sided Flycatchers are fierce defenders of their nests and will harass and chase off squirrels and other predators. • Perched high among the towering, lofty spires of spruce, tamarack and fir, Olive-sided Flycatchers have easy access to an abundance of flying insects that inhabit the sunny forest heights. These feisty birds are difficult to spot, so look for big-headed silhouettes. • Like all flycatchers, this olive-vested songbird perches with a distinctive, attentive, upright profile. Its ready-and-wait stance allows it to quickly launch out and snatch flying insects in mid-air.

ID: dark olive grey "vest"; light throat and belly; olive grey to olive brown upperparts; white tufts on sides of rump; dark upper mandible; base of lower mandible is dull yellow-orange; inconspicuous eye ring.
Size: *L* 18–20 cm.
Status: uncommon to locally fairly common breeder from June to early August; rare to fairly common migrant from early May to early June and from mid-August to early October.
Habitat: semi-open mixed and coniferous forests near water; burned areas and wetlands are preferred.

Nesting: high in a conifer, nest of twigs and plant fibres is bound with spider silk; female incubates 3 white to pinkish-buff eggs, with dark spots concentrated at the larger end, for 14–17 days.
Feeding: flycatches insects from a perch.
Voice: *Male:* chipper and lively *quick-three-beers!*, with the 2nd note highest in pitch; descending *pip-pip-pip* when excited.
Similar Species: *Eastern Wood-Pewee* (p. 199): smaller; lacks white rump tufts; grey breast; 2 faint wing bars. *Eastern Phoebe:* lacks white rump tufts; all-dark bill; often wags its tail. *Eastern Kingbird* (p. 205): lacks white rump tufts; all-dark bill; white-tipped tail.
Best Sites: wetter sites, especially flooded spruce forests, but also in burn areas.

198

EASTERN WOOD-PEWEE
Contopus virens

Perched on an exposed tree branch in a suburban park, woodlot edge or neighbourhood yard, the male Eastern Wood-Pewee whistles his plaintive *pee-ah-wee pee-oh* all day long throughout the summer. Some of the keenest suitors even sing their charms late into the evening, long after most birds have silenced their weary courtship songs. • Like other flycatchers, the Eastern Wood-Pewee loops out from exposed perches to snatch flying insects in mid-flight, a technique often referred to as "flycatching" or "hawking." • The Eastern Wood-Pewee is less aggressive and showy than most of its close relatives. • Many insects have evolved defence mechanisms to avert potential predators such as the Eastern Wood-Pewee. Some flying insects are camouflaged; others are distasteful or poisonous and flaunt their foul nature with vivid colours.

ID: olive grey to olive brown upperparts; 2 narrow white wing bars; whitish throat; grey breast and sides; whitish or pale yellow belly, flanks and undertail coverts; dark upper mandible; base of lower mandible is dull yellow-orange; no eye ring.
Size: *L* 15–16 cm.
Status: common migrant and breeder from early May to mid-September; some birds may arrive as early as mid-April and remain until early November, times when it is most likely to be seen beyond its breeding range.
Habitat: open mixed and deciduous woodlands with a sparse understorey, especially woodland openings and edges; rarely in open coniferous woodlands.
Nesting: open cup of grass, plant fibres and lichen, bound with spider webs; placed on the fork of a horizontal deciduous

branch well away from the trunk; female incubates 3 whitish eggs, with dark blotches concentrated at the larger end, for 12–13 days.
Feeding: flycatches insects from a perch; may also glean insects from foliage, especially while hovering.
Voice: *chip* call. *Male:* clear, slow, plaintive *pee-ah-wee,* with the 2nd note lower, followed by a down-slurred *pee-oh,* given with or without intermittent pauses.
Similar Species: *Olive-sided Flycatcher* (p. 198): larger; white rump tufts; olive grey "vest"; lacks conspicuous white wing bars. *Eastern Phoebe:* lacks conspicuous white wing bars; all-dark bill; often pumps its tail. *Eastern Kingbird* (p. 205): larger; white-tipped tail; brighter white underparts; all-dark bill. Empidonax *flycatchers* (pp. 200–03): smaller; more conspicuous wing bars; eye rings.
Best Sites: *Summer:* open broadleaf woodlands with glades. *In migration:* coastal second-growth.

YELLOW-BELLIED FLYCATCHER
Empidonax flaviventris

Deep within soggy, mosquito-infested bogs, fens and well-shaded coniferous and mixedwood forests you can expect to find the somewhat reclusive Yellow-bellied Flycatcher. In late spring and early summer, the male spends much of his time singing plain, soft, liquidy *chelek* songs and occasionally zipping out from inconspicuous perches to help reduce the insect population. Once nesting has begun, the male changes his tune to a slow, rising *per-wee*. He focuses his attention on defending his nesting territory and supplying food to his growing young. • The Yellow-bellied Flycatcher is the most elusive and secretive of the confusing clan of *Empidonax* flycatchers. It doesn't habitually perch in the open, except in migration, but it distinguishes itself from others by nesting on the ground and by its yellower underparts. Using a good pair of binoculars and paying close attention to fine details in plumage and voice should help you accurately identify this flycatcher.

ID: olive green upperparts; 2 whitish wing bars; yellowish eye ring; white throat; yellow underparts; pale olive breast.

Size: *L* 13–15 cm.

Status: fairly common to locally common breeder from May to August; fairly common migrant from mid-May to mid-June and from mid-August to late September.

Habitat: *Breeding:* coniferous bogs and fens and shady spruce and pine forests with a dense shrub understorey. *In migration:* coastal scrub and second-growth, especially along coasts and on islands.

Nesting: on the ground in dense sphagnum moss or in the upturned roots of a fallen tree; small cup nest of moss, rootlets and weeds is lined with grass, sedges and fine rootlets; female incubates 3–4 whitish eggs, lightly spotted with brown, for 12–14 days.

Feeding: flycatches for insects at low to middle levels of the forest; also gleans vegetation for larval and adult invertebrates while hovering.

Voice: calls include a chipper *pe-wheep, preee, pur-wee* or *killik. Male:* song is a soft *cheluck* or *chelek* (2nd syllable is lower pitched).

Similar Species: *Acadian, Willow* (p. 202), *Alder* (p. 201) and *Least* (p. 203) *flycatchers:* all lack extensive yellow wash from throat to belly; white eye rings; different songs; all but the Acadian have browner upperparts.

Best Sites: *Summer:* all types of closed forest, especially damp coniferous forests. *In migration:* common in coastal scrub.

ALDER FLYCATCHER

Empidonax alnorum

The Alder Flycatcher is relatively indistinguishable from other *Empidonax* flycatchers until it opens its small, bicoloured bill: with a hearty *fee-bee-o* or *free beer*, it reveals its identity. • This bird is well named, because it is often found in alder and willow shrubs. In fact, habitat choice can be important in its identification, because Yellow-bellied Flycatchers and Least Flycatchers are more likely to be seen in well-wooded areas. However, the Alder Flycatcher may have competition from the occasional Willow Flycatcher for control over dense, riparian alder and willow thickets. • Many birds have to learn their songs and calls, but Alder Flycatchers instinctively know the simple phrase of their species. Even if a young bird is isolated from the sounds of other Alder Flycatchers, it can produce a perfectly acceptable *free beer* when it matures. • The Willow Flycatcher is a close relative of the Alder Flycatcher, and these two species were grouped together as the "Traill's Flycatcher," until 1973.

ID: olive brown upperparts; 2 dull white to buff wing bars; faint, whitish eye ring; dark upper mandible; orange lower mandible; long tail; white throat; pale olive breast; pale yellowish belly.
Size: *L* 14–15 cm.
Status: fairly common to common migrant and breeder from mid-May to mid-September; some stragglers may be seen along the coast and on offshore islands until late October.
Habitat: *Breeding:* alder or willow thickets bordering lakes, streams or muskeg. *In migration:* any low growth, often with other flycatchers and warblers.
Nesting: in a fork in a dense bush or shrub, usually less than 1 m above the ground; small cup nest is loosely woven of grass and other plant materials;

female incubates 3–4 white eggs, with dark spots concentrated around the larger end, for 12–14 days; both adults feed the young.
Feeding: flycatches from a perch for beetles, bees, wasps and other flying insects; also eats berries and occasionally seeds.
Voice: snappy *free beer* or *fee-bee-o*; call is a *wheep* or *peep*.
Similar Species: *Eastern Wood-Pewee* (p. 199): lacks eye ring and conspicuous wing bars. *Willow Flycatcher* (p. 202): different song; mostly found in drier areas. *Least Flycatcher* (p. 203): bolder white eye ring; greener upperparts; pale grey-and-white underparts; different song and habitat. *Acadian Flycatcher* and *Yellow-bellied Flycatcher* (p. 200): yellowish eye rings; greener upperparts; yellower underparts; different songs and habitats.
Best Sites: alder and second-growth forest edges, often near water; more widespread in migration.

201

WILLOW FLYCATCHER

Empidonax traillii

Upon arriving in a suitable shrubby area with thick willows and tangled shrubbery, male Willow Flycatchers swing energetically on advantageous perches. They utter their characteristic sneezing *fitz-bew* call and battle vocally over preferred territories. Early spring is the only time these birds can be safely distinguished from Alder Flycatchers, because it is the only time that the two species sing very different songs.

• Once the boundaries are drawn and the business of nesting begins, Willow Flycatchers become shy, inconspicuous birds that prefer to remain out of sight. Only when an avian intruder violates an established boundary does the resident Willow Flycatcher aggressively reveal itself. By late August, the few birds that prospect in Atlantic Canada are already on their journey to Central and South America.

• Thomas Stewart Traill was an Englishman who helped John James Audubon find a British publisher for his book *Ornithological Biography* in the 19th century.

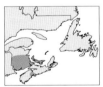

ID: olive brown upperparts; 2 whitish wing bars; no eye ring; white throat; yellowish belly; pale olive breast.

Size: *L* 14–15 cm.

Status: uncommon to locally common migrant and breeder from May to September.

Habitat: shrubby areas of hawthorn, apple, red-osier dogwood, willow or other low growth on abandoned farmlands and in riparian corridors.

Nesting: in a fork or on the branch of a dense shrub, usually 1–2 m above the ground; female builds an open cup nest with grass, bark strips and plant fibres and lines it with down; female incubates 3–4 whitish to pale buff eggs, with brown spots concentrated toward the larger end, for 12–15 days.

Feeding: flycatches insects; also gleans insects from vegetation, usually while hovering.

Voice: call is a quick *whit. Male:* quick, sneezy *fitz-bew* that drops off at the end; may sing up to 30 times per minute.

Similar Species: *Eastern Wood-Pewee* (p. 199): lacks eye ring and conspicuous wing bars. *Alder Flycatcher* (p. 201): different song; usually found in wetter areas. *Least Flycatcher* (p. 203): bold white eye ring; greener upperparts; pale grey-and-white underparts; different song and habitat. *Acadian Flycatcher* and *Yellow-bellied Flycatcher* (p. 200): yellowish eye rings; greener upperparts; yellower underparts; different songs and habitats.

Best Sites: *NB:* Cape Jourimain; Cap St. Louis (Kouchibouguac NP); Sussex; Keswick Ridge; Fredericton; Mactaquac; Castalia. *PEI:* Carleton. *NS:* Windsor Road.

LEAST FLYCATCHER

Empidonax minimus

This bird might not look like a bully, but the Least Flycatcher is one of the boldest and most pugnacious songbirds of Atlantic Canada's deciduous woodlands. During the nesting season, it is noisy and conspicuous, forcefully repeating its simple, two-part *che-bec* call, which many people in Québec say is an expression of its patriotism. Intense song battles normally eliminate the need for physical aggression, but feather-flying fights are occasionally required to settle disputes over turf and courtship privileges. • Even though it is not as colourful and glamorous as other songbirds, the Least Flycatcher is the most common and widespread *Empidonax* flycatcher in mature broadleaf woodlands in most parts of Atlantic Canada. • These birds often fall victim to nest parasitism by the Brown-headed Cowbird, whose hatched young often smother the much smaller Least Flycatcher nestlings.

ID: olive brown upperparts; 2 white wing bars; bold, white eye ring; fairly long, narrow tail; mostly dark bill has yellow-orange lower base; white throat; grey breast; grey-white to yellowish belly and undertail coverts.

Size: *L* 12–14 cm.

Status: fairly common migrant and breeder from early May to mid-September; occasionally at coastal locations and offshore islands until October.

Habitat: open deciduous or mixed woodlands; forest openings and edges; often in second-growth woodlands and occasionally near human habitation.

Nesting: in the crotch or fork of a small tree or shrub, often against the trunk; female builds a small cup nest with plant fibres and bark and lines it with fine grass, plant down and feathers; female incubates 4 creamy white eggs for 13–15 days; both adults feed the young.

Feeding: flycatches insects and gleans trees and shrubs for insects while hovering; may also eat some fruit and seeds.

Voice: constantly repeated, dry *che-bec che-bec.*

Similar Species: *Eastern Wood-Pewee* (p. 199): lacks eye ring and conspicuous wing bars. *Alder Flycatcher* (p. 201): faint eye ring; different song; usually found in wetter areas. *Willow Flycatcher* (p. 202): lacks eye ring; greener upperparts; yellower underparts; different song. *Acadian Flycatcher* and *Yellow-bellied Flycatcher* (p. 200): yellowish eye rings; greener upperparts; yellower underparts; different songs. *Ruby-crowned Kinglet* (p. 232): broken eye ring; much daintier bill; shorter tail.

Best Sites: mature hardwoods; more widespread in migration.

GREAT CRESTED FLYCATCHER
Myiarchus crinitus

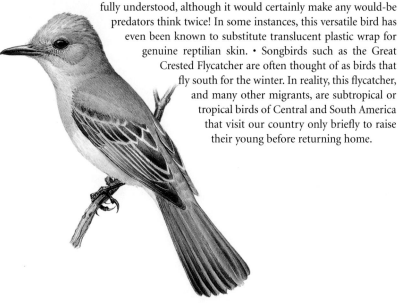

The Great Crested Flycatcher's nesting habits are unusual for a flycatcher: it is a cavity nester. Although natural tree cavities and abandoned woodpecker nests offer this bird a preferred nesting place, it will occasionally use a nest box intended for a bluebird. Once in a while, the Great Crested Flycatcher will even decorate the entrance of its nest with a shed snakeskin. The purpose of this practice is not fully understood, although it would certainly make any would-be predators think twice! In some instances, this versatile bird has even been known to substitute translucent plastic wrap for genuine reptilian skin. • Songbirds such as the Great Crested Flycatcher are often thought of as birds that fly south for the winter. In reality, this flycatcher, and many other migrants, are subtropical or tropical birds of Central and South America that visit our country only briefly to raise their young before returning home.

ID: bright yellow belly and undertail coverts; grey throat and upper breast; reddish-brown tail; peaked "crested" head; dark olive brown upperparts; black bill.

Size: *L* 20–23 cm.

Status: rare to locally uncommon migrant and breeder from mid-May to mid-October; some may remain into early November.

Habitat: deciduous and mixed woodlands and forests, usually near openings or edges.

Nesting: in a tree cavity, nest box or other artificial cavity, often lined with grass, bark strips and feathers; female incubates 5 creamy white to pale buff eggs, marked with lavender, olive and brown, for 13–15 days.

Feeding: often in the upper branches of deciduous trees, where it flycatches for flying insects; may also glean caterpillars and occasionally fruit.

Voice: loud, whistled *wheep!* and a rolling *prrrrreet!*

Similar Species: *Yellow-bellied Flycatcher* (p. 200): much smaller; yellow throat; lacks reddish-brown tail and large, all-black bill. *Western Kingbird:* all-grey head, neck and breast; acks head crest; darker tail with white outer margins. *Baltimore Oriole* (p. 304): immatures are generally browner on head and back, yellower on throat and breast and have pale blue bill and legs. *Ash-throated Flycatcher:* slightly smaller; duller plumage with paler yellow and rufous on body.

Best Sites: *NB:* widespread, except in l'Acadie. *PEI:* Balsam Hollow Trail (PEI NP); Murray River. *NS:* Wolfville Ridge; Grafton Lake Trail (Kejimkujik NP); Seal I.; Lake Echo; Chéticamp River; Ingonish. *PQ:* New Carlisle–New Richmond area.

EASTERN KINGBIRD

Tyrannus tyrannus

When you think of a tyrant, images of an oppressive dictator or large carnivorous dinosaur are much more likely to come to mind than a little bird. True as that might be, no one familiar with the pugnacity of the Eastern Kingbird is likely to refute its scientific name, *Tyrannus tyrannus*. This bird is a brawler, and it will fearlessly attack crows, hawks and even humans that pass through its territory. Intruders are often vigorously pursued, pecked and plucked for some distance until the kingbird is satisfied that there is no further threat. • Eastern Kingbirds are common and widespread in most of Atlantic Canada, so during a drive in the country it is likely you will spot at least one bird sitting on a fenceline or utility wire along a roadside. These birds can be very common close to the coast in migration, especially in late April and early May.

ID: dark grey to black upperparts; white underparts; white-tipped tail; black bill; small head crest; thin, orange-red crown (rarely seen); no eye ring; black legs.
Size: *L* 22 cm.
Status: common to very common migrant and breeder from mid-April to mid-September; a few remain until mid-October and rarely into early December.
Habitat: rural fields with scattered trees or hedgerows, clearings in fragmented forests, open roadsides, burned areas and near human settlements.
Nesting: on a horizontal tree or shrub limb; also on a standing stump or an upturned tree root; pair builds a cup nest of weeds, twigs and grass and lines it with root fibres, fine grass and fur; female incubates 3–4 darkly blotched, white to pinkish-white eggs for 14–18 days.
Feeding: flycatches aerial insects; infrequently eats berries.
Voice: call is a quick, loud, chattering *kit-kit-kitter-kitter;* also a buzzy *dzee-dzee-dzee.*
Similar Species: *Tree Swallow* (p. 217): iridescent, dark blue back; lacks white-tipped tail; more streamlined body; smaller bill. *Olive-sided Flycatcher* (p. 198): lacks white-tipped tail and all-white underparts; 2 white tufts above rump. *Eastern Wood-Pewee* (p. 199): smaller; lacks white-tipped tail and all-white underparts; bicoloured bill.
Best Sites: open fields and marshes close to water; often perched on roadside wires and fence posts.

NORTHERN SHRIKE

Lanius excubitor

Each autumn, Northern Shrikes retreat from their taiga breeding grounds and visit Atlantic Canada. During their winter visits, they typically perch like hawks on exposed treetops, surveying open and semi-open habitats. Winter feeding stations also tempt many shrikes to test their hunting skills on the feeding birds. • When this bird strikes a large target, it relies on its sharp, hooked bill to dispatch its quarry, although it may use its feet to help. It specializes in catching and killing small birds and rodents. • The adult Northern Shrike looks a little bit like a grey robin with the bill of a small hawk. The juvenile is buffish-brown and is more heavily barred below than the adult. • The Northern Shrike's habit of impaling its kills on thorns and barbs has earned it the names "Butcher Bird" and "Nine-Killer." *Lanius* is Latin for "butcher," and *excubitor* is Latin for "watchman" or "sentinel"—"watchful butcher" is an appropriate description of the Northern Shrike's foraging behaviour.

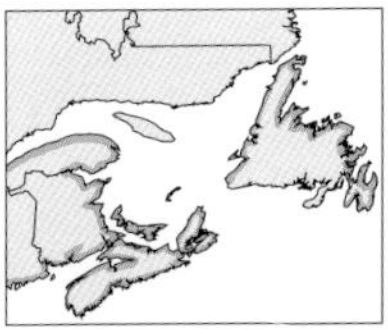

ID: black tail and wings; pale grey upperparts; finely barred, light underparts; black mask does not extend above hooked bill. *In flight:* white wing patches; white-edged tail. *Juvenile:* faint mask; light brown upperparts; brown or grey barring on underparts.

Size: *L* 25 cm.

Status: uncommon and erratic migrant and visitor from October to mid-May.

Habitat: open country, including fields, shrubby areas, forest clearings and roadsides.

Nesting: nests on coast of Labrador; in spruce, willows or shrubs; loose, bulky nest of sticks, bark and moss is lined with feathers and animal hair; female incubates 4–7 darkly spotted, greenish-white to pale grey eggs for 15–17 days.

Feeding: swoops down on prey from a perch or chases prey through the air; regularly eats small birds, shrews, rodents and large insects; may also take snakes and frogs; prey may be impaled on a thorn or barb for later consumption.

Voice: usually silent; infrequently gives a long, grating laugh: *raa-raa-raa-raa. Male:* high-pitched, hiccupy *hee-toodle-toodle-toodle* during summer.

Similar Species: *Loggerhead Shrike:* generally absent in winter; adult's mask extends above bill onto forehead; adult lacks barring on underparts; juvenile has barred underparts, crown and back. *Northern Mockingbird* (p. 244): slim bill; no mask; slimmer overall; paler wings and tail.

Best Sites: *NB:* Kouchibouguac NP; Cape Tormentine; Harvey; Cambridge-Narrows. *PEI:* Dalvay. *NS:* Chebucto Head; Cape North–Ingonish area; Louisbourg. *NF:* Gros Morne NP; Parson's Pond; South Glovertown; Cape Bonavista; Ferryland; Cape Race. *PQ:* Pointe-au-Père.

BLUE-HEADED VIREO

Vireo solitarius

The purposeful, liquid notes of the Blue-headed Vireo penetrate the dense foliage of mixedwood forests. During courtship, male Blue-headed Vireos fluff out their yellowish flanks and bob ceremoniously to their prospective mates. Once mating is complete and the eggs are in the nest, the parents become extremely quiet. Once the young hatch, however, Blue-headed parents will readily scold an intruder long before its approach. Blue-headed Vireos nest throughout most of Atlantic Canada. In Newfoundland, they are more likely to be seen as migrants. • The Blue-eyed Vireo prefers different habitat than many of its relatives, which prefer broadleaf trees or immature stands. • The distinctive "spectacles" that frame this bird's eyes provide a good field mark. They are among the boldest of the eye rings seen on our songbirds. • Until very recently, Blue-headed, Cassin's and Plumbeous vireos were lumped together as one species, the Solitary Vireo.

ID: white "spectacles"; 2 white wing bars; blue-grey head; olive green upperparts; white underparts; yellow sides and flanks; dark wings and tail have yellow highlights; stout bill; dark legs.

Size: *L* 13–15 cm.

Status: widespread but uncommon breeder and locally common migrant from late April to mid-October; a few may remain into December.

Habitat: *Breeding:* primarily remote mixed coniferous–deciduous forests; also pure coniferous forests and pine plantations. *In migration:* coastal woods and shrubby growth, sometimes gardens and urban parks.

Nesting: in a horizontal fork in a coniferous tree or tall shrub; hanging, basket-like cup nest is made of grass, roots, plant down, spider silk and cocoons; pair incubates 3–5 whitish eggs, lightly spotted with black and brown, for 12–14 days.

Feeding: gleans branches for insects; frequently hovers to pluck insects from vegetation.

Voice: *churr* call. *Male:* slow, purposeful, slurred, robin-like notes with moderate pauses in between: *chu-wee, taweeto, toowip, cheerio, teeyay.*

Similar Species: none.

Best Sites: *Summer:* mixed woods with a good conifer component. *In migration:* also on headlands well outside its breeding range.

WARBLING VIREO
Vireo gilvus

The charming Warbling Vireo lacks flashy field marks; it is only when this vireo moves from one leaf-hidden stage to another that it is readily observed. Searching treetops for this generally inconspicuous vireo may literally be "a pain in the neck," but the satisfaction of visually confirming its identity is exceptionally rewarding. Its bubbly, warbling song is often confused with the song of the Purple Finch, which may be found in the same habitat. • During their brief stay in Atlantic Canada, Warbling Vireos prefer mature deciduous trees as foraging and nest sites. In migration, however, they can be found in urban shade trees, second-growth, and alder and willow thickets, often with other vireos and warblers. • The hanging nests of vireos are usually much harder to find than the birds themselves. However, in winter nests are revealed as they swing precariously from bare deciduous branches.

ID: partial dark eye line bordering white eyebrow; no wing bars; olive grey upperparts; yellowish flanks; white to pale grey underparts; grey crown.

Size: *L* 13–14 cm.

Status: rare to uncommon but widespread breeder in NB, rare elsewhere, from late May to August; uncommon migrant throughout from late July to late September; a few remain until mid-November.

Habitat: *Breeding:* open deciduous woodlands and parks and gardens with deciduous trees. *In migration:* any kind of deciduous growth from tall trees to low willow and alder thickets, rarely tuckamore.

Nesting: in a horizontal fork in a deciduous tree or shrub; hanging, basket-like cup nest is made of grass, roots, plant down, spider silk and a few feathers; pair incubates 4 darkly specked, white eggs for 12–14 days.

Feeding: gleans foliage for insects; occasionally hovers to glean insects from vegetation.

Voice: *Male:* long, musical warble of slurred whistles.

Similar Species: *Philadelphia Vireo* (p. 209): yellow breast, sides and flanks; full, dark eye line bordering white eyebrow. *Red-eyed Vireo* (p. 210): black eye line extends to bill; blue-grey crown; red eyes. *Tennessee Warbler* (p. 250): blue-grey cap and nape; olive green back; slimmer bill. *Orange-crowned Warbler* (p. 251): yellow overall; slimmer bill.

Best Sites: *NB:* widespread in open woodlands and forest edges. *PEI:* Brackley Beach. *NS:* Seal I.; Antigonish; Margaree Valley. *NF:* Codroy Pond; Bear Cove Point. *PQ:* Ste-Blandine; Neigette; Ste-Anne-des-Monts.

PHILADELPHIA VIREO
Vireo philadelphicus

While many similar-looking birds sound quite different, the Philadelphia Vireo and the Red-eyed Vireo are two species that sound very similar but are easy to tell apart once you locate them with your binoculars. Most forest songbirds are initially identified by voice, however, so the Philadelphia Vireo is often overlooked because its song is almost identical to the more abundant Red-eyed Vireo. • The Philadelphia Vireo nests throughout maritime Québec, New Brunswick and southwestern Newfoundland. However, it shows up in all provinces in migration, usually along the coast and on islands. • This bird bears the name of the city in which the first specimen was collected. Philadelphia was the centre of America's budding scientific community in the early 1800s, and much of the study of birds and other natural sciences originated in Pennsylvania.

ID: grey cap; dark eye line, bordered by bold, white eyebrow; dark olive green upperparts; pale yellow breast, sides and flanks; white belly (underparts may be completely yellow in autumn); robust bill; pale eyes.
Size: *L* 12–13 cm.
Status: locally fairly common breeder in southern and western NB and uncommon breeder elsewhere from late May to early August; rare to uncommon migrant in mid-May to mid-June and from mid-August to early November.
Habitat: *Breeding:* open broadleaf and mixed woodlands with aspen, willow and alder components; second-growth on burns and cutovers. *In migration:* any deciduous growth, usually along the coast but occasionally in gardens and urban parks.

Nesting: high up in a deciduous tree or low in a shrub; basket-like cup nest hangs from a horizontal fork; nest is made of grass, roots, plant down and spider silk; pair incubates 4 white eggs, with dark spots on the larger end, for about 14 days.
Feeding: gleans vegetation for insects; frequently hovers to glean food from foliage.
Voice: the male's voice is like that of the Red-eyed Vireo, but it is usually slower, slightly higher pitched and not as variable: *look-up way-up tree-top see-me.*
Similar Species: *Red-eyed Vireo* (p. 210): black-bordered, blue-grey cap; lacks yellow breast; red eyes; song is very similar. *Warbling Vireo* (p. 208): partial, dark eye line (mostly behind eye); lacks yellow breast. *Tennessee Warbler* (p. 250): blue-grey cap and nape; olive green back; slimmer bill; lacks yellow breast.
Best Sites: open woods, edges, second-growth on cutovers and burns.

RED-EYED VIREO
Vireo olivaceus

The male Red-eyed Vireo is persistent in his pursuit and defence of a mate. In spring and early summer, a male will sing continuously through the day, continuing long after most songbirds have curtailed their courtship melodies, usually until five or six hours after sunrise. One particularly vigorous Red-eyed Vireo male holds the record for most songs delivered in a single day: approximately 21,000! • Red-eyed Vireos adopt a particular stance when they hop up and along branches. They tend to be more hunched over than other songbirds, and they hop with their bodies diagonal to their direction of travel. • There is no firm agreement about the reason for this vireo's eye colour. Most other vireos, as well as young Red-eyes, have brown irises. Red eyes are very uncharacteristic among songbirds and tend to be more prevalent in non-passerines, such as accipiters, grebes and some herons.

ID: dark eye line; white eyebrow; black-bordered, blue-grey crown; olive green upperparts; olive "cheek"; white to pale grey underparts; may have yellow wash on sides, flanks and undertail coverts, especially in autumn; no wing bars; red eyes in adults (seen only at close range).

Size: *L* 15 cm.

Status: common to very common migrant and breeder from early May to late October; some birds may remain in coastal locations and urban gardens and parks until mid-November.

Habitat: *Breeding:* deciduous woodlands with a shrubby understorey. *In migration:* any deciduous growth at coastal headlands, shade trees and shrubbery in urban parks and gardens.

Nesting: in a horizontal fork in a deciduous tree or shrub; hanging, basket-like cup nest is made of grass, roots, spider silk and cocoons; female incubates 4 white eggs, with dark spots around the larger end, for 11–14 days.

Feeding: gleans foliage for insects, especially caterpillars; often hovers; also eats berries.

Voice: call is a short, scolding *neeah. Male:* song is a continuous and variable, robin-like run of quick, short phrases, with distinct pauses in between: *look-up, way-up, tree-top, see-me, here-I-am.*

Similar Species: *Philadelphia Vireo* (p. 209): yellow breast; lacks black border to blue-grey cap; song is very similar (slightly higher pitched). *Warbling Vireo* (p. 208): dusky eye line does not extend to bill; lacks black border on grey cap. *Tennessee Warbler* (p. 250): blue-grey cap and nape; olive green back; slimmer bill.

Best Sites: mature broadleaf forests and parklands.

GRAY JAY

Perisoreus canadensis

Unexciting in plumage but bold and impudent by nature, the trustful and friendly Gray Jay wins over Atlantic Canadians as it steals their lunch. Some birds have even learned that a billycan of tea is always accompanied by something edible. • Gray Jays lay their eggs and begin incubation as early as late February. Their nests are well insulated to conserve heat, and getting an early start on nesting means that young jays learn how to forage efficiently and store food before the next cold season approaches. These birds' specialized salivary glands coat food with a sticky mucous that helps to preserve it. • This common bird was formerly known as "Canada Jay" because most of its range is within Canada. It also has some interesting alternate names: "Whiskey Jack" is derived from the Algonquin name for this bird, *wiskedjack*; others affectionately call this bird "Camp Robber."

ID: fluffy, pale grey plumage; fairly long tail; white forehead, "cheek," throat and undertail coverts; dark grey nape and upperparts; light grey breast and belly; dark bill. *Juvenile:* dark sooty grey overall; pale bill with dark tip.
Size: *L* 28–33 cm.
Status: uncommon to common year-round resident.
Habitat: dense and open coniferous and mixed forests, bogs and fens, picnic sites and campgrounds.
Nesting: on a branch in a conifer tree; bulky, well-insulated nest is made of plant fibres, roots, moss, twigs, feathers and fur; female incubates 3–4 pale grey to greenish eggs, marked with brown, greenish or reddish dots, for 17–22 days.
Feeding: searches the ground and vegetation for insects, fruit, seeds, fungi, bird eggs and nestlings, carrion and berries; stores food items at scattered cache sites; will visit feeders in hard times.
Voice: complex vocal repertoire includes a soft, whistled *quee-oo*, a chuckled *cla-cla-cla* and a *churr*; also imitates other birds.
Similar Species: *Northern Shrike* (p. 206) and *Loggerhead Shrike:* black mask; black-and-white wings and tail; hooked bill. *Northern Mockingbird* (p. 244): darker wings and tail; white patch in wings; white outer tail feathers; longer, slimmer bill.
Best Sites: in conifers, mixed woods, coastal tuckamore and upland bogs; visits suburban feeders in winter.

BLUE JAY

Cyanocitta cristata

The woodlots and bushy ornamental shrubs of Atlantic Canada's suburban neighbourhoods and rural communities are perfect habitat for the adaptable Blue Jay. Common wherever backyard feeding stations are maintained with a generous supply of sunflower seeds and peanuts, this jay is one of the most recognizable songbirds. • The Blue Jay embodies all the traits and qualities of the corvid family, which also includes crows and ravens. It is beautiful, resourceful and vocally diverse, but it occasionally raids nests and bullies other feeder occupants. • Whether on its own or gathered in a mob, the Blue Jay will rarely hesitate to drive away smaller birds, squirrels or even cats when threatened. There seems to be no predator, not even the Great Horned Owl, too formidable for this bird to cajole or harass. • Blue Jays often form loose flocks in migration and winter. What may appear to be a dozen or so individual regulars at a feeder are often, in fact, three or four parties "doing the rounds."

ID: blue crest; black "necklace"; blue upperparts; white underparts; white bar and flecking on wings; dark bars and white corners on blue tail; black bill.
Size: *L* 28–31 cm.
Status: common breeder from April to August; common to abundant migrant and winter resident.
Habitat: mixed and deciduous forests, agricultural areas, scrubby fields and woodlots; townsites in winter.
Nesting: in the crotch of a tree or tall shrub; pair builds a bulky stick nest and incubates 4–5 greenish, buff or pale blue eggs, spotted with grey and brown, for 16–18 days; young leave the nesting area immediately after fledging.

Feeding: forages on the ground and among vegetation for nuts, berries, eggs, nestlings and birdseed; also eats insects and carrion.
Voice: noisy, screaming *jay-jay-jay*; nasal *queedle queedle queedle-queedle* sounds a little like a muted trumpet; often imitates various sounds.
Similar Species: *Belted Kingfisher* (p. 190); larger; unpatterned face; breast band; very different habits. *Eastern Bluebird* (p. 235): smaller; brighter blue on upperparts; no white markings; reddish on breast.
Best Sites: *Summer:* deciduous and mixed woodlands; less common in conifers. *In migration:* forms loose flocks and can be common on headlands and alongside roads and river courses. *Winter:* common at feeders.

AMERICAN CROW

Corvus brachyrhynchos

American Crows are wary and intelligent birds that have flourished in spite of considerable human efforts, over many generations, to reduce their numbers because of the damage they do to crops. These birds are ecological generalists, and much of their strength lies in their ability to adapt to the variety of habitats provided by human settlement. Agricultural areas offer American Crows everything they need for nesting, feeding and roosting. These birds also thrive around lakes and coastal marshes. • Many American Crows make local migrations to more hospitable wintering sites, where hundreds of birds may roost together on any given winter night. The lengthening days of late winter entice American Crows to disperse and migrate northward to breed. Other birds do not migrate; they join gulls and ravens at landfill sites in winter. • *Corvus brachyrhynchos*, despite sounding cumbersome, is Latin for "raven with the small nose."

ID: all-black body; square-shaped tail; black bill and legs; slim, sleek head and throat.
Size: *L* 43–53 cm; *W* 94 cm.

Status: common to locally abundant resident, with noticeable local migration in winter.

Habitat: urban areas, agricultural fields and other open areas with scattered woodlands; also among clearings, marshes, lakes and rivers in dense forested areas.

Nesting: in a conifer or deciduous tree or on a utility pole; large stick-and-branch nest is lined with fur and soft plant materials; female incubates 4–6 brown- and

grey-blotched, grey-green to blue-green eggs, for about 18 days.

Feeding: very opportunistic; feeds on carrion, small vertebrates, other birds' eggs and nestlings, berries, seeds, invertebrates and human food waste.

Voice: distinctive, far-carrying, repetitive *caw-caw-caw*.

Similar Species: *Common Raven* (p. 214): larger; wedge-shaped tail; shaggy throat; heavier bill. *Gray Jay* (p. 211): smaller; juvenile is dark grey with longer tail; smaller, straighter bill.

Best Sites: *Summer:* in urban areas and all habitats except dense forest, subalpine areas and large bogs. *Winter:* roosts in towns and agricultural areas.

COMMON RAVEN

Corvus corax

The Common Raven is a crow that has convinced itself that it is a raptor. Whether stealing food from a flock of gulls, harassing a soaring hawk in mid-air, dining from a roadside carcass or confidently strutting among campers at a park, this bird is worthy of its reputation as a bold and clever bird. The Common Raven is glorified in native cultures across the Northern Hemisphere, perhaps because it exhibits behaviours that many people once thought of as exclusively human. • Breeding ravens maintain loyal, lifelong pair bonds, which are reinforced each winter in courtship chases consisting of drag races, barrel rolls, dives and tumbles. Pairs can be found gliding and soaring together and enduring everything from food scarcity and harsh weather to the raising of young. • Few birds occupy as large of a natural range as the Common Raven. Distributed throughout the Northern Hemisphere, it is found along coastlines, in deserts, on mountaintops and even on arctic tundra.

Status: common year-round resident; locally abundant in winter.
Habitat: coniferous and mixed forests and woodlands, townsites, campgrounds and landfills; arctic tundra.
Nesting: on steep cliffs, ledges, bluffs, tall coniferous trees and utility poles; large stick-and-branch nest is lined with fur and soft plant materials; female incubates 4–6 brown or olive-blotched greenish eggs for 18–21 days.

ID: black overall; heavy, black bill; wedge-shaped tail; shaggy throat; rounded wings.
Size: *L* 61 cm; *W* 1.3 m.

Feeding: very opportunistic; some birds forage along roadways; feeds on carrion, small vertebrates, other birds' eggs and nestlings, berries, invertebrates and human food-waste.
Voice: deep, guttural, far-carrying, repetitive *craww-craww* or *quork quork*; also many other vocalizations.
Similar Species: *American Crow* (p. 213): smaller; square-shaped tail; slim throat; slimmer bill; call is a higher-pitched *caw-caw-caw*.
Best Sites: in urban areas and forests; found in subalpine areas and mountains more than other corvids; garbage dumps attract large concentrations, especially in winter.

HORNED LARK

Eremophila alpestris

C alled "Shore Larks" in Europe, these open-country inhabitants are most common in migration and in early winter. At these times, they congregate on beaches, fields and any open country, often in the company of Snow Buntings and Lapland Longspurs. Their pale plumage makes them almost invisible in some of the sandy habitats they choose to inhabit. • Horned Larks are also common along the shoulders of gravel roads, where they search for seeds. However, they fly off into adjacent fields or open ground at the approach of any vehicle. • Birds of the *praticola* subspecies are among the earliest of the wintering birds to leave for arctic and subarctic breeding grounds. They are replaced by birds of the *alpestris* subspecies, which return from southern wintering sites to breed in Atlantic Canada. Breeding birds have paler plumage than the winter visitors. • Despite this bird's widespread choice of habitat, its scientific name, which means "lark of the mountains," refers only to its alpine haunts.

ID: *Male:* small black "horns" (rarely raised); black line under eye extends from bill to "cheek"; light yellow to white face; dull brown upperparts; black breast band; dark tail with white outer tail feathers; light throat. *Female:* duller plumage overall.

Size: *L* 18 cm.

Status: locally uncommon breeder from April through mid-August, mostly along coasts; common to locally abundant migrant and winter resident from late September to April.

Habitat: *Breeding:* open areas, including pastures, croplands, sparsely vegetated fields, weedy meadows, airfields, coastal barrens and subalpine tundra. *In migration and winter:* shorelines, dunes, croplands, fields, roadside ditches and fields.

Nesting: on the ground; in a shallow scrape lined with grass, plant fibres and roots; female chooses the nest site and incubates 3–4 pale grey to greenish-white eggs, blotched and spotted with brown, for 10–12 days.

Feeding: gleans the ground for seeds; feeds insects to its young during the breeding season.

Voice: call is a tinkling *tsee-titi* or *zoot*; flight song is a long series of tinkling, twittered whistles.

Similar Species: *Sparrows* (pp. 276–92) and *American Pipit* (p. 247): all lack distinctive facial pattern, "horns" and solid black breast band.

Best Sites: *Summer: NB:* Miscou I.; Tabusintac; Bouctouche; Salisbury; Sussex; Hartland; Grand Falls. *PEI:* Rustico I.; Pinette. *NS:* Kingston; Enfield. *NF:* Gros Morne NP; St. Paul's; L'Anse aux Meadows; Cape St. Mary's; Cape Race.

PURPLE MARTIN
Progne subis

Purple Martins are a local feature in parts of New Brunswick and Nova Scotia. They used to nest in natural tree hollows and cliff crevices, but with today's martin "apartment" complexes, these birds have all but abandoned natural nest sites. To be successful in attracting these large swallows to your backyard, a martin complex should be placed high on a pole in a large, open area, preferably near water. The apartment complex must be designed with perfectly sized cavity openings and should be cleaned out each winter. Purple Martins provide an endlessly entertaining summer spectacle. Adults spiral around the house in pursuit of flying insects, and juveniles perch clumsily at the opening of their apartment cavity. Unfortunately, there is always the chance that aggressive House Sparrows and European Starlings will chase away any Purple Martins that dare to move in. • *Progne* refers to the Pandion's daughter Procne, who, according to Greek mythology, was transformed into a swallow.

ID: dark blue, glossy body; slightly forked tail; pointed wings; small bill. *Male:* dark underparts. *Female:* sooty grey underparts.
Size: *L* 18–20 cm.
Status: locally uncommon breeder from late April to August; common migrant in April and September; a few may arrive as early as late March, and some may remain until late October.
Habitat: semi-open areas, including gardens and fields, almost always near water.
Nesting: communal; usually in a human-made, apartment-style birdhouse; rarely in tree cavities or cliff crevices; nest materials include feathers, grass, mud and vegetation; female incubates 4–5 white eggs for 15–18 days.

Feeding: mostly while in flight; usually eats flies, ants, bugs, dragonflies and mosquitoes; may also walk on the ground, taking insects and rarely berries.
Voice: rich, fluty, robin-like *pew-pew*, often heard in flight.
Similar Species: *European Starling* (p. 246): longer bill (yellow in summer); lacks forked tail. *Barn Swallow* (p. 221): deeply forked tail; buff-orange to reddish-brown throat; whitish to cinnamon underparts. *Tree Swallow* (p. 217): white underparts. *Blue Grosbeak* (p. 295) and *Indigo Bunting* (p. 296): smaller; males are brighter blue; rounded wings.
Best Sites: *NB:* Kouchibouguac NP; Cambridge-Narrows; Hammond River; Gagetown; Florenceville. *PEI:* North Cape. *NS:* Amherst; Southampton area; Margaree Valley; Chéticamp River. *PQ:* Trois-Pistoles; Gaspé Bay.

TREE SWALLOW

Tachycineta bicolor

Tree Swallows, our most common summer swallows, are often seen perched beside their fence-post nest boxes. When conditions are favourable, these busy birds may return to their young 10 to 20 times per hour, providing observers with numerous opportunities to watch and photograph the birds in action. • Tree Swallows prefer to nest in natural tree hollows or woodpecker cavities in standing dead trees. However, where cavities are scarce nest boxes are used as temporary sites. Increasingly, landowners, park managers and forestry companies are realizing the value of dead trees as homes for wildlife and are choosing to leave them standing. • Unlike other North American swallows, female Tree Swallows do not acquire full adult plumage until their second or third year. • In bright spring sunshine, the iridescent back of the Tree Swallow appears dark blue; prior to autumn migration, it appears green. • *Bicolor* is refers to the contrast between the bird's dark upperparts and light underparts.

ID: *Male:* iridescent, dark blue or green head and upperparts; white underparts; no white on "cheek"; dark rump; small bill; long, pointed wings; shallowly forked tail. *Female:* slightly duller. *Immature:* brown upperparts; white underparts.
Size: *L* 14 cm.
Status: common migrant and breeder from April to mid-October; a few may arrive as early as March; some may remain into mid-December.
Habitat: open areas, such as beaver ponds, marshes, lakeshores, field fencelines, townsites and open woodlands.
Nesting: in a tree cavity or nest box lined with weeds, grass and feathers; female incubates 4–6 eggs for up to 19 days.

Feeding: catches flies, midges, mosquitoes, beetles and ants on the wing; also takes stoneflies, mayflies and caddisflies over water; may eat some berries and seeds.
Voice: alarm call is a metallic, buzzy *klweet. Male:* song is a liquid, chattering twitter.
Similar Species: *Purple Martin* (p. 216): female has sooty grey underparts; male is dark blue overall. *Bank Swallow* (p. 219) and *Northern Rough-winged Swallow* (p. 218): brown upperparts. *Barn Swallow* (p. 221): buff-orange to reddish-brown throat; deeply forked tail.
Best Sites: *Summer:* urban areas, and fairly open woodlands with water courses and wetlands. *In migration:* estuaries and large lakes.

NORTHERN ROUGH-WINGED SWALLOW

Stelgidopteryx serripennis

The inconspicuous Northern Rough-winged Swallow typically nests in sandy banks along rivers and streams, enjoying its own private piece of waterfront. Rare in other parts of Atlantic Canada, it is widespread in western New Brunswick, especially along the banks of the Saint John River. Once in a while, a pair may nest among a large colony of Bank Swallows, but most are happy in the company of their own species. In the wheeling flocks of feeding birds, the Rough-wings are regularly completely overlooked among their similar-looking cousins. • Unlike other Canadian swallows, male Northern Rough-wings have curved barbs along the outer edge of their primary wing feathers. The purpose of this saw-toothed edge remains a mystery. The ornithologist who gave this bird its scientific name must have been very impressed with its wings: *Stelgidopteryx* means "scraper wing" and *serripennis* means "saw feather."

ID: brown upperparts; dark rump; light brownish-grey underparts; small bill; dark "cheek." *In flight:* long, pointed wings; notched tail.

Size: *L* 14 cm.

Status: rare to uncommon migrant and breeder from early May to mid-October, very few birds seen at other times.

Habitat: open and semi-open areas, including fields and open woodlands, usually near water.

Nesting: occasionally in small colonies; at the end of a burrow lined with leaves and dry grass; sometimes reuses kingfisher burrows, rodent burrows and other land

crevices; mostly female incubates 4–8 white eggs for 12–16 days.

Feeding: catches flying insects on the wing; occasionally eats insects from the ground; drinks on the wing.

Voice: generally quiet; occasionally a quick, short, squeaky *brrrtt.*

Similar Species: *Bank Swallow* (p. 219): dark breast band. *Tree Swallow* (p. 217): dark, iridescent bluish to greenish upperparts; clean white underparts. *Cliff Swallow* (p. 220): brown-and-blue upperparts; buff forehead and rump patch.

Best Sites: *NB:* Saints Rest Marsh (Saint John); St. George–Pennfield area; St. Andrews; Florenceville; Hartland. *NS:* Maitland Bridge; Ohio River; Roseway River; Shad Bay.

BANK SWALLOW

Riparia riparia

A colony of Bank Swallows can be a constant flurry of activity as eager parents pop in and out of their earthen burrows with mouthfuls of insects for their insatiable young. Not surprisingly, all this activity tends to attract attention, but few predators are able to catch these swift and agile birds. • Bank Swallows usually excavate their own nest burrows, first using their small bills and later digging with their feet. Most nestlings are safe from predators within their nest chamber, which is typically 60 to 90 centimetres in length. However, persistent diggers can reach the burrow from above as it is usually close to the top of a bank or cliff face. • In medieval Europe, it was believed that swallows spent winter in the mud at the bottom of swamps, because they were not seen during that season. In those days, it was beyond imagination that these birds might fly south for the winter. • *Riparia* is from the Latin for "riverbank," which is a common nesting site for these birds.

ID: brown upperparts; light underparts; brown breast band; long, pointed wings; shallowly forked tail; white throat; dark "cheek"; small legs.

Size: *L* 13 cm.

Status: locally common breeder from late May to early August; common migrant from late April to May and from late August to September; some birds may remain as late as mid-November.

Habitat: steep banks, shoreline bluffs and open areas, such as gravel pits.

Nesting: colonial; pair excavates or reuses a long burrow in a steep earthen bank or sandstone cliff; end of the burrow is lined with grass, rootlets, weeds, straw and feathers; pair incubates 4–5 white eggs for 14–16 days.

Feeding: catches flying insects; drinks on the wing.

Voice: twittering chatter: *speed-zeet speed-zeet.*

Similar Species: *Northern Rough-winged Swallow* (p. 218): lacks dark breast band. *Tree Swallow* (p. 217): lacks dark breast band; dark, iridescent bluish to greenish upperparts. *Cliff Swallow* (p. 220): lacks dark breast band; brown and blue upperparts; buff forehead and rump.

Best Sites: *Summer:* usually near water. *In migration:* along the coasts.

CLIFF SWALLOW

Petrochelidon pyrrhonota

If the Cliff Swallow were to be renamed in the 20th century, it would probably be called "Bridge Swallow," because so many bridges in eastern North America seem to have a colony living under them. If you stop to inspect the underside of a bridge, you might see hundreds of gourd-shaped mud nests stuck to the pillars and structural beams. Cliff Swallows may also construct their nests under the eaves of houses and other buildings, where they are susceptible to eviction by House Sparrows. • Master mud masons, Cliff Swallows roll mud into balls with their bills and press the pellets together to form their characteristic nests within several days. Brooding parents peer out of the circular neck of the nest, their gleaming eyes watching the world go by. • Cliff Swallows are also brood parasites: females often lay one or more of their eggs in the temporarily vacant nests of neighbouring Cliff Swallows. Upon returning to a parasitized nest, adults accept the foreign eggs and raise them as though they were their own.

ID: orangey rump; buff forehead; blue-grey head and wings; rusty "cheek," nape and throat; buff breast; white belly; spotted undertail coverts; nearly square tail.
Size: *L* 14 cm.
Status: uncommon to locally common breeder from May to August; common migrant from late April to late September; some birds may remain until late October.
Habitat: steep banks, cliffs, bridges and buildings near watercourses; forages over water, fields and marshes.
Nesting: colonial; under bridges and on cliffs and buildings; pair builds a gourd-shaped mud nest with a small opening near the bottom; pair incubates 4–5 brown-spotted, white to pinkish eggs for 14–16 days.
Feeding: catches flying insects on the wing; occasionally eats berries; drinks on the wing.
Voice: twittering chatter: *churrr-churrr*; also an alarm call: *nyew*.
Similar Species: *Barn Swallow* (p. 221): deeply forked tail; dark rump; usually has rust-coloured underparts and forehead. *Other swallows* (pp. 216–21): lack buff forehead and rump patch.
Best Sites: canyons and river valleys, often close to towns and by highways.

BARN SWALLOW

Hirundo rustica

Barn Swallows once nested on cliffs, but their cup-shaped mud nests are now found under house eaves, in barns and boathouses, under bridges or in any other structure that provides shelter from predators and inclement weather. Unfortunately, not everyone appreciates nesting Barn Swallows—the young can be very messy. Nests are often scraped off buildings as the nesting season is just beginning. However, these graceful birds are natural pest controllers. In addition, their close association with urban areas and tolerance for human activity affords us the wondrous opportunity to observe and study the normally secretive reproductive cycle of birds. • "Swallow-tailed" is a term used to describe something that is deeply forked. In Atlantic Canada, the Barn Swallow is the only swallow that displays this feature. • *Hirundo* is Latin for "swallow," and *rustica* refers to this bird's preference for rural habitats.

ID: long, deeply forked tail; rust-coloured throat and forehead; blue-black upper-parts; rust- to buff-coloured under-parts; long, pointed wings.

Size: *L* 18 cm.

Status: common to abundant migrant and breeder from mid-April to late September; a few birds arrive in early April; some birds remain until December.

Habitat: in open rural and urban areas where bridges, culverts and buildings are found near rivers, lakes, marshes or ponds.

Nesting: singly or in small, loose colonies; on a vertical or horizontal building structure under a suitable overhang, on a bridge or in a culvert; half or full cup nest is made of mud and grass or straw; pair incubates 4–7 white eggs, spotted with brown, for 13–17 days.

Feeding: catches flying insects on the wing.

Voice: continuous twittering chatter: *zip-zip-zip*; also *kvick-kvick*.

Similar Species: *Cliff Swallow* (p. 220): squared tail; buff rump and forehead; light-coloured underparts. *Purple Martin* (p. 216): shallowly forked tail; male is completely blue-black; female has sooty grey underparts. *Tree Swallow* (p. 217): clean, white underparts; notched tail.

Best Sites: *Summer:* urban areas with watercourses and small ponds. *In migration:* estuaries and large lakes.

BLACK-CAPPED CHICKADEE

Poecile atricapilla

In winter, Black-capped Chickadees often join the company of kinglets, nuthatches, creepers, small woodpeckers and sometimes Boreal Chickadees in what appears to be a celebration of life in the forest. At this time of year, these chickadees are common visitors to well-stocked feeders. They are even occasionally enticed to land on an outstretched hand offering a sunflower seed. In summer, the best place to look for Black-caps is wherever there are birch stands; they like to feast on the many insect pests found in these trees. In autumn, adult Black-caps and their fledged young are often joined by vireos and warblers. • When foraging, Black-capped Chickadees swing upside down on tree branches, snatching up insects and berries. • Most songbirds have both songs and calls. The chickadee's *swee-tee* song is heard primarily during spring courtship. Its *chick-a-dee-dee-dee* call keeps flocks together and maintains contact between flock members. • The scientific name *atricapilla* is Latin for "black crown."

ID: black cap and "bib"; white "cheek"; grey back and wings; white underparts; light buff sides and flanks; dark legs; conspicuous white edging on wing feathers.

Size: *L* 13–15 cm.

Status: common year-round resident.

Habitat: deciduous and mixed forests, woodlots, riparian woodlands, birch stands, wooded urban parks and backyards with birdfeeders.

Nesting: excavates a cavity in a soft rotting stump or tree; cavity is lined with fur, feathers, moss, grass and cocoons; female incubates 6–8 white eggs, with fine reddish-brown dots, for 12–13 days.

Feeding: gleans vegetation, branches and the ground for small insects and spiders; visits backyard feeders; also eats conifer seeds and invertebrate eggs.

Voice: call is a chipper, whistled *chick-a-dee-dee-dee*; song is a slow, whistled *swee-tee* or *fee-bee*.

Similar Species: *Boreal Chickadee* (p. 223): grey-brown cap, sides and flanks. *Blackpoll Warbler* (p. 266): breeding male has 2 white wing bars, dark streaking on white underparts, orange legs and longer, paler bill.

Best Sites: all habitats that include birch; flocks occasionally concentrate at coastal headlands and islands.

BOREAL CHICKADEE

Poecile hudsonica

Birders generally love chickadees, and the Boreal Chickadee is especially sought-after as the northern representative of this endearing clan. As its name suggests, this soft-spoken resident is found primarily in Atlantic Canada's expansive boreal forest. Unlike the more common and familiar Black-capped Chickadee, the Boreal Chickadee prefers the seclusion of coniferous forests, and it rarely leaves its cover except in winter. During the nesting season, these birds are so quiet that you would never know they were there at all. • Chickadees burn so much energy that they must replenish their stores daily to survive winter—they have insufficient fat reserves to endure a prolonged stretch of cold weather. Chickadees store food in holes and bark crevices for such an emergency. During a cold night, a chickadee enters a state of torpor, which slows the bird's metabolism so that it uses less energy. • The scientific name *hudsonica* refers to the northern (Hudsonian) region of Canada.

ID: grey-brown cap, back, sides and flanks; black "bib"; whitish to light grey breast and belly; whitish "cheek" patch; grey wings and tail.
Size: *L* 13–14 cm.
Status: fairly common to locally common year-round resident; some occasionally move south of their breeding range in winter.
Habitat: *Breeding:* spruce, fir and pine forests; occasionally in mixed coniferous forests with a small deciduous component. *In migration* and *winter:* birds move to coastal tuckamore and suburban feeders.

Nesting: excavates a cavity in soft, rotting wood or uses a natural cavity or abandoned woodpecker nest in a conifer; female lines the nest with fur, feathers, moss and grass; female incubates 5–8 white eggs, with fine, reddish-brown dots, for 11–16 days.
Feeding: gleans vegetation, branches and infrequently the ground for small tree-infesting insects (including their pupae and eggs) and spiders; also eats conifer seeds.
Voice: soft, nasal, wheezy *sick-a day day day.*
Similar Species: *Black-capped Chickadee* (p. 222): black cap; buffy flanks; more greyish than brownish overall.
Best Sites: conifers and mixed woods.

RED-BREASTED NUTHATCH

Sitta canadensis

The Red-breasted Nuthatch stands out from other songbirds because of its unusual body form and its habit of moving headfirst down tree trunks. Its loud, nasal *yank-yank-yank* calls, which are frequently heard in spring, are also distinctive. A Red-breasted Nuthatch looks a lot like a red rocket as it streaks toward a neighbourhood birdfeeder from the cover of a coniferous tree. • Red-breasted Nuthatches tend to make large-scale migrations every three or more years, perhaps because of cone crop failure on their breeding grounds. In such years, they often join groups of other foraging songbirds in woodlands. • This bird smears the entrance of its nest cavity with pitch from pine or spruce trees. This sticky doormat might inhibit ants and other animals from entering the nest chamber. Invertebrates can be the most serious threat to nesting success, because they can transmit fungal infections or parasitize nestlings. • *Sitta* means "nuthatch" in Greek; *canadensis* refers to this bird's partially Canadian distribution.

ID: rusty underparts; grey-blue upperparts; white eyebrow; black eye line; black cap; straight bill; short tail; white "cheek." *Male:* deeper rust on breast; black crown. *Female:* light red wash on breast; dark grey crown.

Size: *L* 11 cm.

Status: fairly common year-round resident; occasionally locally abundant in migration, as either immigrants or short-distance migrants.

Habitat: *Breeding:* spruce–fir and pine forests; pine plantations. *In migration and winter:* mixed woodlands, especially those near birdfeeders.

Nesting: excavates a cavity or uses an abandoned woodpecker nest; usually smears the entrance with pitch; nest is made of bark shreds, grass and fur; female incubates 5–6 white eggs, spotted with reddish-brown, for about 12 days.

Feeding: forages down trees while probing under loose bark for larval and adult invertebrates; eats pine and spruce seeds during winter; often frequents feeders.

Voice: slow, continually repeated, nasal *yank-yank-yank* or *rah-rah-rah-rah*; also a short *tsip*.

Similar Species: *White-breasted Nuthatch* (p. 225): larger; lacks black eye line and red underparts.

Best Sites: *Summer:* in conifers and mixed forests. *In migration:* more widespread. *Winter:* visits feeders.

WHITE-BREASTED NUTHATCH

Sitta carolinensis

Moving headfirst down a tree trunk, the White-breasted Nuthatch forages for invertebrates, occasionally issuing a noisy call. Unlike woodpeckers and creepers, nuthatches do not use their tails to brace themselves against tree trunks—nuthatches grasp the tree through foot power alone. • To a novice bird-watcher, seeing a White-breasted Nuthatch call repeatedly while clinging to the underside of a branch is an odd sight. To the bird, however, this gravity-defying act is totally natural. • Although White-breasted Nuthatches are regular visitors to backyard feeders, they never stick around longer than it takes to grab a seed and dash. Only an offering of suet can persuade this tiny bird to remain in a single spot for any length of time. • The scientific name *carolinensis* means "of Carolina"—the first White-breasted Nuthatch specimen was collected in the Carolina mountains of the eastern US.

ID: white under-parts; white face; grey-blue back; rusty undertail coverts; short tail; straight bill; short legs. *Male:* black cap. *Female:* dark grey cap.
Size: *L* 15 cm.
Status: uncommon year-round resident in NB, PEI and NS but rare and very local in maritime PQ.
Habitat: mixed forests, woodlots and backyards, with mature trees.
Nesting: in a natural cavity or an abandoned woodpecker nest in a large decidu-ous tree; lines the cavity with bark, grass, fur and feathers; female incubates 5–8

white eggs, spotted with reddish brown, for 12–14 days.
Feeding: forages down trees headfirst in search of larval and adult invertebrates; also eats many nuts and seeds; regularly visits feeders.
Voice: song is a frequently repeated *wer-werwerwerwer;* calls include *ha-ha-ha ha-ha-ha, ank ank* and *ip.*
Similar Species: *Red-breasted Nuthatch* (p. 224): black eye line; rusty underparts. *Black-capped Chickadee* (p. 222): black "bib."
Best Sites: *NB:* widespread. *PEI:* Victoria; Charlottetown. *NS:* Amherst; Truro; Wolfville Ridge; Annapolis Valley; Kejimkujik NP; Antigonish; Ingonish. *PQ:* New Carlisle–New Richmond area.

BROWN CREEPER
Certhia americana

Brown Creepers are never easy to find. They often go unnoticed until a flake of bark suddenly takes the shape of a bird. If a creeper is frightened, it will freeze and flatten against a tree trunk, becoming even tougher to see. • The Brown Creeper spirals up tree trunks, searching for hidden invertebrates. When it reaches the upper branches, it floats down to the base of a neighbouring tree to begin another foraging ascent. Its long, stiff tail feathers prop it up against vertical tree trunks as it hitches its way skyward. • Like the call of the Golden-crowned Kinglet, the thin whistle of the Brown Creeper is so high-pitched that birders often fail to hear it. To further the confusion, the creeper's song, which is sung by the male during courtship, often takes on the boisterous warbling quality of a wood-warbler song. • There are many species of creepers in Europe and Asia, but the Brown Creeper is the only member of its family found in North America.

ID: brown back is heavily streaked with buffy white; white eyebrow; white underparts; downcurved bill; long, pointed tail feathers; rusty rump.
Size: *L* 13 cm.
Status: fairly common resident; uncommon to locally common migrant from early April to early May and from late September to early November; occasionally visits urban parks and suet feeders in winter.
Habitat: mature deciduous, coniferous and mixed forests and woodlands, especially in wet areas with large dead trees; also found near bogs.

Nesting: under loose bark; nest of grass and conifer needles is woven together with spider silk; female incubates 5–6 whitish eggs with reddish-brown dots for 14–17 days.
Feeding: hops up tree trunks and large limbs, probing loose bark for adult and larval invertebrates.
Voice: song is a faint, high-pitched *trees-trees-trees see the trees*; call is a high *tseee*.
Similar Species: *Nuthatches* (pp. 224–25): grey-blue back; straight or slightly up-turned bill. *Woodpeckers* (pp. 191–97): all lack brown back streaking; straight bills.
Best Sites: *Summer:* mixed woods. *Winter:* may appear in urban areas.

HOUSE WREN

Troglodytes aedon

The House Wren's small size, overall brown colour and secretive habits are enhanced in summer by its bubbly song and energetic demeanor. Pairs often nest in gardens, where the male will burst into song at any time throughout the summer. Wrens often build numerous nests, which later serve as decoys or dummy nests. If a nest box is abandoned by a pair, it usually means that they have found another suitable nest site, which could be in any kind of cavity, natural or unnatural. In such a case, your only option is be to clean out the nest-box and hope that another pair of wrens will find your real estate more appealing.

ID: brown upper-parts with fine dark barring on upper wings and lower back; faint, pale eyebrow and eye ring; short, "cocked-up" tail is finely barred with black; whitish throat; whitish to buff underparts; faintly barred flanks.

Size: *L* 12 cm.

Status: rare, local breeder from early April to late August; rare migrant from early April to early June and rare to uncommon from early September to early November.

Habitat: thickets and shrubby openings in or at the edge of deciduous or mixed woodlands; often in shrubs and thickets near buildings.

Nesting: in a natural cavity or abandoned woodpecker nest; also in nest boxes or other artificial cavities; nest of sticks and grass is lined with feathers, fur and other soft materials; female probably incubates the 6–8 white eggs, with heavy reddish-brown dotting, for 12–15 days.

Feeding: gleans the ground and vegetation for insects, especially beetles, caterpillars, grasshoppers and spiders.

Voice: call is a harsh, scolding rattle; song is a rapid, chattering, somewhat unmusical, but pleasant *tsi-tsi-tsi-tsi oodle-oodle-oodle-oodle* (lasting about 2–3 seconds).

Similar Species: *Winter Wren* (p. 228): smaller; darker overall; much shorter, stubby tail; prominent dark barring on flanks. *Sedge Wren* (p. 229): faint white streaking on dark crown and back.

Best Sites: *NB:* Saint John West; St. Stephen; St. Andrews; Grand Manan I.; Fredericton. *NS:* Pubnico; Cape Sable I.; Antigonish. *PQ:* Rivière-du-Loup.

227

WINTER WREN

Troglodytes troglodytes

Winter Wrens boldly announce their claims to patches of moist coniferous woodland, where they often make their homes in the green moss and gnarled, upturned roots of decomposing tree trunks. The song of the Winter Wren is distinguished by its explosive delivery, melodious, bubbly tone and extended duration. Few other singers can sustain their song for up to 10 music-packed seconds. • When they're not singing or nesting, Winter Wrens skulk through the forest understorey, quietly probing the myriad of nooks and crannies for invertebrates, especially spiders and mites. • While the female raises the young, the male brings food to the nest and also defends the territory through song. At night, the male sleeps away from his family in an unfinished nest. • *Troglodytes* is Greek for "creeping in holes" or "cave dweller." • The Winter Wren is the only North American wren also found across Europe and Asia, where it is a common garden bird often referred to as "Jenny Wren."

ID: very short, stubby, "cocked-up" tail; fine, pale buff eyebrow; dark brown upperparts; lighter brown underparts; prominent dark barring on flanks.

Size: *L* 10 cm.

Status: common migrant and breeder from mid-April to mid-November; rare winter visitor from November to March.

Habitat: *Breeding:* moist boreal forest, spruce bogs, cedar swamps and mixed forests dominated by mature pine and hemlock; often near water. *In migration* and *winter:* tuckamore and shrubbery near the coast and tangles close to dense, wooded cover.

Nesting: in a natural hole, under bark or upturned tree roots or, rarely, in an abandoned woodpecker cavity; bulky nest is made of twigs, moss, grass and fur; male frequently builds up to 4 "dummy" nests prior to egg-laying; female incubates 5–7 white eggs, with reddish-brown dots toward the larger end, for 14–16 days.

Feeding: forages on the ground and on trees for beetles, wood borers and other invertebrates.

Voice: *Male:* song is a warbled, tinkling series of quick trills and twitters, often more than 8 seconds long and repeated many times with undiminished enthusiasm; call is a sharp *chip-chip*.

Similar Species: *House Wren* (p. 227): tail is longer than leg; less conspicuous barring on flanks; paler overall. *Carolina Wren:* long, bold white eyebrow; much larger; long tail. *Marsh Wren* (p. 230): white streaking on black back; bold white eyebrow. *Sedge Wren* (p. 229): white streaking on black back and crown; longer tail; paler underparts.

Best Sites: *Summer:* dark, moist woods, especially in areas where trees are covered with mosses and lichens; in cutover areas. *Winter:* urban areas.

SEDGE WREN

Cistothorus platensis

L ike most wrens, the Sedge Wren is secretive and difficult to observe. It is the least familiar of all the North American wrens because it keeps itself well concealed in dense stands of sedges and tall, wet grass. Sedge Wrens are also less loyal to specific sites than other wrens are. They may totally disappear from an area after a few years for no apparent reason. More often than not, birders must end a day of birdwatching with only an aural recognition of the Sedge Wren, rather than a visual record. • Sedge Wrens are feverish nest builders. Each energetic male may build several incomplete nests throughout his territory before females arrive. The decoys or "dummy" nests are not wasted: they often serve as dormitories for young and adult birds later in the season.

ID: short, narrow tail (often cocked up); faint, pale eyebrow; dark crown and back are faintly streaked with white; barring on wing coverts; buff-orange sides, flanks and undertail coverts on otherwise whitish underparts.

Size: *L* 10–11 cm.

Status: very local and rare from late April to mid-October; a few may remain into December.

Habitat: wet sedge meadows, wet grassy fields, marshes, bogs and beaver ponds; often in abandoned wet fields with low, shrubby willows and alders.

Nesting: usually less than 1 m from the ground; well-built globe nest with a side entrance is woven from sedges and grass;

female incubates 4–8 unmarked, white eggs for about 14 days.

Feeding: forages low in dense vegetation, where it picks and probes for adult and larval insects and spiders; occasionally catches flying insects.

Voice: a few short *tsip* notes are followed by an unmusical series of descending notes and often a dry trill; more like the song of an insect than the song of a bird.

Similar Species: *Marsh Wren* (p. 230): broad, conspicuous white eyebrow; prominent white streaking on black back; unstreaked crown; prefers cattail marshes. *Winter Wren* (p. 228): darker overall; shorter, stubby tail; unstreaked crown. *House Wren* (p. 227): unstreaked, dark brown crown and back.

Best Sites: *NB:* Jolicure Marsh (Sackville); New Horton Marsh. *NS:* Missaguash Marsh.

MARSH WREN

Cistothorus palustris

Like many wrens, the Marsh Wren is a very local breeding species in our region. Where it does occur in cattails and bulrushes, it is a reclusive bird that prefers to remain hidden deep within its dense marshland habitat. A patient observer might be rewarded with a brief glimpse of a Marsh Wren. However, it is more likely that this bird's distinctive song, reminiscent of an old-fashioned sewing machine, will inform you of its presence. • Marsh Wrens occasionally destroy the nests and eggs of other Marsh Wrens as well as other marsh-nesting songbirds, such as the Red-winged Blackbird. Other birds are usually prevented from doing the same because the wren's globe nest keeps the eggs well hidden, and several "dummy" nests help to divert predators from the real nest. • Until recently this bird was known as the "Long-billed Marsh Wren." The scientific name *palustris* is Latin for "marsh."

ID: white "chin" and belly; white to light brown upperparts; black triangle on upper back is streaked with white; bold, white eyebrow; unstreaked brown crown; long, thin, downcurved bill.

Size: *L* 13 cm.

Status: locally rare to common breeder from mid-May to August; rare migrant from late March to early May and locally uncommon from September to late November; some may linger until early January.

Habitat: *Breeding:* large cattail and bulrush marshes interspersed with open water; occasionally in tall grass–sedge marshes. *In migration* and *winter:* any wet grassy or shrubby area, usually in coastal locations.

Nesting: in marshes among cattails or tall emergent vegetation; globe-like nest is woven with cattails, bulrushes, weeds and grass and is lined with cattail down; female incubates 4–6 white to pale brown eggs, heavily dotted with dark brown, for 12–16 days.

Feeding: gleans vegetation and flycatches for adult aquatic invertebrates, especially dragonflies and damselflies.

Voice: *Male:* rapid, rattled, staccato warble sounds like an old sewing machine; call is a harsh *chek*.

Similar Species: *Sedge Wren* (p. 229): smaller; streaked crown. *House Wren* (p. 227): faint eyebrow; lacks white streaking on black back. *Carolina Wren:* larger; lacks white streaking on black back; buff underparts.

Best Sites: *Summer* and *in migration: NB:* Tantramar Marshes; Germantown Marsh; Hazen Creek & Red Head Marsh (Saint John); Jemseg. *NS:* Missaguash Marsh; Athol Marsh; Seal I.; Hartlen's Point. *Winter:* coastal areas and islands.

GOLDEN-CROWNED KINGLET

Regulus satrapa

G olden-crowned Kinglets are living proof that bulk is not a prerequisite for surviving brutal Atlantic Canadian winters. At this time of year, they are commonly seen and heard among multi-species flocks that often include chickadees, Red-breasted Nuthatches and Brown Creepers. These small flocks move through forests, decorating tall spruces, pines, firs and naked deciduous hardwoods like Christmas ornaments. As they engage in refueling exercises, these birds use tree branches as swings and trapezes, flashing their regal crowns and constantly flicking their tiny wings. Not much larger than hummingbirds, Golden-crowned Kinglets can be difficult to spot as they flit and hover among coniferous treetops. During summer, these dainty forest sprites are often too busy to make an appearance for admiring observers. • This kinglet's extremely high-pitched call is very faint and is often lost in the slightest woodland breeze.

ID: olive back; darker wings and tail; light underparts; dark "cheek"; 2 white wing bars; black eye line; white eyebrow; black border around crown. *Male:* reddish-orange crown. *Female:* yellow crown.
Size: *L* 10 cm.
Status: common to abundant year-round resident, with populations augmented by migrants in spring and autumn.
Habitat: *Breeding:* mixed and pure, mature coniferous forests, especially those dominated by spruce; also uses some conifer plantations. *In migration* and *winter:* coniferous, deciduous and mixed forests and woodlands; sometimes visits urban parks and gardens.

Nesting: usually in a spruce or conifer; hanging nest is made of moss, lichens, twigs and leaves; female incubates 8–9 whitish to pale buff eggs, spotted with grey and brown, for 14–15 days.
Feeding: gleans and hovers among the forest canopy for insects, berries and occasionally sap.
Voice: song is a faint, high-pitched, accelerating *tsee-tsee-tsee-tsee, why do you shilly-shally?*; call is a very high-pitched *tsee tsee tsee.*
Similar Species: *Ruby-crowned Kinglet* (p. 232): bold, broken white eye ring; lacks black border around crown; powerful song. *Chickadees* (pp. 222–23): lack bright, colourful crowns.
Best Sites: conifers and mixed woods; more urban areas in winter.

231

RUBY-CROWNED KINGLET

Regulus calendula

I n early summer, the forest emerges from its long winter sleep, and the sound of cold wind blowing through conifer boughs is replaced by the joyful sound of singing birds. The loud, rolling song of the Ruby-crowned Kinglet echoes through Atlantic Canada's boreal forest in May and June. Its loudness and exuberance is somewhat unexpected from so small a bird, considering the abilities of its close relatives. • The male kinglet erects his brilliant red crown while he sings to impress prospective mates during courtship. Throughout most of the year, however, the crown is impossible to see, even through binoculars—it remains hidden among dull feathers on his head. • While in migration, Ruby-crowned Kinglets regularly flit around treetops, mingling with a colourful assortment of warblers and vireos. These kinglets can be mistaken for *Empidonax* flycatchers, but the Ruby-crowned Kinglets' frequent hovering techniques and energetic wing-flicking behaviour set them apart from look-alikes.

ID: bold, broken eye ring; 2 bold white wing bars; olive green upperparts; dark wings and tail; whitish to yellowish underparts; short tail; flicks its wings. *Male:* small, red crown (usually hidden). *Female:* lacks red crown.
Size: *L* 10 cm.
Status: common to abundant migrant from mid-April to late May and from September to late October; fairly common to locally common breeder from May to late August; rare lingerer, occasionally into December.
Habitat: *Breeding:* mixed woodlands and pure coniferous forests, especially those dominated by spruce; often found around wet forest openings and edges. *In migration* and *winter:* variety of woods, scrubby tuckamore, parks and gardens, mostly near the coast.

Nesting: usually in a spruce or other conifer; female builds a hanging nest made of moss, lichens, twigs and leaves and lines it with feathers, fur and plant down; female incubates 7–8 brown-spotted, whitish to pale buff eggs for 13–14 days.
Feeding: gleans and hovers for insects and spiders; will also eat seeds and berries.
Voice: *Male:* song is an accelerating and rising *tea-tea-tea-tew-tew-tew look-at-Me, look-at-Me, look-at-Me*.
Similar Species: *Golden-crowned Kinglet* (p. 231): dark "cheek"; black border to crown; male has orange crown with yellow border; female has yellow crown. *Orange-crowned Warbler:* no eye ring or wing bars. Empidonax *flycatchers* (pp. 200–03): complete eye ring or no eye ring at all; larger bill; longer tail; lack red crown; perch upright.
Best Sites: *Summer:* in mixed forests and wetter sites. *In migration:* very common at headlands.

BLUE-GRAY GNATCATCHER

Polioptila caerulea

The tiny, long-tailed Blue-gray Gnatcatcher is the most widespread of its genus and is the only gnatcatcher found in cooler temperate regions. Populations have been expanding northward on both coasts since the 1960s. The Blue-gray Gnatcatcher is now regularly found across southern Canada from coast to coast. • This gnatcatcher is a restless inhabitant of woodlands and brushy areas. It flits from shrub to shrub with its long, cocked-up tail moving from side to side. Scratchy, banjo-like twanging calls announce progress and keep pairs close together. During courtship, which may start early as late April, the male follows his prospective mate around his territory. Once a bond is established, the paired birds are inseparable. Male Blue-gray Gnatcatchers take a greater part in nesting and raising the young than males in closely related species. • Although these birds undoubtedly eat gnats, this food item is not the major part of their varied diet. The scientific name *caerulea* is from the Latin word for "sky blue."

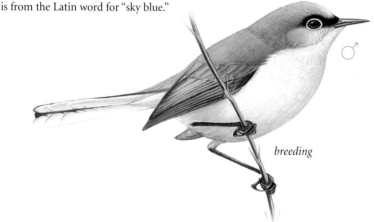

breeding

ID: tiny hyperactive songbird; blue-grey upperparts; long, thin tail; white eye ring; pale grey underparts; dark legs; thin, dark bill (pale in winter). *Breeding male:* black forehead. *Juvenile:* similar to adult; pale bill; brown-washed upperparts. *In flight:* long-tailed and broad-winged; long, fan-shaped tail with flashy white outer feathers.
Size: *L* 11 cm.
Status: rare migrant from early May to mid-June and rare to locally uncommon migrant from mid-September to late October; occasional breeder.
Habitat: scrubby growth and moist, riparian woods; occasionally in overgrown gardens and parks.

Nesting: on a branch, usually halfway to the trunk; cup nest is made of plant fibres and bark chips, decorated with lichens and well lined with fine vegetation, hair and feathers; female incubates 4–5 pale, spotted eggs for 11–15 days; male feeds female and young.
Feeding: moves up and down through foliage, flicking its tail constantly, possibly to flush prey into view; eats small insects and spiders.
Voice: calls are thin and high-pitched: single *see* notes, or a short series of "mewing" or chattering notes; can mimic several species.
Similar Species: no other songbird has the same shape and pattern.
Best Sites: offshore islands, especially Seal I. and Brier I., NS.

NORTHERN WHEATEAR

Oenanthe oenanthe

There are almost 20 species of wheatears in the Old World, and most of them inhabit desert regions. This wheatear, by contrast, nests in the arctic tundra of North America and Eurasia. In autumn, most birds fly via Greenland and Europe to Africa, but a few birds may stopover in Atlantic Canada. • These nervous birds restlessly forage on the ground or on foliage for insects, actively flicking their tails. They often perch on rocks and posts at coastal headlands. Sometimes Northern Wheatears join Snow Buntings and Lapland Longspurs. • Unfortunately, Atlantic Canadians very rarely get to see Northern Wheatears in their attractive breeding attire. When they arrive in Atlantic Canada, most birds are in non-breeding or immature plumage. • *Oenanthe* is derived from Aristotle's name for this bird meaning "vine blossom"; this wheatear arrived in Greece around the time that the vines began flowering.

breeding

ID: white rump and tail base; pale cream belly. *Breeding male:* grey cap, nape and back; thick, black eye line; cinnamon breast; black wings and tip of tail. *Female* and *non-breeding male:* grey-brown cap, nape and back; dark brown wings and tip of tail.

Size: *L* 15 cm.

Status: rare local breeder along the northern coast of Labrador; very rare vagrant in May and rare, but increasing, migrant from mid-August to mid-October.

Habitat: *Breeding:* rocky tundra. *In migration:* any open country, including coastal meadows, vacant lots and barren fields.

Nesting: on ground, usually in a crevice under rocks or in an abandoned burrow; cup nest is built from grass, twigs and fur and is lined with mosses, lichens and grass; mostly the female incubates 5–6 pale blue eggs, which may have reddish markings, for 13–14 days.

Feeding: run-and-stop foraging on ground; may fly out from a perch to catch insects; eats mostly insects and other hard-bodied invertebrates; occasionally feeds on berries.

Voice: song is a jumble of warbled notes; calls are a clicking *chack-chack* and a whistled *hweet*.

Similar Species: *American Pipit* (p. 247): slimmer; streaked on back and underparts; narrow, white outer tail feathers; brown rump.

Best Sites: *Summer:* nests in Labrador, south to at least Grady I. *In migration: NB:* Miscou I. *NS:* Seal I. *NF:* L'Anse aux Meadows; St. Anthony; Cape Freels; Cape Bonavista; Cape Race. *PQ:* Mont-Joli; Ste-Anne-des-Monts; Godbout.

EASTERN BLUEBIRD

Sialia sialis

With the colours of the cool sky on its back and the warm setting sun on its breast, the male Eastern Bluebird looks like a piece of pure sky come to life. It is too bad that it is now a rare bird in most of Atlantic Canada. • When House Sparrows and European Starlings were introduced to North America, Eastern Bluebirds were forced to compete with them for nest sites, and bluebird populations suffered. The development of "bluebird trails" (nest boxes mounted on fence posts that stretch along highways and rural roads) across parts of Canada has allowed bluebird populations to gradually recover in some areas. Because Eastern Bluebirds are still quite rare in Atlantic Canada, bluebird trails are not common—the nest boxes are often taken over by sparrows, European Starlings and Tree Swallows. • Even though Atlantic Canada is at the edge of the Eastern Bluebird's breeding range, nesting birds can be found in all provinces except Newfoundland.

ID: chestnut red "chin," throat, breast and sides; white belly and undertail coverts; dark bill and legs. *Male:* deep blue upperparts. *Female:* thin white eye ring; grey-brown head and back tinged with blue; blue wings and tail; paler chestnut on underparts.
Size: *L* 18 cm.
Status: rare to uncommon migrant and breeder from March to October.
Habitat: cropland fencelines, meadows, fallow and abandoned fields, pastures, forest clearings and edges, golf courses, large lawns and cemeteries.
Nesting: in an abandoned woodpecker cavity, natural cavity or nest box; mostly the female incubates 4–5 pale blue eggs for 13–16 days.
Feeding: swoops from a perch and pursues flying insects; also forages on the ground for invertebrates.
Voice: song is a rich, warbling *turr, turr-lee, turr-lee*; call is a chittering *pew*.
Similar Species: *Mountain Bluebird:* lacks red underparts; exceptionally rare in Atlantic Canada.
Best Sites: in open areas, especially near farm fences and in orchards.

235

VEERY

Catharus fuscescens

Navigating its way across the forest floor, the Veery travels in short, springy hops, flipping leaves and scattering leaf litter in search of worms and grubs. This shy, camouflaged bird is always well tuned to the sounds of wiggling prey or approaching danger. It is the most terrestrial of the North American thrushes, and it is often difficult to find. Listen for the Veery in spring and early summer, when its fluty, cascading song is easily detected, especially after other songbirds have called it a day. • These birds migrate to South America each winter, so there is a very good chance that the Veery pairs nesting in your local ravine might soon be travelling to the rainforests of the Amazon! • When startled by an intruder, the Veery either flushes or faces the threat with its faintly streaked buffy breast exposed, hoping for concealment. • The name "Veery" is an onomatopoeic version of this bird's airy song. The scientific name *fuscescens* is from the Latin word for "dusky," in reference to the bird's colour.

ID: reddish-brown or tawny upperparts; very thin, greyish eye ring; faintly streaked buff throat and upper breast; light underparts; grey flanks and face patch.
Size: *L* 16–19 cm.
Status: fairly common to common migrant and breeder from late April to October.
Habitat: cool, moist deciduous and mixed forests and woodlands with a dense understorey of shrubs and ferns; often in disturbed woodlands.
Nesting: on the ground or in a shrub; female builds a bulky nest of leaves, weeds, bark strips and rootlets; female incubates 3–4 pale greenish-blue eggs for 10–15 days.
Feeding: gleans the ground and lower vegetation for invertebrates and berries.
Voice: *Male:* song is a fluty, descending *da-vee-ur, vee-ur, vee-ur, veer, veer, veer;* call is a high, whistled *feeyou.*
Similar Species: *Swainson's Thrush* (p. 239): bold eye ring; olive brown upperparts; darker spotting on throat and upper breast. *Hermit Thrush* (p. 240): reddish rump and tail; brownish back; bold eye ring; buff-brown flanks; large dark spots on throat and breast. *Gray-cheeked Thrush* (p. 237) and *Bicknell's Thrush* (p. 238): grey-brown upperparts; dark breast spots; brownish-grey flanks.
Best Sites: open broadleaf and mixed woods with a shrubby understorey.

GRAY-CHEEKED THRUSH

Catharus minimus

Few Atlantic Canadians have ever heard of the Gray-cheeked Thrush, but keen birders find this inconspicuous bird a source of great interest. This champion migrant of thrushes overwinters as far south as Peru and regularly summers in the Arctic—farther north than any other North American thrush. In Atlantic Canada, a few birds nest in the Gaspé, Cape Breton and Newfoundland. • The *minimus* subspecies that is found throughout Newfoundland is greyer than the subspecies found in the rest of Atlantic Canada. • The Gray-cheeked Thrush will settle in almost any habitat while migrating, but it does not stay for long. It rarely utters more than a simple warning note during its brief refueling stop. On territory, the somewhat squeaky, rising repetitions of this bird's song make the Gray-cheeked Thrush a little bit easier to find.

ID: grey-brown upperparts; grey face; inconspicuous eye ring may not be visible; heavily spotted breast; light underparts; brownish-grey flanks.

Size: *L* 18–20 cm.

Status: rare migrant from late April to early June and from late August to mid-October in most of the region; rare to common breeder from early May to mid-August.

Habitat: *Breeding:* dwarf black spruce near the treeline and on coastal islands; muskeg and coniferous forest; locally in mixed woods and open conifers in NF. *In migration:* a variety of forested areas, parks and backyards.

Nesting: in a tree or willow, usually quite low to the ground; nest is woven from twigs, moss, grass, weeds, bark strips and rootlets; female incubates 4 pale blue eggs with pale brown spots for 12–14 days.

Feeding: hops along the ground, picking up insects and other invertebrates; may also feed on berries during migration.

Voice: typically thrush-like in tone, ending with a clear, usually 3-part whistle with the middle note higher-pitched: *wee-o, wee-a, titi wheeee*; call is a Veery-like, slurred *fee-oo*.

Similar Species: *Bicknell's Thrush* (p. 238): different song; base of lower mandible is noticeably yellow. *Swainson's Thrush* (p. 239): prominent eye ring; buff "cheek" and upper breast. *Hermit Thrush* (p. 240): reddish tail; olive brown upperparts; lacks grey "cheek." *Veery* (p. 236): reddish-brown upperparts; very light breast streaking.

Best Sites: *NS:* French Mountain; Cape North. *NF:* Gros Morne NP; L'Anse aux Meadows; Malady Head & Louil Hills (Terra Nova NP); Oxen Pond (St. John's); Cape Shore. *PQ:* Forillon NP.

BICKNELL'S THRUSH

Catharus bicknelli

Prior to 1995, the Bicknell's Thrush was considered a subspecies of the Gray-cheeked Thrush. The two species are very difficult to tell apart. Both thrushes may summer in Cape Breton, Nova Scotia and the Gaspé, Québec. Identification problems are compounded when browner Newfoundland Gray-cheeks appear in other parts of Atlantic Canada in migration. The best way to distinguish the two species is not by appearance but by song, although even this may be challenging. • On both its breeding and wintering grounds it is vulnerable to habitat loss from timber harvesting and forest fragmentation. It has a small breeding range that extends from Québec City to Nova Scotia and south to New York. Its wintering range is even smaller—this thrush is regularly found only on islands in the Greater Antilles.

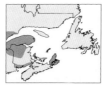

ID: warm brown upperparts; buff breast heavily spotted with brown; white belly.
Size: *L* 16 cm.
Status: rare to locally uncommon breeder from mid-June to early August; rare to uncommon migrant from late April to early June and from late August to mid-November.
Habitat: *Breeding:* open and closed canopy coniferous and mixed forests, mainly in darker, moister boreal forests.
In migration: mainly coastal scrub and tuckamore, but occasionally second-growth and overgrown gardens.
Nesting: up to 6 m high in short, stunted conifers; female builds cup nest made of grass, leaves, bark, mud and moss; female incubates 3–6 bluish eggs for 13–14 days.
Feeding: forages on the ground or picks food from branches and foliage; eats mostly insects, spiders and earthworms.

Voice: a high-pitched, nasal *ch-ch zreee p-zreeew p-p-zreeee* with the last note rising; call note is a buzzy, descending *vee-ah*, higher-pitched and less slurred than the Gray-cheeked Thrush.
Similar Species: *Gray-cheeked Thrush* (p. 237): slightly larger; upperparts more grey-brown (except NF race *minimus*); darker lower mandible. *Swainson's Thrush* (p. 239): buffy lores and more buff on face and breast; more greyish upperparts. *Hermit Thrush* (p. 240): distinct white eye ring; buff rump. *Wood Thrush* (p. 241): very reddish upperparts; dark spots extend onto belly. *Veery* (p. 236): reddish upperparts; reddish spotting on breast.
Best Sites: *NB:* Mount Carleton; Doaktown; Fundy NP; Riley Brook–Nictau area. *PEI:* North Cape; Bubbling Springs Trail (PEI NP). *NS:* Wolfville Ridge; Cape Breton Highlands NP; Cape North; St. Peter's. *PQ:* L'Anse-au-Griffon (Forillon NP); Percé; Îles de la Madeleine.

SWAINSON'S THRUSH

Catharus ustulatus

The upward spiral of this bird's song lifts the soul of each listener with every rising note. The Swainson's Thrush is an integral part of the morning chorus, and its inspiring song is also heard at dusk. In fact, the Swainson's Thrush is routinely the last of the forest singers to be silenced by nightfall. • Most thrushes feed on the ground, but the Swainson's Thrush is also adept at gleaning food from the airy heights of trees, sometimes briefly hover-gleaning like a warbler or vireo. On its breeding grounds, it is often seen as a silhouette against the colourful sky as it perches high in a treetop. In migration, this thrush skulks low on the ground under shrubs and tangles, occasionally finding itself in backyards and neighbourhood parks. A wary bird, the Swainson's Thrush does not allow many viewing opportunities, and it often gives a sharp warning call from some distance. • William Swainson was an English zoologist and illustrator. His name also graces the Swainson's Hawk.

ID: grey-brown upperparts; noticeable buff eye ring; buff wash on "cheek" and upper breast; spots arranged in streaks on throat and breast; white belly and undertail coverts; brownish-grey flanks.
Size: *L* 18 cm.
Status: common to very common migrant from late April to early June and from mid-August to late October; common breeder from May to late October; a few may remain until early January.
Habitat: edges and openings of coniferous and mixed boreal forests to treeline; prefers moist areas with spruce and fir.
Nesting: usually in a shrub or small tree; small cup nest is made of grass, moss, leaves, roots and lichens and is lined with fur and soft fibres; female incubates 3–4 pale blue eggs, with brown spots toward the larger end, for 12–14 days.
Feeding: gleans vegetation and forages on the ground for invertebrates; also eats berries.
Voice: song is a slow, rolling, rising spiral: *Oh, Aurelia will-ya, will-ya will-yeee*; call is a sharp but pleasant *wick* or *prit*.
Similar Species: *Gray-cheeked Thrush* (p. 237) and *Bicknell's Thrush* (p. 238): grey "cheeks"; less or no buff wash on breasts; lack conspicuous eye ring. *Hermit Thrush* (p. 240): reddish tail and rump; greyish-brown upperparts; darker spotting on whiter breast. *Veery* (p. 236): lacks bold eye ring; upperparts are more reddish; faint breast streaking.
Best Sites: broadleaf and mixed woods throughout; in conifers in NF and Cape Breton, NS.

HERMIT THRUSH

Catharus guttatus

The Hermit Thrush's ethereal song is as much a part of the forest ecosystem as the trees and wildflowers. If the beauty of forest birds was gauged by sound rather than appearance, there is no doubt that the Hermit Thrush would be deemed one of the most beautiful birds in Atlantic Canada. • This bird often hides its cryptic cup nest under the low branches of a spruce or fir in a natural hollow between raised mossy hummocks. It may seem unfair that the female incubates the eggs on her own while the male defends the territory, but less activity around the nest probably benefits the vulnerable eggs. • This bird's plumage is quite ordinary. However, the Hermit Thrush distinguishes itself when it raises its reddish tail after landing on a perch or when disturbed.

ID: reddish-brown tail and rump; greyish-brown upperparts; black-spotted throat and breast; light underparts; grey flanks; thin, whitish eye ring.

Size: *L* 18 cm.

Status: common to abundant breeder from May to September; very common migrant from early April to mid-May and from mid-September through October; a few may remain through winter.

Habitat: *Breeding:* deciduous, mixed or coniferous woodlands; wet coniferous bogs bordered by trees. *In migration* and *winter:* coastal tuckamore and second-growth; parklands and gardens with low ground cover.

Nesting: usually on the ground; occasionally in a small tree or shrub; female builds a bulky cup nest of grass, twigs, moss, ferns and bark strips; female incubates 4 pale blue to greenish-blue eggs, sometimes with dark flecks, for 11–13 days.

Feeding: forages on the ground and gleans vegetation for insects and other invertebrates; also eats berries.

Voice: song is a series of beautiful, ethereal flute-like notes, both rising and falling in pitch; calls include a faint *chuck* and a fluty *treee.*

Similar Species: *Swainson's Thrush* (p. 239): buff "cheek" and wash on breast; greyish-brown back and tail. *Veery* (p. 236): lightly streaked upper breast; reddish-brown upperparts and tail. *Gray-cheeked Thrush* (p. 237) and *Bicknell's Thrush* (p. 238): grey "cheek"; lack conspicuous eye ring; may have chestnut tail. *Fox Sparrow* (p. 284): stockier build; conical bill; brown breast spots.

Best Sites: *Summer:* mixed woods and conifers, locally in scrubby growth and tuckamore. *In migration:* also in urban woodlots.

WOOD THRUSH

Hylocichla mustelina

M any tracts of forest that have been urbanized or developed for agriculture now host families of American Robins rather than the once prominent Wood Thrush. Broken forests and small woodlots have allowed for the invasion of common open-area predators and parasites, such as raccoons, skunks, crows, jays and cowbirds, to areas that used to be insulated deep within vast stands of hardwood forest. Now the Wood Thrush is restricted to mature broadleaf woodlands in New Brunswick and Nova Scotia. • There is some evidence that birds are returning northward to areas where forest fragmentation and urban sprawl previously eliminated much of their nesting habitat. • Henry David Thoreau, naturalist and author, considered the Wood Thrush's song to be the most beautiful of avian sounds.

ID: plump body; large black spots on white breast, sides and flanks; bold white eye ring; rusty head and back; brown wings, rump and tail.

Size: *L* 20 cm.

Status: rare to locally uncommon migrant and breeder from mid-April to early November; a few may remain into December.

Habitat: moist, mature and preferably undisturbed deciduous woodlands and mixed forests.

Nesting: low in the fork of a deciduous tree; female builds a bulky cup nest of grass, twigs, moss, weeds, bark strips and mud; nest is lined with softer materials; female incubates 3–4 pale greenish-blue eggs for 13–14 days.

Feeding: forages on the ground and gleans vegetation for insects and other invertebrates; also eats berries.

Voice: *Male:* 3–6-note bell-like phrases, with each note at a different pitch and followed by a trill: *Will you live with me? Way up high in a tree, I'll come right down and...seeee!*; calls include a *pit pit* and *bweebeebeep.*

Similar Species: *Other thrushes* (pp. 234–40): smaller spots on underparts; most have coloured wash on sides and flanks; all lack bold white eye ring and rusty cap and back. *Ovenbird* (p. 269): much smaller and browner; black and russet crown stripes; streaky spots on underparts.

Best Sites: mature broadleaf woods.

AMERICAN ROBIN

Turdus migratorius

American Robins are widely recognized as harbingers of spring. When March rolls around we look forward to their arrival in all parts of Atlantic Canada. Although many American Robins migrate, some birds overwinter wherever mountain-ash berries are plentiful. These birds may even come to feeders if berries and other fruit are provided. • A hunting American Robin may appear to be listening for prey, but it is actually looking for movements in the soil—it tilts its head because its eyes are placed on the sides of its head. The bird's tendency to stamp is designed to get earthworms to betray their presence by moving. • The darker-backed Newfoundland subspecies is often seen in Nova Scotia in winter. • The American Robin was named by English colonists after the Robin (*Erithacus rubecula*) of their native land. Both birds look and behave similarly, even though they are only distantly related. The American Robin's closest European relative is, in fact, the Blackbird (*T. merula*), which is identical in all aspects except plumage.

ID: grey-brown back; dark head; white throat streaked with black; white undertail coverts; incomplete white eye ring; yellow, black-tipped bill; NF *nigrideus* subspecies has back almost as dark as head. *Male:* deep brick red breast; black head. *Female:* dark grey head; light red-orange breast. *Immature:* heavily spotted breast.
Size: *L* 25 cm.
Status: abundant year-round resident; migratory and local movements from October to March.
Habitat: *Breeding:* residential lawns and gardens, pastures, urban parks, broken forests, bogs and river shorelines.

In migration and *winter:* coastal tuck-amore, beaches and urban sites.
Nesting: in a coniferous or deciduous tree or shrub; sturdy cup nest is built of grass, moss and loose bark and is cemented with mud; female incubates 4 light blue eggs for 11–16 days; may raise up to 3 broods each year.
Feeding: forages on the ground and among vegetation for larval and adult insects, earthworms, other invertebrates and berries.
Voice: song is an evenly spaced warble: *cheerily cheer-up cheerio;* call is a rapid *tut-tut-tut.*
Similar Species: *Thrushes* (pp. 234–41): paler on back, whiter on underparts than immature.
Best Sites: *Summer:* in all habitats except treeless uplands. *Winter:* moves to urban areas and farmlands.

GRAY CATBIRD

Dumetella carolinensis

G ray Catbirds are most common in summer, when nesting pairs build their loose cup nests deep within impenetrable tangles of shrubs, brambles and thorny thickets. Gray Catbirds vigorously defend their nesting territories, and their defence tactics are so effective that the nesting success of neighbouring warblers and sparrows may increase as a result of this bird's constant vigilance. Females are very loyal to their nests, so Gray Catbirds are less susceptible to parasitism by cowbirds. Even if a Brown-headed Cowbird sneaks past the watchful female to deposit an egg in the nest, the foreign egg is often recognized and ejected from the nest. • True to its name, the Gray Catbird's call sounds much like the scratchy mewing of a house cat. • In some parts of Atlantic Canada, Gray Catbirds may successfully raise two broods in a single nesting season, which can keep the parents busy from May to early September.

ID: dark grey overall; black cap; long tail may be dark grey to black; chestnut undertail coverts; black eyes, bill and legs.

Size: *L* 22–23 cm.

Status: uncommon to fairly common migrant and breeder from mid-May to October; very rare visitor from November to February.

Habitat: dense thickets, brambles, shrubby or brushy areas and hedgerows, often near water.

Nesting: in a dense shrub or thicket; bulky cup nest is loosely built with twigs, leaves and grass and is lined with fine material; female incubates 4 greenish-blue eggs for 12–15 days.

Feeding: forages on the ground and in vegetation for a wide variety of ants, beetles, grasshoppers, caterpillars, moths and spiders; also eats berries and visits feeders.

Voice: calls include a cat-like *meoow* and a harsh *check-check*; song is a variety of warbles, squeaks and mimicked phrases repeated only once and often interspersed with a *mew* call.

Similar Species: *Gray Jay* (p. 211) and *Northern Mockingbird* (p. 244): lack black cap and chestnut undertail coverts. *Brown Thrasher* (p. 245): rusty brown upperparts; streaked underparts; repeats each song phrase twice.

Best Sites: *Summer* and *in migration:* in tangles and shrubbery of forest glades and gardens, especially near water.

243

NORTHERN MOCKINGBIRD

Mimus polyglottos

Northern Mockingbirds are slowly establishing themselves as year-round residents in Maritime parks and gardens. In winter, they rely heavily on wild and ornamental fruits, especially nutritious rose hips. Generous offerings of suet, raisins and fruit can go a long way toward luring mockingbirds and other birds into your yard. • The Northern Mockingbird thrills people with its impressive vocal repertoire and its springtime courtship dances. Northern Mockingbirds have been known to sing more than 400 different song types, and they can imitate other birds, barking dogs and even musical instruments. They imitate sounds so closely that a computerized auditory analysis is often unable to detect differences between the original source and the mockingbird. • The Northern Mockingbird's energetic courtship dance is interesting to watch. The male and female square off in what appears to be a swordless fencing duel. • The scientific name *polyglottos* is Greek for "many tongues."

ID: grey upperparts; dark wings; 2 thin white wing bars; long, dark tail with white outer tail feathers; light grey underparts. *Immature:* paler overall; spotted breast. *In flight:* large white patch at base of black primaries.

Size: *L* 25 cm.

Status: rare to locally uncommon breeder; rare to locally common migrant in October and November; a few birds overwinter at feeders.

Habitat: hedges, suburban gardens and orchard margins with an abundance of available fruit; hedgerows of multiflora roses are especially important in winter.

Nesting: often in a small shrub or small tree; cup nest is built with twigs, grass, fur and leaves; female incubates 3–4 brown-blotched, bluish-grey to greenish eggs for 12–13 days.

Feeding: gleans vegetation and forages on the ground for beetles, ants, wasps and grasshoppers; also eats berries and wild fruit; visits feeders for suet and raisins.

Voice: song is a medley of mimicked phrases, with the phrases often repeated 3 times or more; calls include a harsh *chair* and *chewk*.

Similar Species: *Northern Shrike* (p. 206) and *Loggerhead Shrike:* thicker, hooked bill; black mask; immatures are stockier and less vocal. *Gray Catbird* (p. 243): grey overall; black cap; chestnut undertail coverts; lacks white outer tail feathers.

Best Sites: in tangles, hedgerows, ornamental shrubbery and shade trees in suburban and urban areas.

BROWN THRASHER

Toxostoma rufum

Amid the various chirps and warbles that rise from woodland and lakefront edges in spring and early summer, the song of the male Brown Thrasher stands alone—its lengthy, complex chorus of twice-repeated phrases is unique. This thrasher has the most extensive vocal repertoire of any North American bird. Biologists estimate that it is capable of up to 3000 distinctive combinations of various phrases. • Despite its size, the Brown Thrasher goes unnoticed in its shrubby domain. A typical sighting of this thrasher consists of nothing more than a flash of rufous as it zips from one tangle to another. • Because it nests on or close to the ground, this bird's eggs and nestlings are particularly vulnerable to predation by snakes, weasels, skunks and other animals. The pair's spirited defence, sometimes to the point of drawing blood, is not always enough to protect its progeny. • Unlike other notable singers, such as the Northern Mockingbird and the similarly shaped, shrub-dwelling Gray Catbird, the Brown Thrasher lives well away from urban areas.

ID: reddish-brown upperparts; light-coloured under-parts with heavy brown streaking; long, downcurved bill; orange-yellow eyes; long, rufous tail; 2 white wing bars.
Size: *L* 29 cm.
Status: rare breeder from late April to early August; rare to locally uncommon migrant from September to November; a few birds overwinter.
Habitat: dense shrubs and thickets, overgrown pastures (especially those with hawthorns), woodland edges and brushy areas, rarely close to human habitation.
Nesting: usually in a low shrub; often on the ground; cup nest, made of grass, twigs and leaves, is lined with fine vegetation; pair

incubates 4 reddish-brown dotted, bluish-white to pale blue eggs for 11–14 days.
Feeding: gleans the ground and vegetation for larval and adult invertebrates; occasionally tosses leaves aside with its bill; also eats seeds and berries.
Voice: sings a variety of phrases, with each phrase usually repeated twice: *dig-it dig-it, hoe-it hoe-it, pull-it-up, pull-it-up;* calls include a loud crackling note, a harsh *shuck,* a soft *churr* and a whistled 3-note *pit-cher-ee.*
Similar Species: *Hermit Thrush* (p. 240) and *Wood Thrush* (p. 241): spots, not streaks, on underparts; dark eye with pale eye ring; shorter tail; lacks wing bars.
Best Sites: *Summer* and *in migration: NB:* widespread, especially in the south. *PEI:* Cape Turner. *NS:* Seal I.; Cape Sable I.; Halifax; Cape North. *NF:* Ramea. *PQ:* Rimouski; Bic; Gaspé Bay.

EUROPEAN STARLING

Sturnus vulgaris

The European Starling was introduced to North America in 1890 and 1891, when about 60 individuals were released into New York's Central Park. It was part of the local Shakespeare society's plan to introduce all the birds mentioned in their favorite author's writings. The starling quickly established itself in New York, then spread quickly across the continent, often at the expense of many native, cavity-nesting birds, such as the Tree Swallow, Eastern Bluebird and Yellow-bellied Sapsucker. Despite many concerted efforts to control or even eradicate the European Starling, it will doubtless continue to assert its claim in the New World. • Courting European Starlings are infamous for their ability to reproduce the sounds of other birds such as Killdeers, Red-tailed Hawks and Soras.

breeding

ID: short, squared tail; dark eyes. *Breeding:* blackish, iridescent plumage; yellow bill. *Non-breeding:* blackish wings; feather tips are heavily spotted with white and buff. *Juvenile:* grey-brown plumage; brown bill. *In flight:* pointed, triangular wings.
Size: *L* 22 cm.
Status: abundant year-round.
Habitat: agricultural areas, townsites, woodland and forest edges, landfills and roadsides.
Nesting: in a tree cavity, nest box or other artificial cavity; nest is made of grass, twigs and straw; mostly female incubates 4–6 bluish to greenish-white eggs for 12–14 days.

Feeding: very diverse diet includes many invertebrates, berries, seeds and garbage; forages mostly on the ground.
Voice: variety of whistles, squeaks and gurgles; imitates other birds throughout the year.
Similar Species: *Rusty Blackbird* (p. 301): longer tail; black bill; lacks spotting; yellow eyes; rusty tinge on upperparts in autumn. *Brewer's Blackbird:* longer tail; black bill; lacks spotting; male has yellow eyes; female is brown overall. *Brown-headed Cowbird* (p. 303): lacks spotting; adult male has longer tail, shorter, dark bill and brown head; juvenile has streaked underparts, stout bill and longer tail.
Best Sites: in all habitats except barren mountains and densely forested areas; winter roosts are mainly in urban areas or marshes.

AMERICAN PIPIT

Anthus rubescens

Each autumn, agricultural fields and open shorelines serve as refueling stations for large concentrations of migratory American Pipits. Flocks of pipits may go unnoticed to untrained eyes, because their dull, brown-and-buff plumage blends into the landscape. To keen observers, however, their plain attire, white outer tail feathers and habit of continuously wagging their tails makes them readily identifiable. • Like their relatives around the world, American Pipits perform marvellous courtship flights. The male flies up to a great height and starts singing as he glides back down to earth, often landing on the same perch that he started from. • American Pipits are found around mountaintops in maritime Québec and northern New Brunswick. However, it is much easier to find them around sea bird colonies in Newfoundland, where they use the cliffs as sounding boards for their tinkling song. • This bird was formerly known as "Water Pipit" (*A. spinoletta*).

breeding

ID: faintly streaked grey-brown upperparts; lightly streaked "necklace" on upper breast; streaked sides and flanks; dark legs; dark tail with white outer tail feathers; buff-coloured underparts; slim bill and body.

Size: *L* 15–18 cm.

Status: rare to common breeder and migrant from mid-April to late July; common to locally abundant migrant from mid-September to early November; a few may remain into January along coasts.

Habitat: *Breeding:* coastal tundra. *In migration* and *winter:* agricultural fields, pastures and shores of wetlands, lakes and rivers; coastal headlands and marshes; sometimes seaweed-covered beaches.

Nesting: in a shallow depression; small cup nest is made of coarse grass and sedges and is sometimes lined with fur; frequently has an overhanging canopy; female incubates 4–6 heavily spotted, whitish to pale buff eggs for 13–15 days.

Feeding: gleans the ground and vegetation for terrestrial and freshwater invertebrates and seeds.

Voice: familiar flight call is *pip-it pip-it*. *Male:* harsh, sharp *tsip-tsip* or *chiwee*.

Similar Species: *Horned Lark* (p. 215): black "horns"; facial markings. *Blackpoll Warbler* (p. 266): females and immatures have white wing bars and shorter tail without white sides.

Best Sites: *Summer: NB:* Mount Carleton. *NF:* Gros Morne NP; St. Paul's; L'Anse aux Meadows; Cape St. Mary's; Cape Race and any alpine or cliff site. *PQ:* Parc de la Gaspésie.

BOHEMIAN WAXWING

Bombycilla garrulus

Descending upon mountain ash and other ornamental plantings, great flocks of Bohemian Waxwings thrill us with their unpredictable appearances. The faint, quavering whistles of these birds attract attentive naturalists who take pleasure in watching the birds descend on berry-filled trees. In most years, Bohemians are seen only in small groups, usually intermingled with wintering flocks of similar-looking Cedar Waxwings (the Bohemian's chestnut undertail coverts readily distinguishes it from its cedar counterpart). • Waxwings get their name from the colourful spots on their secondary feathers. These "waxy" spots are actually colourful enlargements of the feather shafts. The pigments are derived from the birds' berry-filled diet. *Garrulus* is derived from *Garrulus glandarius*, the scientific name for the noisy European Jay, which has a similar forehead crest.

ID: grey and cinnamon crest; black mask and throat; soft brownish-grey body; yellow terminal tail band; chestnut undertail coverts; small white, red and yellow markings on wings. *Juvenile:* brown-grey above; streaked underparts; light throat; no mask; white wing patches.
Size: *L* 20 cm.
Status: irregularly rare to fairly common visitor from mid-October to mid-May, very rarely into June.
Habitat: natural and residential areas with wild berries and fruit.

Nesting: does not nest in Atlantic Canada.
Feeding: gleans vegetation for insects and wild fruit or catches flying insects on the wing; depends on berries and fruit in winter.
Voice: faint, high-pitched, quavering whistle.
Similar Species: *Cedar Waxwing* (p. 249): smaller; browner overall; slight yellow wash on belly; white undertail coverts; lacks yellow on wings.
Best Sites: *NB:* Dalhousie; Alma; Rockwood Park (Saint John); Fredericton. *NS:* Amherst; Antigonish; Halifax; Sydney. *NF:* South Glovertown; St. John's. *PQ:* Rimouski; Cap Gaspé; Penouille.

CEDAR WAXWING

Bombycilla cedrorum

Flocks of handsome Cedar Waxwings take turns gorging on berries from bushes or trees during late summer and autumn. If a bird's crop is full, it will continue to pluck fruit and pass it down the line of birds as if it were in a bucket brigade, until the fruit is gulped down by a still-hungry bird. Waxwings have a remarkable ability to digest a wide variety of berries, some of which are inedible or even poisonous to humans. If the fruits have fermented, these birds will show definite signs of tipsiness—they might fly erratically or flop around on the ground. • Unlike Bohemian Waxwings, which nest in remote northern areas, Cedar Waxwings are familiar summer residents. They are late nesters, which ensures that the berry crops will be ripe when nestlings are ready to be fed. • Planting native berry-producing trees and shrubs in your backyard can attract Cedar Waxwings, often encouraging them to nest in your area.

ID: cinnamon crest; brown upperparts; black mask; yellow wash on belly; grey rump; yellow terminal tail band; white undertail coverts; small red "drops" on wings. *Juvenile:* no mask; streaked underparts; grey-brown body.
Size: *L* 18 cm.
Status: common migrant and breeder from mid-May to late September; uncommon to locally abundant visitor from October to November; irregularly common throughout winter.
Habitat: *Breeding:* wooded residential parks and gardens, overgrown fields, forest edges, second-growth, riparian and open woodlands. *In migration* and *winter:* second-growth and low growth at headlands, riparian edges, urban gardens and parks.

Nesting: in a coniferous or deciduous tree or shrub; cup nest of twigs, grass, moss and lichens is often lined with fine grass; female incubates 3–5 pale grey to bluish-grey eggs, with fine dark spotting, for 12–16 days.
Feeding: catches flying insects on the wing or gleans vegetation; also eats large amounts of berries and wild fruit, especially in autumn and winter.
Voice: faint, high-pitched, trilled whistle: *tseee-tseee-tseee.*
Similar Species: *Bohemian Waxwing* (p. 248): larger; chestnut undertail coverts; small white, red and yellow markings on wings; juvenile has chestnut undertail coverts and white wing patches.
Best Sites: *Summer* and *in migration:* wherever berries are found, especially in parklands and gardens. *Winter: NB:* Saint John. *NS:* Halifax–Dartmouth.

TENNESSEE WARBLER

Vermivora peregrina

Tennessee Warblers lack the bold, bright features found on other warblers. Even so, they are difficult birds to miss, because they have a loud, familiar song, and they are relatively common in Atlantic Canada. • Migrating birds often sing their tunes and forage for insects high in the forest canopy. However, inclement weather or the need for food after a long flight will often force them to lower levels in the forest. • Spruce budworm outbreaks are welcomed by Tennessee Warblers, which thrive on these insects.

During times of plenty, these warblers may produce more than seven young in a single brood. • The species name *peregrina,* Latin for "wandering," refers to this bird's nomadic habits. Alexander Wilson discovered it along Tennessee's Cumberland River and named it after that state. It is only a migrant in Tennessee, however—it breeds almost exclusively in Canada.

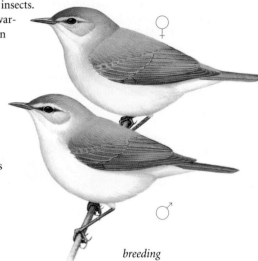

breeding

ID: *Breeding male:* blue-grey cap; olive green back, wings and tail edgings; white eyebrow; black eye line; clean white underparts; thin bill. *Breeding female:* yellow wash on breast and eyebrow; olive grey cap. *Non-breeding:* olive yellow upperparts; yellow eyebrow; yellow underparts except for white undertail coverts; male may have white belly.

Size: *L* 12 cm.

Status: common to abundant migrant and breeder from early May to October; a few birds linger into late November.

Habitat: *Breeding:* coniferous or mixed mature forests; occasionally spruce bogs; in NF, in alder and willow thickets close to water, roads or power lines. *In migration:* any woodland or tall-shrubbed area; coastal tuckamore.

Nesting: on the ground or on a raised hummock; female builds a cup nest of grass, moss and roots and lines it with fur; female incubates 5–6 white eggs, marked with brown or purple, for 11–12 days.

Feeding: gleans foliage and buds for small insects, caterpillars and other invertebrates; also eats berries; occasionally visits suet feeders.

Voice: male's song is a loud, sharp, accelerating *ticka-ticka-ticka swit-swit-swit-swit chew-chew-chew-chew-chew;* call is a sweet *chip*.

Similar Species: *Warbling Vireo* (p. 208): stouter overall; thicker bill; much less green on upperparts. *Philadelphia Vireo* (p. 209): stouter overall; thicker bill; yellow breast and sides. *Orange-crowned Warbler* (p. 251): lacks white eyebrow and blue-grey head.

Best Sites: damp woodlands with dense undergrowth, often in alder and willow thickets alongside rivers and ditches; in all woodland habitats in migration.

ORANGE-CROWNED WARBLER

Vermivora celata

When encountered, this bird usually appears as a blurred olive or greyish-yellow bundle flitting nervously among the leaves and branches of low shrubs. Even worse, its drab, olive yellow appearance makes it frustratingly similar to females of other warbler species. Don't be disappointed if you can't see the Orange-crowned Warbler's tell-tale orange crown, because its most distinguishing characteristic is its lack of field marks: wing bars, eye rings and colour patches are all conspicuously absent. Moreover, Orange-crowned Warblers seen in Atlantic Canada are generally of the palest and greyest race and are thus even more drab than elsewhere.

• *Vermivora* is Latin for "worm eating"; *celata* is derived from the Latin word for "hidden," a reference to this bird's inconspicuous crown.

ID: olive yellow to olive grey body; faintly streaked underparts; bright yellow undertail coverts; thin, faint dark eye line; bright yellow eyebrow and broken eye ring; thin bill; faint orange crown patch (rarely seen).
Size: *L* 13 cm.
Status: rare migrant from mid-April to mid-June and from late August to early November; increasingly regular early winter visitor at feeders.
Habitat: any woodland or tall-shrubbed area, including urban parks and gardens.
Nesting: on the ground or in a small shrub; well-hidden cup nest is made of coarse grass, twigs, bark, moss and leaves and is lined with hair and fine grasses; female incubates

4–5 creamy white eggs, speckled with reddish-brown, for 11–14 days.
Feeding: gleans foliage for invertebrates, berries, nectar and sap; often hover-gleans.
Voice: *Male:* faint trill that breaks downward halfway through.
Similar Species: *Tennessee Warbler* (p. 250): blue-grey head; white underparts, including undertail coverts. *Ruby-crowned Kinglet* (p. 232): broken white eye ring; white wing bars. *Wilson's Warbler* (p. 273): complete bright yellow eye ring; brighter yellow underparts. *Yellow Warbler* (p. 254): brighter head and underparts; reddish breast streaks (faint or absent on female). *Common Yellowthroat* (p. 272): female has darker face and upperparts.
Best Sites: *NB:* Kouchibouguac NP. *PEI:* Rustico I.; Blooming Point. *NS:* Seal I.; Argyle–Pubnico area; Cape North. *NF:* St. John's; Blackhead (Cape Spear); Bear Cove Point (Renews). *PQ:* Rimouski.

251

NASHVILLE WARBLER

Vermivora ruficapilla

The Nashville Warbler has two widely separated summer populations, one in eastern North America and the other in the West. These populations are believed to have been created thousands of years ago when a single core population split apart during continental glaciation. • This warbler was first described near Nashville, Tennessee, but it does not breed in that state. This misnomer is not an isolated incident: the Tennessee, Cape May and Connecticut warblers all bear names that misrepresent their breeding distributions. • Nashville Warblers are fairly common migrants and breeders in most of Atlantic Canada. They are best found in overgrown farmland and second-growth forest as they forage low in trees and thickets, often at the edge of a dry forest or burn area. Considered a rare bird in the 1800s, Nashville Warblers have benefited from the clearing of old-growth forests for timber and agriculture.

ID: bold white eye ring; yellow-green upperparts; yellow underparts; white between legs. *Male:* blue-grey head; may show small, chestnut-red crown. *Female and immature:* duller overall; light eye ring; olive grey head; blue-grey nape.
Size: *L* 12 cm.
Status: common migrant from early May to early June and from September to October; locally common breeder from May to August; a few may arrive in early April; some may remain into December; rare in NF.
Habitat: prefers second-growth mixed woodlands; also in wet coniferous forests, riparian woodlands, cedar spruce swamps and moist, shrubby, abandoned fields.

Nesting: on the ground under a fern, sapling or shrubby cover; female builds a cup nest of grass, bark strips, ferns and moss and lines it with conifer needles, fur and fine grasses; female incubates 4–5 white eggs, with reddish-brown spots toward the larger end, for 11–12 days.
Feeding: gleans foliage for insects, such as caterpillars, flies and aphids.
Voice: male's song begins with a thin, high-pitched *see-it see-it see-it see-it* followed by a trilling *ti-ti-ti-ti-ti*; call is a metallic *chink*.
Similar Species: *Common Yellowthroat* (p. 272) and *Wilson's Warbler* (p. 273): females lack greyish head and bold white eye ring; all-yellow underparts. *Mourning Warbler* (p. 271): females have greyish to brownish "hood"; yellow between legs.
Best Sites: second-growth forest and open brush with birch or aspen stands.

NORTHERN PARULA

Parula americana

Young Northern Parulas spend the first few weeks of their lives enclosed in a fragile, sock-like nest suspended from a tree branch. Once they have grown too large for the nest and their wing feathers are strong enough to allow for a short, awkward flight, the young leave their warm abode, dispersing themselves among the surrounding trees and shrubs. As warm summer nights slip away to be replaced by cooler autumn weather, newly fledged Northern Parulas migrate to the warmer climes of Central America, but mature birds winter in the US. • These warblers are typically found in older forests where the lichens that they use during nesting have had a chance to mature. Males spend most of their time singing and foraging among the tops of tall coniferous spires, where they are often fearless and easily approached. *Parula* is Latin for "little titmouse."

ID: blue-grey upperparts; olive patch on back; 2 bold white wing bars; bold white eye ring broken by black eye line; yellow "chin," throat and breast; white belly and flanks. *Male:* 1 black breast band and 1 orange band.
Size: *L* 11 cm.
Status: uncommon to locally common migrant and breeder from late April to late October; a few may remain into December.
Habitat: moist coniferous forests, humid riparian woodlands and swampy deciduous woodlands, especially where lichens hang from branches.

Nesting: usually in a conifer; female weaves a small hanging nest into hanging strands of tree lichens; pair incubates 4–5 brown-marked, whitish eggs for 12–14 days.
Feeding: forages for insects and other invertebrates by hovering, gleaning or hawking; feeds from tips of branches and occasionally on ground.
Voice: song is a rising, buzzy trill that ends with an abrupt lower-pitched *zip.*
Similar Species: *Yellow-rumped Warbler* (p. 259): lacks yellow throat; yellow rump and crown. *Canada Warbler* (p. 274): larger; more uniform blue-and-yellow plumage; blackish streaking on breast; no wing bars.
Best Sites: *Summer:* fairly moist mixed and coniferous forests with abundant *Usnea* tree lichen for nest-building. *In migration:* along coasts.

YELLOW WARBLER

Dendroica petechia

Yellow Warblers usually arrive in early May with the first main wave of spring warblers. Flitting from branch to branch among open woodland edges and riparian shrubs, these inquisitive birds seem to be in perpetual motion. • Yellow Warblers are among the most frequent victims of cowbird parasitism. Unlike many birds, however, they can recognize the foreign eggs, and many pairs will either abandon their nests or build another nest overtop the old eggs. Some persistent Yellow Warblers build over and over, creating bizarre, multi-layered high-rise nests. • During autumn migration, silent, plain-looking Yellow Warblers, often with other, similar-looking warblers, can confuse birders who know them from summer. Yellow Warblers are unique, however, in having yellow flashes on the sides of their tails. • Because of their bright yellow plumage, Yellow Warblers are also called "Wild Canaries" or, in Newfoundland, "Yellowhammers."

breeding

Size: L 13 cm.
Status: common migrant and breeder from late April to October; a few may remain into November.
Habitat: *Breeding:* usually near water, in moist, open woodlands with dense, low scrub, shrubby meadows, willow tangles and riparian woodlands. *In migration:* almost any shrubby growth, including gardens.
Nesting: in a fork in a deciduous tree or small shrub; female builds a compact cup nest made of grass, weeds and shredded bark and lines it with plant down and fur;

ID: yellow body; black bill and eyes; yellow highlights in dark olive tail and wings. *Breeding male:* red breast streaks.

female incubates 4–5 speckled or spotted, greenish-white eggs for 11–12 days.
Feeding: gleans foliage and vegetation for invertebrates; occasionally hover-gleans.
Voice: male's song is a fast, frequently repeated *sweet-sweet-sweet summer sweet.*
Similar Species: *Orange-crowned Warbler* (p. 251): lacks reddish breast streaks; darker olive plumage overall. *American Goldfinch* (p. 313): black wings and tail; male often has black forehead. *Wilson's Warbler* (p. 273): male has black cap; female has darker crown and upperparts; shorter, darker tail. *Common Yellowthroat* (p. 272): female lacks yellow highlights in wings; darker face and upperparts.
Best Sites: *Summer:* second-growth and suburban areas. *In migration:* alder swales and undergrowth.

CHESTNUT-SIDED WARBLER

Dendroica pensylvanica

Chestnut-sided Warblers favour early-succession forests, which have become abundant over the past century. Although clear-cut logging and prescribed forest burns have adversely affected other species of warblers, they have created suitable habitat for the Chestnut-sided Warbler in many parts of Atlantic Canada. A good indicator of this species' success is the fact that each spring and summer you can easily see more of these warblers in a single day than John J. Audubon saw in his entire life—he saw only one! • Although other warblers lose some of their brighter colours in autumn yet look familiar, the Chestnut-sided Warbler undergoes a complete transformation and masquerades as a flycatcher or kinglet in its green-and-grey coat.

♂

breeding

ID: *Breeding:* chestnut sides; white underparts; yellow cap; black legs; yellowish wing bars; black facial mask. *Male:* bold colours. *Female:* washed-out colours; dark streaking on yellow cap. *Non-breeding:* yellow-green crown, nape and back; white eye ring; grey face and sides; white underparts.
Size: *L* 11–14 cm.
Status: common breeder from May to August; uncommon migrant in May and from late August to October.
Habitat: *Breeding:* shrubby, second-growth deciduous woodlands, abandoned fields and orchards; especially in areas that are regenerating after logging or fire. *In migration:* more widespread, usually in alder and willow thickets with other warblers.

Nesting: low in a shrub or sapling; small cup nest is made of bark strips, grass, roots and weed fibres and is lined with fine grasses, plant down and fur; female incubates 4 brown-marked, whitish eggs for 11–12 days.
Feeding: gleans trees and shrubs at mid-level for insects.
Voice: loud, clear song: *so pleased, pleased, pleased to MEET-CHA!*; musical *chip* call.
Similar Species: *Bay-breasted Warbler* (p. 265): black face; dark chestnut hind-crown, upper breast and sides; buff belly and undertail coverts; white wing bars. *American Redstart* (p. 268): female has large yellow patches on wings and tail; more greyish overall. *Flycatchers* (pp. 198–205): less obvious eye ring; perch upright. *Ruby-crowned Kinglet* (p. 232): smaller; buffer underparts; more active.
Best Sites: almost always in second-growth and thickets. *PQ:* Bas St-Laurent.

MAGNOLIA WARBLER

Dendroica magnolia

The Magnolia Warbler is widely regarded as one of the most beautiful wood-warblers. Like a customized Cadillac, the Magnolia comes fully loaded with all the fancy features—bold eyebrows, flashy wing bars and tail patches, an elegant "necklace," a bright yellow rump and breast and a dark mask. It frequently forages along the lower branches of trees and among shrubs, allowing for reliable close-up observations. Autumn birds lose the dark mask and black "necklace," but they are immediately identifiable by the distinctive white tail flash. • Magnolia Warblers and many other songbirds migrate at night. Unfortunately, many birds are killed each year when they collide with buildings, radio towers and tall smokestacks. • These warblers may well feed in magnolia trees in migration and at wintering sites, but the preferred breeding habitat is almost strictly conifers.

breeding

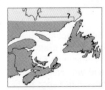

ID: *Breeding male:* yellow underparts with bold black streaks; black mask; white eyebrow; blue-grey crown; dark upperparts; white wing bars often blend into larger patch. *Female* and *non-breeding male:* duller overall; light facial mask; 2 distinct white wing bars; streaked olive back. *In flight:* yellow rump; white tail patches.
Size: *L* 12–13 cm.
Status: very common breeder from June to August; common to locally abundant migrant from early to late May and from late August to mid-October.
Habitat: *Breeding:* open coniferous and mixed forests, mostly in natural openings and along edges, often near water. *In migration:* all types of low growth, especially alder and willow thickets with a few conifers.
Nesting: on a horizontal limb in a conifer; loose cup nest is made of grass, twigs

and weeds and is lined with rootlets; female incubates 4 white eggs, marked with olive, brown, grey and lavender, for 11–13 days.
Feeding: gleans vegetation and buds; occasionally flycatches for beetles, flies, wasps, caterpillars and other insects; sometimes eats berries.
Voice: male's song is a quick, rising *pretty pretty lady* or *wheata wheata wheet-zu*; call is a *clank*.
Similar Species: *Yellow-rumped Warbler* (p. 259): white throat; yellow hindcrown patch; white belly. *Cape May Warbler* (p. 257): chestnut "cheek" patch on yellow face; lacks white tail patches. *Prairie Warbler* (p. 263): dusky jaw stripe; faint yellowish wing bars; immature lacks white tail patches.
Best Sites: conifers and mixed woods in all stages of succession, but particularly eastern hemlock and balsam fir; often at headlands in large numbers during autumn migration.

CAPE MAY WARBLER

Dendroica tigrina

Cape May Warblers require forests that are least 50 years old for secure nesting habitat and an abundance of canopy-dwelling insects. Throughout most of their almost exclusively Canadian breeding range, these small birds seem to be spruce budworm specialists—in years of budworm outbreaks, Cape Mays can successfully fledge more young. Pesticide use to control budworms and the cutting of old-growth forests might adversely affect populations of this warbler. • The Cape May uses its tubular tongue, unique among wood-warblers, to feed on nectar and fruit juices while on its tropical wintering grounds. • Named after Cape May County, New Jersey, where the first scientific specimen was collected in 1811, this bird was not recorded there again for more than 100 years!

breeding

ID: dark streaking on yellow underparts; yellow side collar; dark olive green upperparts; yellow rump; clean white undertail coverts. *Breeding male:* chestnut "cheek" on yellow face; dark crown; large white wing patch. *Female:* paler overall; 2 thin, faint white wing bars; greyish "cheek" and crown.
Size: *L* 12–14 cm.
Status: locally common migrant from mid- to late May and from late August to mid-October; a few may remain into December; uncommon to locally common breeder from May to August.
Habitat: *Breeding:* mature coniferous and mixed forests, especially in dense old-growth stands of white spruce and balsam fir. *In migration:* coastal second-growth and tuckamore.

Nesting: near the top of a spruce or fir, often near the trunk; cup nest of moss, weeds and grass is lined with feathers and fur; female incubates 6–7 whitish eggs with reddish-brown spots for about 12 days.
Feeding: gleans treetop branches and foliage for spruce budworms, flies, beetles, moths, wasps and other insects; occasionally hover-gleans.
Voice: weak, very high-pitched: *see see see see;* call is a very high-pitched *tsee.*
Similar Species: *Bay-breasted Warbler* (p. 265): male has black face and chestnut throat, upper breast and sides; buff underparts lack black streaking. *Black-throated Green Warbler* (p. 260): black throat or upper breast or both; white lower breast and belly; lacks chestnut "cheek." *Magnolia Warbler* (p. 256): lacks chestnut "cheek" patch and yellow side collar.
Best Sites: mature conifers and mixed woods; common at headlands in migration.

BLACK-THROATED BLUE WARBLER

Dendroica caerulescens

Dark and handsome, the male Black-throated Blue Warbler is a treasured sight to the eyes of any bird enthusiast or casual admirer. The female looks nothing like her male counterpart, however, appearing more like a vireo or a plain-coloured Tennessee Warbler. • This warbler prefers to work deliberately and methodically over a small area, snatching up insects among branches and foliage. It is generally shy and inconspicuous, foraging secretly in deciduous foliage or within the dense confines of low shrubs and saplings. • Black-throated Blue Warblers prefer solitude among deciduous forests, but agriculture and urban development have forced them from many of these haunts in Atlantic Canada. They tend to come out into the open in migration, joining Black-and-white Warblers to glean insects from tree branches or competing with Palm Warblers for food on the ground.

ID: *Male:* black face, throat, upper breast and sides; dark blue upperparts; clean white underparts and wing patch.
Female: olive brown upperparts; unmarked buff underparts; faint white eyebrow; small, buff to whitish wing patch (may not be visible).
Size: *L* 13–14 cm.
Status: uncommon to fairly common migrant and breeder from mid-May to September; smaller numbers may remain into October and November, when they may reach NF.
Habitat: *Breeding:* drier mixed woods and riparian hardwood areas. *In migration:* shrubs and thickets at coastal headlands; occasionally in gardens and at feeders.
Nesting: in the fork of a dense shrub or sapling, usually within 1 m of the ground;

female builds an open cup of weeds, bark strips and spider webs and lines it with moss, hair and pine needles; female incubates 4 creamy white eggs, with reddish-brown and grey blotches toward the larger end, for 12–13 days.
Feeding: thoroughly gleans the main branches and understorey for caterpillars, moths, spiders and other insects; occasionally eats berries and seeds.
Voice: song is a slow, wheezy *I am soo lay-zeee*, rising slowly throughout; call is a short *tip*.
Similar Species: male is distinctive. *Tennessee Warbler* (p. 250): lighter "cheek"; greener back; lacks white wing patch. *Philadelphia Vireo* (p. 209) and *Warbling Vireo* (p. 208): stouter bill; lighter "cheek"; more yellow-white below; lacks white wing patch.
Best Sites: dense broadleaf or mixed woods with a fairly dense understorey, especially in cutover areas and old clearings.

YELLOW-RUMPED WARBLER

Dendroica coronata

One of the earliest wood-warblers to arrive in Atlantic Canada in spring, the Yellow-rumped Warbler is the most abundant and widespread wood-warbler in North America. The best time to find one is shortly after dawn, when most Yellow-rumps will be foraging among streamside and shoreline trees. Many Yellow-rumps continue on to Hudson Bay or Labrador, but later arrivals stay to nest here. They may join Blackpoll Warblers in spindly or stunted black spruce stands. In migration, Yellow-rumps are the least choosy of all warblers, spreading out and using all manner of growth. If the wax-myrtle (bayberry) crop is abundant, some birds may overwinter—this species is one of the few wood-warblers to do so in good numbers. • All but a few stray Yellow-rumps in Atlantic Canada are of the "Myrtle" (*coronata*) subspecies. • The scientific name *coronata* is Latin for "crowned," referring to this bird's yellow crown.

"Myrtle Warbler"

ID: yellow fore-shoulder patches and rump; white underparts with dark streaking; faint, white wing bars; thin eyebrow. *Male:* yellow crown; blue-grey upperparts with black streaking; black "cheek" and breast band. *Female:* grey-brown upperparts.
Size: *L* 13–15 cm.
Status: common to abundant migrant from early April to mid-May and from mid-September to early November; common to locally abundant breeder from May to September; a few overwinter.
Habitat: *Breeding:* coniferous and mixed forests; rarely in pure deciduous woodlands. *In migration* and *winter:* all kinds of habitats, especially in low growth along shorelines.
Nesting: in the crotch or on a horizontal limb of a conifer; female builds a compact cup nest with grass, bark strips, moss, lichen and spider silk and lines it with feathers and fur; female incubates 4–5 brown- and grey-marked, creamy white eggs for about 12 days.
Feeding: hawks and hovers for insects; gleans vegetation; sometimes eats berries.
Voice: male's song is a tinkling trill, often given in 2-note phrases that rise or fall at the end; there can be much variation between individuals; call is a sharp *chip* or *check*.
Similar Species: *Magnolia Warbler* (p. 256): yellow underparts; lacks yellow crown. *Chestnut-sided Warbler* (p. 255): chestnut sides on otherwise clean white underparts; lacks yellow rump. *Cape May Warbler* (p. 257): heavily streaked yellow throat, breast and sides; lacks yellow crown.
Best Sites: forested areas of all types and successional stages. *Winter:* Northumberland Strait and NS's Lighthouse Route.

BLACK-THROATED GREEN WARBLER

Dendroica virens

Before the first warm rays of dawn brighten the spires of Atlantic Canada's forests, male Black-throated Green Warblers offer up their distinctive *see-see-see SUZY!* tunes. Unlike other warblers, they continue to sing throughout summer, although song quality tends to suffer late in the season. Not only do males use song to defend their turf, they also seem to thrive on chasing each other, and even other songbirds, from their territories. When foraging among the forest canopy, males are highly conspicuous as they dart from branch to branch, chipping noisily as they go. Females often prefer to feed at lower levels among the foliage of tall shrubs and sapling trees.• In some parts of its range, the Black-throated Green Warbler prefers old-growth coniferous forests. In Atlantic Canada, however, it also nests in mixed woodlands, pure deciduous forests and even second-growth and forest edges.

ID: yellow face; may show faint dusky "cheek" or eye line; black upper breast band; streaking along sides; olive crown, back and rump; dark wings and tail; 2 bold white wing bars; white lower breast, belly and undertail coverts. *Male:* black throat. *Female:* yellow throat; thinner wing bars.
Size: *L* 11–13 cm.
Status: common breeder from May to August; common to locally abundant migrant from September to late October but uncommon as a migrant in May.
Habitat: *Breeding:* coniferous and mixed forests; also in some deciduous woodlands with beech, maple, aspen or birch; may inhabit cedar swamps, hemlock ravines, second-growth and open parklands. *In migration:* coastal woods, second-growth and tuckamore.

Nesting: in a crotch or on a horizontal limb, usually in a conifer; compact cup nest of grass, weeds, twigs, bark, lichen and spider silk is lined with moss, fur, feathers and plant fibres; female incubates 4–5 creamy white to grey eggs, scrawled or spotted with reddish-brown, for 12 days.
Feeding: gleans vegetation and buds for beetles, flies, wasps, caterpillars and other insects; sometimes takes berries; frequently hover-gleans.
Voice: fast *see-see-see SUZY!* or *zoo zee zoo zoo zee*, more languid in late summer; call is a fairly soft *tick*.
Similar Species: *Blackburnian Warbler* (p. 261): female has yellowish underparts and angular dusky facial patch. *Cape May Warbler* (p. 257): heavily streaked yellow throat, breast and sides. *Pine Warbler* (p. 262): lacks black upper breast band; yellowish breast and upper belly.
Best Sites: open coniferous and mixed woods, especially in birch and aspen stands.

BLACKBURNIAN WARBLER

Dendroica fusca

High among the towering conifers lives the colourful Blackburnian Warbler, ablaze in spring with a fiery orange throat. Widely regarded as one of the most beautiful species of warblers in Canada, the Blackburnian stays hidden in the upper canopy for much of the summer. • Different species of wood-warblers are able to coexist through a partitioning of foraging niches and feeding strategies. This intricate partitioning reduces competition for food sources and avoids the exhaustion of particular resources. Some warblers inhabit high treetops, a few feed and nest along outer tree branches—some at high levels and some at lower levels—and others restrict themselves to inner branches and tree trunks. Blackburnians have found their niche predominantly in the outermost branches of each tree. • This bird's name is thought to honour the Blackburne family of England, which collected the type specimen and

managed the museum in which it was housed. • The scientific name *fusca* is Latin for "dusky," an odd reference to the duller winter plumage of this bird.

breeding

ID: *Breeding male:* fiery, reddish-orange upper breast and throat; orange-yellow head with black markings; blackish upperparts; large white wing patch; yellowish to whitish underparts; dark streaking on sides and flanks. *Female:* brown version of male; upper breast and throat are more yellowish than male's.
Size: *L* 12–14 cm.
Status: uncommon to locally common breeder, except locally uncommon in southwest NF and very rare in central NF; rare to uncommon migrant in May and from late August to mid-October.
Habitat: *Breeding:* mature conifers, especially tall spruce and hemlock; mixed forests. *In migration:* wooded areas, including deciduous second-growth; coastal tuckamore.

Nesting: high in a mature conifer, often near a branch tip; cup nest of bark, twigs and plant fibres is lined with conifer needles, moss and fur; female incubates 3–5 white to greenish-white eggs, blotched with reddish-brown toward the larger end, for about 13 days.
Feeding: forages on the uppermost branches, gleaning budworms, flies, beetles and other invertebrates; occasionally hover-gleans.
Voice: soft, faint, high-pitched song: *ptoo-too-too-too tititi zeee* or *see-me see-me see-me see-me*; call is a short *tick*.
Similar Species: *Prairie Warbler* (p. 263): faint yellowish wing bars; black facial stripes do not form solid angular patch. *Black-throated Green Warbler* (p. 260): unstreaked greenish-olive on back and rump.
Best Sites: mature conifers and mixed woods.

PINE WARBLER

Dendroica pinus

Pine Warblers are often difficult to find, because they typically forage near the tops of very tall pine trees. During breeding, these unassuming birds are particularly attracted to mature stands of long-needled white pine and red pine. The species may have been more widespread before many tall pines were cut for shipbuilding in the 1800s and early 1900s. • Although male Pine Warblers are bright enough in summer, the otherwise modest appearance of this species is very similar to that of a number of immature and autumn-plumaged vireos and warblers, making identification more challenging. This warbler is most often confused with the Bay-breasted Warbler or Blackpoll Warbler in drab autumn plumage.

ID: *Male:* olive green head and back; dark greyish wings and tail; whitish to dusky wing bars; yellow throat and breast; faded dark streaking or dusky wash on sides of breast; white undertail coverts and belly; faint yellow, broken eye ring; a little duller in autumn. *Female:* like male, but duller, especially in autumn.

Size: *L* 13–14 cm.

Status: rare to locally uncommon migrant from April to early June; very locally rare to uncommon breeder from May to September; a few may remain into November.

Habitat: *Breeding:* prefers open, mature pine woodlands and mature pine plantations for nesting. *In migration* and *winter:* mixed and deciduous woodlands with other warblers; rare in winter, usually at suet feeders.

Nesting: toward the end of a pine limb; female builds a deep, open cup nest of twigs, bark, weeds, pine needles and spider webs and lines it with feathers; pair incubates 3–5 whitish eggs, with brown specks toward the larger end, for about 10 days.

Feeding: eats mostly insects, berries and seeds; gleans from the ground or foliage by climbing around trees and shrubs; may hang upside down on branch tips.

Voice: song is a short, musical trill; call is a sweet *chip*.

Similar Species: *Prairie Warbler* (p. 263): distinctive dark facial stripes; darker streaking on sides; yellowish wing bars. *Bay-breasted Warbler* (p. 265) and *Blackpoll Warbler* (p. 266): immature and autumn birds have dark streaking on head or back or both; long, thin yellow eyebrow. *Palm Warbler* (p. 264): lacks wing bars; yellow undertail not white.

Best Sites: *Summer* and *in migration: NB:* St. Stephen; Brockway; Douglas; Minto. *NS:* Seal I.; Argyle; Cape Sable I.; Halifax. *NF:* St. John's; Blackhead (Cape Spear); Bear Cove Point (Renews).

PRAIRIE WARBLER

Dendroica discolor

Although Prairie Warblers are considered quite common in many parts of the eastern US, they are very rare in Atlantic Canada and are seen only as vagrants. Most birds have appeared in autumn in the wave of southbound warblers passing through the US eastern seaboard or Ontario and brought to the East Coast by autumn storms. • The increase in birdwatching—and especially feeder operations—since the 1960s has contributed to a major increase in sightings of this conspicuous, tail-wagging yellow warbler with its flashy facial and flank markings. Another factor has been the expansion of its breeding range into coastal Massachusetts and Maine. A further move into Atlantic Canada would be much appreciated.

ID: *Male:* bright yellow face and underparts, except for white undertail coverts; dark "cheek" stripe and eye line; black streaking on sides; olive grey upperparts; inconspicuous chestnut streaks on back; 2 faint yellowish wing bars. *Female* and *immature:* like male, but duller.

Size: *L* 12–13 cm.

Status: uncommon, but increasingly observed, migrant from early August to late October; very rare spring migrant and early winter visitor, mainly at headlands and feeders.

Habitat: usually at headlands and gardens in second-growth; alder and willow thickets.

Nesting: does not nest in Atlantic Canada.

Feeding: mainly insectivorous; gleans, hover-gleans and occasionally hawks for prey; caterpillars are a favoured item for nestlings; will also eat berries and tree sap exposed by sapsuckers.

Voice: buzzy song is an ascending series of *zee* notes; call is sweet *chip*.

Similar Species: *Pine Warbler* (p. 262): lacks distinctive dark streaking on face; lighter streaking on sides; whitish wing bars. *Palm Warbler* (p. 264): usually much duller; fainter streaks on underparts; yellow undertail; no wing bars. *Bay-breasted Warbler* (p. 265) and *Blackpoll Warbler* (p. 266): non-breeding and immature have white bellies and wing bars as well as lighter upperparts with dark streaking.

Best Sites: *NB:* Saint John; Grand Manan I. *NS:* Brier I.; Seal I.; Cape Sable I.; Fall River–Waverley area. *NF:* Ramea; St. John's; Blackhead (Cape Spear); Bear Cove Point (Renews).

PALM WARBLER

Dendroica palmarum

The Palm Warbler, which doesn't forage in palm trees, was apparently named to indicate its subtropical winter range. It is just as comfortable in its summer range, which lies almost exclusively in Canada. Therefore, it could just as easily have been named "Tamarack Warbler" to reflect its preferred breeding habitat. • Whether hopping on the ground or perched momentarily on a tree limb, the Palm Warbler incessantly bobs its tail. This trait is a prominent field mark, particularly in autumn, when its distinctive chestnut crown fades to olive brown. • To all but the most discerning ears, the Palm Warbler's monotonous trill is virtually indistinguishable from the songs of both the Dark-eyed Junco and the Swamp Sparrow, which often nest in adjoining habitats.

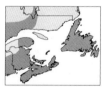

ID: chestnut cap (may be inconspicuous in autumn); yellow eyebrow; yellow throat and undertail coverts; yellow or white breast and belly; dark streaking on breast and sides; olive brown upperparts; frequently bobs its tail; may show dull yellowish rump.

Size: *L* 11–14 cm.

Status: fairly common migrant from mid-April to mid-May and common to locally abundant from early September to late October; uncommon to locally common breeder from May to August; a few may remain into January.

Habitat: *Breeding:* edges of mature bogs with scattered tamarack and black spruce; less frequently in openings of spruce–tamarack forests with sphagnum moss and shrubs. *In migration:* coastal vegetation, including gardens and cemeteries.

Nesting: on the ground or in a low shrub or stunted spruce; often on a sphagnum hummock concealed by grass; female builds a cup nest of grass, weeds and bark and lines it with feathers; 4–5 brown-marked, creamy white eggs are incubated for about 12 days.

Feeding: gleans the ground and vegetation for a variety of insects and berries while perched or hovering; occasionally hawks for insects; may take some seeds.

Voice: male's song is a weak, buzzy trill with a quick finish; call is a sharp *check* or *sup.*

Similar Species: *Yellow-rumped Warbler* (p. 259): female has bright yellow rump, crown patch and foreshoulder patch; white wing bars, throat and undertail coverts. *Prairie Warbler* (p. 263): dark jaw stripe; darker eye line; lacks chestnut crown and dark streaking on breast. *Chipping Sparrow* (p. 278) and *American Tree Sparrow* (p. 277): stouter bodies; unstreaked, greyish underparts; lack yellow plumage. *Pine Warbler* (p. 262): lacks chestnut cap and bold yellow eyebrow; faint whitish wing bars; white undertail coverts.

Best Sites: *Summer* and *in migration:* tamarack and black spruce bogs, especially in Cape Breton and NF.

BAY-BREASTED WARBLER

Dendroica castanea

In summer the handsome Bay-breasted Warbler can be difficult to spot, because it typically forages deep within a stand of old-growth spruce and fir, often on a tree's inner branches. • Bay-breasted Warblers are invaluable when it comes to long-term suppression of spruce budworm outbreaks, typically moving to where the larvae are most numerous. It is estimated that in outbreak years Bay-breasted Warblers can eat 13,000 budworms per hectare through the breeding season. • The Bay-breasted Warbler's scientific name *castanea* (meaning "chestnut" in Latin) comes from its being discovered sitting in a chestnut tree.

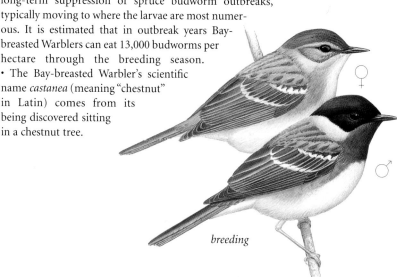

breeding

ID: *Breeding male:* black face and "chin"; chestnut crown, throat and flanks; creamy yellow belly, undertail coverts and patch on side of neck; 2 white wing bars. *Breeding female:* paler overall; dusky face; whitish to creamy underparts and neck patch; faint chestnut cap; rusty wash on sides and flanks. *Non-breeding:* yellow olive head and back; dark streaking on crown and back; whiter underparts.
Size: *L* 13–15 cm.
Status: fairly common migrant from early May to early June and from late August to late October; uncommon to locally common breeder from May to August; a few may remain into November.
Habitat: *Breeding:* mature coniferous and mixed boreal forest; almost exclusively in stands of spruce and fir. *In migration:* coastal woods and scrubby tuckamore.
Nesting: usually on a horizontal conifer branch; open cup nest is built of grass,

twigs, moss, roots and lichen and is lined with fine bark strips and fur; female incubates 4–5 whitish eggs, with dark marks toward the larger end, for about 13 days.
Feeding: usually forages at the mid-level of trees; gleans vegetation and branches for spruce budworms, other caterpillars and adult invertebrates.
Voice: song is an extremely high-pitched *seee-seese-seese-seee*; call is a high *see*.
Similar Species: *Cape May Warbler* (p. 257): chestnut "cheek" on yellow face; dark streaking on mostly yellow underparts; lacks reddish flanks and crown. *Chestnut-sided Warbler* (p. 255): yellow crown; white "cheek" and underparts; non-breeding has white eye ring, unmarked whitish face and underparts and lacks bold streaking on lime green upperparts. *Blackpoll Warbler* (p. 266): non-breeding and immature have dark streaking on breast and sides and lack chestnut on sides and flanks; white undertail coverts.
Best Sites: coniferous areas with a few mature birch and second-growth edges.

BLACKPOLL WARBLER

Dendroica striata

Birdwatchers get a break from the Blackpoll Warbler in Atlantic Canada, where it is one of the commonest nesting warblers, and where it nests in upland conifers and in tuckamore at headlands—elsewhere, this bird summers in remote, insect-swarmed muskeg. • The Blackpoll is the greatest warbler migrant: weighing less than a wet teabag, eastern migrants are known to fly south over the Atlantic, leaving land on the east coast of Newfoundland and not resting until they reach the northern coast of Venezuela. In a single year, a Blackpoll Warbler may fly as far as 16,000 kilometres! • Blackpoll Warblers in autumn plumage are easily confused with very similar-looking Bay-breasted Warblers. Most Blackpolls migrate later in autumn than their Bay-breasted counterparts, leaving as late as early December.

breeding

ID: 2 white wing bars; black streaking on white underparts; white undertail coverts. *Breeding male:* black cap and "chin" stripe; white "cheek"; black-streaked, olive grey upperparts. *Breeding female:* streaked olive yellow head and back; white underparts; small, dark eye line and pale eyebrow. *Non-breeding:* olive yellow head, back, rump, breast and sides; yellow eyebrow; dark legs.
Size: *L* 13–14 cm.
Status: common migrant from mid-May to mid-June and locally abundant from early September to late November; locally common to rare breeder.
Habitat: *Breeding:* coniferous and mixed scrub, open coniferous growth on dry fens and bogs, the backsides of ridged river-banks and sparsely vegetated beach ridges. *In migration:* coastal vegetation, especially tuckamore and mixed woods.

Nesting: well concealed in a stunted spruce tree; nest of twigs, bark shreds, grass and lichen is lined with feathers, fur and rootlets; female incubates 4–5 whitish eggs, spotted with lavender and brown, for about 12 days.
Feeding: gleans buds, leaves and branches for aphids, mosquitoes, beetles, wasps, caterpillars and many other insects; often flycatches for insects.
Voice: song is an extremely high-pitched, uniform trill: *tsit tsit tsit*; call is a loud *chip*.
Similar Species: *Black-and-white Warbler* (p. 267): dark legs; striped, black-and-white crown; male has black "chin," throat and "cheek" patch. *Black-capped Chickadee* (p. 222): lacks wing bars and black streaking on underparts; black "chin" and throat. *Bay-breasted Warbler* (p. 265): non-breeding and immature lack dark streaking on underparts; chestnut sides and flanks; buff undertail coverts.
Best Sites: *Summer:* conifers, especially spruce tuckamore and burn areas. *In migration:* coastal locations in eastern NF.

BLACK-AND-WHITE WARBLER

Mniotilta varia

This bird looks pretty normal for a warbler, but its foraging behaviour stands in sharp contrast to that of most of its kin. Rather than dancing or flitting quickly between twig perches, Black-and-white Warblers behave like creepers and nuthatches—a distantly related group of birds. Birders with frayed nerves and tired eyes from watching flitty warblers will be refreshed by the sight of this bird as it methodically creeps up and down tree trunks. • Novice birders can easily identify this unique two-toned warbler, which retains its standard plumage throughout the year. A keen ear also helps to identify this forest-dweller: its gentle oscillating song—like a wheel in need of greasing—is easily recognized and remembered. *Mniotilta* is from the Greek word for "moss-plucking."

breeding

ID: black-and-white striped crown; dark upperparts with white streaking; 2 white wing bars; white underparts with black streaking on sides, flanks and undertail coverts; black legs. *Breeding male:* black "cheek" and throat. *Breeding female:* grey "cheek"; white throat.
Size: *L* 11–14 cm.
Status: common migrant from late April to May and from late August to mid-October; fairly common to very common breeder from May to August; a few may remain into December.
Habitat: *Breeding:* deciduous or mixed forests, often near water; cedar swamps and alder and willow thickets bordering muskeg and beaver ponds. *In migration:* mixed woods, woodlots and coastal tuckamore and scrub.

Nesting: usually on the ground next to a tree, log or large rock; in a shallow scrape, often among a pile of dead leaves; female builds a cup nest with grass, leaves, bark strips, rootlets and pine needles and lines it with fur and fine grasses; female incubates 5 creamy white eggs, with brown flecks toward the larger end, for 10–12 days.
Feeding: gleans insect eggs, larval insects, beetles, spiders and other invertebrates while creeping along tree trunks and branches.
Voice: series of high, thin, 2-syllable notes: *weetsee weetsee weetsee weetsee weetsee weetsee*; call is a sharp *pit* and a soft, high *seat*.
Similar Species: *Blackpoll Warbler* (p. 266): breeding male has solid black cap and clean white undertail coverts.
Best Sites: *Summer:* forests dominated by hardwoods. *In migration:* urban gardens and parks.

AMERICAN REDSTART

Setophaga ruticilla

American Redstarts are consistently a favourite among birders. These super-charged birds flit from branch to branch in dizzying pursuit of prey. Even when perched, their tails sway rhythmically back and forth. Few birds can rival a mature male redstart for his contrasting black-and-orange plumage, his approachability and his animated behaviour. • Although American Redstarts are common in Atlantic Canada, their high-pitched, lisping, trilly songs are so variable that identifying one is a challenge to birders of all levels. • Redstarts are typically found in small, rural woodlots and wooded parks in suburban residential areas, wherever there is a dense understorey of saplings. • On its wintering grounds, this bird is called "Butterfly-Bird" in the US and *candelita* (little candle) in Central America.

ID: *Male:* black overall; red-orange foreshoulder, wing and tail patches; white belly and undertail coverts. *Female:* olive brown upperparts; grey-green head; yellow foreshoulder, wing and tail patches; clean white underparts.

Size: *L* 13 cm.

Status: common migrant and breeder from early May to early October; a few may remain into November.

Habitat: *Breeding:* shrubby woodland edges, open and semi-open deciduous and mixed forests with a regenerating decidu-ous understorey of shrubs and saplings; often near water. *In migration:* prefers alder swales and thickets.

Nesting: in the fork of a shrub or sapling, usually 1–7 m above the ground; female builds an open cup nest with plant down, bark shreds, grass and rootlets and lines it with feathers; female incubates 4 brown- or grey-marked, whitish eggs for 11–12 days.

Feeding: actively gleans foliage and hawks for insects and spiders on leaves, buds and branches; often hover-gleans.

Voice: male's song is a highly variable series of *tseet* or *zee* notes, often given at different pitches; call is a sharp, sweet *chip*.

Similar Species: none.

Best Sites: widespread.

OVENBIRD

Seiurus aurocapillus

The Ovenbird's loud and joyous "ode to teachers" is a common sound that echoes through Atlantic Canada's deciduous and mixed forests in spring. The Ovenbird also issues a dusk flight song that may continue into the night.
• In summer, this bird is most comfortable hidden in tangles of low shrubs or among conifer branches, but it seems to lose some of its inhibitions in autumn.
• "Ovenbird" refers to this bird's unusual oven-shaped ground nest. The nest is so well camouflaged that few people ever find one, even if it is near a public path. An incubating female usually feels so secure in her nest that when approached, unless closely, she will sit tight rather than flee. A female may have up to three mates to call on for protection and feeding the young.
• The genus and species names translate as "golden-haired tail-waver."

ID: olive brown upperparts; white eye ring; heavy, dark streaking on white breast, sides and flanks; rufous crown bordered by black; pink legs; white undertail coverts; no wing bars.

Size: *L* 15 cm.

Status: common migrant from mid-May to early June, and more widespread but less common from mid-August to early October; fairly common to common breeder from May to August; a few may remain as late as the end of November.

Habitat: *Breeding:* undisturbed, mature deciduous, mixed and coniferous forests with a closed canopy and very little under-storey; often in ravines and riparian areas. *In migration:* dense riparian shrubbery and thickets and coastal woodlands.

Nesting: on the ground; female builds an oven-shaped, domed nest made of grass, weeds, bark, twigs and dead leaves and lines it with animal hair; female incubates 4–5 white eggs, with grey and brown spots, for 11–13 days.

Feeding: gleans the ground for worms, snails, insects and occasionally seeds.

Voice: loud, distinctive *tea-cher tea-cher tea-CHER tea-CHER*, increasing in speed and volume; night song is an elaborate series of bubbly, warbled notes, often ending in *teacher-teacher*; call is a brisk *chip*, *cheep* or *chock*.

Similar Species: *Northern Waterthrush* (p. 270) and *Louisiana Waterthrush:* bold yellowish or white eyebrow; lack rufous crown; darker upperparts. *Thrushes* (pp. 236–41): larger; lack rufous crown outlined in black.

Best Sites: mature broadleaf woods, locally in conifers and mixed woods in Cape Breton and NF; at headlands in October.

269

NORTHERN WATERTHRUSH

Seiurus noveboracensis

This bird mostly skulks along the shores of deciduous swamps or coniferous bogs, so fallen logs, shrubby tangles and soggy ground might discourage human visitors. Birders who are not satisfied with simply hearing a Northern Waterthrush in its nesting territory must literally get their feet wet if they hope to see one in summer. During the relatively bug-free months of spring and autumn, however, birders can typically find migrating Northern Waterthrushes in drier, upland forests or in coastal scrub and tuckamore as well. • Waterthrushes tip and teeter while walking on logs over water or along shorelines and forest vegetation, a habit similar to that of Spotted Sandpipers and perhaps intended to disturb ground- and water-dwelling insects. • This small bird's loud and raucous voice seems fitting for its species name, *noveboracensis*, which is Latin for "of New York," a city well known for its decibels.

ID: pale yellowish to buff eyebrow and underparts; dark streaking on underparts; finely spotted throat; olive brown upperparts; pinkish legs; frequently bobs tail.

Size: *L* 13–15 cm.

Status: common migrant from early May to early June and uncommon from late August to early October; fairly common breeder from May to August.

Habitat: *Breeding:* wooded edges of swamps, lakes, beaver ponds, bogs and rivers; also in moist, wooded ravines and riparian thickets. *In migration:* wetter habitats and coastal tuckamore.

Nesting: on the ground, usually near water; female builds a cup nest made of moss, leaves, bark shreds, twigs and pine needles and lines it with moss, hair and rootlets; female incubates 4–5 whitish eggs, spotted and blotched with brown and purple-grey, for 13 days.

Feeding: distinctive "teeter-totter" walk; gleans foliage and the ground for invertebrates, often tossing aside ground litter with its bill; may also take aquatic invertebrates and small fish from shallow water.

Voice: song is a loud, 3-part *sweet sweet sweet, swee wee wee, chew chew chew chew;* call is a brisk *chip* or *chuck.*

Similar Species: *Ovenbird* (p. 269): russet crown bordered by black stripes; white eye ring; lacks pale eyebrow; unspotted throat. *Palm Warbler* (p. 264): immature is yellower on underparts; indistinct wing bars; wags tail.

Best Sites: tangles and thickets in open conifers and mixed woods, usually near running water.

MOURNING WARBLER

Oporornis philadelphia

ourning Warblers seldom leave the protection of their dense, shrubby, often impenetrable habitat, and they tend to utter their *cheery* song only on their breeding territory. Riparian areas, regenerating clear-cuts and patches of forest recently cleared by fire provide the low shrubs and saplings that this warbler relies on for nesting and foraging. Although essentially birds of broadleaf shrubs, Mourning Warblers can sometimes be found deep in boreal conifers, as long as there is some ground cover. • Mourning Warblers are best seen during migration, when backyard shrubs and raspberry thickets may attract small, silent flocks. They are also seen in coastal locations where cover is more limited. • This bird's dark "hood" reminded pioneering ornithologist Alexander Wilson of someone dressed in mourning. Some birders like to remember this bird's name by thinking that it is mourning the loss of its eye ring.

breeding

ID: yellow under-parts; olive green upperparts; short tail; pinkish legs. *Breeding male:* usually no eye ring, but may have broken eye ring; blue-grey "hood"; black upper breast patch. *Female:* grey "hood"; whitish "chin" and throat; may show thin eye ring. *Immature:* grey-brown "hood"; pale grey to yellow "chin" and throat; thin, incomplete eye ring.
Size: *L* 13–14 cm.
Status: uncommon to locally common breeder from June to August; rare to uncommon migrant from mid-May to late June and from late August to mid-September; a few may remain into late October.
Habitat: dense and shrubby thickets, tangles and brambles, often in moist areas of forest clearings and along the edges of ponds, lakes and streams; boreal forest.

Nesting: on the ground; at the base of a shrub or plant tussock or in a small shrub; bulky nest made with leaves, weeds and grass is lined with fur and fine grass; female incubates 3–4 brown-spotted or brown-blotched creamy white eggs for about 12 days.
Feeding: forages in dense, low shrubs for caterpillars, beetles, spiders and other invertebrates.
Voice: husky, 2-part song is variable and lower at the end: *churry, churry, churry, churry, chorry, chorry;* call is a loud, low *check.*
Similar Species: *Nashville Warbler* (p. 252): bright yellow throat; dark legs. *Common Yellowthroat* (p. 272): less obvious "hood"; yellow throat; duller yellow underparts.
Best Sites: deciduous undergrowth in broadleaf woods or scrubby clearings in conifers; most common in boreal forest of Cape Breton and NF.

COMMON YELLOWTHROAT

Geothlypis trichas

This energetic, black-masked male songster is a favourite among birders—his small size, bright plumage and spunky disposition quickly endear him to all who cross his path. • Common Yellowthroats favour cattail marshes and wet, overgrown meadows, shunning the forest habitat preferred by most of their wood-warbler relatives. • In May and June, the male yellowthroat issues his distinctive songs while perched atop a series of tall cattails or shrubs that he visits in rotation. These strategic outposts mark the boundary of his territory, which he will fiercely guard from intrusions by other males. • Common Yellowthroat nests are commonly parasitized by Brown-headed Cowbirds.

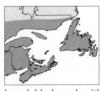

ID: yellow throat, breast and under-tail coverts; dingy white belly; olive green to olive brown upperparts; orangey legs. *Male:* broad, black mask with white upper border. *Female:* no mask; may show faint white eye ring.

Size: *L* 11–14 cm.

Status: locally common migrant and breeder from early May to late October; a few may remain as late as early January.

Habitat: *Breeding:* cattail marshes, riparian willow and alder clumps, sedge wetlands, beaver ponds and wet, overgrown meadows; sometimes on dry, abandoned fields. *In migration:* any wetter vegetation or tuckamore near coastal ponds and bogs.

Nesting: on or near the ground, often in a small shrub or among emergent aquatic vegetation; female builds a bulky open cup nest made of weeds, grass, sedges and other materials and lines it with hair and soft plant fibres; female incubates 3–5 brown- and black-spotted, creamy white eggs for 12 days.

Feeding: gleans vegetation and hovers for adult and larval insects; occasionally eats seeds.

Voice: clear, oscillating *witchety witchety witchety-witch* or other 3-syllable (rarely 2-syllable) repetitions; call is a sharp *tcheck* or *tchet*.

Similar Species: male's black mask is distinctive. *Yellow Warbler* (p. 254): brighter yellow overall; yellow highlights in wings; all-yellow underparts. *Wilson's Warbler* (p. 273): forehead, eyebrow and "cheek" are as bright as all-yellow under-parts; may show dark cap. *Orange-crowned Warbler* (p. 251): dull olive yellow overall; faint breast streaks. *Nashville Warbler* (p. 252): bold, complete eye ring; blue-grey crown.

Best Sites: *Summer* and *in migration:* any brushy sites, usually near water.

WILSON'S WARBLER

Wilsonia pusilla

You are almost sure to catch sight of the energetic Wilson's Warbler at any migration hotspot. This lively bird flickers quickly through tangles of leaves and trees, darting frequently into the air to catch flying insects. Birders often become exhausted while pursuing a Wilson's Warbler, but the bird itself never seems to tire during its lightning-fast performances. • This bird may make brief stopovers in the shrubs of almost any backyard during spring or autumn migration, but its nesting habitat is mostly in early successional stages of willow and alder near bogs and shrub-lined beaver ponds and in pioneering trees on drier sites. • The Wilson's Warbler is richly deserving of its name. Named after Alexander Wilson, this species epitomizes the energetic devotion that the pioneering ornithologist exhibited in the study of North American birds.

ID: yellow under-parts; yellow-green upperparts; black bill; orange legs. *Male:* black cap. *Female:* cap very faint or absent.

Size: *L* 11–13 cm.

Status: uncommon to fairly common breeder from May to August; uncommon migrant from mid-May to mid-June and from early September to October; a few may remain into late December in urban woodlots.

Habitat: *Breeding:* riparian woodlands, willow and alder thickets, bogs and wet, shrubby meadows. *In migration:* second-growth and alder thickets, locally in garden shrubbery.

Nesting: on the ground in moss or at the base of a shrub; female builds a nest made of moss, grass and leaves and lines it with animal hair and fine grass; female incubates 4–6 brown-marked, creamy white eggs for 10–13 days.

Feeding: hovers, flycatches and gleans vegetation for insects.

Voice: song is a rapid chatter that drops in pitch at the end: *chi chi chi chi chet chet*; call is a flat, low *chet* or *chuck*.

Similar Species: black cap is distinctive. *Yellow Warbler* (p. 254): male has red breast streaks; brighter yellow upperparts. *Common Yellowthroat* (p. 272): female has darker face. *Orange-crowned Warbler* (p. 251): dull olive yellow overall; faint breast streaks. *Nashville Warbler* (p. 252): bold, complete eye ring; blue-grey crown. *Canada Warbler* (p. 274): bluish-black on head and back; black "necklace" on male, grey on female.

Best Sites: *Summer:* widespread in open habitat. *In migration:* islands.

CANADA WARBLER

Wilsonia canadensis

To find nesting Canada Warblers, seek out the wettest and most tangled patches of cover imaginable and then await their unwarbler-like, staccato song. Nesting pairs have little competition from other warblers and do not have to go far from the nest for food. • Male Canada Warblers, with their bold white eye rings, have a wide-eyed, alert appearance. • Both sexes are fairly inquisitive and will occasionally pop up from dense shrubs in response to passing hikers. • Canada Warblers live in open defiance of winter: they never stay in one place long enough to experience one! As the summer nesting season in Canada comes to a close, these warblers migrate to South America. • Although there are several wood-warblers that breed exclusively in Canada, the Canada Warbler isn't one of them. Most Canada Warblers nest in eastern Canada, but some can be found nesting in the US.

ID: yellow "spectacles"; yellow underparts (except white undertail coverts); blue-grey upperparts; pale legs. *Male:* streaky black "necklace"; dark, angular half mask. *Female:* blue-green back; faint "necklace."
Size: *L* 13–14 cm.
Status: uncommon to fairly common migrant from mid-May to early June and from mid-August to late September; uncommon to fairly common breeder from May to August, except rare in NF.
Habitat: wet, low-lying areas of mixed forests with a dense understorey, especially riparian willow-alder thickets; also cedar woodlands and swamps.

Nesting: on a mossy hummock or upturned root or stump; female builds a loose, bulky cup nest made of leaves, grass, ferns, weeds and bark and lines it with animal hair and soft plant fibres; 4 brown-spotted, creamy white eggs are incubated for about 10–14 days.
Feeding: gleans the ground and vegetation for beetles, flies, hairless caterpillars, mosquitoes and other insects; occasionally hovers.
Voice: song begins with 1 sharp *chip* note and continues with a rich, variable warble; call is a loud, quick *chick* or *chip*.
Similar Species: *Northern Parula* (p. 253): white wing bars; broken white eye ring. *Common Yellowthroat* (p. 272), *Mourning Warbler* (p. 271) and *Wilson's Warbler* (p. 273): greenish on back; lack "necklace."
Best Sites: wet, shrubby growth and tangles alongside streams.

SCARLET TANAGER

Piranga olivacea

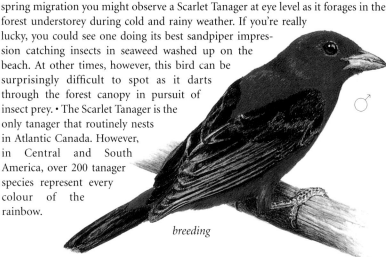

Each spring, birders eagerly await the sweet, rough-edged song of the lovely Scarlet Tanager. The return of the brilliant red male to wooded ravines and traditional migratory sites is always a much-anticipated event. • During spring migration you might observe a Scarlet Tanager at eye level as it forages in the forest understorey during cold and rainy weather. If you're really lucky, you could see one doing its best sandpiper impression catching insects in seaweed washed up on the beach. At other times, however, this bird can be surprisingly difficult to spot as it darts through the forest canopy in pursuit of insect prey. • The Scarlet Tanager is the only tanager that routinely nests in Atlantic Canada. However, in Central and South America, over 200 tanager species represent every colour of the rainbow.

breeding

ID: *Breeding male:* bright red overall with pure black wings and tail; pale bill. *Autumn male:* patchy red and green-yellow plumage; black wings and tail. *Non-breeding male:* bright yellow underparts; olive upperparts; black wings and tail. *Female:* uniformly olive upperparts; yellow underparts; greyish-brown wings.

Size: *L* 17–19 cm.

Status: uncommon migrant from early May to mid-June and from mid-August to October; rare to locally uncommon breeder from May to August; a few birds linger into December and beyond.

Habitat: *Breeding:* fairly mature, upland deciduous and mixed forests and large woodlands. *In migration:* shade trees and coastal shrubbery.

Nesting: on a high branch (usually deciduous) away from the trunk; female builds a flimsy, shallow cup of grass, weeds and twigs and lines it with rootlets and fine grass; female incubates 2–5 pale blue-green eggs, with reddish-brown to brown spots, for 12–14 days.

Feeding: gleans insects from the tree canopy; may hover-glean or hawk insects in mid-air; may forage at lower levels during cold weather; also takes seasonally available berries.

Voice: song is a series of 4–5 sweet, clear, whistled phrases like a slurred version of the American Robin's song; call is a *chip-burrr* or *chip-churrr*.

Similar Species: *Summer Tanager:* larger bill; male has red tail and red wings; female has paler wings and is duskier overall, often with orange or reddish tinge. *Northern Cardinal* (p. 293): red bill, wings and tail; prominent head crest; male has black mask and "bib." *Orchard Oriole* and *Baltimore Oriole* (p. 304): females have sharper bills and wing bars.

Best Sites: *NB:* Edmundston; Sunny Corner (Miramichi); Florenceville. *NS:* Kentville; Bear River; Grafton Lake Trail (Kejimkujik NP); Yarmouth; Seal I.; Chéticamp River. *NF:* Grand Codroy Estuary. *PQ:* Rimouski; St-Anaclet.

EASTERN TOWHEE

Pipilo erythrophthalmus

Eastern Towhees are often heard before they are seen. These noisy foragers rustle about in dense undergrowth, craftily scraping back layers of dry leaves to expose the seeds, berries or insects hidden beneath. • Although you wouldn't guess it, this colourful bird is a member of the American Sparrow family—a group that is usually drab in colour. • The Eastern Towhee and its western relative, the Spotted Towhee (*P. maculatus*), were once grouped together as a single species known as "Rufous-sided Towhee," although they could equally be called the "Red-eyed Towhee." Both towhees act in the same way, and both are eager to see what is going on around them. • The scientific name *Pipilo* is derived from the Latin *pipo*, meaning "to chirp or peep"; *erythrophthalmus* is derived from Greek words that mean "red eye."

ID: rufous sides and flanks; white wing patches; white outer tail corners; white lower breast and belly; buff undertail coverts; red eyes; dark bill. *Male:* black "hood" and upperparts. *Female:* brown "hood" and upperparts. *Immature:* brownish, with distinct streaking above and below; pale bill.

Size: *L* 18–21 cm.

Status: uncommon migrant from April to mid-June and from late August to October; some birds may attempt to winter at feeders; occasional breeder.

Habitat: often along woodland edges and in shrubby, abandoned fields; readily takes to feeders as long as there is dense, low cover available.

Nesting: on the ground or in a dense, low shrub; cup nest is made of twigs, bark strips, grass, weeds, rootlets and animal hair; mostly the female incubates 3–6 spotted, creamy white to pale grey eggs for 10–12 days.

Feeding: scratches at leaf litter for insects, seeds and berries; sometimes forages in low shrubs and saplings.

Voice: song is 2 high, whistled notes followed by a trill: *drink your teeeee*; call is a scratchy, slurred *cheweee!* or *chewink!*

Similar Species: *Dark-eyed Junco* (p. 290): much smaller; pale bill; black eyes; white outer tail feathers. *Sparrows* (pp. 277–89): smaller; lack wing patch of immature. *Purple Finch* (p. 306): more heavily streaked; darker legs; conical bill.

Best Sites: *NB:* Sackville; Bocabec (St. Andrews); Saint John; Summerville; Jemseg; Fredericton. *NS:* Digby; Brier I.; Kejimkujik NP; Sable I.; Port Joli Bay. *NF:* Corner Brook. *PQ:* Trois-Pistoles.

AMERICAN TREE SPARROW

Spizella arborea

Most of us in the south know these rufous-capped, spot-breasted sparrows as winter visitors to backyard feeders, but few of us realize that American Tree Sparrows also visit parts of Atlantic Canada in summer. They typically nest among patches of shrubs along Newfoundland's far northern coast and at the subarctic treeline, so most people find it easier to see them in late March and April when they are in migration. As the small flocks migrate north, they offer bubbly, bright songs between bouts of foraging along the ground or in low, budding shrubs. In autumn, flocks reappear with Dark-eyed Juncos and Chipping Sparrows and spread out over weedy fields, wastelands and roadside thickets.

• Although its name suggests a close relationship with trees, this bird actually prefers treeless fields and semi-open, shrubby habitats; it might more appropriately be named "Subarctic Shrub Sparrow."

breeding

ID: grey under-parts; dark, central breast spot; pale rufous cap; rufous stripe behind eye; grey face; mottled brown upperparts; notched tail; 2 white wing bars; dark legs; dark upper mandible; yellow lower mandible. *Non-breeding:* grey central crown stripe. *Immature:* streaky breast and head.

Size: *L* 15–16 cm.

Status: common to locally abundant from late September to late November; fairly common in winter; fairly common migrant from late March to mid-May; rare breeder in northern NF from May to August.

Habitat: *Breeding:* treeline and coastal shrubby areas of willow, alder and dwarf birch. *Winter* and *in migration:* brushy thickets, roadside shrubs, semi-open fields and agricultural cropland.

Nesting: usually on the ground; on a raised tussock or in a shrub; female builds an open cup nest made of grass, moss, bark shreds and twigs and lines it with feathers and fine grass; female incubates 4–6 pale greenish or bluish eggs, with brown spots toward the larger end, for 11–13 days.

Feeding: scratches exposed soil or snow for seeds in winter; eats mostly insects in summer; takes some berries and occasionally visits birdfeeders.

Voice: a high, whistled *tseet-tseet* is followed by a short, sweet, musical series of slurred whistles; song may be given in late winter and during spring migration; call is a 3-note *tsee-dle-eat*.

Similar Species: *Chipping Sparrow* (p. 278): clear black eye line; white eyebrow; lacks dark breast spot. *Swamp Sparrow* (p. 287): lacks dark breast spot and white wing bars; white throat. *Field Sparrow* (p. 280): white eye ring; orange-pink bill; lacks dark breast spot.

Best Sites: *Summer: NF:* Gros Morne; L'Anse-aux-Meadows. *In migration:* fairly common near the coast throughout, except locally only in NF. *Early winter:* locally uncommon.

CHIPPING SPARROW

Spizella passerina

The Chipping Sparrow and Dark-eyed Junco do not share the same tailor, but they must have attended the same voice lessons, because their songs are very similar. Though the rapid trill of the Chipping Sparrow is slightly faster, drier and less musical, even experienced birders can have difficulty identifying this singer. • Chipping Sparrows commonly nest at eye level, so you can easily watch their breeding and nest-building rituals. They are well known for their preference for conifers as a nest site and hair as a lining material for the nest. By planting conifers in your backyard and offering samples of your pet's hair—or even your own—in backyard baskets in spring, you could attract nesting Chipping Sparrows to your area and contribute to their nesting success. • "Chipping" refers to this bird's call; *passerina* is Latin for "little sparrow."

breeding

ID: *Breeding:* prominent rufous cap; white eyebrow; black eye line; light grey unstreaked underparts; mottled brown upperparts; all-dark bill; 2 faint wing bars; pale legs. *Non-breeding:* paler crown with dark streaks; brown eyebrow and "cheek"; pale lower mandible. *Immature:* brown-grey overall with dark brown streaking; pale lower mandible. **Size:** *L* 13–15 cm.
Status: common to abundant migrant and breeder from mid-April to early November; occasional visitor from November to April.
Habitat: open conifers or mixed woodland edges, especially conifer parklands; often in yards and gardens with tree and shrub borders.
Nesting: usually at mid-level in a tree; female builds a compact cup nest of woven grass and rootlets, which is often lined

with hair; female incubates 4 pale blue eggs for 11–12 days.
Feeding: gleans seeds while hopping along the ground and on outer tree or shrub branches; prefers seeds from grass, dandelions and clovers; also eats adult and larval invertebrates; occasionally visits feeding stations.
Voice: rapid, dry trill of *chip* notes; call is a high-pitched *chip.*
Similar Species: *American Tree Sparrow* (p. 277): dark central breast spot; lacks bold white eyebrow; rufous stripe extends behind eye. *Swamp Sparrow* (p. 287): lacks white eyebrow, black eye line and white wing bars. *Field Sparrow* (p. 280): lacks bold white eyebrow; rufous stripe extends behind eye; white eye ring; grey throat; orange-pink bill.
Best Sites: *Summer:* woodland openings and edges, parklands, orchards and gardens. *In migration:* locally abundant along coasts and on islands.

CLAY-COLORED SPARROW

Spizella pallida

For the most part, Clay-colored Sparrows go completely unnoticed, because their plumage, habit and voice all contribute to a cryptic lifestyle. Even when males are singing at the top of their "air sacs," they are usually mistaken for buzzing insects. Their eastward breeding range expansion has reached Québec and New Brunswick, but they remain a rare commodity in Atlantic Canada, and even keen birders in suitable habitat have difficulty finding these sparrows.
• Although subtle in plumage, the Clay-colored Sparrow still possesses an unassuming beauty. Birders looking closely at this sparrow to confirm its identity can easily appreciate its delicate shading, texture and form—features so often overlooked in birds with more colourful plumage. • Often found in shrubby, open bogs and willow scrub habitat, Clay-colored Sparrows will tag along with migrant and wintering Chipping Sparrows and Dark-eyed Juncos and show up in a variety of open-ground habitats.

ID: unstreaked white underparts; buff breast wash; grey nape; light brown "cheek," edged with darker brown; brown crown with dark streak and pale central stripe; pale eyebrow; white jaw stripe bordered by brown; white throat; mostly pale bill. *Immature:* dark streaks on buff breast, sides and flanks.
Size: *L* 13–14 cm.
Status: rare migrant and very local breeder from mid-May to mid-November.
Habitat: *Breeding:* brushy open areas along forest and woodland edges; in forest openings, regenerating burn sites, abandoned fields and riparian thickets. *In migration* and *winter:* variety of open-ground habitats, including cemeteries and gardens.

Nesting: in a grassy tuft or small shrub; female builds an open cup nest made of twigs, grass, weeds and rootlets and lines it with rootlets, fine grass and fur; mostly the female incubates 4 bluish-green eggs, speckled with brown, for 10–12 days.
Feeding: forages for seeds and insects on the ground and in low vegetation.
Voice: song is a series of 2–5 slow, low-pitched, insect-like buzzes; call is a soft *chip*.
Similar Species: *Chipping Sparrow* (p. 278): breeding adult has prominent rufous cap, grey "cheek" and underparts, 2 faint white wing bars and all-dark bill; immature lacks grey nape and buff on sides and flanks but may look almost identical.
Best Sites: *Summer* and *in migration:* NB: St-Simon–Shippegan area; Rexton; Grand Manan I.; Fredericton. *NS:* Seal I. *NF:* St. John's, Cape Race. *PQ:* Gaspé.

279

FIELD SPARROW

Spizella pusilla

This pink-billed sparrow frequents overgrown fields, pastures and forest clearings. Deserted farmland may seem "unproductive" to some people, but to the Field Sparrow it is heaven. For nesting purposes, this bird usually chooses pastures that are scattered with shrubs, herbaceous plants and plenty of tall grass. • A few birds have colonized New Brunswick, and summer sightings elsewhere suggest that others may follow. Having this bird around adds a lot to a summer day, because its song is a pleasant combination of two or more languid whistles and a rapid trill. • The Field Sparrow has learned to recognize when its nest has been parasitized by the Brown-headed Cowbird. Because the unwelcome eggs are usually too large for this small sparrow to eject, the nest is simply abandoned. This sparrow can be so stubborn in refusing to raise young cowbirds that affected pairs may make many nesting attempts in a single season.

ID: orange-pink bill; grey face and throat; rusty crown with grey central stripe; rusty streak behind eye; white eye ring; 2 white wing bars; unstreaked grey underparts with buffy-red wash on breast, sides and flanks; pinkish legs. *Immature:* duller version of adult, with streaked breast and faint buff-white wing bars.
Size: *L* 13–15 cm.
Status: uncommon migrant and rare, local breeder from early April to mid-November; rare from late November to March.
Habitat: abandoned or weedy and overgrown fields and pastures; woodland edges and clearings; extensive shrubby riparian areas and young conifer plantations.
Nesting: on or near the ground, often sheltered by a grass clump, shrub or sapling; female weaves an open cup

nest made of grass and lines it with animal hair and soft plant material; female incubates 3–5 brown-spotted, whitish to pale bluish-white eggs for 10–12 days.
Feeding: forages on the ground; takes mostly insects in summer; takes mostly seeds in winter.
Voice: song is a series of woeful, musical, down-slurred whistles accelerating into a trill; call is a *chip* or *tsee*.
Similar Species: *American Tree Sparrow* (p. 277): dark central breast spot; lacks white eye ring; dark upper mandible. *Swamp Sparrow* (p. 287): lacks 2 white wing bars and white eye ring; white throat; dark upper mandible. *Chipping Sparrow* (p. 278): all-dark bill; white eyebrow; black eye line; lacks buffy-red wash on underparts.
Best Sites: *Summer* and *in migration:* NB: St. Stephen; Pennfield Ridge; Fredericton. *NS:* South Milford; Caledonia; Seal I. *PQ:* Rimouski; Carleton–New Richmond area.

VESPER SPARROW

Pooecetes gramineus

For birders who live near grassy fields and agricultural lands with multitudes of confusing little brown sparrows, the Vesper Sparrow offers a welcome relief—white outer tail feathers and a chestnut shoulder patch announce its identity whether it's perched or in flight. • The Vesper Sparrow is also known for its bold and easily distinguished song, which begins with two sets of memorable double notes: *here-here! there-there!* • More often than not, a Vesper Sparrow nest is built in a grassy hollow at the base of a clump of weeds or small shrub. This set-up provides camouflage and functions as a windbreak and an umbrella to protect the young. Unfortunately, modern land management practices work against the Vesper Sparrow: keeping grass short destroys the very habitat it prefers, just as it lays its eggs. • "Vesper" is Latin for "evening," a time when this bird often sings; *Pooecetes* is Greek for "grass dweller."

ID: chestnut shoulder patch; white outer tail feathers; pale yellow lores; weak flank streaking; white eye ring; dark upper mandible; lighter lower mandible; light-coloured legs.

Size: *L* 15–17 cm.

Status: uncommon migrant and breeder from mid-April to mid-November; rare in winter, although some birds have overwintered.

Habitat: open fields bordered or interspersed with shrubs, semi-open shrub lands and grasslands; also in agricultural areas, open, dry conifer plantations and scrubby gravel pits.

Nesting: in a scrape on the ground, often under a canopy of grass or at the base of a shrub; loosely woven cup nest made of grass is lined with rootlets, fine grass and hair; mostly the female incubates 3–5 brown- and grey-blotched, whitish to greenish-white eggs for 11–13 days.

Feeding: walks and runs along the ground, picking up grasshoppers, beetles, cutworms, other invertebrates and seeds.

Voice: 4 characteristic preliminary notes, with the second higher in pitch, followed by a bubbly trill: *here-here there-there, everybody-down-the-hill.*

Similar Species: *American Pipit* (p. 247): thinner bill; greyer upperparts lack brown streaking; lacks chestnut shoulder patch. *Lapland Longspur* (p. 291): broad, pale eyebrow and reddish edgings to wing feathers in non-breeding plumage; blackish or buff wash on upper breast. *Other sparrows* (pp. 277–89): lack white outer tail feathers and chestnut shoulder patch.

Best Sites: *Summer* and *in migration: NB:* Tabusintac; Kellys Beach (Kouchibouguac NP); Tantramar Marshes; Salisbury; New River Beach; St. Andrews. *PEI:* North Cape; Victoria; Pinette. *NS:* Oxford–River Philip area; Parrsboro; Grand Pré; Margaree Valley. *PQ:* Bic; Presqu'île de Forillon.

281

SAVANNAH SPARROW

Passerculus sandwichensis

The Savannah Sparrow is one of the most common open-country birds in Atlantic Canada. At one time or another, most residents have probably seen or heard this sparrow, although they may not have been aware of it. This bird's streaky, dull brown, buff-and-white plumage makes it resemble so many of the other grassland sparrows that it is easily overlooked. The very pale *princeps* sub-species, the "Ipswich Sparrow," is mostly found on Nova Scotia's Sable Island, but it has also nested on the mainland coast at Martinique Beach, Nova Scotia, and appeared at other locations in winter. • From early spring to early summer, males belt out their distinctive, buzzy, thoroughly unprofessional tunes while perched atop a prominent shrub, strategic fence post or tall weed. Like most sparrows, however, Savannahs generally stay out of sight. When danger appears, they fly only as a last resort—they prefer to run swiftly and inconspicuously through the grass, like feathered voles. • The common and scientific names of this bird reflect its broad North American distribution: "Savannah" refers to the city in Georgia; *sandwichensis* is derived from Sandwich Bay in the Aleutians off Alaska.

ID: finely streaked breast and flanks; mottled brown upperparts; light-coloured, streaked underparts; yellow lores; light jaw line; light-coloured legs and bill; may show dark breast spot.
Size: *L* 11–16 cm.
Status: common to abundant migrant and breeder from late March to late October; rare visitor from November to March.
Habitat: *Breeding:* agricultural fields (especially hay and alfalfa), moist sedge and grass meadows, pastures, salt marshes, beaches, dunes, bogs and fens, locally in forest clearings. *In migration* and *winter:* along shorelines, in weedy fields and in overgrown gardens.

Nesting: on the ground; in a shallow scrape well concealed by grass or a shrub; female builds an open cup nest that is woven and lined with grass; female incubates 3–6 whitish to greenish or pale tan eggs, marked with brown, for 10–13 days.
Feeding: walks or runs on the ground to glean insects and seeds; occasionally scratches.
Voice: song is a high-pitched, clear, buzzy *tea tea tea teeeeea today;* call is a high, thin *tsit.*
Similar Species: *Vesper Sparrow* (p. 281): white outer tail feathers; chestnut shoulder patches. *Lincoln's Sparrow* (p. 286): buff jaw line; buff wash across breast; broad, grey eyebrow. *Song Sparrow* (p. 285): lacks yellow lores; triangular "moustache" stripes; pale central crown stripe; rounded tail.
Best Sites: *Summer* and *in migration:* widespread.

NELSON'S SHARP-TAILED SPARROW

Ammodramus nelsoni

Although spotting a Nelson's Sharp-tailed Sparrow in other parts of Canada requires a careful search among dense, concealing stands of cattails and bulrushes, the duller *subvirgatus* subspecies found throughout the Maritimes is as easy to find as any other sparrow fond of concealing itself in low, coastal marsh grasses. A few even venture into inland freshwater marshes and riparian margins. • This sparrow's buzzy song is probably seldom recognized, and some people say it should not even be considered to be a song! Nonetheless, Sharp-tails announce their presence well into the summer and then abruptly disappear. • Nelson's Sharp-tailed Sparrows have a very unusual breeding strategy among songbirds: the males rove around the marsh mating with all available females, which are also promiscuous. These sparrows do not establish pair bonds or territories. • Edward William Nelson was the chief of the US Biological Survey and president of the American Ornithologists' Union. His greatest contribution to ornithology was the creation of the Migratory Bird Treaty, which is still in effect today.

ID: buff-orange face, breast, sides and flanks; grey "cheek," central crown stripe and nape; dark line behind the eye; indistinct streaking on the underparts; brown stripes on a grey back; white to light-buff throat.

Size: *L* 13–15 cm.

Status: uncommon to locally common breeder from June to August; rare migrant from mid-May to mid-June and from September to mid-November.

Habitat: *Breeding:* coastal sedge and salt marshes; very local in wet meadows and along the edges of marshes and lakes. *In migration* and *winter:* marshlands with tall emergent vegetation and shoreline vegetation; coastal salt marshes and dunes.

Nesting: on the ground or low in upright grass or sedge stems; bulky cup nest is woven with dry grass and sedges and lined with fine grass; female incubates 3–5 pale blue-green to greenish-white eggs, heavily dotted with reddish-brown, for 11–12 days.

Feeding: gleans ants, beetles, grasshoppers and other invertebrates from the ground and low vegetation; also eats seeds.

Voice: song is a short, raspy buzz: *ts tse-sheeeee*.

Similar Species: *Savannah Sparrow* (p. 282): notched tail; heavily streaked underparts.

Best Sites: *Summer* and *in migration:* coastal marshes. *NB:* lower Saint John River Valley; Keswick Ridge. *NS:* along the Shubenacadie River.

FOX SPARROW

Passerella iliaca

Like the Eastern Towhee, the Fox Sparrow eagerly scratches out a living, using both feet to stir up leaves and scrape organic matter along the forest floor. This sparrow's preference for impenetrable, brushy habitat makes it a difficult species to observe, even though its noisy foraging habits often reveal its whereabouts. Its loud, whistled courtship songs are as easily recognized, and to the attentive listener they can often be as moving as a loon's wail or a wolf's howl. • Unlike other songbirds, which often filter through the region in a series of lingering waves, most Fox Sparrows appear in the Maritimes for only a few short weeks before moving on to their nesting grounds. They are among the first sparrows to appear in spring and one of the last to leave in autumn. • The overall reddish-brown appearance of this bird inspired taxonomists to name it after the red fox. Fox Sparrows in western Canada are sooty-brown, which can cause a moment's confusion for Atlantic Canadian birders travelling there.

ID: whitish underparts; reddish-brown spotting and streaking; central breast spot; reddish-brown wings, rump and tail; grey crown; brown-streaked back; grey eyebrow and nape; stubby, conical bill; pale legs.

Size: *L* 17–19 cm.

Status: common to locally abundant migrant from late March to mid-April and from early October to mid-November; locally rare to common breeder from May to September; rare to locally uncommon winter visitor from November to April.

Habitat: *Breeding:* moist riparian thickets of willow and alder; dense vegetation in mixedwood forests; coastal headlands; highland barrens. *In migration:* also in brushy woodland clearings, edges and parklands. *Winter:* some birds visit feeders.

Nesting: on the ground or low in a shrub or sapling; often in sphagnum moss or Labrador tea; cup nest, woven with twigs, grass, moss and bark shreds, is lined with fine grass and animal hair; female incubates 3–4 greenish-white to pale green eggs, heavily blotched with reddish-brown, for about 12 days.

Feeding: scratches the ground to uncover seeds, berries and invertebrates; visits feeders.

Voice: song is a variable, long series of melodic whistles: *All I have is what's here dear, won't you won't you take it?*; calls include *chip* and *click* notes.

Similar Species: *Song Sparrow* (p. 285): pale central crown stripe; dark "moustache"; dark brownish rather than reddish streaking and upperparts. *Hermit Thrush* (p. 240): longer, thinner bill; light eye ring; dark breast spots; lacks heavy streaking on underparts; unstreaked olive brown and reddish-brown upperparts.

Best Sites: *Summer: NB:* Eel River Lagoon; Mount Carleton PP; Plaster Rock–Nictau area. *NS:* islands; Peggys Cove–Herring Cove area; Sherbrooke; Canso; Cape Breton Highlands NP; Aspy Bay. *NF:* widespread. *PQ:* widespread. *In migration:* urban areas and along coasts.

SONG SPARROW

Melospiza melodia

The Song Sparrow's heavily streaked, low-key plumage doesn't prepare you for its symphonic song. This well-named sparrow is known for the complexity, rhythm and emotion of its springtime rhapsodies, although many residents will insist that the Fox Sparrow and Lincoln's Sparrow carry the best tunes. • Young Song Sparrows (and many other songbirds) learn to sing by eavesdropping on their fathers or on rival males. By the time a young male is a few months old, he will have formed the basis for his own courtship tune. • In recent decades, mild winters and an abundance of backyard birdfeeders have enticed an increasing number of Song Sparrows to overwinter here. The species is also expanding its range eastward in Newfoundland and will soon occupy all of Atlantic Canada. • The scientific name *melodia* means "melody" in Greek.

ID: whitish underparts with heavy brown streaking that converges into central breast spot; greyish face; dark line behind eye; white jaw line is bordered by dark stripes; dark crown with pale central stripe; mottled brown upperparts; rounded tail tip.

Size: *L* 14–18 cm.

Status: common to abundant migrant and breeder from early March through November; uncommon but increasing visitor from November to March.

Habitat: *Breeding:* shrubby areas, often near water, including willow shrub lands, riparian thickets, forest openings and pastures. *In migration* and *winter:* any brushy area and overgrown field, often in urban areas.

Nesting: usually on the ground or low in a shrub or small tree; female builds an open cup nest made of grass, weeds, leaves and bark shreds and lines it with rootlets, fine grass and hair; female incubates 3–5 greenish-white eggs, heavily spotted with reddish-brown, for 12–14 days; may raise 2–3 broods each summer.

Feeding: gleans the ground, shrubs and trees for cutworms, beetles, grasshoppers, ants, other invertebrates and seeds; also eats wild fruit and visits feeding stations.

Voice: 1–4 bright, distinctive introductory notes, such as *sweet, sweet, sweet*, followed by a buzzy *towee*, then a short, descending trill; calls include a short *tsip* and a nasal *tchep*.

Similar Species: *Fox Sparrow* (p. 284): heavier breast spotting and streaking; lacks pale central crown stripe and dark "moustache"; reddish rather than dark brownish streaking and upperparts. *Lincoln's Sparrow* (p. 286): lightly streaked breast with buff wash; buff jaw line. *Savannah Sparrow* (p. 282): lightly streaked breast; yellow lores; lacks greyish face and dark triangular "moustache"; notched tail.

Best Sites: brushy growth and waterside edges—absent only from densely forested areas and uplands.

LINCOLN'S SPARROW

Melospiza lincolnii

There is a certain beauty in the plumage of a Lincoln's Sparrow that is greater than the sum of its feathers. Everything about it is refined and, dare we say, "feminine," in comparison to the scruffier, chunkier and more "masculine" Song Sparrow. Sightings of this bird can bring joy to the hearts of perceptive bird-watchers, especially if they are lucky enough to hear its song. • Most Lincoln's Sparrows build their nests in the cool, moist muskeg of northern Canada, but in Atlantic Canada they are birds of boreal bogs, fens and the margins of wetland areas. • Lincoln's Sparrows seem to be more timid than other Atlantic Canadian sparrows. Males will sit openly on exposed perches and sing their bubbly, wren-like songs, but as soon as they are approached they tend to slip under the cover of nearby shrubs. When they're not singing their courtship songs, Lincoln's Sparrows remain well hidden in tall grass and dense brushy growth. • This sparrow bears the name of Thomas Lincoln, a young companion to John J. Audubon on his voyage to Labrador.

ID: buff breast band, sides and flanks with fine dark streaking; buff jaw stripe; grey eyebrow, face and collar; dark line behind eye; dark reddish cap with grey central stripe; white throat and belly; mottled grey-brown to reddish-brown upperparts; very faint white eye ring.
Size: *L* 14 cm.
Status: fairly common to locally abundant breeder from late May to late August; uncommon to locally common migrant from early May to early June and from mid-September to November; occasionally lingers to late December.
Habitat: *Breeding:* shrubby edges of bogs, swamps, beaver ponds and meadows; also in the shrubby growth of recent forest burns or clearings. *In migration:* variety of open and scrubby habitats, mostly along coasts and usually with other sparrows.

Nesting: on the ground, often on soft moss or concealed beneath shrubs; female builds a well-hidden cup nest made of grass and sedges and lines it with fine grass and hair; female incubates 4–5 greenish-white to pale green eggs, heavily spotted with reddish-brown, for 11–14 days.
Feeding: scratches at the ground, exposing invertebrates and seeds; occasionally visits feeding stations.
Voice: wren-like musical mixture of buzzes, trills and warbled notes; calls include a buzzy *zeee* and *tsup*.
Similar Species: *Song Sparrow* (p. 285): heavier breast streaking; dark, triangular "moustache"; lacks buff wash on breast, sides and flanks. *Savannah Sparrow* (p. 282): yellow lores; white eyebrow and jaw line. *Swamp Sparrow* (p. 287): generally lacks streaking on breast; more contrast between red and grey crown stripes.
Best Sites: in open bogs, wet, scrubby areas and wet meadows.

SWAMP SPARROW

Melospiza georgiana

breeding

Swamp Sparrows are well adapted to life near water. These wetland inhabitants skulk about the emergent vegetation of cattail marshes, foraging for a variety of invertebrates, including beetles, caterpillars, spiders, leafhoppers and flies. Like other sparrows, they are unable to swim, but that is no deterrent—they nevertheless snatch many of their meals directly from the water's surface. • Swamp Sparrows must keep a lookout for daytime predators such as Northern Harriers, Great Blue Herons and large snakes; at night the key to survival is finding a secluded, concealing perch that will keep them safe from raccoons, skunks and weasels. • Male Swamp Sparrows are easily seen in spring, when they sing their familiar trills from atop cattails or shoreline shrubs, and both sexes can be seen in autumn, when they join other sparrows in alder and willow thickets along the coasts.

ID: grey face; reddish-brown wings; brownish upperparts; dark streaking on back; dull grey breast; white throat and jaw line outlined by black stripes; dark line behind eye. *Breeding:* rusty cap; streaked buff sides and flanks. *Non-breeding:* streaked brown cap with grey central stripe; more brownish sides. *Immature:* buffy eyebrow and faint streaking on breast.
Size: *L* 13–14 cm.
Status: fairly common to common migrant and breeder from April to late October; rare to locally uncommon from November to December, sometimes overwinters in urban areas and sheltered coastal areas.
Habitat: cattail marshes, open wetlands, wet meadows and open, riparian deciduous thickets; joins other sparrows in migration.
Nesting: in emergent aquatic vegetation or shoreline bushes; cup nest is woven with coarse grass and marsh vegetation and is lined with fine grass; usually has a partial canopy and a side entrance; female incubates 4–5 greenish-white to pale green eggs, heavily marked with reddish-brown, for 12–15 days.
Feeding: gleans insects from the ground, vegetation and the water's surface; takes seeds in late summer and autumn.
Voice: song is a slow, sharp, metallic trill: *weet-weet-weet-weet*; call is a harsh *chink*.
Similar Species: *Chipping Sparrow* (p. 278): clean white eyebrow; full black eye line; uniformly grey underparts; white wing bars. *American Tree Sparrow* (p. 277): dark central breast spot; white wing bars; 2-toned bill. *Song Sparrow* (p. 285): heavily streaked underparts; lacks grey collar. *Lincoln's Sparrow* (p. 286): fine breast streaking; less contrast between brown and grey crown stripes.
Best Sites: *Summer* and *in migration:* in wet areas, including meadows, cattail marshes and shrubbery around lakes and ponds.

WHITE-THROATED SPARROW
Zonotrichia albicollis

This patriot of Canada's northern forests arrives each spring to sing its glorious, familiar tribute: *dear sweet Canada Canada Canada*. Listeners often find pleasure at the soothing sound of these few simple notes announcing the arrival of spring. Like many "snowbirds," most White-throated Sparrows move to warmer climates in autumn and early winter, but the few birds that overwinter at feeders are equally welcome, because they add a touch of colour to the host of drabber finches and sparrows. • This handsome sparrow is easily identified by its bold white throat and striped crown. Two colour morphs are common throughout Atlantic Canada: one has black and white stripes on the head; the other has brown and tan stripes. • In spring and autumn, White-throated Sparrows can appear anywhere in great abundance. They are often found in loose, active bands with other sparrows, often acting as sentinels on guard for neighbourhood cats and other predators. • *Zonotrichia* means "hair-like," a reference to the striped heads of birds in this genus; *albicollis* is Latin for "white neck."

white-striped morph

ID: black-and-white (or brown-and-tan) striped head; white throat; grey "cheek"; yellow lores; black eye line; grey unstreaked underparts; mottled brown upperparts; greyish bill.
Size: *L* 17–18 cm.
Status: common to abundant migrant from April to mid-May and from mid-September to early November; common breeder from May to September; rare to locally uncommon visitor from November to April.
Habitat: *Breeding:* semi-open coniferous and mixed forests, especially in disturbed woods, regenerating clearings and along shrubby forest edges. *In migration:* woodlots, wooded parks and riparian brush. *Winter:* feeders and sheltered coastal lagoons.
Nesting: on or near the ground, often concealed by low shrubs or a fallen log;

female builds an open cup nest made of grass, weeds, twigs and conifer needles and lined with rootlets, fine grass and hair; female incubates 4–5 greenish-blue to pale blue eggs, marked with lavender and reddish-brown, over 11–14 days.
Feeding: scratches the ground to expose invertebrates, seeds and berries; also gleans insects from vegetation and while in flight; eats seeds from birdfeeders in winter.
Voice: variable song is a clear and distinct whistled *dear sweet Canada Canada Canada*; call is a sharp *chink*.
Similar Species: *White-crowned Sparrow* (p. 289): lacks bold white throat and yellow lores; pinkish bill; grey collar. *Swamp Sparrow* (p. 287): smaller; lacks head pattern; grey and chestnut on crown; streaked underparts.
Best Sites: in forest edge habitats and disturbed woodlands, including coniferous and mixed woodlands.

WHITE-CROWNED SPARROW

Zonotrichia leucophrys

Large, bold and smartly patterned, White-crowned Sparrows brighten brushy expanses and suburban parks and gardens across much of the region with their striped crowns and cheeky songs for a few short weeks in spring and autumn. Some of the spring birds are of the yellow-billed western subspecies *gambelii*. Most White-crowned Sparrows then disappear to their northern tundra home, except for a small population that crosses over to Newfoundland's northern peninsula. Some of this small group nest in coastal tuckamore. The rest make their ascent to the scrubby growth of subalpine mountaintop barrens, where their melancholy, whistled song is just what you want to hear after a long uphill slog. • The White-crowned Sparrow is one of North America's most studied sparrows. Research on this bird has given science tremendous insight into bird physiology, homing behaviour and the geographic variability of song dialects.

ID: black-and-white striped head; black eye line; pink-orange bill; grey face; unstreaked grey underparts; pale grey throat; mottled grey-brown upperparts; 2 faint white wing bars. *Immature:* broad grey eyebrow bordered by brown eye line and crown.

Size: *L* 14–18 cm.

Status: common to locally abundant migrant from mid-September to mid-November; uncommon to locally common migrant from late April to early June; uncommon local breeder from June to early September; rare visitor from November to April, often at feeders.

Habitat: *Breeding:* shrubby open meadows, bogs, forest edges, forest clearings, riparian thickets and willow clumps on tundra; locally coastal in tuckamore and occasionally shrubby growth on field edges. *In migration:* also woodlots and brushy tangles.

Nesting: on or near the ground, usually in a depression of moss and lichen sheltered by a shrub or small tree; female builds an open cup nest made of twigs, grass, leaves, weeds and bark shreds and lines it with feathers, hair and fine grass; female incubates 3–5 creamy-white to pale greenish eggs, heavily spotted with reddish-brown, for 11–14 days.

Feeding: scratches the ground to expose insects and seeds; also eats berries, buds and moss caps; may take seeds from bird feeders.

Voice: song is a frequently repeated variation of *I gotta go wee-wee now;* call is a high, thin *seet* or a sharp *pink.*

Similar Species: *White-throated Sparrow* (p. 288): bold white throat; greyish bill; yellow lores; browner overall. *Chipping Sparrow* (p. 278): smaller; greyish rump; finer bill.

Best Sites: *Summer: NF:* Gros Morne; Parson's Pond; Eddies Cove East; Cape Norman; L'Anse-aux-Meadows. *In migration:* headlands; very rarely inland.

DARK-EYED JUNCO

Junco hyemalis

Most Dark-eyed Juncos in the Canadian interior migrate south for winter, but you can manage to find a few birds here and there in Atlantic Canada even during the coldest years. Juncos usually congregate in backyards with bird feeders and sheltering conifers—they are, in fact, the original "snowbird" that Anne Murray sang about in the 1970s. • Juncos spend most of their time on the ground, and they are readily flushed from wooded trails and backyard feeders. Their distinctive white outer tail feathers will flash in alarm as they rush for the cover of a nearby tree or shrub. • Juncos rarely perch at feeders, preferring to snatch up seeds that are knocked to the ground by other visitors, such as chickadees, sparrows, nuthatches and jays. • Western Canada boasts a great diversity of junco subspecies, some of which occasionally visit Atlantic Canada, but most of the home-grown variety belong to the subspecies *hyemalis*, the "Slate-colored Junco."

"Slate-colored Junco"

ID: white outer tail feathers; pale bill. *Male:* dark slate grey overall, except for white lower breast, belly and undertail coverts. *Female:* brown rather than grey. *Immature:* brown like female but streaked with darker brown.
Size: *L* 14–17 cm.
Status: common breeder from May to late August; common to abundant migrant and visitor from September to late April; many overwinter in urban areas, especially where there are ground feeders.
Habitat: *Breeding:* coniferous and mixed forests, especially in young conifer stands, burned-over areas and shrubby, regenerating clearings. *In migration* and *winter:* forest edges and clearings, weedy fields, wastelands, coastal tuckamore and overgrown gardens.

Nesting: on the ground, occasionally in a stump crevice, usually concealed by a shrub, tree, root, log or rock; female builds a cup nest made of twigs, bark shreds, grass and moss and lines it with fine grass and hair; female incubates 3–5 whitish to bluish-white eggs, marked with grey and brown, for 12–13 days.
Feeding: scratches the ground for invertebrates; also eats berries and seeds.
Voice: song is a long, dry trill, very similar to the call of the Chipping Sparrow but more musical; call is a smacking *chip* note, often given in series.
Similar Species: *Eastern Towhee* (p. 276): larger; female has rufous sides, red eyes and greyish bill. *Other sparrows* (pp. 277–89): brownish and streaked; most lack white outer tail feathers of immature juncos.
Best Sites: in forest openings and edges, usually in drier sites than other sparrows.

LAPLAND LONGSPUR

Calcarius lapponicus

Lapland Longspurs are birds of autumn and early winter in much of Atlantic Canada. As flocks wheel about in masses over the fields and coastal barrens, they seem to be blown hither and thither like the falling autumn leaves, while their companions the Snow Buntings look like snowflakes. Flocks of longspurs can be surprisingly inconspicuous until closely approached—anyone attempting a closer look at the flock will be awed by the sight of the birds suddenly erupting into the skies, flashing their white outer tail feathers. • When farmers work their fields in spring, Lapland Longspurs have already moulted into their bold breeding plumage, which they will wear through summer. In autumn these birds arrive from their breeding grounds looking like mottled, brownish sparrows, and they retain their drab plumage throughout winter. • The Lapland Longspur breeds in northern polar regions, including the area of northern Europe known as Lapland.

non-breeding

ID: white outer tail feathers; pale yellowish bill. *Breeding male:* black crown, face and "bib"; chestnut nape; broad white stripe curving down to shoulder from eye (may be tinged with buff behind eye). *Female:* mottled, brown-and-black upperparts; lightly streaked flanks; narrow, lightly streaked buff breast band. *Non-breeding male:* like female but with faint chestnut on nape and diffuse black breast.
Size: *L* 16 cm.
Status: uncommon to locally common from late September to early May.

Habitat: coastal barrens, dunes, wasteland, pastures, meadows and croplands.
Nesting: does not nest in Atlantic Canada.
Feeding: gleans the ground and snow for seeds and waste grain.
Voice: flight song is a rapid, slurred warble; musical calls; flight calls include a rattled *tri-di-dit* and a descending *teew*.
Similar Species: *Snow Bunting* (p. 292): black-and-white wing pattern. *Sparrows* (pp. 277–89): most lack distinctive head pattern; most have pale legs.
Best Sites: low, open beaches, dunes, coastal grasslands and headlands, and any open fields and inland marshes.

SNOW BUNTING

Plectrophenax nivalis

I n early winter, when flocks of Snow Buntings descend on Atlantic Canada, their startling black-and-white plumage flashes in contrast with the snow-covered backdrop. It may seem strange that Snow Buntings are whiter in summer than they are in winter, but the darker winter plumage may help these birds absorb heat on clear, cold winter days. • Snow Buntings do not stay in Atlantic Canada once the longer days of summer begin, and they venture farther north than any other songbird in the world. A single individual, probably misguided and lost, was recorded not far from the North Pole in May 1987. • In winter, Snow Buntings prefer expansive areas, such as grain croplands, fields and pastures, where they join Lapland Longspurs and sparrows to scratch and peck at exposed seeds and grains. On occasion they will ingest small grains of sand or gravel from roadsides as a source of minerals and to help digestion.

non-breeding

ID: black-and-white wings and tail; white underparts. *Breeding male:* black back; all-white head and rump; black bill. *Breeding female:* streaky, brown-and-whitish crown and back; dark bill. *Non-breeding male:* yellowish bill; golden brown crown. *Non-breeding female:* like male but with blackish forecrown and dark-streaked golden back.
Size: *L* 15–18 cm.
Status: common to irregularly abundant from late September to mid-May.
Habitat: coastal barrens and headlands, shorelines, fields, feedlots, pastures, grassy meadows, lakeshores, roadsides and railways; birds visit feeders in Cape Breton and NF.
Nesting: does not nest in Atlantic Canada.
Feeding: gleans the ground and snow for seeds and waste grain; also takes insects when they are available.
Voice: spring song is a musical, high-pitched *chi-chi-churee*; call is a whistled *tew*.
Similar Species: *Lapland Longspur* (p. 291): brownish upperparts; lacks black-and-white wing pattern. *Sparrows* (pp. 277–89): lack white wing and tail patches.
Best Sites: low-lying coastal areas; open fields inland.

NORTHERN CARDINAL

Cardinalis cardinalis

A bird as beautiful as the Northern Cardinal rarely fails to capture our attention and admiration; it is often the first choice for Christmas cards and bird calendars. • Cardinals prefer the tangled shrubby edges of woodlands, but they are easily attracted to backyards with feeders and sheltering trees and shrubs. • Cardinals form one of the most faithful pair bonds of the bird world. The male and female remain in close contact year-round, singing to one another through the seasons with soft, bubbly whistles. • Few people realize that the Northern Cardinal is a relative newcomer to Canada. This bird's range has expanded northward over the years into Atlantic Canada, probably because of the wealth of backyard birdfeeders here, the warm microclimate of our urban centres and forest fragmentation.

ID: *Male:* red over-all; pointed crest; black mask and throat; red, conical bill. *Female:* shaped like male; brown-buff to buff olive overall; red bill, crest, wings and tail. *Immature male:* like female but with dark bill and crest.
Size: *L* 19–23 cm.
Status: very rare to uncommon local year-round resident.
Habitat: brushy thickets and shrubby tangles along forest and woodland edges, in backyards and in suburban and urban parks.
Nesting: in dense shrubs, thickets or vine tangles or low in a coniferous tree; female builds an open cup nest made of twigs, bark shreds, weeds, grass, leaves and rootlets and lines it with hair and fine grass; female incubates 3–4 whitish to bluish- or greenish-white eggs, marked with grey, brown and purple, for 12–13 days.
Feeding: hops on the ground or in low shrubs, gleaning seeds, insects and berries.
Voice: song is a variable series of clear, bubbly whistled notes: *what cheer! what cheer! birdie-birdie-birdie what cheer;* call is a metallic *chip.*
Similar Species: *Scarlet Tanager* (p. 275) and *Summer Tanager:* lack head crest, black mask and throat and red, conical bill.
Best Sites: *NB:* Sussex; The Whistle & North Head (Grand Manan I.); St. Stephen; St. Andrews; Kennebecasis Peninsula. *NS:* Digby; Granville Ferry; Seal I.; Yarmouth; Pubnico.

293

ROSE-BREASTED GROSBEAK

Pheucticus ludovicianus

It's difficult to miss the boisterous, whistled tune of the Rose-breasted Grosbeak. This bird's hurried, robin-like song is easily recognized, and it's one of the more common songs heard among the Maritime deciduous forests in spring and summer. Although the female lacks the magnificent colours of the male, she shares his talent for beautiful song. • Rose-breasted Grosbeaks usually build their nests low in a tree or tall shrub, but they typically forage high in the canopy, where they can be difficult to spot. Luckily for birdwatchers, the abundance of autumn berries often draws these birds to ground level. • Rose-breasted Grosbeaks migrate primarily at night and because of their wandering habits a few birds turn up unexpectedly in remote northern communities. • The species name *ludovicianus*, Latin for "from Louisiana," is misleading, because this bird is only a migrant in Louisiana and other southern US states.

breeding

ID: pale, conical bill; dark wings with small, white patches; dark tail. *Male:* black "hood" and back; red breast and inner underwings; white underparts and rump. *Female:* bold whitish eyebrow; thin crown stripe; brown upperparts; buff underparts with dark brown streaking.
Size: *L* 18–21 cm.
Status: uncommon to fairly common migrant and breeder from late April to mid-October; a few may remain as late as December and may even overwinter; very rare in the Gaspé, PQ.
Habitat: *Breeding:* deciduous and mixed forests with shrubs and second-growth. *In migration:* woodlots, parklands and gardens; sometimes visits feeders in early winter.

Nesting: fairly low in a tree or tall shrub, often near water; mostly the female builds a flimsy cup nest made of twigs, bark strips, weeds, grass and leaves and lines it with rootlets and hair; pair incubates 3–5 pale greenish-blue eggs, spotted with reddish-brown, for 13–14 days.
Feeding: gleans vegetation for insects, seeds, buds, berries and some fruit; occasionally hover-gleans or catches flying insects on the wing; may also visit feeding stations.
Voice: song is a long, melodious series of whistled notes, much like a fast version of a robin's song; call is a distinctive squeak.
Similar Species: male is distinctive. *Purple Finch* (p. 306) and *House Finch* (p. 307): female is much smaller and has heavier streaking on underparts. *Sparrows* (pp. 277–89): smaller; all lack large, conical bill.
Best Sites: deciduous woods.

BLUE GROSBEAK

Guiraca caerulea

Male Blue Grosbeaks owe their spectacular spring plumage not to a fresh moult but, oddly enough, to feather wear. While Blue Grosbeaks are wintering in Mexico and Central America, their brown feather tips slowly wear away, leaving the crystal blue plumage that is seen as they arrive on their breeding grounds. • Blue Grosbeaks are very expressive during courtship. If you are lucky enough to spot one of these birds in spring, watch for the tail-spreading, tail-flicking and crown-raising behaviours that suggest the bird might be breeding—you could be witness to the first Blue Grosbeak nesting attempt in Atlantic Canada. • Look carefully for the rusty wing bars that distinguish this bird from the similar-looking and much more common Indigo Bunting. • *Caerulea* is from the Latin for "blue," a description that just doesn't reveal this bird's true beauty.

ID: large, pale greyish, conical bill. *Male:* blue overall; 2 rusty wing bars; black around base of bill. *Female:* soft brown plumage overall; whitish throat; rusty wing bars; rump and shoulders are faintly washed with blue. *1st-spring male:* similar to female but has blue head.

Size: *L* 15–19 cm.

Status: rare but increasingly regular from April to early June and from September to January.

Habitat: thick brush, riparian thickets, shrubby areas and dense, weedy fields near water; sometimes found at feeders on peninsulas or headlands that jut into the Atlantic Ocean.

Nesting: does not nest in Atlantic Canada.

Feeding: gleans insects from the ground while hopping; occasionally takes seeds; may visit feeding stations.

Voice: sweet, melodious, warbling song with phrases that rise and fall; call is a loud *chink*.

Similar Species: *Indigo Bunting* (p. 296): smaller body and bill; male lacks wing bars; female has dark brown streaking on breast.

Best Sites: *NB:* Grand Manan I. *NS:* Seal I.; Argyle–Pubnico area; Halifax–Dartmouth; Canso. *NF:* St. John's; Bear Cove Point (Renews).

295

INDIGO BUNTING

Passerina cyanea

I n the shadow of a towering tree, a male Indigo Bunting can look almost black. If possible, quickly reposition yourself to a place from which you can see the sun strike and enliven this bunting's incomparable indigo colour—the rich shade of blue is rivalled only by the sky. • A few of the Indigo Buntings seen in Atlantic Canada are heading for southwestern New Brunswick and southern Québec to nest, but most of them appear to have no intention of nesting in the region. Yet, every spring, dozens to hundreds arrive as early as April, stay until late May and then disappear again. For most of these visitors, their time here appears to be a spring vacation. They reappear in autumn, when few traces of blue are visible.

breeding

ID: stout, grey, conical bill; beady, black eyes; black legs; no wing bars. *Breeding male:* blue overall; black lores; wings and tail may show some black. *Non-breeding male:* similar to female, but usually with some blue in wings and tail. *Female:* soft brown overall; brown streaks on breast; whitish throat.
Size: *L* 14 cm.
Status: irregularly common migrant from April to May and again from mid-September to mid-November; rare and very local breeder from May to early September; a few birds overwinter.
Habitat: deciduous forest and woodland edges, regenerating forest clearings, shrubby fields, orchards.
Nesting: usually in an upright fork of a small tree or shrub or within a vine tangle;

female builds a cup nest made of grass, leaves and bark strips and lines it with rootlets, hair and feathers; female incubates 3–4 white to bluish-white eggs, rarely spotted with brown or purple, for 12–13 days.
Feeding: gleans low vegetation and the ground for insects; also eats the seeds of native plants.
Voice: song consists of paired warbled whistles: *fire-fire, where-where, here-here, see-it see-it*; call is a quick *spit*.
Similar Species: *Blue Grosbeak* (p. 295): larger overall; larger, more robust bill; 2 rusty wing bars; female lacks streaking on breast.
Best Sites: *NB:* Millerton (Miramichi); St. Stephen–St. Andrews area; Cambridge-Narrows–Hampton area; Fredericton; Plaster Rock. *NS:* Truro; Brier I.; Seal I.; Wedgeport–Pubnico area; Canso. *NF:* Long Point (Port au Port); St. John's; Ferryland. *PQ:* Dégelis; Cap-des-Rosiers.

DICKCISSEL

Spiza americana

Following the first Dickcissel sighting in North Sydney in 1929, there were no Nova Scotian sightings for two decades, but since then the birds have appeared every year in all the Atlantic provinces. The erratic and irregular behaviour of Dickcissels both befuddles the motivation of would-be observers and ignites their imagination. Dickcissels are sometimes seen foraging in small flocks during migration, but they are most regularly seen among troupes of House Sparrows at backyard feeders over winter. These birds gradually assume their full breeding colours, and what most observers thought was simply a particularly well-marked sparrow becomes a local celebrity. Once identified, Dickcissels don't hang around very long, and summer sightings are almost non-existent.

breeding

ID: yellow eyebrow; grey head, nape and sides of yellow breast; brown upperparts; pale greyish underparts; rufous shoulder patch; dark, conical bill. *Male:* white "chin" and black "bib"; duller colours in non-breeding plumage. *Female:* duller version of male; white throat. *Immature:* dull like female but has very faint eyebrow and dark streaking on crown, breast, sides and flanks.
Size: *L* 15–18 cm.
Status: increasingly common annual visitor from August to early June; very rare visitor from April to May.
Habitat: abandoned fields, weedy meadows, croplands, grasslands and grassy roadsides; most often seen in winter at feeders.

Nesting: does not nest in Atlantic Canada.
Feeding: insects and seeds are gleaned from the ground and low vegetation; small flocks may visit birdfeeders, especially in winter.
Voice: song consists of 2–3 single notes followed by a trill, often paraphrased as *dick dick dick-cissel*; flight call is a buzzer-like *bzrrrrt.*
Similar Species: *Eastern Meadowlark* (p. 300): much larger; long, pointed bill; yellow "chin" and throat with black "necklace." *American Goldfinch* (p. 313): lacks black "bib"; white or yellow-buff bars on dark wings; may show black forecrown.
Best Sites: *NB:* Grand Manan I.; St. Andrews; Sussex. *PEI:* Kensington; Stanhope. *NS:* Brier I.; Seal I.; Halifax–Dartmouth; Louisbourg. *NF:* Ramea; Glovertown; St. John's. *PQ:* Cap Gaspé.

BOBOLINK

Dolichonyx oryzivorus

During the nesting season, male and female Bobolinks rarely interact with one another. For the most part, males perform aerial displays and sing their bubbly, tinkling songs from exposed grassy perches while females carry out the nesting duties. Once the young have hatched, males become scarce, spending much of their time hunting along the ground for insects. • At first glimpse, the female Bobolink resembles a sparrow, but the male, with his dark belly and buff-and-black upper-parts, is coloured like no other bird in the region. • Bobolinks once benefited from increased agriculture in Atlantic Canada, but modern practices, such as harvesting hay early in the season, now often thwart the reproductive efforts of this bird.

breeding

ID: *Breeding male:* black overall; buff nape; white rump and wing patch. *Breeding female:* yellowish bill; brown-buff overall; streaked upperparts; pale eyebrow; dark eye line; light central crown stripe bordered by dark stripes. *Non-breeding male:* similar to a breeding female, but darker above and rich golden-buff below.
Size: *L* 15–20 cm.
Status: uncommon to locally common migrant and breeder from early May to late October.
Habitat: tall, grassy meadows and ditches, hayfields and some croplands; increasingly uses coastal meadowlands and sand dunes with wax myrtle and other low growth.

Nesting: on the ground, usually in hay-fields; well-concealed cup nest made of grass and forb stems is lined with fine grass; female incubates 5–6 greyish to light reddish-brown eggs, heavily blotched with lavender and brown, for 11–13 days.
Feeding: gleans the ground and low vegetation for adult and larval invertebrates; also eats many seeds.
Voice: song is a series of banjo-like twangs: *bobolink bobolink spink spank spink*, often given in flight; also issues a *pink* call in flight.
Similar Species: male is distinctive. *Savannah Sparrow* (p. 282): dark breast streaking; yellow lores. *Vesper Sparrow* (p. 281): breast streaking; white outer tail feathers.
Best Sites: meadowlands, shorelines of lakes, ponds and marshes, and coastal dunes.

RED-WINGED BLACKBIRD

Agelaius phoeniceus

A birder's winter blahs might be remedied by the sound of the season's first Red-winged Blackbird. The males get an early start on the season, arriving in rural communities with other blackbirds as early as mid-March, a week or so before females arrive. In the females' absence, the males stake out territories in cattail marshes, pond margins and roadside ditches through song and visual displays. A male's bright red shoulders and short, raspy song are his most important tools in the often intricate strategy he employs to defend his territory from rivals. A flashy and richly voiced male that has managed to establish a large and productive territory can attract several mates to his cattail kingdom. • After a male has wooed her, a female starts the busy work of weaving a nest amidst the cattails. Cryptic coloration allows her to sit inconspicuously upon her nest, blending perfectly with the surroundings.

ID: *Male:* all black, except for the large, red shoulder patch edged in yellow (occasionally concealed). *Female:* heavily streaked underparts; mottled brown upperparts; faint red shoulder patch; light eyebrow.
Size: *L* 18–24 cm.
Status: abundant migrant and common breeder from mid-March to October; rare to locally uncommon from November to early March; visits feeders in winter.
Habitat: *Breeding:* cattail marshes, wet meadows and ditches, croplands and shoreline shrubs. *In migration* and *winter:* farmlands, grain sheds and barns; urban ponds, shrubbery and feeders.
Nesting: colonial and polygynous; in cattails or shoreline bushes; female weaves an open cup nest made of dried cattail leaves and grass and lines it with fine grass; female incubates 3–4 darkly marked, pale blue-green eggs for 10–12 days.
Feeding: gleans the ground for seeds, waste grain and invertebrates; also gleans vegetation for seeds, insects and berries; occasionally catches insects in flight; may visit feeding stations.
Voice: song is a loud, raspy *konk-a-ree* or *ogle-reeeee*; calls include a harsh *check* and a high *tseert*; female may give a loud *che-che-che chee chee chee*.
Similar Species: male is distinctive when the shoulder patch shows. *Rusty Blackbird* (p. 301): females lack streaked underparts. *Brown-headed Cowbird* (p. 303): juvenile is smaller and has stubbier, conical bill.
Best Sites: wetlands near farming areas but also marshes and brushy areas on sand dunes and shorelines.

EASTERN MEADOWLARK

Sturnella magna

The male Eastern Meadowlark's bright yellow underparts, black V-shaped "necklace" and white outer tail feathers help attract mates. Females share these colourful attributes for a slightly different purpose: when a predator approaches too close to a nest, the incubating female explodes from the grass in a burst of flashing colour. Most predators cannot resist chasing the moving target, and once the female has led the predator away from the nest, she simply folds away her white tail flags, exposes her camouflaged back and disappears into the grass without a trace. • Because of their bright plumage, Eastern Meadowlarks don't seem to fit in with the blackbird family. When they're seen in silhouette, however, the similarities become very apparent. • Eastern Meadowlarks are relatively hard to come by in Atlantic Canada. Wintering birds join up with flocks of European Starlings, providing safety in numbers and a chance to feast on the tasty morsels stirred up by so many feet.

breeding

ID: yellow underparts; broad, black breast band; mottled brown upperparts; short, wide tail with white outer tail feathers; long, pinkish legs; yellow lores; long, sharp bill; blackish crown stripes and eye line border; pale eyebrow and median crown stripe; dark streaking on white sides and flanks.

Size: *L* 23–24 cm.

Status: rare to uncommon migrant and breeder from mid-March to mid-November; rare visitor from November to March.

Habitat: *Breeding:* grassy meadows and pastures; also in some croplands, weedy fields, grassy roadsides and old orchards. *In migration* and *winter:* coastal barrens and fields, croplands and wasteland.

Nesting: in a depression or scrape on the ground, concealed by dense grass; domed grass nest is woven into the surrounding vegetation; female incubates 3–7 white eggs, heavily spotted with brown and purple, for about 13–15 days.

Feeding: walks or runs along the ground gleaning grasshoppers, crickets, beetles and spiders from the ground and vegetation; extracts grubs and worms by probing its bill into the soil; also eats seeds.

Voice: song is a rich series of 2–8 melodic, distinct, slurred whistles: *see-you at school-today* or *this is the year*; gives a rattling flight call and a high, buzzy *dzeart*.

Similar Species: *Dickcissel* (p. 297): much smaller; solid dark crown; white throat; lacks brown streaking on sides and flanks. *European Starling* (p. 246): immatures are more uniform grey-brown with indistinct markings; no trace of yellow anywhere in plumage. *Bobolink* (p. 298): smaller; more conical bill; less yellow on underparts; lacks black breast band.

Best Sites: *Summer* and *in migration: NB:* Shediac; Petitcodiac; Sussex; Hampton; McAdam–Mactaquac area; Glassville; St. Leonard. *NS:* Hantsport; Annapolis Valley; Granville Centre. *NF:* Cuslett–St. Bride's area. *PQ:* Cacouna; Mont-Joli; Presqu'île de Forillon.

RUSTY BLACKBIRD

Euphagus carolinus

This bird owes its name to the rusty colour of its autumn plumage, but its name could just as well reflect its grating, squeaky song, which sounds very much like a rusty hinge. • Unlike many blackbirds, the Rusty Blackbird nests in isolated pairs or very small, loose colonies in flooded woodlands and treed boreal bogs, not in wetlands. • During migration and over winter, Rusty Blackbirds often intermingle with flocks of other blackbirds, sometimes blackening rural skies. Their days are spent foraging along the wooded edges of fields and wetlands, and they will occasionally pick through the manure-laden ground of cattle feedlots. At day's end, foraging is curtailed, and most birds seek the shelter of trees and shrubs and the stalks of emergent marshland vegetation. • Rusty Blackbirds are generally less abundant and less aggressive than their relatives, and they tend to avoid disturbed environments.

breeding

ID: yellow eyes; dark legs; long, sharp bill. *Breeding male:* dark plumage; subtle green gloss on body; subtle bluish or greenish gloss on head. *Breeding female:* paler than male; without gloss. *Non-breeding male:* rusty wings, back and crown. *Non-breeding female:* less dark than male; buffy underparts; rusty "cheek."
Size: *L* 23 cm.
Status: fairly common to common migrant from mid-March to late April and from late September to November; uncommon, local breeder from May to mid-September; rare but increasing winter visitor.
Habitat: *Breeding:* treed bogs, fens, beaver ponds, wet meadows and the shrubby shorelines of lakes, rivers and swamps. *In migration* and *winter:* marshes,

open fields, feedlots and woodland edges near water; occasionally at feeders in winter.
Nesting: low in a shrub or small conifer, often over or very near water; female builds a bulky nest made of twigs, grass and lichens, with an inner cup of mud and decaying vegetation, and lines it with fine grass; female incubates 4–5 pale blue-green eggs, spotted with grey and brown, for about 14 days.
Feeding: walks along shorelines gleaning water bugs, beetles, dragonflies, snails, grasshoppers and occasionally small fish; also eats waste grain and seeds.
Voice: song is a squeaky, creaking *kush-leeeh ksh-lay*; call is a harsh *chack*.
Similar Species: *Common Grackle* (p. 302): longer, keeled tail; larger body and bill; more iridescent. *European Starling* (p. 246): bill is yellow in summer; speckled appearance; dark eyes.
Best Sites: *Summer* and *in migration:* wetter woods, treed bogs, flooded forest edges and beaver ponds.

COMMON GRACKLE

Quiscalus quiscula

The male Common Grackle is a poor but spirited singer. Usually while perched in a shrub, he will slowly take a deep breath to inflate his breast, causing his feathers to spike outward; then he closes his eyes and gives out a loud, strained *tssh-schleek*. Despite his lack of musical talent, the male remains smug and proud, posing with his bill held high. • In autumn and over winter, large and often noisy flocks of Common Grackles are common in rural areas, where they forage for waste grain in open fields. Smaller bands occasionally venture into urban neighbourhoods, where they assert their dominance at backyard feeders—even bullying Blue Jays yield feeding rights to these cocky and aggressive birds. Grackles have also learned to disable feeding finches and sparrows by pecking out their eyes. • At night, grackles commonly roost with groups of European Starlings, Red-winged Blackbirds and even Brown-headed Cowbirds.

ID: *Male:* often black-looking, iridescent plumage (purple-blue head and breast, bronze back and sides, and purple wings and tail); long, keeled tail; yellow eyes; long, heavy bill. *Female:* smaller, duller and browner than male. *Immature:* dull brown overall; dark eyes.
Size: *L* 28–34 cm.
Status: common to abundant migrant and breeder from mid-March to mid-November; formerly uncommon but now locally abundant from late November to March.
Habitat: wetlands, fields, riparian woodlands, along the edges of coniferous forests and woodlands, shrubby gardens and urban and suburban parks.
Nesting: singly or in small colonies; in dense tree or shrub branches or emergent vegetation, often near water; female builds a bulky open cup nest made of twigs, grass, forbs and mud and lines it with fine grass or feathers; female incubates 4–5 brown-blotched, pale blue eggs for 12–14 days.
Feeding: slowly struts along the ground, gleaning, snatching and probing for insects, earthworms, seeds, waste grain and fruit; also catches insects in flight and eats small vertebrates; may take some bird eggs.
Voice: song is a series of harsh, strained notes ending with a metallic squeak: *tssh-schleek* or *gri-de-leeek*; call is a quick, loud *swaaaack* or *chaack*.
Similar Species: *Rusty Blackbird* (p. 301): smaller overall; lacks heavy bill and keeled tail. *Red-winged Blackbird* (p. 299): shorter tail; male has red shoulder patch and dark eyes. *European Starling* (p. 246): very short tail; long, thin bill (yellow in summer); speckled appearance; dark eyes.
Best Sites: *Summer* and *in migration:* widespread.

BROWN-HEADED COWBIRD

Molothrus ater

The Brown-headed Cowbird's song, a bubbling, liquidy *glug-ahl-whee*, might translate to other bird species as "here comes trouble!" Historically, Brown-headed Cowbirds followed bison herds across the plains and prairies of the Prairie Provinces—they now follow cattle—and their nomadic lifestyle made it impossible for them to construct and tend a nest. Instead, cowbirds engage in "nest parasitism": laying their eggs in the nests of other songbirds. Many of the parasitized songbirds do not recognize that the eggs are not theirs, so they incubate them and raise the cowbirds as their own. Cowbird chicks typically hatch first and develop much more quickly than their nestmates, which are pushed out of the nest or out-competed for food. • The expansion of ranching, the fragmentation of forests and the extensive network of transportation corridors through Atlantic Canada has significantly increased the cowbird's range. It now parasitizes more than 140 bird species in North America, including species that probably had no contact with it prior to widespread human settlement.

ID: thick, conical bill; short, squared tail; dark eyes. *Male:* iridescent green-blue body plumage (usually looks glossy black); dark brown head. *Female:* brown plumage overall; faint streaking on light brown underparts; pale throat.
Size: *L* 15–20 cm.
Status: uncommon to locally common migrant and breeder from late March to November; uncommon to locally abundant from December to March.
Habitat: open agricultural and residential areas.
Nesting: does not build a nest; each female may lay up to 40 eggs per year in the nests of other birds, usually laying 1 egg per nest (larger numbers, up to 8 eggs per nest, are probably from several different cowbirds); whitish eggs, marked with grey and brown, hatch after 10–13 days.
Feeding: gleans the ground for seeds, waste grain and invertebrates, especially grasshoppers, beetles and true bugs.
Voice: song is a high, liquidy gurgle *glug-ahl-whee* or *bubbloozeee*; call is a squeaky, high-pitched *seep, psee* or *wee-tse-tse*, often given in flight; also a fast, chipping *ch-ch-ch-ch-ch-ch*.
Similar Species: *Rusty Blackbird* (p. 301): lacks contrasting brown head; darker body; slimmer, longer bill; longer tail; yellow eyes. *Common Grackle* (p. 302): much larger overall; longer, heavier bill; longer, keeled tail.
Best Sites: *Summer* and *in migration:* open areas, especially farmlands, and urban parklands. *Winter:* farmland areas.

BALTIMORE ORIOLE

Icterus galbula

The male Baltimore Oriole has a striking, Halloween-style black-and-orange plumage that flickers like smoldering embers amidst our neighbourhood treetops. As if its brilliant plumage wasn't enough to secure our admiration, its rich courtship whistles drip to the ground like manna from the heavens. • Baltimore Orioles are fairly common local breeders in the Maritimes but they are often difficult to find because they spend most of their time in the forest heights. Developing an ear for their whistled *peter peter peter here peter* tune and more frequent gazing up into your neighbourhood's deciduous trees will no doubt produce many enchanting views of this beloved oriole. • "Oriole" is derived from Latin and means "golden."

ID: *Male:* black "hood," back, wings and central tail feathers; bright orange underparts, shoulder, rump and outer tail feathers; white wing patch and feather edgings. *Female:* olive brown upperparts (darkest on head); dull yellow-orange underparts and rump; white wing bar.

Size: *L* 18–20 cm.

Status: uncommon migrant and local breeder from late April to mid-October; increasingly widespread and common from November on, with some birds successfully overwintering at feeders.

Habitat: deciduous and mixed forests, particularly riparian woodlands, natural openings, shorelines, roadsides, orchards, gardens and parklands.

Nesting: high in a deciduous tree, suspended from a branch; female builds a hanging pouch nest made of grass, bark shreds, rootlets, plant stems and grapevines and lines it with fine grass, rootlets and fur; occasionally adds string and fishing line; female incubates 4–5 pale grey to bluish-white eggs with dark markings for 12–14 days.

Feeding: gleans canopy vegetation and shrubs for invertebrates; also eats some fruit and nectar; may visit hummingbird feeders and feeding stations that offer orange halves.

Voice: song consists of slow, loud, clear whistles: *peter peter peter here peter*; calls include a 2-note *tea-too* and a rapid chatter: *ch-ch-ch-ch-ch*.

Similar Species: *Orchard Oriole:* male has darker chestnut plumage; female is olive yellow and lacks orange overtones. *Scarlet Tanager* (p. 275) and *Summer Tanager:* females have thicker, pale bills and lack wing bars.

Best Sites: in southern NB, PEI and central NS; increasingly common in migration along the coasts and becoming more regular at feeders in winter.

PINE GROSBEAK

Pinicola enucleator

The Pine Grosbeak, a colourful nomad of the Boreal Forest region, is one of the more widespread breeding birds in maritime Québec, Cape Breton and Newfoundland as well as a regular visitor to other parts of Atlantic Canada. • Much of their survival depends on the availability of conifer seeds, so Pine Grosbeaks are always in search of a good crop. In the recent past, they were regular winter visitors to city streets, where they feasted on maple and ash seeds. They also caused consternation to orchard owners, who did not appreciate their taste for spring buds. However, the arrival of Evening Grosbeaks at urban feeders seems to have inhibited the gentler Pine Grosbeaks. • It is a great moment in a typical Atlantic Canadian winter when Pine Grosbeaks emerge from the wilds to settle on your backyard feeder. Every so often, they flock in huge numbers to all parts of Atlantic Canada in winter. These erratic winter invasions thrill local naturalists—the birds' bright colours and exciting flock behaviour are certainly a welcome sight.

ID: stout, dark, conical bill; 2 white wing bars; black wings and tail. *Male:* rosy red head, upperparts and breast; grey sides, flanks, belly and undertail coverts. *Female* and *immature:* grey overall; yellow or russet wash on head and rump.
Size: L 20–25 cm.
Status: uncommon to common transient and year-round resident; irregularly uncommon to abundant visitor outside of breeding habitats, usually from October to March.
Habitat: *Breeding:* spruce-fir coniferous forests. *Winter:* conifer plantations, deciduous woodlands with fruiting mountain-ash, crabapple and woody nightshade as well as backyard feeding stations.
Nesting: in a conifer or tall shrub; bulky cup nest, loosely made of twigs, grass, forbs and rootlets, is lined with lichens,

rootlets and moss; female incubates 4 bluish-green eggs, spotted with black, brown and purple, for 13–15 days.
Feeding: gleans buds, berries and seeds from trees; also forages on the ground; visits feeding stations in winter.
Voice: song is a short, sweet, musical warble; call is a 3-note whistle with a higher middle note; short, muffled trill is often given in flight; chatters when feeding in flocks.
Similar Species: *White-winged Crossbill* (p. 309): much smaller; lacks stubby bill and prominent grey coloration. *Red Crossbill* (p. 308): lacks stubby bill and white wing bars. *Evening Grosbeak* (p. 314): female has light-coloured bill, dark "whisker" stripe, tan underparts and broad, white wing patches.
Best Sites: open conifers and coastal tuckamore; in some years large numbers of birds invade urban parks and gardens in winter.

PURPLE FINCH

Carpodacus purpureus

The courtship of Purple Finches is a gentle and appealing ritual. The liquid warbling song of the male bubbles through conifer boughs, announcing his presence to potential mates. Upon the arrival of an interested female, the colourful male dances lightly around her, beating his wings until he softly lifts into the air. • Flat, raised, table-style feeding stations with nearby tree cover are sure to attract Purple Finches, and erecting one may keep a small flock in your area over winter. • "Purple" (*purpureus*) is simply a false description of the male's reddish coloration. Roger Tory Peterson said it best when he described the Purple Finch as "a sparrow dipped in raspberry juice."

ID: *Male:* light bill; raspberry red (occasionally yellow to salmon-pink) head, throat, breast and nape; brown- and red-streaked back and flanks; reddish-brown "cheek"; red rump; notched tail; light, unstreaked belly and undertail coverts. *Female:* dark brown "cheek" and "jaw line"; white eyebrow and lower "cheek" stripe; heavily streaked underparts; unstreaked undertail coverts.
Size: *L* 13–15 cm.
Status: fairly common migrant and breeder from March to October; rare to locally uncommon visitor from October to March.
Habitat: *Breeding:* open coniferous and mixed forests. *In migration* and *winter:* coniferous, mixed and deciduous forests, shrubby open areas; small flocks

accompanied by other boreal species will often visit feeding stations with nearby tree cover.
Nesting: on a conifer branch, far from the trunk; cup nest woven with twigs, grass and rootlets is lined with moss and hair; female incubates 4–5 pale greenish-blue eggs, marked with black and brown, for about 13 days.
Feeding: gleans the ground and vegetation for seeds, buds, berries and insects; readily visits table-style feeding stations.
Voice: song is a bubbly, continuous warble; call is a single metallic *cheep* or *weet*.
Similar Species: *House Finch* (p. 307): squared tail; male lacks reddish cap; female lacks distinct "cheek" patch. *Red Crossbill* (p. 308): larger bill with crossed mandibles; male has more red overall and dark "V"s on whitish undertail coverts.
Best Sites: open, mixed woodlands and parkland, quite often close to urban areas.

HOUSE FINCH

Carpodacus mexicanus

Since its first appearance here in the late 1970s, the House Finch has established itself in many communities in southwestern Atlantic Canada and is now expanding into the rest of the region. A native to western North America, the House Finch was brought to eastern parts of the continent as an illegally captured cage bird known as "Hollywood Finch." In the early 1940s, New York pet shop owners released their birds to avoid prosecution and fines, and it is the descendants of those birds that are now colonizing eastern Canada. • The resourceful House Finch usually gains the upper hand on the more even-tempered Purple Finch, and it is the only bird aggressive and stubborn enough to outcompete the House Sparrow, which also prospers in urban environments.

ID: streaked undertail coverts; brown-streaked back; square tail. *Male:* brown cap; bright red eye-brow, forecrown, throat and breast; heavily streaked flanks. *Female:* indistinct facial patterning; heavily streaked underparts.
Size: *L* 13–15 cm.
Status: rare to locally uncommon year-round resident and wanderer; irregular breeder.
Habitat: cities, towns and agricultural areas.
Nesting: in a cavity, building, dense foliage or abandoned bird nest—especially in evergreens and ornamental shrubs near buildings; mostly the female builds an open cup nest made of grass, twigs, forbs, leaves, hair and feathers, often adding string and other debris; female incubates 4–5 pale blue eggs, dotted with lavender and black, for 12–14 days.
Feeding: gleans vegetation and the ground for seeds; also takes berries, buds and some flower parts; often visits feeding stations.
Voice: song is a bright, disjointed warble lasting about 3 seconds, often ending with a harsh *jeeer* or *wheer;* flight call is a sweet *cheer,* given singly or in series.
Similar Species: *Purple Finch* (p. 306): notched tail; male has more burgundy red cap, upper back and flanks; female has distinct "cheek" patch. *Red Crossbill* (p. 308): bill has crossed mandibles; male has more red overall and darker wings.
Best Sites: *NB:* Newcastle; Kouchibouguac River; Moncton; St. Andrews; Saint John. *PEI:* Charlottetown. *NS:* Wolfville; Granville Ferry; Bear River; Brier I.; Seal I.; Yarmouth; Pubnico; Halifax; Lake Echo; Antigonish.

RED CROSSBILL

Loxia curvirostra

Red Crossbills are the great gypsies of Canada's bird community, wandering through the forests in search of cones. They might breed at any time of the year if they discover a bumper crop—it's not unusual to hear them singing and see them nest-building in midwinter. Their nomadic ways make them difficult to find, and even during years of plenty there is no guarantee these birds will surface in every province. Winter is typically the time to see crossbills here, and in some years large flocks suddenly appear in southern parts of the region. • In Atlantic Canada, two subspecies share pine, fir, spruce and tamarack seeds and also eat buds and berries. Most of the breeding birds in the Maritimes are of the *minor* subspecies, whereas those in Newfoundland are the heavier-billed *pusilla* subspecies. Both subspecies wander in winter, when a third, western *sitkensis* subspecies may also appear in maritime Québec and New Brunswick in small numbers. • The scientific name *curvirostra* is Latin for "curve-billed."

ID: bill has crossed tips. *Male:* dull orange-red to brick red plumage; dark wings and tail; always has colour on throat. *Female:* olive grey to dusky yellow plumage; plain, dark wings.

Size: *L* 13–16 cm.

Status: erratic and irruptive, uncommon to locally abundant transient year-round resident; particularly irruptive in winter.

Habitat: coniferous forests of all types, coastal and montane tuckamore; mixed forests and urban parks during irruptions.

Nesting: high on the outer branch of a conifer; female builds an open cup nest made of twigs, grass, bark shreds and rootlets and lines it with moss, lichens, rootlets, feathers and hair; female incubates 3–4 pale bluish-white to greenish-white eggs, dotted with black and purple, for 12–18 days.

Feeding: primarily conifer seeds (especially pine); also eats buds, deciduous tree seeds and occasionally insects; often licks road salt or minerals in soil and along roadsides; rarely visits feeders.

Voice: distinctive *jip-jip* call note, often given in flight; song is a varied series of warbles, trills and *chips* (similar to other finches).

Similar Species: *White-winged Crossbill* (p. 309): 2 broad, white wing bars. *Pine Siskin* (p. 312): similar to immature Red Crossbill, but is smaller, lacks crossed bill and has yellow highlights on wing. *Pine Grosbeak* (p. 305): stubby, conical bill; white wing bars. *House Finch* (p. 307) and *Purple Finch* (p. 306): conical bills; less red overall; lack red on lower belly; lighter brownish wings.

Best Sites: conifers with seed-bearing cones.

WHITE-WINGED CROSSBILL

Loxia leucoptera

People are often amazed by the colourful and bizarre shapes of bird bills. Although this bird's bill lacks the colourful flair of the tropical toucan's and the massive proportions of the hornbill's, its cross-mandible design is shared by only two bird species in North America. White-winged Crossbills eat primarily spruce and tamarack seeds, and their oddly shaped bills are adapted to pry open cones. They then use their nimble tongues to extract the soft, energy-rich seeds hidden within. • Crossbills overwinter in flocks. The presence of a foraging group high in a spruce tree creates an unforgettable shower of conifer cones and crackling chatter. Like many finches, White-winged Crossbills can be abundant one year, then absent the next. • When not foraging in spruce spires, White-winged Crossbills often drop to ground level, where they drink water from shallow forest pools or lick salt from winter roads, which often results in crossbill fatalities.

ID: bill has crossed tips; 2 bold white wing bars. *Male:* pinkish-red overall; black wings and tail. *Female:* streaked brown upperparts; dusky yellow underparts slightly streaked with brown; dark wings and tail.

Size: *L* 15–17 cm.

Status: uncommon to fairly common, transient year-round resident; uncommon to locally abundant erratic, irruptive visitor from October to March.

Habitat: coniferous forests, primarily spruce, fir, tamarack and eastern hemlock; occasionally townsites, urban parks and deciduous forests.

Nesting: on an outer branch in a conifer; female builds an open cup nest made of twigs, grass, bark shreds and forbs and lines it with moss, lichen, rootlets, hair and soft plant down; female incubates 2–4 whitish to pale blue-green eggs, spotted with brown and lavender, for 12–14 days.

Feeding: prefers conifer seeds (mostly spruce and tamarack); also eats deciduous tree seeds and occasionally insects; often licks salt and minerals from roads when available.

Voice: song is a high-pitched series of warbles, trills and *chips*; call is a series of harsh, questioning *cheat* notes, often given in flight.

Similar Species: *Red Crossbill* (p. 308): lacks white wing bars; male is deeper red (less pinkish). *Pine Siskin* (p. 312): similar to immature White-winged Crossbill but smaller; yellow highlights in wing; lacks crossed bill. *Pine Grosbeak* (p. 305): stubby, conical bill; thinner wing bars; female is very grey; male has grey sides. *House Finch* (p. 307) and *Purple Finch* (p. 306): conical bills; less red overall; lighter brownish wings.

Best Sites: open woodlands, forest edges and conifer groves.

COMMON REDPOLL

Carduelis flammea

A predictably unpredictable winter visitor, the Common Redpoll is seen in varying numbers—it might appear in flocks of hundreds or in groups of a dozen or fewer, depending on the year. • Renowned for their effective winter adaptations, redpolls can endure lower temperatures than any other songbirds. Because they do not have much body fat, to avoid dying from hypothermia they maintain a high metabolic rate and eat almost constantly—redpolls are continually gleaning waste grain from bare fields or stocking up on seed at winter feeders. Their focus on food helps make wintering redpolls remarkably fearless of humans. The highly insulative feathers also help enable these birds to withstand bitter cold, especially when the feathers are fluffed out to trap layers of warm, insulating air.

ID: red forecrown; black "chin"; yellowish bill; streaked upper-parts, including rump; lightly streaked sides, flanks and undertail coverts; notched tail. *Male:* pinkish-red breast (brightest in breeding plumage). *Female:* whitish to pale grey breast.

Size: *L* 13 cm.

Status: fairly common but local year-round breeding resident; uncommon to locally abundant erratic, irruptive migrant and visitor from October to early April.

Habitat: *Breeding:* coastal and alpine tundra with low shrubs and patches of dwarf spruce, willow and alder; locally in alder thickets. *Winter:* coastal barrens and scrubby growth, open fields, roadsides, forest edges and backyards with feeders.

Nesting: low in a shrub or dwarf spruce; occasionally in grass clumps; open cup nest, made of fine twigs, grass, plant stems, lichen and moss, is lined with feathers, hair or plant down; female incubates 4–5 pale blue eggs with fine dark speckles for about 12 days.

Feeding: gleans the ground, snow and vegetation in large flocks for seeds in winter; often visits feeding stations; takes some insects in summer.

Voice: song is a twittering series of trills; calls are a soft *chit-chit-chit-chit* and a faint *swe-eet*; indistinguishable from the Hoary Redpoll's songs and calls.

Similar Species: *Hoary Redpoll* (p. 311): unstreaked or partly streaked rump; usually has faint or no streaking on sides and flanks; generally paler and more plump overall; bill may look stubbier; lacks streaking on undertail coverts. *Pine Siskin* (p. 312): heavily streaked overall; yellow highlights in wings and tail.

Best Sites: *Summer: NS:* Cape Breton Highlands NP. *NF:* Gros Morne; Broom Point; L'Anse aux Meadows; St. Anthony; Lumsden–Cape Freels area; Louil Hills (Terra Nova NP); Cape Bonavista. *PQ:* Parc de la Gaspésie.

HOARY REDPOLL

Carduelis hornemanni

Mixed in with the abundant Common Redpolls you will often see a more lightly coloured bird with noticeably less streaking. Could it be an aberrant subspecies of the Common Redpoll, or could it be one of two subspecies of Hoary Redpoll? If the rump is white or pink with little or no streaking and the bill is small, you've got an unambiguous Hoary. • Hoary Redpolls are well adapted to life in the cold. They have a high level of food intake, in part because they can store it in a special pouch in the esophagus (the esophageal diverticulum), which allows them to carry large quantities of energy-rich seeds. When seed crops fail or icy winds become intolerably cold, however, Hoary Redpolls do not hesitate to move south, where numbers occasionally "irrupt" every few years. • The scientific name honours Jens Wilken Hornemann, one of Denmark's leading botanists, who helped organize an expedition to Greenland, where the first scientific specimen of this bird was taken.

ID: red forecrown; black "chin"; yellowish bill; frosty white plumage overall; lightly streaked upperparts, except for the unstreaked rump; unstreaked underparts (flanks may have faint streaking); notched tail. *Male:* pinkish-tinged breast. *Female:* white to light grey breast.

Size: *L* 13–14 cm.

Status: very rare to uncommon erratic, irruptive migrant and visitor from November to March.

Habitat: open fields, meadows, roadsides, utility cutlines, railways, forest edges and backyards with feeders.

Nesting: not known to nest in Atlantic Canada.

Feeding: gleans the ground, snow and vegetation for seeds and buds; occasionally visits feeding stations in winter.

Voice: song is a twittering series of trills; calls are a soft *chit-chit-chit-chit* and a faint *swe-eet*; indistinguishable from the Common Redpoll's songs and calls.

Similar Species: *Common Redpoll* (p. 310): streaked rump, sides, flanks and undertail coverts; generally darker and slimmer overall. *Pine Siskin* (p. 312): heavily streaked overall; yellow highlights on wings and tail.

Best Sites: on headlands and wasteland along coasts. *NB:* Lamèque, Cape Jourimain. *PEI:* East Point. *NS:* Amherst, Canard–Gaspereau area, Halifax. *NF:* L'Anse aux Meadows, St. Anthony, St. Bride's. *PQ:* St-Tharcisius, Presqu'île de Forillon.

PINE SISKIN

Carduelis pinus

In many parts of Canada, you can spend days, weeks and even months in pursuit of Pine Siskins, only to meet with frustration, aching feet and a sore, crimped neck. In Atlantic Canada, however, it is the Pine Siskins that do all the travelling—they go everywhere throughout the year. The lazy way to meet these birds is to set up a finch feeder filled with niger seed in your backyard and wait for them to appear. If the feeder is in the right location, you can expect your backyard to be visited by Pine Siskins at just about any time of year, but particularly in winter. • Once you learn to recognize the characteristic rising *zzzreeeee* calls and boisterous chatter of these finches, you can confirm their presence by simply listening. Along the coast, they regularly meet up with redpolls, which attempt to outcompete them in terms of exuberance and noise with their combined twittering calls. These excitable winter flocks can be so large that they look like a flock of shorebirds or a swarm of giant bees as they whirl overhead.

ID: heavily streaked underparts; yellow highlights at base of tail feathers and on wings (easily seen in flight); dull wing bars; darker, heavily streaked upperparts; slightly forked tail; indistinct facial pattern. *Immature:* similar to adult, but overall yellow tint fades through summer.
Size: *L* 11–13 cm.
Status: uncommon to common, irruptive and erratic year-round resident.
Habitat: *Breeding:* coniferous and mixed forests; urban and rural ornamental and shade trees. *Winter:* coniferous and mixed forests, forest edges, meadows, roadsides, agricultural fields and backyards with feeders.
Nesting: usually loosely colonial; typically at mid-height on an outer branch of a conifer; female builds a loose cup made of twigs, grass and rootlets and lines it with feathers, hair, rootlets and fine plant fibres; female incubates 3–5 pale blue eggs with dark dots for about 13 days.
Feeding: gleans the ground and vegetation for seeds (especially thistle seeds), buds and some insects; attracted to road salts, mineral licks and ashes; regularly visits feeding stations, sometimes in huge numbers.
Voice: song is a variable, bubbly mix of squeaky, metallic, raspy notes, sometimes resembling a jerky laugh; call is a buzzy, rising *zzzreeeee.*
Similar Species: *Common Redpoll* (p. 310) and *Hoary Redpoll* (p. 311): red forecrown; lack yellow on wings and tail. *Purple Finch* (p. 306) and *House Finch* (p. 307): females have thicker bill and no yellow on wings or tail. *Sparrows* (pp. 277–89): all lack yellow on wings and tail.
Best Sites: conifers and mixed woods, occasionally in urban parks. *In migration:* large flocks wander mainly between conifer stands and second-growth deciduous forest. *Winter:* urban feeders.

AMERICAN GOLDFINCH

Carduelis tristis

The American Goldfinch is a bright, cheery songbird that is commonly seen in weedy fields, along roadsides and among backyard shrubs throughout summer and autumn. Goldfinches seem to delight in perching upon late-summer thistle heads as they search for seeds. It's hard to miss the familiar, jubilant *po-ta-to-chip* they issue as they flutter over parks and gardens with their distinctive undulating flight style. • Goldfinches nest late in summer to ensure there is a dependable source of seeds from thistles and dandelions to feed their young. • It is enjoyable to observe a flock of goldfinches raining down to ground level to poke and prod the heads of dandelions. These birds do their best to play up the comedy as they step down on the flower stems to reach the crowning seeds. A dandelion-filled lawn always seems a lot less weedy with a flock of glowing goldfinches hopping through it.

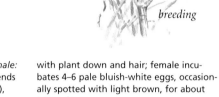

breeding

ID: *Breeding male:* black cap (extends onto forehead), wings and tail; bright yellow body; white wing bars, undertail coverts and tail base; orange bill and legs. *Non-breeding male:* olive brown back; yellow-tinged head; grey underparts. *Female:* yellow-green upperparts and belly; yellow throat and breast.
Size: *L* 11–14 cm.
Status: fairly common to common year-round resident; local in eastern NF; local at feeders, where many overwinter.
Habitat: weedy fields, woodland edges, meadows, riparian areas and parks and gardens.
Nesting: in a fork in a deciduous shrub or tree; female builds a compact cup nest of plant fibres, grass and spider silk, lined with plant down and hair; female incubates 4–6 pale bluish-white eggs, occasionally spotted with light brown, for about 12–14 days.
Feeding: gleans vegetation for seeds, primarily thistle, birch and alder, as well as for insects and berries; commonly visits feeding stations.
Voice: song is a long and varied series of trills, twitters, warbles and hissing notes; calls include *po-ta-to-chip* or *per-chic-or-ee* (often delivered in flight) and a whistled *dear-me, see-me.*
Similar Species: *Evening Grosbeak* (p. 314): much larger; massive bill; lacks black forehead. *Wilson's Warbler* (p. 273): olive upperparts; olive wings without wing bars; thin, dark bill; black cap does not extend onto forehead.
Best Sites: open areas, except in the uplands.

EVENING GROSBEAK

Coccothraustes vespertinus

One chilly winter day, a flock of Evening Grosbeaks descends, unannounced, upon your backyard birdfeeder filled with sunflower seeds. You watch the stunning gold-and-black grosbeaks with delight, but you soon come to realize that these birds are both an aesthetic blessing and a financial curse. The birds will eat great quantities of expensive birdseed and then, in an expression of their wild and independent spirit, suddenly disappear in late winter. Transient residents in much of Atlantic Canada, Evening Grosbeaks are generally encountered in large wintering flocks every two to three years. • It's hard not to notice the massive bill of this seed eater. As any seasoned bird-bander will tell you, the Evening Grosbeak's bill can exert an incredible force per unit area—it may be the most powerful of any North American bird. • It was once thought that the Evening Grosbeak sang only in the evening, a fact that is reflected in both its common and scientific names (*vespertinus* is Latin for "of the evening").

ID: massive, light-coloured, conical bill; black wings and tail; broad white wing patches. *Male:* black crown; bright yellow eyebrow and forehead band; dark brown head gradually fades into golden yellow belly and lower back. *Female:* grey head and upper back; yellow-tinged underparts; white undertail coverts.
Size: *L* 18–22 cm.
Status: fairly common breeder from April to early October (irregular in NF); irregularly rare to locally fairly common migrant and visitor from October to mid-May.
Habitat: *Breeding:* coniferous and mixed forests and woodlands; occasionally in deciduous woodlands, suburban parks and orchards. *Winter:* forests and woodlands; parks and gardens with feeders.

Nesting: on an outer limb in a conifer; female builds a flimsy cup nest made of twigs and lines it with rootlets, fine grass, plant fibres, moss and pine needles; female incubates 3–4 pale blue to blue-green eggs, blotched with purple, grey and brown, for 11–14 days.
Feeding: gleans the ground and vegetation for seeds, buds and berries; also eats insects and licks mineral-rich soil; often visits feeding stations for sunflower seeds.
Voice: song is a wandering, halting warble; call is a loud, sharp *clee-ip* or a ringing *peeer*.
Similar Species: *American Goldfinch* (p. 313): much smaller; small bill; smaller wing bars; male has black cap. *Pine Grosbeak* (p. 305): female has black bill and smaller wing bars; grey overall.
Best Sites: mixed woods and conifers, occasionally in urban parks; also at feeders in migration and winter.

HOUSE SPARROW

Passer domesticus

For most of us, the House Sparrow is the first bird we meet and recognize in our youth. Although it is one of our most abundant and conspicuous birds, many generations of House Sparrows may live out their lives within our backyards with few of us ever knowing much about this omnipresent neighbour. • House Sparrows were introduced to North America in the 1850s around Brooklyn, New York, as part of a plan to control the insects that were damaging grain and cereal crops. Contrary to popular opinion at the time, this sparrow's diet is largely vegetarian, so its impact on crop pests proved to be minimal. Since then, this Eurasian sparrow has managed to colonize most populated areas on the continent, and it has benefited greatly from a close association with humans. Unfortunately, its aggressive behaviour has helped it to usurp territory from many native bird species, especially in rural habitats. • House Sparrows are not closely related to the other North American sparrows: they belong to the family of Old World Sparrows or "Weaver Finches."

ID: *Breeding male:* grey crown; black "bib" and bill; chestnut nape; light grey "cheek"; white wing bar; dark, mottled upperparts; grey underparts. *Non-breeding male:* smaller black bib; light-coloured bill. *Female:* plain grey-brown overall; buffy eyebrow; streaked upperparts; indistinct facial patterns; greyish unstreaked underparts.

Size: *L* 14–17 cm.

Status: abundant year-round resident in populated areas, but absent from many small communities in outlying and exposed areas in NF.

Habitat: townsites, urban and suburban areas, farmyards and agricultural areas, railway yards and other developed areas; absent from undeveloped areas.

Nesting: often communal; in artificial structures, ornamental shrubs or natural cavities; pair builds a large, dome-shaped nest made of grass, twigs, plant fibres and litter and often lines it with feathers; pair incubates 4–6 whitish to greenish-white eggs, dotted with grey and brown, for 10–13 days.

Feeding: gleans the ground and vegetation for seeds, insects and fruit; frequently visits feeding stations for seeds.

Voice: song is a familiar, plain *cheep-cheep-cheep-cheep*; call is a short *chill-up*.

Similar Species: female is distinctively drab. *Harris's Sparrow:* grey face, black cap and pink-orange bill. *Dickcissel* (p. 297): brighter, more heavily streaked plumage; yellowish or buff underparts; chestnut wing coverts, white "chin."

Best Site: urban and suburban areas.

ACCIDENTAL BIRD SPECIES

The following is a selection of 41 of the 151 accidentals (species that are not seen every year) in Atlantic Canada. For a full listing of accidental species, please refer to the checklist (pp. 324–28).

PACIFIC LOON
Gavia pacifica
This northern breeder overwinters mainly along the Pacific Coast, but it is a fairly regular visitor to the Atlantic Coast from September to early April. Most birds are in non-breeding plumage and are difficult to distinguish from the Arctic Loon. Look for Pacific Loons off Rimouski and Northumberland Strait.

CORY'S SHEARWATER
Calonectris diomedea
This broad-winged shearwater from western Europe joins other ocean species to feed over the Continental Shelf from late May to late October. Most birds seen in Atlantic Canada are immatures that are probably migrating from the waters off South Africa and Argentina. Most sightings are from pelagic ferries, in the Bay of Fundy and off the southwest coast of Nova Scotia.

LITTLE BLUE HERON
Egretta caerulea
This medium-sized heron is often confused with egrets in its all-white immature plumage, which is the plumage most likely to be seen in this bird's post-breeding wanderings to Atlantic Canada. Most birds are seen in coastal marshes from July to October, but there are also spring sightings, including blue adults, from April to early June. Check out coastal locations in New Brunswick and Nova Scotia and the Bas Saint-Laurent.

LITTLE EGRET
Egretta garzetta
The Little Egret is a recent arrival from Europe. In the breeding season, it can be distinguished from the very similar Snowy Egret only by its two trailing head plumes and paler yellow lores and feet. At other times the two species are virtually identical. Most sightings have been in late summer. Although they don't breed here, some Little Egrets have been seen in spring and early summer with nesting herons at Bon Portage Island in Nova Scotia.

BARNACLE GOOSE
Branta leucopsis
This small relative of the Canada Goose is popular with waterfowl breeders. A few wild birds also wander here in autumn, probably from breeding grounds in northeastern Greenland. They are usually seen with migrating Canada Geese.

GARGANEY
Anas querquedula
This Eurasian equivalent of the Blue-winged Teal is becoming a more regular vagrant to Atlantic Canada's freshwater marshes. Garganeys appear in mid-May and may remain into the breeding season. They usually accompany the last Green-winged Teals and the main movement of Blue-winged Teals. Most Garganeys identified are males, but there may well be more females and immatures than reported.

PURPLE GALLINULE
Porphyrula martinica
This erratically wandering member of the rail family has been turning up in early winter with increasing regularity. The first arrivals were ferried back to Florida aboard scheduled flights but this practice has been discontinued. Birds have appeared with increasing frequency, especially in southern New Brunswick and Nova Scotia headlands.

SANDHILL CRANE
Grus canadensis
More birds of the smallest, migratory northern race are appearing in Atlantic Canada in spring and autumn. They are easily attracted to pinioned birds at wildlife parks and some have shown courtship activity to the point where they may eventually breed. Both adults and juveniles have been seen in all five provinces.

Sandhill Crane

NORTHERN LAPWING
Vanellus vanellus
A familiar farmland and salt marsh bird in Eurasia, the Northern Lapwing is a wanderer by nature. It is prone to erratic dispersions in winter that take it south and west of its breeding range. Some of these movements deposit flocks on our shores, particularly on the east coast of Newfoundland.

COMMON RINGED PLOVER
Charadrius hiaticula
The presence of Common Ringed Plovers in Atlantic Canada should not be a surprise. They are common nesters in northern Europe and have colonized the eastern arctic islands of Canada from Greenland. These plovers occasionally travel south into Atlantic Canada in autumn with parties of Semipalmated Plovers, which are almost identical in plumage but have a different call.

AMERICAN OYSTERCATCHER
Haematopus palliatus
The breeding range of this striking black-and-white shorebird has been expanding northward from Massachusetts. It appears to be only a matter of time before the American Oystercatcher becomes established in Nova Scotia and New Brunswick, where most sightings have occurred. There has already been one nest at Daniel's Head, Nova Scotia, and summering birds can be found elsewhere.

MARBLED GODWIT
Limosa fedoa
Marbled Godwits are birds of the western plains and prairies, yet they regularly turn up in Atlantic Canada, usually in fairly open coastal locations. Most birds are seen in autumn. Good places to look for them are Rimouski, Îles de la Madeleine, Grand Manan Island and Cape Sable Island.

WESTERN SANDPIPER
Calidris mauri
Although most arctic-nesting Western Sandpipers use the Pacific Coast to reach their wintering grounds, a few join the masses of Semipalmated Sandpipers heading to the Atlantic Coast. It's a challenge to find them in the roosting and feeding flocks from mid-July to early November but well worth the effort. Some of the best locations are Pointe-au-Père, Mary's Point, Lawrencetown Loop and Saint Paul's.

CURLEW SANDPIPER
Calidris ferruginea
As more birders check out the flocks of sandpipers thronging on Atlantic beaches and mud flats, there are more sightings of this trans-Atlantic vagrant. Birds in July and August are still in breeding plumage, but most of the reports from September to late October are of birds in moult or in their non-breeding plumage. Regular locations include Mary's Point, Prince Edward Island National Park, southwestern Nova Scotia and northeast Cape Breton.

RUFF
Philomachus pugnax
Male Eurasian Ruffs come in a variety of colours, but females, called Reeves, are more sombre and shy. The female looks more like a cross between a Buff-breasted Sandpiper and Pectoral Sandpiper. Spring birds are often in breeding plumage, and the more regular late summer and autumn sightings are mostly of juveniles. A few birds have even overwintered in Atlantic Canada. Look for them at Îles de la Madeleine, Cape Jourimain and Lawrencetown.

Ruff

Eastern Screech-Owl

LONG-BILLED DOWITCHER

Limnodromus scolopaceus

Better information to the public about the field marks and traits of Long-billed Dowitchers has led to an increase in the number of reports of these birds on the Atlantic Coast. The best chances of seeing them are at Rimouski, Fredericton, Brier Island, and Lawrencetown.

FRANKLIN'S GULL

Larus pipixcan

Each spring and autumn, a few members of this prairie-breeding species arrive in Atlantic Canada, usually in the company of Bonaparte's Gulls. Most sightings of Franklin's Gulls are at inshore upwellings in the Bay of Fundy, in harbours and coastal bays on the Atlantic Coast and along the Bas Saint-Laurent shore. Spring birds are usually adults in breeding plumage; in late summer and autumn, juveniles are more likely than adults.

LITTLE GULL

Larus minutus

If you have the patience to watch a huge flock of gulls gathered at an ocean upwelling in the Bay of Fundy, or if you spend enough time watching smaller gulls in Atlantic harbours, eventually you will find an adult or first-winter Little Gull. This is the smallest gull species in the world. Most sightings have been from the St. Lawrence North Shore ferries, off Grand Manan Island and at L'Anse aux Meadows.

ROSS'S GULL

Rhodostethia rosea

Most people never get to see a Ross's Gull, because its breeding range is in the Arctic and it overwinters well out to sea on pack ice. Occasionally one bird gets caught up with other small gulls and appears inshore. Aside from northern Newfoundland, the best places to see this gull are the Cabot Strait and Canso Causeway.

FORSTER'S TERN

Sterna forsteri

Fortunately for birders in Atlantic Canada, most Forster's Terns are seen in autumn and early winter, when their head pattern is quite different from the earlier-departing Common, Arctic and Roseate terns. Most years, single birds fish in shallows and coastal marshes. However, autumn storms may sometimes deposit this and other species on their way to the Carolinas. Birds have turned up in all five provinces, but Grand Manan Island is the only regular location.

EASTERN SCREECH-OWL

Otus asio

The secretive Eastern Screech-Owl may nest in small numbers throughout the mainland of Atlantic Canada. There are so few records that it is uncertain if they appear each summer. This bird is most likely found in southwestern and central New Brunswick, where there have been nesting records, or in the Bas Saint-Laurent region of maritime Québec.

GREAT GRAY OWL

Strix nebulosa

Small mammals may dispute this bird's designation as "Gentle Giant," but anyone fortunate enough to see a regal Great Gray Owl marvels at its patience and its ability to remain hidden even in sparse vegetation. In winters when other arctic owls move south to find food, the chances of finding a Great Gray Owl are the greatest. Plaster Rock in northern New Brunswick offers the best hope of seeing this infrequent visitor.

RED-HEADED WOODPECKER

Melanerpes erythrocephalus

The main reason for a decline in Red-headed Woodpecker populations in neighbouring New England was competition for nest sites from the introduced European Starling, and the same is probably true in Atlantic Canada. The best chance of seeing this woodpecker is on offshore islands in Québec, New Brunswick and Nova Scotia during migration. The alternative is to check birding hotlines for sightings at urban feeders.

WESTERN KINGBIRD
Tyrannus verticalis
Common in dry, open country in western North America, this bird is a rare spring and early summer vagrant and a regular straggler in autumn and early winter. Most Western Kingbirds appear on headlands and offshore islands, but a few wander into urban areas and occasionally visit gardens to catch flying insects and eat winter berries. Locations around the Bay of Fundy and in southwestern Nova Scotia provide the most sightings, but any open headland is worth checking.

LOGGERHEAD SHRIKE
Lanius ludovicianus
The Loggerhead Shrike was once a common summer resident in southern Canada and an uncommon breeding species in the Maritimes. Today, it is a rare migrant, briefly seen perched on wires and shrubs before it swoops down to catch its prey. There have been a few summer reports in the Maritime provinces, but no confirmed nesting records for some time, suggesting that its endangered species status is well deserved.

YELLOW-THROATED VIREO
Vireo flavifrons
The Yellow-throated Vireo could be the stunt double for the Pine Warbler—their plumages are so similar that you have to check for the thicker bill, unstreaked underparts and grey rump of this vireo. A few birds are heard singing in most summers, but breeding records are lacking, and more birds are seen in autumn migration. A few birds nest close by in extreme southwestern Québec. Offshore islands in Nova Scotia provide the most records.

CAROLINA WREN
Thryothorus ludovicianus
As colonies of Carolina Wrens grow, more birds push the limits of their breeding range north and east into Atlantic Canada, where frigid winter temperatures and midwinter ice storms can decimate populations. Those birds that make it through such winters survive to sustain the colony. Look for these wrens in southern Québec and New Brunswick and northern Nova Scotia. Occasionally they are also seen on offshore islands in migration.

TOWNSEND'S SOLITAIRE
Myadestes townsendi
Every autumn, some Townsend's Solitaires flying over the Continental Divide get caught up in weather systems from the West that eventually deposit them in eastern Canada. Birds that reach Atlantic Canada usually arrive in October and may attempt to overwinter in urban locations and close to headlands. A few birds have made it through the winter by surviving on berries and food provided at

Yellow-throated Vireo

feeders. Other birds tag along with wintering robins or waxwings and follow them to assured winter food sources.

FIELDFARE
Turdus pilaris
When this Eurasian thrush first appeared in residential St. John's, Newfoundland, in the early 1980s, it caused quite a stir. A winter migration of sorts came into being as birders flocked from all parts of the continent to look for it among wintering flocks of American Robins. When it was followed a few winters later by the Redwing *(T. iliacus)*, another migratory Eurasian thrush, St. John's achieved international recognition. Two decades later, Fieldfares and Redwings have been reported in several Atlantic Canadian cities, mostly in the winter months. Hard-core birders are still irresistibly drawn to them.

BLUE-WINGED WARBLER
Vermivora pinus
The Blue-winged Warbler's range expansion into southern Ontario and Québec has led to more sightings of this attractive little warbler in Atlantic Canada. Most birds are found on offshore islands and headlands, but a few of these warblers make it to urban gardens. Look for them at Grand Manan, Kent, Brier, Seal and Bon Portage islands, as well as southwestern Nova Scotia.

YELLOW-THROATED WARBLER
Dendroica dominica
The strikingly plumaged Yellow-throated Warbler nests in the southeastern US and overwinters in the West Indies and Central America. A few overshoot their range, however, and appear in Atlantic Canada with the early wave of warblers from early May to early June. Another invasion occurs from late August to November, when more birds get diverted north by strong winds. A few birds linger into January at feeders, where they forage like Black-and-white Warblers and pick at seeds and suet. The offshore islands of New Brunswick and Nova Scotia get most of the wanderers.

Summer Tanager

CONNECTICUT WARBLER
Oporornis agilis
Most of Atlantic Canada's Connecticut Warblers pass by unnoticed, because they are not birds that seek attention. Secretive by nature and largely silent, these birds seek the solitude of cover that they find in open forests, bogs and fens well to the northwest of Atlantic Canada. A few birds arrive off Nova Scotia with the later warblers in spring. More birds reach New Brunswick and Nova Scotia in autumn, when they are more likely to be seen inland.

HOODED WARBLER
Wilsonia citrina
Hooded Warblers reach the northeastern limit of their range in southwestern Ontario and head south at the end of the breeding season. All the birds that reach offshore islands near Nova Scotia and inland New Brunswick and maritime Québec from April to mid-June have been diverted by unfavourable winds or by other warblers pushing them northeast. The same thing happens from August to October, when these birds appear with other migrants all over Atlantic Canada.

YELLOW-BREASTED CHAT
Icteria virens
The Yellow-breasted Chat has puzzled ornithologists ever since it was first discovered. DNA testing has confirmed that it is, indeed, a wood-warbler, but its habits and vocalizations suggest a closer link to mimic thrushes. Almost all birds arrive in Atlantic Canada between August and December, and several have stayed into early February, usually at feeders.

SUMMER TANAGER
Piranga rubra
Unlike most other songbird vagrants, Summer Tanagers are much more likely to be seen in spring than in autumn. These tanagers pass through in May in full breeding plumage, and they often appear in shade trees and gardens. Most Summer Tanagers frequent offshore islands and the southwestern tip of Nova Scotia, but birds have been seen as far east as Glace Bay, Nova Scotia, and as far north as Île Bonaventure, Québec.

LARK SPARROW
Chondestes grammacus
Appropriately nondescript when feeding, Lark Sparrows distinguish themselves in flight by flashing their conspicuous white outer tail feathers. This feature gets the attention of birders, who then notice the distinctive facial pattern. Most sightings are from around the Bay of Fundy and along the east coast of Nova Scotia.

GRASSHOPPER SPARROW
Ammodramus savannarum
Grasshopper Sparrows are open-country birds that like weedy fields free of trees and shrubs. This kind of habitat is in limited supply in Atlantic Canada. A few birds appear every spring and summer, but most sightings are from late September to early November. Offshore islands provide most of the sightings, but these birds have been recorded on urban Christmas bird counts in New Brunswick and Nova Scotia.

YELLOW-HEADED BLACKBIRD
Xanthocephalus xanthocephalus
Yellow-headed Blackbirds have been reported in Nova Scotia for more than a century, yet they remain unknown to most people in Atlantic Canada. These birds often appear with other blackbirds from late August to October, with a few birds staying at feeders well into winter. The Yellow-headed Blackbird is one vagrant species that can find enough food to survive cold snaps. A few breeding-plumaged birds have appeared from mid-April to early June, but none has stayed into summer.

ORCHARD ORIOLE
Icterus spurius
A few Orchard Orioles that arrive after mid-April linger into summer. These orioles are widespread but less common from mid-August to late October. They appear to get caught up in major East Coast bird movements or are sent north by storms. It is possible that these birds will eventually breed in Atlantic Canada, because their range is expanding north into other parts of Canada.

SELECT REFERENCES

American Ornithologists' Union. 1998. *Check-list of North American Birds.* 7th ed. (and its supplements). American Ornithologists' Union, Washington, D.C.

Burrows, R. 1988. *Birding in Atlantic Canada: Nova Scotia.* Jesperson Press Ltd., St. John's, NF.

Burrows, R. 1989. *Birding in Atlantic Canada: Newfoundland.* Jesperson Press Ltd., St. John's, NF.

Burrows, R. 1990. *Birding in Atlantic Canada: Acadia.* Jesperson Press Ltd., St. John's, NF.

Choate, E.A. 1985. *The Dictionary of American Bird Names.* Rev. ed. Harvard Common Press, Cambridge, MA.

COSEWIC. 2001. *Canadian Species at Risk.* Committee on the Status of Endangered Wildlife in Canada.

Erskine, A.J. 1992. *Atlas of Breeding Birds of the Maritime Provinces.* Nimbus Publishing Ltd. & Nova Scotia Museum, Halifax.

Finlay, J.C., ed. 2000. *A Bird-finding Guide to Canada.* McClelland and Stuart, Toronto.

Godfrey, W.E. 1986. *The Birds of Canada.* Rev. ed. National Museum of Natural Sciences, Ottawa.

Jones, J.O. 1990. *Where The Birds Are.* William Morrow and Company, Inc., New York.

Kaufman, K. 1996. *Lives of North American Birds.* Houghton Mifflin Co., Boston.

Kaufman, K. 2000. *Birds of North America.* Houghton Mifflin Co., New York.

Montevecchi, W.M. and L.M. Tuck. 1987. *Newfoundland Birds: Exploitation, Study, Conservation.* Nuttall Ornithological Club, Cambridge, MA.

National Geographic Society. 1999. *Field Guide to the Birds of North America.* 3rd ed. National Geographic Society, Washington, D.C.

Sibley, D.A. 2000. *National Audubon Society The Sibley Guide to Birds.* Alfred A. Knopf, New York.

Tufts, R.W. 1986. *Birds of Nova Scotia.* 3rd ed. Nova Scotia Museum, Halifax.

Great Cormorant

GLOSSARY

accipiter: a forest hawk (genus *Accipiter*), characterized by a long tail and short, rounded wings; feeds mostly on birds.

brood: *n.* a family of young from one hatching; *v.* to incubate the eggs.

brood parasite: a bird that lays its eggs in other birds' nests.

buteo: a high-soaring hawk (genus *Buteo*), characterized by broad wings and a short, wide tail; feeds mostly on small mammals and other land animals.

cere: on birds of prey, a fleshy area at the base of the bill that contains the nostrils.

clutch: the number of eggs laid by the female at one time.

dabbling: a foraging technique used by some ducks, in which the head and neck are submerged but the body and tail remain on the water's surface; dabbling ducks can usually walk easily on land, can take off without running and have brightly coloured speculums.

"eclipse" plumage: a cryptic plumage, similar to that of females, worn by some male ducks in autumn when they moult their flight feathers and consequently are unable to fly.

endangered: a species facing imminent extirpation or extinction.*

extinct: a species that no longer exists.*

extirpated: a species no longer existing in the wild in Canada but occurring elsewhere.*

flushing: when frightened birds explode into flight in response to a disturbance.

flycatching: a feeding behaviour in which the bird leaves a perch, snatches an insect in mid-air and returns to the same perch; also known as "hawking" or "sallying."

lek: a place where males gather to display for females in the spring.

peep: a sandpiper of the *Calidris* genus.

pelagic: refers to open ocean habitat very far from land.

polyandry: a mating strategy in which one female breeds with many males.

polygyny: a mating strategy in which one male breeds with several females.

precocial: a bird that is relatively well developed at hatching; precocial birds usually have open eyes, extensive down and are fairly mobile.

raft: a gathering of birds.

riparian: habitat along riverbanks.

sexual dimorphism: a difference in plumage, size or other characteristics between males and females of the same species.

special concern: a species of special concern because of characteristics that make it particularly sensitive to human activities or natural events.*

speculum: a brightly coloured patch on the wings of many dabbling ducks.

stage: to gather in one place during migration, usually when birds are flightless or partly flightless during moulting.

stoop: a steep dive through the air, usually performed by birds of prey while foraging or during courtship displays.

threatened: a species likely to become endangered if limiting factors are not reversed.*

vent: the single opening for excretion of uric acid and other wastes and for sexual reproduction; also known as the "cloaca."

* from COSEWIC, 2001.

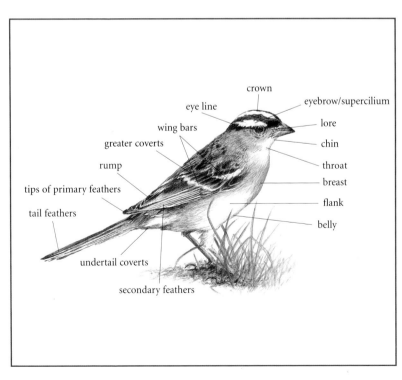

CHECKLIST

The following checklist contains 477 species of birds that have been officially recorded in New Brunswick, Prince Edward Island, Nova Scotia, Newfoundland and Labrador, and Québec. Species are grouped by family and listed in taxonomic order in accordance with the A.O.U. *Check-list of North American Birds* (7th ed.) and its supplements.

Accidentals (species that are not seen on a yearly basis) are listed in italics. An asterisk (*) identifies species that are known to nest in one or more of the provinces. A plus (+) identifies introduced species. In addition, the following COSEWIC (Committee on the Status of Endangered Wildlife in Canada) risk categories are also noted: extinct or extirpated (ex), endangered (en), threatened (th) and special concern (sc).

Loons (Gaviidae)
❏ Red-throated Loon*
❏ Pacific Loon
❏ Common Loon*
❏ *Yellow-billed Loon*

Grebes (Podicipedidae)
❏ Pied-billed Grebe*
❏ Horned Grebe
❏ Red-necked Grebe
❏ *Eared Grebe*
❏ *Western Grebe*

Albatrosses (Diomedeidae)
❏ *Yellow-nosed Albatross*
❏ *Black-browed Albatross*

Petrels & Shearwaters (Procellariidae)
❏ Northern Fulmar*
❏ *Black-capped Petrel*
❏ Cory's Shearwater
❏ Greater Shearwater
❏ Sooty Shearwater
❏ Manx Shearwater*
❏ *Audubon's Shearwater*

Storm-Petrels (Hydrobatidae)
❏ Wilson's Storm-Petrel
❏ *White-faced Storm-Petrel*

❏ *European Storm-Petrel*
❏ Leach's Storm-Petrel

Tropicbirds (Phaethontidae)
❏ *White-tailed Tropicbird*

Gannets & Boobies (Sulidae)
❏ *Brown Booby*
❏ Northern Gannet*

Pelicans (Pelecanidae)
❏ *American White Pelican*
❏ *Brown Pelican*

Cormorants (Phalacrocoracidae)
❏ Double-crested Cormorant*
❏ Great Cormorant*

Frigatebirds (Fregatidae)
❏ *Magnificent Frigatebird*

Herons (Ardeidae)
❏ American Bittern*
❏ Least Bittern* (sc)
❏ Great Blue Heron*
❏ Great Egret
❏ *Little Egret*
❏ Snowy Egret

❏ Little Blue Heron
❏ *Tricolored Heron*
❏ Cattle Egret
❏ Green Heron*
❏ Black-crowned Night-Heron*
❏ Yellow-crowned Night-Heron

Ibises (Threskiornithidae)
❏ *White Ibis*
❏ *Glossy Ibis*

Storks (Ciconiidae)
❏ *Wood Stork*

Vultures (Cathartidae)
❏ *Black Vulture*
❏ Turkey Vulture

Flamingoes (Phoenicopteridae)
❏ *Greater Flamingo*

Waterfowl (Anatidae)
❏ *Black-bellied Whistling-Duck*
❏ *Fulvous Whistling-Duck*
❏ *Pink-footed Goose*
❏ Greater White-fronted Goose
❏ Snow Goose

❏ Ross's Goose
❏ Canada Goose*
❏ Brant
❏ *Barnacle Goose*
❏ Mute Swan*+
❏ *Tundra Swan*
❏ Wood Duck*
❏ Gadwall*
❏ Eurasian Wigeon
❏ American Wigeon*
❏ American Black Duck*
❏ Mallard*
❏ Blue-winged Teal*
❏ *Cinnamon Teal*
❏ Northern Shoveler*
❏ Northern Pintail*
❏ *Garganey*
❏ Green-winged Teal*
❏ Canvasback
❏ Redhead*
❏ Ring-necked Duck*
❏ Tufted Duck
❏ Greater Scaup*
❏ Lesser Scaup
❏ King Eider
❏ Common Eider*
❏ Harlequin Duck* (sc)
❏ Labrador Duck (ex)
❏ Surf Scoter*
❏ White-winged Scoter*
❏ Black Scoter*
❏ Long-tailed Duck
❏ Bufflehead
❏ Common Goldeneye*
❏ Barrow's Goldeneye* (sc)
❏ *Smew*
❏ Hooded Merganser*
❏ Common Merganser*
❏ Red-breasted Merganser*
❏ Ruddy Duck*

Kites, Hawks & Eagles (Accipitridae)
❏ Osprey*
❏ *Swallow-tailed Kite*
❏ *Mississippi Kite*
❏ Bald Eagle*
❏ Northern Harrier*

❏ Sharp-shinned Hawk*
❏ Cooper's Hawk*
❏ Northern Goshawk*
❏ Red-shouldered Hawk (sc)
❏ Broad-winged Hawk
❏ *Swainson's Hawk*
❏ *Zone-tailed Hawk*
❏ Red-tailed Hawk*
❏ Rough-legged Hawk*
❏ Golden Eagle*

Falcons (Falconidae)
❏ *Eurasian Kestrel*
❏ American Kestrel*
❏ Merlin*
❏ Gyrfalcon*
❏ Peregrine Falcon* (th)

Grouse & Allies (Phasianidae)
❏ Chukar*+
❏ Gray Partridge*
❏ Ring-necked Pheasant*
❏ Ruffed Grouse*
❏ Spruce Grouse*
❏ Willow Ptarmigan*
❏ Rock Ptarmigan*
❏ Sharp-tailed Grouse*+

Rails & Coots (Rallidae)
❏ Yellow Rail* (sc)
❏ *Black Rail*
❏ *Corn Crake*
❏ *Clapper Rail*
❏ *King Rail* (en)
❏ Virginia Rail*
❏ Sora*
❏ *Purple Gallinule*
❏ Common Moorhen*
❏ *Eurasian Coot*
❏ American Coot*

Cranes (Gruidae)
❏ Sandhill Crane

Plovers (Charadriidae)
❏ Northern Lapwing
❏ Black-bellied Plover
❏ Eurasian Golden-Plover
❏ American Golden-Plover
❏ *Pacific Golden-Plover*
❏ *Wilson's Plover*
❏ *Common Ringed Plover*
❏ Semipalmated Plover*
❏ Piping Plover* (en)
❏ Killdeer*

Oystercatchers (Haematopodidae)
❏ *Eurasian Oystercatcher*
❏ *American Oystercatcher*

Stilts & Avocets (Recurvirostridae)
❏ *Black-necked Stilt*
❏ *American Avocet*

Sandpipers & Allies (Scolopacidae)
❏ *Common Greenshank*
❏ Greater Yellowlegs
❏ Lesser Yellowlegs
❏ *Common Redshank*
❏ *Spotted Redshank*
❏ *Wood Sandpiper*
❏ Solitary Sandpiper*
❏ Willet*
❏ Spotted Sandpiper*
❏ Upland Sandpiper*
❏ *Little Curlew*
❏ Eskimo Curlew (en)
❏ Whimbrel
❏ *Eurasian Curlew*
❏ Long-billed Curlew (sc)
❏ *Black-tailed Godwit*
❏ Hudsonian Godwit
❏ *Bar-tailed Godwit*
❏ *Marbled Godwit*
❏ Ruddy Turnstone
❏ Red Knot
❏ Sanderling
❏ Semipalmated Sandpiper
❏ Western Sandpiper

- ❑ *Red-necked Stint*
- ❑ *Little Stint*
- ❑ Least Sandpiper
- ❑ White-rumped Sandpiper
- ❑ Baird's Sandpiper
- ❑ Pectoral Sandpiper
- ❑ *Sharp-tailed Sandpiper*
- ❑ Purple Sandpiper
- ❑ Dunlin
- ❑ *Curlew Sandpiper*
- ❑ Stilt Sandpiper
- ❑ *Broad-billed Sandpiper*
- ❑ Buff-breasted Sandpiper
- ❑ *Ruff*
- ❑ Short-billed Dowitcher
- ❑ Long-billed Dowitcher
- ❑ Common Snipe
- ❑ *Eurasian Woodcock*
- ❑ American Woodcock*
- ❑ Wilson's Phalarope*
- ❑ Red-necked Phalarope*
- ❑ Red Phalarope*

Gulls & Allies (Laridae)
- ❑ Great Skua
- ❑ South Polar Skua
- ❑ Pomarine Jaeger
- ❑ Parasitic Jaeger
- ❑ Long-tailed Jaeger
- ❑ Laughing Gull*
- ❑ Franklin's Gull
- ❑ Little Gull
- ❑ Black-headed Gull*
- ❑ Bonaparte's Gull
- ❑ *Black-tailed Gull*
- ❑ Mew Gull
- ❑ Ring-billed Gull*
- ❑ *California Gull*
- ❑ Herring Gull*
- ❑ *Yellow-legged Gull*
- ❑ Thayer's Gull
- ❑ Iceland Gull
- ❑ Lesser Black-backed Gull
- ❑ Glaucous Gull
- ❑ Great Black-backed Gull*
- ❑ Sabine's Gull
- ❑ Black-legged Kittiwake*
- ❑ Ross's Gull (sc)

- ❑ Ivory Gull (sc)
- ❑ *Gull-billed Tern*
- ❑ Caspian Tern*
- ❑ *Royal Tern*
- ❑ *Sandwich Tern*
- ❑ Roseate Tern* (en)
- ❑ Common Tern*
- ❑ Arctic Tern*
- ❑ Forster's Tern
- ❑ *Least Tern*
- ❑ *Bridled Tern*
- ❑ *Sooty Tern*
- ❑ *White-winged Tern*
- ❑ Black Tern*
- ❑ *Black Skimmer*

Alcids (Alcidae)
- ❑ Dovekie
- ❑ Common Murre*
- ❑ Thick-billed Murre*
- ❑ Razorbill*
- ❑ Great Auk (ex)
- ❑ Black Guillemot*
- ❑ *Long-billed Murrelet*
- ❑ *Marbled Murrelet*
- ❑ Atlantic Puffin*

Pigeons & Doves (Columbidae)
- ❑ Rock Dove*
- ❑ *Band-tailed Pigeon*
- ❑ *White-winged Dove*
- ❑ Mourning Dove*
- ❑ Passenger Pigeon (ex)
- ❑ *Common Ground-Dove*

Cuckoos (Cuculidae)
- ❑ Black-billed Cuckoo*
- ❑ Yellow-billed Cuckoo

Barn Owls (Tytonidae)
- ❑ *Barn Owl* (en)

Owls (Strigidae)
- ❑ Eastern Screech-Owl*
- ❑ Great Horned Owl*
- ❑ Snowy Owl
- ❑ Northern Hawk Owl*

- ❑ *Burrowing Owl* (en)
- ❑ Barred Owl*
- ❑ *Great Gray Owl*
- ❑ Long-eared Owl*
- ❑ Short-eared Owl* (sc)
- ❑ Boreal Owl*
- ❑ Northern Saw-whet Owl*

Nightjars (Caprimulgidae)
- ❑ Common Nighthawk*
- ❑ *Chuck-will's-widow*
- ❑ Whip-poor-will*

Swifts (Apodidae)
- ❑ Chimney Swift*

Hummingbirds (Trochilidae)
- ❑ Ruby-throated Hummingbird*
- ❑ *Black-chinned Hummingbird*
- ❑ *Rufous Hummingbird*

Kingfishers (Alcedinidae)
- ❑ Belted Kingfisher*

Woodpeckers (Picidae)
- ❑ *Lewis's Woodpecker*
- ❑ Red-headed Woodpecker* (sc)
- ❑ Red-bellied Woodpecker
- ❑ Yellow-bellied Sapsucker*
- ❑ Downy Woodpecker*
- ❑ Hairy Woodpecker*
- ❑ Three-toed Woodpecker*
- ❑ Black-backed Woodpecker*
- ❑ Northern Flicker*
- ❑ Pileated Woodpecker*

Flycatchers (Tyrannidae)
- ❑ Olive-sided Flycatcher*
- ❑ Eastern Wood-Pewee*
- ❑ Yellow-bellied Flycatcher*
- ❑ *Acadian Flycatcher* (en)
- ❑ Alder Flycatcher*

❏ Willow Flycatcher*
❏ Least Flycatcher*
❏ *Dusky Flycatcher*
❏ Eastern Phoebe*
❏ *Say's Phoebe*
❏ *Vermillion Flycatcher*
❏ *Ash-throated Flycatcher*
❏ Great Crested Flycatcher*
❏ *Sulphur-bellied Flycatcher*
❏ *Tropical Kingbird*
❏ *Couch's Kingbird*
❏ *Cassin's Kingbird*
❏ Western Kingbird*
❏ Eastern Kingbird*
❏ *Gray Kingbird*
❏ *Scissor-tailed Flycatcher*
❏ *Fork-tailed Flycatcher*

Shrikes (Laniidae)
❏ *Brown Shrike*
❏ Loggerhead Shrike* (en)
❏ Northern Shrike*

Vireos (Vireonidae)
❏ *White-eyed Vireo*
❏ *Yellow-throated Vireo*
❏ *Plumbeous Vireo*
❏ Blue-headed Vireo*
❏ Warbling Vireo*
❏ Philadelphia Vireo*
❏ Red-eyed Vireo*

Jays & Crows (Corvidae)
❏ Gray Jay*
❏ Blue Jay*
❏ *Black-billed Magpie*
❏ *Eurasian Jackdaw*
❏ American Crow*
❏ *Pied Crow*
❏ *Fish Crow*
❏ Common Raven*

Larks (Alaudidae)
❏ Horned Lark*

Swallows (Hirundinidae)
❏ Purple Martin*
❏ Tree Swallow*
❏ *Violet-green Swallow*
❏ Northern Rough-winged Swallow*
❏ Bank Swallow*
❏ Cliff Swallow*
❏ *Cave Swallow*

Chickadees and Titmice (Paridae)
❏ Black-capped Chickadee*
❏ Boreal Chickadee*
❏ *Tufted Titmouse* *
❏ *Great Titmouse*

Nuthatches (Sittidae)
❏ Red-breasted Nuthatch*
❏ White-breasted Nuthatch*

Creepers (Certhiidae)
❏ Brown Creeper*

Wrens (Troglodytidae)
❏ Carolina Wren*
❏ *Bewick's Wren*
❏ House Wren*
❏ Winter Wren*
❏ Sedge Wren*
❏ Marsh Wren*

Kinglets (Regulidae)
❏ Golden-crowned Kinglet*
❏ Ruby-crowned Kinglet*

Gnatcatchers (Sylviidae)
❏ Blue-gray Gnatcatcher*

Thrushes (Turdidae)
❏ Northern Wheatear*
❏ *Stonechat*
❏ Eastern Bluebird*
❏ *Mountain Bluebird*
❏ *Townsend's Solitaire*

❏ Veery
❏ Gray-cheeked Thrush*
❏ Bicknell's Thrush* (sc)
❏ Swainson's Thrush*
❏ Hermit Thrush*
❏ Wood Thrush*
❏ *Eurasian Blackbird*
❏ Fieldfare
❏ *Redwing*
❏ American Robin*
❏ *Varied Thrush*

Mockingbirds & Thrashers (Mimidae)
❏ Gray Catbird*
❏ Northern Mockingbird*
❏ Brown Thrasher*

Starlings (Sturnidae)
❏ European Starling*

Wagtails & Pipits (Motacillidae)
❏ *White Wagtail*
❏ American Pipit*

Waxwings (Bombycillidae)
❏ Bohemian Waxwing
❏ Cedar Waxwing*

Wood-Warblers (Parulidae)
❏ Blue-winged Warbler
❏ *Golden-winged Warbler*
❏ *Virginia's Warbler*
❏ Tennessee Warbler*
❏ Orange-crowned Warbler*
❏ Nashville Warbler*
❏ Northern Parula*
❏ Yellow Warbler*
❏ Chestnut-sided Warbler*
❏ Magnolia Warbler*
❏ Cape May Warbler*
❏ Black-throated Blue Warbler*
❏ Yellow-rumped Warbler*

- ❏ Black-throated Gray Warbler
- ❏ Black-throated Green Warbler*
- ❏ *Townsend's Warbler*
- ❏ *Hermit Warbler*
- ❏ Blackburnian Warbler*
- ❏ *Yellow-throated Warbler*
- ❏ Pine Warbler*
- ❏ Prairie Warbler*
- ❏ Palm Warbler*
- ❏ Bay-breasted Warbler*
- ❏ Blackpoll Warbler*
- ❏ *Cerulean Warbler* (sc)
- ❏ Black-and-white Warbler*
- ❏ American Redstart*
- ❏ *Prothonotary Warbler* (en)
- ❏ *Worm-eating Warbler*
- ❏ *Swainson's Warbler*
- ❏ Ovenbird*
- ❏ Northern Waterthrush*
- ❏ *Louisiana Waterthrush* (sc)
- ❏ *Kentucky Warbler*
- ❏ Mourning Warbler*
- ❏ Connecticut Warbler
- ❏ Common Yellowthroat*
- ❏ Hooded Warbler (th)
- ❏ Wilson's Warbler*
- ❏ Canada Warbler*
- ❏ Yellow-breasted Chat (sc)

Tanagers (Thraupidae)
- ❏ Summer Tanager
- ❏ Scarlet Tanager*
- ❏ *Western Tanager*

Sparrows & Allies (Emberizidae)
- ❏ *Green-tailed Towhee*
- ❏ *Spotted Towhee*
- ❏ Eastern Towhee*
- ❏ Cassin's Sparrow
- ❏ American Tree Sparrow*
- ❏ Chipping Sparrow*
- ❏ Clay-colored Sparrow*

- ❏ *Brewer's Sparrow*
- ❏ Field Sparrow*
- ❏ Vesper Sparrow*
- ❏ Lark Sparrow
- ❏ *Lark Bunting*
- ❏ Savannah Sparrow* (sc)
- ❏ Grasshopper Sparrow
- ❏ *Henslow's Sparrow* (en)
- ❏ *Le Conte's Sparrow*
- ❏ Nelson's Sharp-tailed Sparrow*
- ❏ *Seaside Sparrow*
- ❏ Fox Sparrow*
- ❏ Song Sparrow*
- ❏ Lincoln's Sparrow*
- ❏ Swamp Sparrow*
- ❏ White-throated Sparrow*
- ❏ White-crowned Sparrow*
- ❏ *Harris's Sparrow*
- ❏ *Golden-crowned Sparrow*
- ❏ Dark-eyed Junco*
- ❏ Lapland Longspur
- ❏ *Smith's Longspur*
- ❏ *Chestnut-collared Longspur*
- ❏ Snow Bunting

Grosbeaks & Buntings (Cardinalidae)
- ❏ Northern Cardinal*
- ❏ Rose-breasted Grosbeak*
- ❏ *Black-headed Grosbeak*
- ❏ Blue Grosbeak
- ❏ Indigo Bunting*
- ❏ *Painted Bunting*
- ❏ Dickcissel

Blackbirds & Allies (Icteridae)
- ❏ Bobolink*
- ❏ Red-winged Blackbird*
- ❏ Eastern Meadowlark*
- ❏ *Western Meadowlark*
- ❏ Yellow-headed Blackbird
- ❏ Rusty Blackbird*
- ❏ *Brewer's Blackbird*
- ❏ Common Grackle*
- ❏ *Great-tailed Grackle*

- ❏ *Shiny Cowbird*
- ❏ Brown-headed Cowbird*
- ❏ Orchard Oriole
- ❏ Baltimore Oriole*
- ❏ *Bullock's Oriole*

Finches (Fringillidae)
- ❏ *Common Chaffinch*
- ❏ Pine Grosbeak*
- ❏ Purple Finch*
- ❏ House Finch*
- ❏ Red Crossbill*
- ❏ White-winged Crossbill*
- ❏ Common Redpoll*
- ❏ Hoary Redpoll
- ❏ Pine Siskin*
- ❏ *Eurasian Siskin*
- ❏ American Goldfinch*
- ❏ *European Goldfinch*
- ❏ Evening Grosbeak*

Old World Sparrows (Passeridae)
- ❏ House Sparrow*

Eastern Meadowlark

INDEX OF SCIENTIFIC NAMES

This index references only the primary species accounts.

329

INDEX OF COMMON NAMES

This index includes only standardized common names; local names are mentioned in the species accounts. Page numbers in boldface type refer to the primary, illustrated species accounts.

INDEX

ABOUT THE AUTHOR

Since immigrating to Canada in 1970 from England, Roger Burrows has traveled North America extensively. While completing his B.Sc. in Nova Scotia, he worked for Parks Canada in the four Atlantic provinces as a naturalist, interpretive planner and avifaunal consultant. He then became a writer/photographer for, and then owner of, a rural lifestyle magazine in Newfoundland. He took part in breeding bird surveys, Maritime shorebird surveys and Christmas bird counts in all four provinces. A keen birder, Roger self-published one volume of *A Birdwatcher's Guide to Atlantic Canada*, which evolved into the three published volumes of *Birding in Atlantic Canada*. In 1993, Roger set off across the country to British Columbia, and since then he has been an active birder, bird identification workshop provider, avifaunal surveyor and naturalist on cruise ships.